I0868507

ECONOMIC HISTORY

ALEXANDER DALRYMPLE (1737–1808) AND THE EXPANSION OF BRITISH TRADE

COLONIAL AND IMPERIAL

ALEXANDER DALRYMPLE (1737–1808) AND THE EXPANSION OF BRITISH TRADE

HOWARD T. FRY

Routledge
Taylor & Francis Group
LONDON AND NEW YORK

First published 1970 by Routledge

2 Park Square, Milton Park, Abingdon, Oxfordshire OX14 4RN
711 Third Avenue, New York, NY 10017

Routledge is an imprint of the Taylor and Francis Group, an informa business

First issued in paperback 2018

British Library Cataloguing in Publication Data
A CIP catalogue record for this book
is available from the British Library

Alexander Dalrymple (1937–1808) and the Expansion of British Trade

ISBN 978-0-415-38006-5 (subset)
ISBN 978-0-415-28619-0 (set)

ISBN 13: 978-0-415-38165-9 (hbk)
ISBN 13: 978-1-138-86515-0 (pbk)

Routledge Library Editions: Economic History

IMPERIAL STUDIES NO. XXIX

General Editor: GERALD S. GRAHAM

Rhodes Professor of Imperial History in the University of London

Alexander Dalrymple (1737-1808)

and the Expansion of British Trade

IMPERIAL STUDIES SERIES

1927–1969

I *Political Unrest in Upper Canada, 1816–1836*, by AILEEN DUNHAM.
II *The British West African Settlements, 1750–1821*, by EVELINE C. MARTIN.
III *British Colonial Policy and the South African Republics, 1848–1872*, by C. W. DE KIEWIET.
IV *British Policy and Canada, 1774–1791: A Study in 18th Century Trade Policy*, by GERALD S. GRAHAM.
V *Colonial Admiralty Jurisdiction in the Seventeenth Century*, by HELEN J. CRUMP.
VI *Education for Empire Settlement*, by ALEC G. SCHOLES.
VII *The Provincial System of Government in New Zealand, 1852–76*, by W. P. MORRELL.
VIII *Railway and Customs Policies in South Africa, 1885–1910*, by JEAN VAN DER POEL.
IX *The 1820 Settlers in South Africa: A Study in British Colonial Policy*, by ISOBEL EIRLYS EDWARDS.
X *Governor Arthur's Convict System: Van Diemen's Land, 1824–36*, by W. D. FORSYTH.
XI *Canada and the British Army, 1846–1871*, by C. P. STACEY.
XII *The Earth Goddess*, by G. HOWARD JONES.
XIII *The Colonial Office, a History*, by HENRY L. HALL.
XIV *European Beginnings in West Africa, 1454–1578*, by J. W. BLAKE.
XV *The Crucial Problem of Imperial Development*. A Record of the Conference on Imperial Development convened by The Royal Empire Society in November 1937, edited by Professor A. P. NEWTON.
XVI *The Struggle for Imperial Unity, 1868–1895*, by J. E. TYLER.
XVII *The Establishment of Constitutional Government in Newfoundland, 1783–1832*, by A. H. MCLINTOCK.
XVIII *European Powers and South East Africa, 1796–1856*, by MABEL V. JACKSON-HAIGHT.
XIX *The Berlin West African Conference, 1884–1885*, by S. E. CROWE.
*XX *The Free Port System in the British West Indies: A Study in Commercial Policy, 1766–1822*, by FRANCES ARMYTAGE.
*XXI *Forerunners of Drake: A Study of English trade with Spain in the early Tudor Period*, by GORDON CONNELL-SMITH.
*XXII *The Colonial Office in the early Nineteenth Century*, by D. M. YOUNG.
*XXIII *Anglo-Portuguese Relations in South-Central Africa 1890–1900*, by P. R. WARHURST.
*XXIV *The British Search for the Northwest Passage in the Eighteenth Century*, by GLYNDWR WILLIAMS.
*XXV *British India's Northern Frontier, 1865–1895*, by G. J. ALDER.
*XXVI *Social Policy and Missionary Organisations in Ceylon, 1840–1855*, by K. M. DE SILVA.
*XXVII *Royal Government and Political Conflict in Jamaica, 1729–1783*, by G. METCALFE.
*XXVIII *The Colonial and Imperial Conferences 1887–1911*, by J. E. KENDLE.

* In print, available from Longmans, Green & Co., Ltd.

* *

Engraved by Ridley, from an original drawing by John Brown

Dalrymple

Alexander Dalrymple (1737-1808) and the Expansion of British Trade

HOWARD T. FRY

Lecturer in the History of South-East Asia
at the James Cook University of North Queensland

With a Foreword by R. A. Skelton

PUBLISHED FOR
THE ROYAL COMMONWEALTH SOCIETY
BY
FRANK CASS & CO. LTD.
1970

First published in 1970 by
FRANK CASS AND COMPANY LIMITED
67 Great Russell Street, London WC1B 3BT

ISBN 0 7146 2594 9

Publisher's Note
This is the twenty-ninth volume in the
Imperial Studies Series
and is published for
The Royal Commonwealth Society
by Frank Cass and Company Limited

TO THE MEMORY OF
EDITH ALICE AND LINDSAY BOWRING FRY

CONTENTS

MAPS

* I am grateful to Marjorie Matthews of Sydney for her careful preparation of these maps.

ABBREVIATIONS USED

Add.Mss.	*Additional Manuscripts.*
B.M.	*British Museum.*
I.O.Lbry.	*India Office Library.*
J.M.B.R.A.S.	*Journal of the Malay Branch of the Royal Asiatic Society.*
J.R.Lbry.	*John Rylands Library, Manchester.*
Nat.Lbry.	*National Library.*
Nat.Mar.Mus.	*National Maritime Museum Library, Greenwich.*
P.R.O.	*Public Record Office*
Univ.Libry.	*University Library.*
Hisp.Am.Hist.Rev.	*Hispanic American Historical Review.*

FOREWORD

Few historical revaluations have been so long overdue as that of Alexander Dalrymple. It is often the fate of prophets that, when their message has won the general ear, their advocacy is forgotten. Only in the last twenty years, in the work of the late Professor V. T. Harlow, has Dalrymple's far-sighted contribution to the concept of a 'second British Empire', focused on markets rather than colonies, begun to receive its due appreciation. In Dr Fry's perceptive biography the full stature of this generously gifted man can now be discerned.

For the first time the paradoxes inherent in the commonly accepted view of Dalrymple have been effectively resolved. His dictum that 'errors may lead to the truth' is exemplified in his own career. His geographical hypotheses motived the great voyages of discovery made to test them, although their immediate objectives proved to be illusory. There was no Southern Continent, there was no navigable passage from the Atlantic to the Pacific south of the Arctic Circle; but in the search for them Cook and Vancouver drew the modern map of the Pacific Ocean. Dalrymple's patient collection and analysis of geographical information supplied the explorers with a compendium of previous experience. And in the long term, as Dr Fry demonstrates, Dalrymple's vision was to be realized in the swing from colonization to discovery, at the service of trade, as the dominant purpose in British overseas expansion.

His profoundly imaginative insight into the ends of commercial policy has perhaps been observed, in the eyes of posterity, by the very force of his convictions, supported by the power of his propagandist writing and by a pertinacity never defeated by frustration and disappointment. Yet he was no 'closet philosopher'. Before 1768 he had proved himself as an administrator, a commander, and a man of action. In the organization of hydrographic information for the greater safety of shipping he was a notable pioneer; and he wrote the first English manual on nautical survey.

This thoroughly documented biography does justice to a hitherto underrated man. We can now see Dalrymple's character, in all his manifold activities, as essentially simple: intensely enthusiastic, even romantic, with impressive powers of application and synthesis, unshakeable honesty and respect for fact, and far greater flexibility of mind than is usually credited to him. Finally Dr Fry has demonstrated that, as the achievement of Captain Cook looms larger, Dalrymple's stature is not thereby diminished but increased.

Tilford, Surrey
May 1970

R. A. SKELTON.

PREFACE

In 1859 the Hakluyt Society published the volume entitled *Early Voyages to Terra Australis, now called Australia.* The editor was R. H. Major who, in his Introduction, remarked that it was to Alexander Dalrymple, 'next to Hakluyt, this Country is the most largely indebted for its commercial prosperity'. Yet for nearly a century the truth of that perceptive observation was overlooked, until V. T. Harlow, in the first volume of *The Founding of the Second British Empire* (1952), once more directed attention to the commercial significance of Alexander Dalrymple's career.

It is the purpose of this book to follow up the late Professor Harlow's lead by studying the ways in which Dalrymple's influence helped to re-shape the pattern of Britain's trade in the late eighteenth and early nineteenth centuries.

His attempt at diverting the China trade from Canton to a free trade port in the Sulu archipelago was of revolutionary significance. In the first place it was the precedent which led to the later foundation of Penang and Singapore. Secondly it was to result in the first cession of an extensive territory in North Borneo to British trading interests. And since the modern state of Malaysia was formed out of the amalgamation of the states which had formerly constituted British North Borneo and British Malaya, the latter of which had in turn developed out of the Straits Settlements of Penang, Malacca and Singapore, it can be seen that Dalrymple's free trade experiment in the Sulu archipelago was, in a sense, the seed from which the concept of Malaysia grew.

In both the North and South Pacific his work was to have equally momentous results. To capitalize on the successful outcome of the Seven Years' War the British government had already initiated a programme for the exploration of the South Pacific when Dalrymple appeared on the London scene. The voyages of Byron, Wallis and Carteret had been rather a disappointment, however, and it needed the enthusiastic conviction and scholarly knowledge of Dalrymple to ensure that the British persevered in their search for a Southern Continent. His case for its existence was so powerfully argued that the problem could not be evaded. At the age of thirty he succeeded in winning the Royal Society's nomination as commander of its 1768 expedition to the South Pacific, and though this decision was rescinded because of the Admiralty's insistence upon a naval appointment, Dalrymple's work had not been wasted. It ensured that Cook was instructed to make the search for a Southern Continent a prime purpose of the expedition, once the transit of Venus had been observed.

Similarly in the North Pacific his influence was decisive in persuading the British government to bring its search for a North-West Passage to a decisive conclusion. This was to result in Vancouver's great survey of the north-west coast of America. Thus Dalrymple's genius for marshalling evidence and posing problems that demanded an answer was as decisive for the history of modern Canada as it was for Australia and New Zealand. Without Vancouver's survey this whole coastline might well have passed, in time, to the United States of America. Canada, Australia and New Zealand are all beneficiaries of Dalrymple's influence for their emergence as Pacific powers, even though he did not foresee the long-term effects of his own work.

Finally, Dalrymple's great work as the Hydrographer, first of the East India Company and then of the Admiralty as well, has been treated in some detail, as this was of particular significance for the expansion of British commerce. Before his time British charts were most inadequate, whereas at the time of his death Britain led the world in the science of hydrography, and all were agreed that this was in large measure due to Dalrymple's lifelong and indefatigable labours in this field. The successful expansion of Britain's commerce depended upon the safety of the seas, and Dalrymple's contribution to that expansion, in all its varying aspects, is the subject of this book.

In the preparation of this work I owe a debt of gratitude to many. In particular I would like to mention Professor E. E. Rich of Cambridge University who first directed my attention to Alexander Dalrymple and whose help and advice have been invaluable, Vice-Admiral Sir Archibald Day, K.B.E., C.B., D.S.O., former Hydrographer of the Navy, who most generously lent me the original draft of his book *The Admiralty Hydrographic Service, 1795–1919* and whose continued encouragement and practical help have been greatly appreciated, and Mr H. E. Maude, Professorial Fellow of the Research School of Pacific Studies in the Australian National University, who first drew my attention to the unfinished 'Life of Alexander Dalrymple' by the late Hugh Carrington. Professor C. E. Carrington has kindly given me permission to quote from this work, and I also wish to express my acknowledgements to the Alexander Turnbull Library, Wellington, the owners of the original typescript.

It is a pleasure to express thanks to the various library staffs who have invariably been so helpful, and in particular I would like to mention the India Office Library; the Public Record Office; The British Museum Reading, Manuscript and Map Rooms; the Library of the Royal Society; the National Library of Scotland; the University of Edinburgh Library; the Cambridge University Library; the Bodleian Library, Oxford; the John Rylands Library, Manchester; the National Maritime Museum Library, Greenwich; the Ministry of Defence (Navy) Library, Earls Court; and the National Register of Archives. The National Library of Australia, Canberra, and the National Archives of India, Janpath, New Delhi were most helpful in supplying me with microfilm and photostat materials, as was the Superintendent of Sailing Directions at the Hydrographic Department, Cricklewood, in allowing me to study the various manuscripts and other relevant materials in his keeping. I also appreciate the ready help so kindly extended to me by Brigadier-General Sir Robert Pigot, Bart., D.S.O., M.C., and Sir Mark Dalrymple, Bart., of Newhailes, as well as the readiness of Dr R. H. Carnie to put at my disposal his thesis on Lord Hailes.

Finally, I wish to acknowledge my indebtedness to the Trustees of the Sir Richard Stapley Trust and of the Sir Bartle Frere Fund, whose financial assistance was invaluable.

INTRODUCTION

As his brother told Boswell in 1763, Alexander Dalrymple was 'a more romantic person than our modern cold times have produced. Bred a merchant upon dry land, he has become an able navigator, and if he lives will be an author voluminous and vast'.[1]

At the beginning of his career it appeared that Dalrymple was marked out for the life of a man of action, for which he showed himself well fitted during his early years in India and the Malay archipelago. Yet this was not to be his destiny. The years 1768–70 were to prove the turning point of his life, for after he had been replaced, first as the commander of the *Endeavour* and then as the leader of the Balambangan trading settlement, he had to re-orient his whole life. That he was able to do this with such success and distinction was a great tribute to his adaptability, and though his new role was less glamorous than the former had promised to be, and was to yield less ready fame, nevertheless it is probable that from his London offices in East India House and the Admiralty he was able to exert a greater influence over the course of history than he could ever have done as an explorer or the chief of a trading settlement.

Dalrymple, in those early years, had shown himself to be a born leader with great self-confidence. Now he had to rely upon other qualities: his immense capacity for hard and unremitting work, his possession of an imaginative insight denied to less able men, and a stubborn courage and persistence that ensured that he would never give up, however great the opposition or whatever the disappointments that lay ahead. This stubbornness sometimes made him a difficult man to work with, but without this quality he could never have exerted the influence that he did. It enabled him to stand up to the scepticism and ridicule

[1] Quoted by R. H. Carnie in *Lord Hailes – a study*, Ph.D. thesis University Library, St Andrews, p. 14, quoting from Yales Mss., letter dated 13 February 1763.

that he invited through his proclaimed faith in a Southern Continent and a North-West Passage. Captain James Cook and George Vancouver were themselves sceptical of the existence of what they were sent out to find, and the realisation of their great achievements was dependent upon the sustained faith of Dalrymple, who was as aware as any man of the reasons for doubt, but who, after long study and deep thought, was convinced that his faith was based upon a rational interpretation of the available evidence. Aware of the immense benefits that would follow if his theories were found to be correct, he refused to rest content until the problems had been fully investigated and proved or disproved beyond all possible doubt.

Dalrymple was fortunate in the family into which he had been born, not merely because of the fame of its name, but because of the quality of its family life. All his elder brothers were men of character. Lord Hailes, the eldest, was a distinguished judge and a noted man of letters; James was a colonel in the army that captured Quebec; Hugh was a naval captain who was a friend of Captain Cook, and the man under whom James Burney, the future admiral and Pacific historian, first served; and John became Lord Provost of Edinburgh. This was a family where the highest standards of integrity prevailed, and whose members were proud to call themselves Christians in an age 'when infidelity was in high fashion'.[2]

Brought up in this strict but kindly family atmosphere, Alexander Dalrymple himself was a man who was utterly upright and unafraid, with a strict regard for truth and honesty and a scorn for dissembling, whether in word or deed. One could cite many examples of his integrity, but a few will suffice. When the East India Company and Dalrymple were trying to come to terms over the remuneration that should be paid to the Chief of Balambangan, for which post Dalrymple was in line, he insisted upon a substantial remuneration, in return for which he was prepared to undertake to accept no presents in money and to keep an account of any other gifts. He knew that a man could

[2] See *Autobiography of Dr. Alexander Carlyle,* London and Edinburgh, 1960, p. 218, and J. Ramsay, *Scotland and Scotsmen in the Eighteenth Century,* London and Edinburgh, 1888, pp. 394, 406–8.

make a very ample fortune '"doing as other men have done", by little dirty jobs and by preying on the people committed to his charge', but this was a mode of behaviour he scorned and was determined to avoid at all costs. And when an Indian Rajah once asked him, in surprise, if it was his practice to refuse large financial presents, Dalrymple assured him: 'I would receive no money . . . and it would be their own fault if any other did, for that if they would let me know, I would prevent it.'[3] This was when he was a Member of Council at Fort St George, and it was characteristic that whereas he criticized the low salary paid to such Members (£800 p.a.), he would not tolerate attempts to make up this deficiency by underhand means.

This same attitude, and not advancing years and declining health as is usually supposed, was responsible for the pause in the production of his maps and other publications at the beginning of the nineteenth century. As he explained in a letter to Viscount Melville in 1805, this was due to the introduction of Income Tax. As a publisher he found it impossible to ascertain his profits 'in an account above 30 years' standing when many early Publications are not yet sold off, where a complex expence has occurred, part defrayed by the East India Company and part by myself, with large disbursements by me for repairing Plates and Printing what may be several years unsold'. For a time these difficulties had induced him to stop the sale of all his publications, but the need of the East India Company and the Admiralty for more of his charts had finally changed his mind. In now suggesting an alternative way of framing the tax, he emphasized that he 'desired to pay the Tax instead of being excused', but disliked the present system which was 'a great Embarrassment to those who do not mean to evade due payment and affords an easy opportunity to elude paying the full Tax by those who may be so inclined'.[4]

Of course, Dalrymple had his shortcomings. He readily admitted to being a warm-tempered man, and himself stated that 'humour was not his talent'. This limited sense of humour no

[3] A. Dalrymple, *A Retrospective View of the Antient System of the East India Company, with a Plan of Regulation*, London, 1784, p. 78.

[4] P.R.O. 30/8, Vol. 128, f.58, Dalrymple to Melville, 9 March 1805.

doubt helps to explain why he tended to lose a sense of proportion when he became involved in controversial argument. His shortness of temper may partly have been due to his service in the East, which had taken its toll of his health. At various times he was described as suffering from erysipelas, scrofula and bile, and there were occasions when his work was interrupted by ill health. In a few of his surviving letters his handwriting, usually so firm and clear, has become very shaky, though this was exceptional and not an effect of old age. A medical writer of the day suggested that the European in India might preserve better health if he 'were to relax a little in his passion for beef-steaks in the morning, a sumptuous dinner at seven in the evening, with a bottle of wine to crown the whole', and were to adopt the eating habits of the Indians themselves which were better suited to the climate. However, Dalrymple's shortness of temper was not wholly attributable to bad health, but was even more the complementary defect to one of his most valuable characteristics, namely his warm enthusiasm for any task that he undertook. Once he was committed to a new cause he would devote to it the whole of his formidable energy. Nothing was allowed to stand in the way of its completion, and both inertia and opposition were liable to produce a temperamental storm of wrath. Being himself a man of imaginative insight, he tended to equate opposition with myopic ignorance and could not tolerate the inaction that this produced. Sometimes this made him difficult to work with, but it did ensure that his ideas were acted upon and were not allowed to remain the mere daydreams of a speculative thinker.

It is for his irascibility, particularly in relation to Captain Cook – a subject that is dealt with in Chapter Ten – that Dalrymple is chiefly remembered today, yet this was the least important aspect of his personality. It was more significant that he was, as Lord Hailes had said, essentially a romantic, a man of warm feelings and high ideals.

His idealism was seen at its best in his ready sympathy for the native peoples with whom he came in contact. This was no mere allegiance to the doctrine of the 'Noble Savage' which was then so fashionable, but a genuine liking for these peoples. His attitude was not marked by sentimentality, for he had too much practical experience in eastern waters to be under any illusions. He had seen piracy at close quarters, he had lost Lascar seamen in Sulu through the treachery of some of the islanders, he had himself experienced a most unfriendly welcome off the coast of Vietnam. Nevertheless, he preserved an understanding attitude which bore testimony to his innate humanity and magnanimity.

It is not surprising that many captains with experience of the East Indian trade, whose ships had suffered frequent piratical attacks, did not share his enlightened views.[5] Dalrymple sensed, however, that it was unreasonable to expect identical sets of human values to prevail in utterly different societies, and he hated 'the odious superiority which too often prevails with Europeans over the natives in all parts of India'. He therefore took every opportunity that offered to stress the finer qualities of these peoples and seems to have shared the fear that haunted his friend Captain Thomas Forrest, who described Britain's assumption of sovereign power in India in the following terms: 'a very distant country, held in subjection by the sword, is a new feature in the annals of England; but, as we have passed the Rubicon, it must be held by the sword; we have gone too far to recede; however, in the long run it may corrupt our manners'.[6] Dalrymple himself wished to see the powers of government in India limited. 'Laws', he remarked, 'are only good as they are fit for the people who receive them . . . an Englishman is the fittest to enact laws for Englishmen: He knows their wants and he feels their grievances. But he is unfit to form laws for the Indians.'[7]

Two particular instances of his regard for the peoples of the Malay archipelago are worth mentioning for the light they throw on his general attitude. In the first place there was Pedro Manuel, his manservant, whom he had originally recruited to his service during one of his visits to the Philippines in the 1760s. In early days Pedro had helped Dalrymple with his survey work

[5] e.g., H. M. Elmore, *The British Mariner's Directory and Guide to the Trade and Navigation of the Indian and China Seas*, London, 1802, passim.

[6] T. Forrest, *Voyage to . . . the Mergui Archipelago*, London, 1792, p.i.

[7] A. Dalrymple, *A Retrospective View . . .*, p. 32.

in the Sulu archipelago, and when Dalrymple had returned to London the Filipino had gone with him, and was to remain in his service for the rest of his days. When Dalrymple drew up his will he referred to Pedro Manuel as 'my old and faithful Companion for I cannot call him Servant'.[8] The second instance related to Sultan Sarapodin of Sulu to whom reference is made later in this book. In his will Dalrymple described him as 'a Man of as much Worth and Honour as any that I ever knew of any colour or faith'.

Dalrymple's respect for their sultan was reciprocated by the Sulu islanders' regard for himself. When McCluer visited Sulu in the 1790s he found that Dalrymple's memory was cherished even after the lapse of twenty-eight years, and this was confirmed by Amaso Delano, the American sailor who accompanied McCluer on that voyage. Writing some years after Dalrymple's death he stated that the islanders had described him as 'thorough, bold, magnanimous and generous . . . They had wanted him to live with them permanently, and said they would cover him with honours'.[9]

Dalrymple's natural generosity was to be seen in the ready help he extended to others. Admiral Beaufort, James Rennell and James Horsburgh were only some of the more notable of those who owed him a debt of gratitude for their success in later years. He had a talent for making and keeping friends, and he was unstinting in his loyalty towards those who had earned his confidence.

The man to whom he felt particularly indebted for the opportunities of his early career was George (later Lord) Pigot. Their friendship dated from the time when Pigot became Governor of Fort St George in 1755. Pigot had taken a particular interest in Dalrymple and had given him full backing for his project of a trading settlement in the Sulu archipelago. When Dalrymple returned to England in 1765 to seek the support of the Court of Directors of the East India Company for this scheme, and to make a bid for the leadership of the Royal Society's expedi-

[8] Somerset House, London, Will no. 555, dated 24 December 1798, with corrections and codicils 25 October 1805.

[9] Amaso Delano, *Voyages and Travels*, Boston, 1817, p. 181.

tion to the South Pacific, he lived with Pigot and his family in Soho Square. He also used to stay with the Pigots at their country home at Patsul, in Staffordshire, and it was during these years that he became increasingly friendly with Pigot's two daughters, Leonora and Sophia.

In 1775 the East India Company decided that the time had come to restore order in the Presidency of Madras, as had already been done by Clive in Bengal. Lord Pigot was chosen for this task, and in several respects there was a considerable similarity between these two men. They had both played a notable part in the Seven Years' War in India. Pigot, as Governor, had been largely responsible for the successful defence of Madras during the French siege of 1758–9, after he had taken the risk of weakening his defence force in order to send Clive north to recapture Calcutta. Pigot, like Clive, had made a fortune in India and now, like Clive, was required to intervene and restore order before unscrupulous fortune-seekers in Madras reduced that Presidency to ruin in the manner that their colleagues had so recently done in Bengal.

Pigot, however, was in a much weaker position than he realized. He had told Dalrymple that he considered that the Company's business should be transacted by the whole Council. He did not expect to find that there would be any members of the Council whose private interests would lead them to oppose the necessary reformation of the Presidency, but considered that a Governor who was determined to do what was right would not find a constant majority of the Council against him.[10] But the facts were to prove otherwise. For in Madras, in a condition of perpetual indebtedness, lived Muhammed Ali, the titular Nawab of the Carnatic, to please whom the Madras authorities in 1773 had deposed the Raja of Tanjore. Also living in Madras was the notorious Paul Benfield who, with others, including servants of the Company high and low, was reaping a handsome living by lending large sums of money to the Nawab in return for the acquisition of large interests in Tanjore. Thus, when Pigot tried to carry out the first duty which the Directors had laid upon

[10] Alexander Dalrymple, *A Paper concerning the general Government of India*, c. 1772, p. 7.

him, namely, to restore the Raja of Tanjore to his territory, he ran up against fierce opposition, and when he persisted he was arrested by a majority of his own Council.

Pigot had arrived in Madras in December 1775, accompanied by his two daughters and by Dalrymple and Claud Russell who were to be Members of his Council, and his arrest was to take place in the following August. Only three Members of Council – Dalrymple, Russell and Stone – stood by him, though there were others in Madras, including a junior servant of the Company called the Hon. Edward Monckton, who also supported the Governor. Immediately after the arrest Dalrymple was despatched to England, travelling by way of the Red Sea to save time, to represent Pigot's case in London.

Over this period it is quite clear that Dalrymple's affection for Pigot's two daughters had deepened, and in the case of Sophia had ripened into love. The latter was presumably considerably younger than Dalrymple, and her own feelings seem to have been more detached. Writing to a friend in England on Sunday, 20 October 1776, Sophy Pigot stated that she was sending the smallest of her three journals 'by Dalrymple le milord Anglois', and a week later confessed: 'I begin now to wish earnestly for news from Dalrymple, this springs from no motive of either generosity or friendship, but interest; however that interest was not originally my own, I have made it so by my filial affection'.[11]

In Madras, however, events moved to a sudden tragic climax when, on 11 May 1777, after a short illness brought on by overexposure to the sun, Lord Pigot died while still under house arrest. This left his two daughters in a most unenviable situation, for they were natural daughters by an Indian mother, and with their father's death they were left in a very precarious position socially. If they returned to England there could be no assurance that they would find a recognized position in English society. Clearly it was of great importance for them to get married, and all this occurred when the unfortunate Dalrymple was at the other side of the world. What chance he would have had of winning Sophy's hand in happier circumstances one will never

[11] Sheffield City Libraries. Vernon Wentworth Papers: Journal of Sophy Pigot. Addressed to 'My dear Peggy', with last page by Leonora, 1776–7.

know. The two girls soon found husbands, Sophia marrying the Hon. Edward Monckton, and Leonora marrying Dalrymple's old friend Claud Russell.[12]

Thus fate had denied Dalrymple marriage with the woman he loved, though his love for Sophia remained. In 1785 he presented her with his own annotated copy of his newly published *Extracts from Juvenilia, or Poems by George Wither*, and in a long dedication in both prose and verse wrote: '... whatever brings to remembrance the Objects that are dear, in our affections or respect, is a perpetual source of exalted pleasure on Earth. If you had been unknown to me, Wither's Poem of "Fair Virtue" would have given me much less pleasure than it has; I should then have read it only as an elegant description of an ideal being: but the many traits in your character, which bear a striking resemblance to the finest parts of his description, bring that description home to the heart, as the picture of truth, and not of fancy'.[13] The dedication was signed 'Your most devoted Aretephil'. Ten years later he wrote a play for her, based upon a seventeenth-century novel, which he dedicated to her 'in testimony of the highest admiration and purest affection'.[14] And in his will he remembered both these sisters. To Leonora at her own request he left a portrait of himself, while to Sophy he left a gift which Sultan Sarapodin of Sulu had given him many years before, and which, one feels, Dalrymple had always intended for Sophia from the beginning, 'pearl earings and cross and rose set round with diamonds'.

To conclude this Introduction it is fitting to close with a few lines from George Wither, whom Dalrymple was the first to try to restore to public favour, for these lines faithfully reflect Dalrymple's own attitude to life:

> I have no pleasure, or delight in ought,
> That by dissembling, must to passe be brought.

[12] The D.N.B. states that Sophia married Monckton on 14 March 1776, but this date is contradicted by the fact that she was still unmarried when writing her journal between October 1776 and February 1777.

[13] Bodleian Library, Oxford. MS Don. f.25.

[14] Bodleian Library, Oxford. MS. Don. e. 55.

If I dislike, I'd sooner tell them so,
Than hide my face, beneath a friendly show.

...
I rather wish to saile with honesty,
Than to prevaile in ought by treachery.

I have no Nation on the earth abhord,
But with a Jewe, or Spaniard can accord,
As well, as with my Brother; if I finde
He bear a Vertuous, and Heroick mind.[15]

[15] These lines are taken from Dalrymple's personal copy of his *Juvenilia*. It is noteworthy that Dalrymple not only preceded Charles Lamb and Southey in championing the poetry of Wither, but that Lamb also worked in East India House, while Southey made use of Dalrymple's 14,000-volume library when writing his *History of Brazil*.

CHAPTER I

The Years of Preparation

BORN on 24 July 1737, Alexander Dalrymple was the eleventh child, and seventh son, of Sir James and Lady Christian Dalrymple of Newhailes, Musselburgh, near Edinburgh.

These were not easy years in which to raise a large family, and certainly not for a Dalrymple, for the family had a tradition of stern opposition to the House of Stuart. This was why the 1745 Jacobite Rebellion forced Sir James to move his wife and children to Berwick-on-Tweed for protection, which interrupted the young boy's education. Shortly before the outbreak of this rebellion, Alexander had been sent to Haddington School, and thither he returned as soon as the family came back to Newhailes, but this, the only formal education he enjoyed, ceased before he was fourteen years old, owing to his father's death in 1750. Sir David, his eldest brother, now took a hand, beginning with an attempt to improve Alexander's Latin. Sir David was later to win literary distinction as an antequarian and a friend of Dr Johnson, and he also became a distinguished Lord of Session under the name of Lord Hailes. He had no success, however, with Alexander's studies, since his younger brother found no pleasure in translating the Odes of Horace. Nor was the attempt to send him to a French Academy in Edinburgh any more successful, since he refused to learn the language of his country's enemies, a wilful and headstrong attitude which he had cause to rue in later years when he developed close ties with several eminent Frenchmen!

As a younger son in a big family Alexander could expect no large patrimony, so at the age of fifteen a decision had to be taken about his future career, and here he had firm views of his own. From an early age he had been fascinated by tales of travel through foreign countries, an interest which his father had encouraged, and two books in particular had fired his imagination, giving him an ambition to visit the Orient. The first of these books was Edward Kimber's *The Life and Adventures of Joe Thompson* (1750), a novel which sought to exploit the contemporary interest in Collections of Voyages. Apart from adventures in India and the East Indies, the tale featured a landfall at Cape Circumcision, which, with its mysterious adjacent coastline, had only recently been discovered by Bouvet, and had yet to be explored. It may well be that this imaginary incident helped to instil in the impressionable mind of the young reader that conviction in the existence of a great southern continent with which his name is so closely linked; certainly he took the earliest opportunity, when he was living in Madras, to study an account of Bouvet's voyage of discovery. The second book which so particularly influenced him was Nieuhoff's *Voyages*. After the flight of the last Ming Emperor in 1644 and the establishment of the new Manchu Dynasty, the Dutch Government had decided to send a trade mission to Peking, and Jan Nieuhoff, who was a member of this embassy, wrote a full account of it. He was an observant traveller who gave an accurate account of the glimpses he had had of the Celestial Empire, as seen from a junk travelling up the Yangtze, the Yellow River and the Grand Canal to Peking. This work had met with a large response, being translated into both French and English, and it was a significant book, as the author of a recent work has pointed out, since it helped to fix 'the vision of Cathay on the European imagination'.[1]

When the boy confessed this strong ambition to go to India, his family had to consider how this could be achieved. To enter the service of the East India Company, a lad was enrolled as a Writer at the age of sixteen. Because of the opportunities which it afforded, service in the Company was keenly sought after, and to have a chance of acceptance it was essential to be nominated by someone of influence. No member of the family had ever served with the Company, but there was one possible opening. The Hon General St Clair, who was Alexander's uncle, was a close friend of Alderman Baker, the Chairman of the Company.

[1] H. Honour, *Chinoiserie: the Vision of Cathay*, London, 1961, pp. 18–21.

Swift action would be needed, however, for the Alderman was shortly due to retire from the chairmanship, and once he did so he would no longer be in a position to help. But Alexander was not yet sixteen, which nearly brought matters to a standstill. Lady Christian strongly objected to a Dalrymple 'even tacitly assenting to countenance what was not true', and it was only with great reluctance that she came to accept Alderman Baker's assurance that it was the spirit rather than the letter of the regulation which counted.

Thus, in the spring of 1752 Alexander Dalrymple left Scotland for London, accompanied by his eldest brother. There he spent some months learning to keep merchants' accounts in preparation for his new duties, and on 1 November 1752 he was officially appointed a Writer in the East India Company's service. A week later he was informed that he would be stationed at Madras.

In mid-December 1752 he embarked at Gravesend on board the *Suffolk* Indiaman, and here he met a man who was to play a significant part in his early years, the ship's commander, Captain William Wilson. But this first meeting does not seem to have been a success, for the captain was unwilling to receive him on board as a passenger, since he felt that he already had as many as he could conveniently carry. It was fortunate indeed that the chief mate was acquainted with General St Clair, and was therefore anxious to help the General's nephew by persuading the captain to relent.

The *Suffolk* sailed from the Downs on 26 December 1752, and after an uneventful voyage arrived at Madras on 11 May 1753. During these months at sea Captain Wilson had changed his mind about his young passenger, and was now ready to befriend him. This was of great benefit, for the boy knew nobody at Madras. Lord Northesk had, indeed, provided him with a letter of introduction to Thomas Saunders, the Governor, but as the two men did not know each other personally, this could only be of marginal value. The other letters he had been given proved useless, as the addressees were either absent or dead, while the Secretary, Charles Bourchier, warned him against presenting his letter to the one exception who was still present, but who had become a complete drunkard whose friendship would be a liability. A letter of introduction, it has been said, was 'a sine qua non of entry into the polite world', without which a new arrival 'had no entry into society, no invitations to public or private breakfasts or dinners for an indefinite period', and he might well have had difficulty, too, in finding suitable accommodation.[2] As it was, however, the kindly Captain Wilson took his young friend under his protection, and for the month that the ship remained at Madras he had him to live at his house as his guest.

Writers in the Company's service were responsible for copying out the correspondence, minutes and proceedings in a fair hand, and every young Writer who wished to make progress desired to be employed in the Secretary's office, for this was the only place where he could gain any general knowledge of the Company's affairs, and so fit himself for promotion. Unfortunately, however, Dalrymple's short and interrupted education had not brought his handwriting up to the high standards of legibility insisted upon from the Company's Writers, and he was therefore made an assistant to the storekeeper, where he could have learnt little of value and would have had no proper chance of promotion. In these circumstances it was a lucky moment for him when, on Saunders' retirement from the Governorship in October 1754, George Pigot was recalled from Vizagapatam to succeed him in that office. George Pigot's brother, Admiral Hugh Pigot, was a friend of General St Clair, and the new Governor had been particularly asked to look after Alexander. Thus when he arrived, and found out why the latter had been relegated to the post of assistant storekeeper, he was kind enough to give him personal instruction and encouragement, with happy results.

Another valuable friend whom Alexander made at this time was Robert Orme, who later became famous for his *History of the Military Transactions of the English Nation in Hindustan*. Orme was several years older than Dalrymple, and was at this time the Accountant and a Member of Council. Some business matter had brought Dalrymple to Orme's notice, and the latter was sufficiently impressed to want him as his assistant. Although

[2] Percival Spear, *The Nabobs: a study in the social life of the English in eighteenth century India*, London, 1963, p. 44.

this did not materialize, the two men struck up a friendship which was to last until Orme's death some forty years later, and Dalrymple benefited immediately by being given the free use of the older man's library, a concession of particular value in view of the Fort's meagre literary resources.

In May 1757 Dupré, the Secretary at Fort St George, decided to appoint Dalrymple as his Deputy. This was relatively swift promotion, and Dalrymple determined to prepare himself for his new duties, and in particular for the eventual succession to the Secretaryship which was now assured, by making a careful study of the old records of the East India Company at Fort St George.[3] He planned to go through all these records systematically, first preparing abstracts of the documents in each class, and then making long extracts of the most important papers. This process was never completed, but he did finish his work on the Letters Received, which many years later he published in his *Oriental Repertory*.[4] These and other papers in the same valuable publication help to portray the Eastern World as he saw it during the years 1757–9, while he studied hard to gain an overall picture of the Company's affairs, and of the opportunities that appeared to offer for an extension of the Company's trade, both on the mainland of South-East Asia and in the Indian Archipelago.

Throughout his life Dalrymple strove to extend the limits of British trade, and it is natural to wonder whether his sponsor, Alderman Baker, had met him before he sailed for India, and had impressed upon him the urgency of this task. Certainly the Alderman himself was alive to this need. The Directors of the

[3] 'Memoirs of Alexander Dalrymple Esq.', *European Magazine*, Vol. 42, (1802), p. 326.

[4] Alexander Dalrymple, *Oriental Repertory*, London, 1794, Vol. II, pp. 169–200. These records consisted of:

(*a*) Consultations – containing the Proceedings of the President in Council, together with an abstract of all Letters Received and Sent.

(*b*) Letters Received.

(*c*) Letters Sent.

(*d*) Country Correspondence – i.e., correspondence with the Indian princes.

(*e*) Cowles and Commissions – i.e., commissions to military officers, contracts, leases, etc.

(*f*) Ship Book – a register of all ships arriving at, and leaving, Madras.

East India Company had seldom been allowed to forget, for long, the jealousy which their monopoly aroused, and a common line of attack was to accuse the Company of neglecting to sell British manufactures, especially woollens. The strength of this argument increased as the century wore on, when the growing productivity of British industry forced the manufacturers to find larger markets for their goods. As Chairman, Alderman William Baker had felt compelled to defend the Company against its critics, and he wrote a letter on the subject to the Duke of Newcastle on 11 October 1751, which must have been at the very time when his help was being sought on behalf of Alexander Dalrymple. The Alderman expressed the pain that he felt on learning that the king had been advised that the Company was not showing sufficient vigour in prosecuting its trade. 'Several schemes for opening new branches of commerce are now in agitation,' he wrote, 'the success of which depends on secrecy, and therefore I shall be excused particularising them; and I will venture to say there are more in Embryo.' New regulations had been introduced to increase the consumption of British manufactures, particularly of woollens. 'Instead of allowing the goods to lie engrost as was formerly the case,' he explained, 'the Court of Directors have ordered publick sales, of all their effects, to be made in all their principal settlements, in such Lots as that every Trader, of any Nation, may be the purchaser at first hand. This method,' he added hopefully, 'I think is now fully established, and with such success, that the annual demand for almost all kinds of goods is remarkably increased, but especially for cloth.' To push this policy still further, the Court of Directors had decided to send a much larger quantity of cloth than had been indented for, being content with a smaller profit on a larger turnover. As for China, that was a difficult market, and the supercargoes experienced in the trade were not optimistic, but he was not without hope. 'In order to encourage the supercargoes to be sedulous in pushing that branch of trade,' he remarked, 'we began this time two year to allow them a commission of 5 per cent on all such manufactures or produce of Great Britain as they should put of in China, with instructions not to endeavour to make proffit in them, but rather to induce the consumption by selling everything low; at the same time we sent for the principal manufacturers in Spitalfields, and gave them almost unlimited orders to make any sorts of goods, that any of the gentlemen who had been at China should direct.' He ended by noting that imports of Chinese raw silk had greatly increased as a result of the House of Commons voting for a reduction of the duty, so that the British were now able to compete with the Dutch in the manufacture of velvet, but otherwise, the Company's main difficulty was to fill its ships on the home run, their numbers having been markedly increased to cope with the great growth of exported goods.[5]

This spirited defence of the Company's policy and record showed good intentions, but to enforce these policies was not easy. Certainly the trade at Madras caused the Directors growing irritation and dissatisfaction, so that in 1761 they were driven to complain that whereas that settlement's revenues had once sufficed to make it and its dependencies self-supporting, since 1746 they had been running at an ever-increasing loss, and there were strong suspicions that this was due, at least in part, to a selfish and short-sighted refusal by the Governor and Council to obey the Court of Directors' orders. To begin with, the complaints had been made in a tone more of sorrow than anger. Thus in 1754 the Directors were acknowledging the difficulties caused by 'the unhappy situation of affairs' round Fort St George, Fort St David, and the Northern Settlements, but were pleading with their servants to watch 'every opportunity to extend your Purchases to make some amends for the vast sums most unhappily sunk in Military Operations'.[6]

Two months later the main concern seemed to be with the 'languishing condition' observable in the Northern Settlements' trade, particularly at Vizagapatam. On 19 December 1755, the Directors were expressing their disappointment with the lack of progress, despite the cessation of hostilities, and they were reporting that as a result of the heavy expenses incurred by the troubles on the Coromandel Coast, it had been found necessary to reduce

[5] Alderman Wm. Baker, Chairman of the E.I.C., to the Duke of Newcastle, Public Records Office, *C.O. 77/19, f68d.*

[6] *Madras Despatches,* Vol. 1, para. 47, p. 309.

the dividend from 8 per cent to 6 per cent, so that the utmost frugality and good management were called for.[7] The Company put the blame not only on bad management, but on dishonesty. 'It is with Infinite concern,' they lamented, 'we must here observe that our Servants in general are contriving and putting every Method in Execution to Enrich themselves at the Company's Expence,' and the threat was added that if they failed to mend their ways 'every Individual of you (will) feel the weight of our Resentment'.[8] Yet two-and-a-half years later there appeared to be no improvement. Only Madras it seems, had complained of being overburdened with woollen goods, and had failed to sell them, and the Directors were convinced that this was because private interests were being allowed to predominate over those of the Company as a whole.[9] The formal closure to all such Dispatches, whereby it was customary for the Directors to sign themselves 'Your Loving Friends', must sometimes have seemed derisory to senders and recipients alike.

As he conscientiously worked his way through all these Dispatches, and noted the mounting strain of censure, the young Deputy Secretary had much food for thought. For Senior Merchants and Members in Council, whose careers were ending and (in many cases) whose fortunes were made, the reality of the threats may well have seemed less ominous than to a young and honest man at the beginning of his service. Public and private interest alike suggested the urgency of discovering new and extensive markets for British and Indian exports.

Dalrymple had already been a close observer of one effort by the Madras Presidency to establish a new factory on the mainland of South-East Asia, for one month before his arrival at Madras Governor Saunders had sent a small force to occupy the island of Negrais, close to the River Bassein, one of the mouths of the Irawaddy. In this case the immediate incentive had been the desire to forestall the French, who had been expected to take the identical action themselves, and strategic considerations had been uppermost in the Governor's mind. The recent struggle

[7] *Madras Despatches,* Vol. 1, para. 139, p. 585.
[8] Ibid., para. 63, p. 318.
[9] Ibid., para. 26, p. 689 and para. 139, p. 767.

with the French under Dupleix had emphasised to the British authorities at Madras the key role which sea-power had to play in the future of the European settlements in India. The great weakness of the British position on the Coromandel Coast was the lack of harbours. Madras itself had no harbour at all, and all visiting shipping had to lie a mile or two offshore, transportation through the notorious lines of breakers being effected by the massoolah boats and their accompanying catamarans. Moreover, for that half of the year when the north-east monsoon prevailed, this coast provided a very dangerous lee shore which no ships could risk. The only naval bases available to the British, where their ships could seek shelter and carry out repairs at such times, were Bombay or in the 'River of Bengal' which, as a paper submitted to Governor Saunders in about 1750 pointed out, 'is full of Dangers for large ships, besides not so convenient, to put to Sea at all times of the Year'.[10] It would clearly be of great benefit if a station could be found on the other side of the Bay of Bengal, where there would be shelter at all times, and where there was ready access to the incomparable Burmese teak wood for shipbuilding and repairs. But it was hoped that besides offering strategic advantages, this capacious harbour, lying near the frontier of the Kingdoms of Ava and Arakan, would develop a flourishing trade by offering security from the civil war on the mainland – which, Dalrymple observed, was uncommonly brutal, even by civil war standards – and by attracting merchants through low customs duties. It was believed that the settlement would prove defensible.

The timing of the operation, however, proved unfortunate, for it was not found possible, as had been hoped, to keep out of the civil war, which was a struggle for mastery between the Burmese in the north (Ava) and the Mons in the south (Pegu). In 1740 the Mons, who for a century had been ruled by the Burmese as a subject people, rose up in revolt and for a time were successful. But at the very moment when the British settlement at Negrais was established, a new leader called Alaung-

[10] *Oriental Repertory*, London, 1793, Vol. 1, pp. 129–32. 'The Paper received from Governor Saunders: The Consequence of Settling an European Colony on the Island Negrais'.

paya became king of the north and determined to reconquer the Mons. Needing outside help he demanded aid from the British at Negrais, just as the Mons vainly sought it from the French. Alaungpaya managed to capture Pegu in 1757, but the British did not benefit, for their response had not matched Alaungpaya's demands. Thus the Company failed to get a firm title to the island. When the Seven Years' War broke out in Europe it was felt that such expensive adventures were not warranted, and the authorities at home decided to withdraw the settlement, which unhappily ended in a massacre before the evacuation had been completed.[11]

Although not privy to the secret discussions which had decided upon this venture, Dalrymple had made his own estimate of the potentialities of this country, which he included in a letter written on the first stage of his exploratory cruise in the *Cuddalore* snow, and which he printed some thirty-two years later in the *Oriental Repertory*.[12] The evacuation of Negrais was then under way, and he could have been under no illusions as to the immediate prospects of success, but he clearly felt that this was a territory of sufficient promise to warrant perseverance. Among its own commodities he listed such important metals as gold, silver, lead, tin and copper, with plentiful supplies of salt-petre (inferior in quality to that of Bengal, but nevertheless significant at a time of recurring Anglo-French wars). In view of the difficulties at Canton, where the authorities had even (temporarily) prohibited the export of silk, it was reassuring to learn that Burma might offer an alternative source of supply, for 'vast quantities of raw silk may be obtained from this and the adjacent Countries'. There was also plentiful cotton, and it seemed reasonable to hope that in time, with encouragement, 'a sufficient quantity for the

[11] 'Letter concerning the Negrais Expedition; and concerning the Adjacent Countries', 23 June 1759. Ibid., pp. 97–128. 'Account of the Loss of Negrais'. Ibid., pp. 343–50. D. G. E. Hall, *Europe and Burma*, London, 1945, pp. 60–73.

[12] *Oriental Repertory*, Vol. 1, pp. 97–128. Here Dalrymple particularly emphasized the need for an accurate survey before attempting to establish a settlement, to save expense and lessen hardships – a significant comment, since that was the purpose of his voyage in the *Cuddalore*, which had just begun.

Investment in Bengal, and on the Choromandel Coast' could be secured. Hopes were also held out of lessening the dangers of famine on that coast, if it was true that the Persaim area could grow enough rice to meet its needs 'from Pondicherry to Masulapatam, 20 miles inland'.

An important geographical advantage in Burma was the Irrawaddy ('Ava River'), which would allow a free flow of exports and imports, including British woollens. The nature of the upper reaches of the river was not known, but Dalrymple's friend and colleague, Captain George Baker, had travelled up it as far as Ava itself, and there seemed no doubt that ships could sail thus far from Negrais at all seasons. Moreover there was every reason to believe that British woollens could be got through to Tibet, which would offer a ready market. It had been reported 'that the Inhabitants of Laos, carry on a considerable Traffick with Thibet: this must be done either through the Province of Yunnan, or through the Dominions of the Bûraghmahns; either way it is evident a Trade may be carried on by the English with these respective Countries.' Laos itself ought to be a market for large quantities of woollens, and Yunnan had considerable possibilities as well, for at the moment it could only buy European goods at a high price, both because of the high customs duties charged at Canton, and because of its distance overland from that city. At the beginning of the seventeenth century the English settlements in Burma had included one on the borders of China at a place called Prammoo, whose location he had been unable to find, but whose purpose seemed to have been to penetrate into the Yunnanese market.

Siam, Dalrymple concluded, offered no prospects for British trade at the present time, but Cambodia and Cochin-China[13] were a different matter. In his search for information about the countries surrounding Pegu, he had been very interested to come across an account of Bowyear's embassy of 1695–7, which he believed was the only occasion when the British had made any attempt to open up trade in that area. Thomas Bowyear was a 'freeman inhabitant' of Madras, who had been sent on an unofficial voyage of reconnaissance by the then President of Fort

[13] The name then used for modern South Vietnam.

St George, Nathaniel Higginson.[14] Although he had reached Faifo, his mission had achieved no concrete success, but Dalrymple noted that the 'ambassador of Camboja' had met Bowyear and had tried to interest him in establishing British trade with his country. It seemed strange to Dalrymple that this was an area which had been ignored by the British, for not only had Bowyear suggested it as a likely market for British woollen goods, but Cambodia was well situated for trade, and was 'plentifully supplied with all the conveniences of ship-building', while its river was navigable 'for vessels of Burthen to the City'.[15]

The growing difficulties of trading direct with China would have been common talk in Fort St George at this time, with up-to-date news being brought by the captains of the homeward-bound China ships. Moreover, his search of the old records had taught Dalrymple of the long-standing difficulties of trading at Amoy,[16] and now there had come the 1757 Imperial Decree confining all foreign trade to Canton, where relations between the Chinese authorities and the Company's representatives were reaching a point of crisis. He was therefore interested to read of the establishment which the Company had formed in 1686, subordinate to Fort St George, at 'Tonqueen', which he assumed was intended to allow the Company 'to obtain a share in the Chinese and Japanese Trade'.[17] This may well have prompted his later interest in making Tourane a base for this trade, backed up by his own experience in the *Cuddalore* in 1760.[18]

In contrast to these opportunities on the mainland of South-East Asia, where no European powers had yet penetrated, the limits within which British commercial expansion could be envisaged in the East Indies were more clearly defined by the presence of the Dutch East India Company, with its head-

[14] D. G. E. Hall, *History of South-East Asia*, London, 1955, pp. 323, 359.

[15] 'Cochin China', dated Fort St George 1757 and 18 Nov. 1758, *Oriental Repertory*, Vol. I, pp. 65–94.

[16] Ibid., Vol. II, pp. 183–9, where, after five months' experience, the local English factors described the Chinese as 'Devils in men's shapes'! (1685).

[17] *Oriental Repertory*, Vol. II, pp. 182–3.

[18] See Chapter II.

quarters at Batavia, and of the Spanish government in the Philippines.

In Sumatra, the British still had a foothold with their settlement at Bencoolen,[19] but its value had steadily declined and there seemed little reason to expect a revival. Elsewhere on the island, only Achin had maintained its political independence, though its former power had been undermined by the Dutch success in breaking its control over the pepper trade. Other states on the island had granted to the Dutch the exclusive right of controlling their most important export crops.[20] Similarly, the latter had gained control over the islands of Bangka and Billiton, famed for their tin deposits, while in Java itself their power was at its most evident.

Batavia, strategically sited so as to control the Straits of Sunda, was the centre of Dutch political power in the Archipelago, but the focal point of their economic power was in the Moluccas, the home of the spice trade, where the Dutch policy of monopoly was seen in its most uncompromizing and ruthless form. Cloves and nutmegs, the spices controlling, perhaps, the most lucrative markets, could be grown on many of the islands in this region. To have numerous sources of supply, however, made control difficult, and it therefore became the accepted Dutch policy to limit the cultivation of nutmegs to the Banda islands, and of cloves to the island of Amboina. Elsewhere, all spice trees were ordered to be destroyed. To make this policy feasible, it had been necessary to force the sultans of Ternate and Tidore, who between them claimed suzerainty over the Moluccas, to agree to these measures, and every year the Dutch sent out expeditions of armed proas, manned by natives from Amboina and the Banda islands and commanded by Dutch officials, to visit the coasts of any islands where unlicensed spice-tree orchards were suspected and to destroy them.[21]

Celebes was an island with possibilities in which both the British and Dutch showed interest, and Dalrymple, after his first

[19] i.e., Fort Marlborough.

[20] B. H. M. Vlekke, *Nusantara: A History of Indonesia*, The Hague and Bandung, 1959, p. 201.

[21] Ibid., pp. 203–4.

voyage, was to be asked by the President and Council of Fort St George to submit what may have been the first British intelligence report on the island. However, that still lay in the future, and all that was known at present was that the Dutch were established on the north-east and south-west coasts, in the former by treaties freely made, but in the latter by the conquest of Macassar (1667–9), whose harbour, once the meeting-place of Portuguese, British, Danish, Chinese and Malay traders, was now largely deserted and dominated by the Dutch fortress called Rotterdam.

In Borneo the Dutch had largely confined their interest to the sultanate of Bandjermasin, whose importance had been increased by the fall of Macassar, which had caused the Portuguese traders (from Timor), and British and Chinese merchants to leave Macassar for Bandjermasin. Their interest lay in the pepper which grew in the neighbourhood, but still more in the spices which were smuggled thither from the Moluccas. This worried the Dutch, as it threatened their monopoly, but in 1756 they were able to regain control of the situation as a result of a trade treaty which they signed with the sultan.[22]

The Lesser Sunda group of islands from Sumbawa to Timor were not much frequented by Europeans, though the Portuguese and Dutch did have settlements in Timor itself. As for the islands still further to the east, including the north-west corner of New Guinea, these were considered to be of little economic significance by Europeans, though Dalrymple was already interested in the geographical puzzles of this area and was well acquainted with Dampier's voyages.

Apart from the Dutch policy of monopoly, effectively enforced by sea-power, two other factors made it difficult for other nations to penetrate this area. Firstly, the Dutch kept the hydrographic knowledge of these seas a close secret. In the words of C. N. Parkinson, the maze of islands between Malaya and New Holland formed 'a world of mystery and complexity', with vast areas 'unsurveyed, ill-surveyed and unexplored'.[23] It is interesting to note that even the Dutch captains themselves complained

[22] Ibid., p. 202.

[23] C. N. Parkinson, *Trade in the Eastern Seas*, Cambridge, 1937. p. 347. Reprinted Frank Cass, 1966.

of the bad charts they had to use; Stavorinus, who wrote an account of the four voyages which he made to the East Indies between 1768–78, compared Dutch laziness in this field with the 'indefatigable assiduity' of other nations, and particularly the English, whose maps he considered to be 'infinitely preferable to ours'. Secondly, pirates swarmed all over the Archipelago, some of their most famous haunts being on the east coast of Borneo (Kutei); on the north-east coast of Halmahera (Tolebo); among the islands off the north-west coast of New Guinea; and in the Sulu group, where the 'Illanos' were considered the most dangerous of all. But the great age of piracy in these seas was a decade or two later than this.[24]

The Spaniards were only in effective control of the northern islands of the Philippines. Mindanao, in particular, had remained largely independent, and Dampier had found the sultan there anxious for relations with the English as security against Spanish or Dutch intrusion. Further to the west, the little-known Sulu islands and the northern part of Borneo had remained free from European domination.

As Dalrymple pondered over the trading prospects of this Eastern world, he could see promising opportunities both on the mainland and in the islands. His studies had shown him 'that the Company were in antient times very solicitous to regain the trade of the Eastern Islands, of which the Nation had been deprived by the intrigues of the Dutch and the Pusilanimity of our own Court: on considering the subject attentively', he concluded, 'I was convinced that this Trade might not only be regained but extended much beyond what it ever was'.[25]

[24] For a discussion of this whole problem, particularly during the first half of the nineteenth century, see N. Tarling, *Piracy and Politics in the Malay World*, Melbourne, etc., 1963.

[25] I. O. Lbry., *Miscellaneous Letters Received*, Vol. 51, f. 32.

CHAPTER II

The Cruise of the Cuddalore

In April 1762 Captain Richard Kempenfelt, then in command of HMS *Norfolk*, sent a letter from Madras to Admiral Pocock, his old Commander-in-Chief. 'The Company,' he wrote, 'has a fair field open to them now to Establish their Trade upon an advantageous footing, but I apprehend it will require a nice Judgment and Dexterous Management to Effect this, in such a manner as not too much to alarm and raise the jealousy of other European states. It must not be my attempting to ingrose much but by a Moderate and Judicious choise of what trade they take to themselves and of the Places they Establish Settlements at. I find we may if we please have a share in the Spice Trade without interfering with those Islands the Dutch have settlements at, as in the S.E. part of those Seas are many islands probably not known to the Dutch abounding with spices some of them producing Cinnamon equal to that of Ceylone besides several other Commodities for Commerce. These discoverys have been made by a young Gentleman of This Settlement (Dalrimple) He is lately returned here having been absent amongst these Islands three years in the Cuddalore Schooner to make discoveryes and observations.'[1]

This voyage of discovery may be said to have begun when the *Pitt* East-Indiaman anchored off Fort St George on 14 September 1758.[2] The *Pitt* was bound for China, but had called at

[1] The original letter, dated 1 April 1762, is among the *Pocock Papers* in the National Maritime Museum, Greenwich. Copies are to be found in the *European Magazine*, Vol. 42 (1802, pp. *321–2, and in the *Orme Mss.* (I.O. Lbry.), Vol. 52, f. 25, p. 183. (*N.B.* the pagination of the Memoirs in the *European Magazine* runs, in this first instalment, from pp. 322–8, and then from *321–*7.

[2] The *Pitt's* Journal is among the *Marine Records* in the India Office Library.

Madras to deliver two companies of infantry, in anticipation of an attack upon the town by the French under Lally. The convoy of which she formed a part had been late in leaving England, and further delays had been caused during the voyage because of sickness.[3] It had therefore been clear, at an early stage, that the *Pitt* could not reach Canton that season if she sailed by way of the China Sea, since ships using that route had to complete their voyage before the onset of the north-east monsoon, which normally occurred in October.

In command of the *Pitt* was Dalrymple's old guardian and friend, William Wilson, who was now Commodore of all the East India Company's ships and vessels. During the long voyage out he had been reflecting upon how he might reach Canton at so late a season. A less enterprising captain would have been content to seek a port en route, wherein to await the return of the south-west monsoon. Such delays were costly, however, and it occurred to Commodore Wilson that there was an alternative. Why should he not make use of the contrary monsoons which prevailed simultaneously on either side of the Equator? This was a normal procedure for ships leaving Madras for the Malabar coast and Persia during the south-west monsoon. In that case, they left Madras on a south-easterly heading until they had crossed the Equator and reached the region where the south-east trade winds blew. They then headed westwards until they were well beyond the meridian of their intended port, after which they headed back north across the Equator, and so sailed before the monsoon to their destination. If he used the same principle to reach China, he could avoid the north-east monsoon in the China Sea by sailing southwards across the Equator until he reached the region of the north-west monsoons. He would then use this wind to carry him so far to the eastward, that when he eventually headed back towards Canton the north-east monsoon would now be a favourable wind.[4]

[3] The *Pitt* was a new ship, and it was notorious that such vessels were unhealthy to sail in. She was overcrowded, for in addition to her crew of 311 officers and men – she had only been designed to carry 250 – she was transporting an additional 164 soldiers. Before India was reached, 28 seamen and 30 soldiers had died; another 32 seamen were lost before she reached England again.

[4] *European Magazine*, Vol. 42 (1802), p. 326.

If he could prove that this ingenious theory was practicable, the Company's ships would in future be able to reach China at any time of the year, with a great saving in time and money. To try out this new route in practice, however, called for considerable moral courage, for none of the Company's ships had ever used this route. Only the Dutch knew anything of these waters, and they had done their best to keep their knowledge secret, and to give the impression that navigation in this area was most hazardous. Moreover, there were no reliable charts of this region, British, French or Dutch. This meant that the Commodore would be hazarding the safety of a unique and irreplaceable ship[5] if he decided to make this experiment.

Before consulting the Governor, Wilson had a word with his young friend Alexander Dalrymple, who had already become an authority on earlier voyages. Dalrymple was able to confirm that this was a practical proposition, by referring to the example of John Saris, whose voyage from Bantam to Japan in 1613 had been carried out between the months of January and June, the very season when Wilson was planning to be in that area. Presumably he also mentioned the voyages of William Dampier which he had closely studied.

Armed with this information, Wilson sought the advice and permission of the Governor, and Pigot gave him discretionary permission to make the experiment if the conditions promised to be favourable. This enabled Wilson to proceed with his plans, and his next step was to buy a small vessel, the *Success* snow,[6]

[5] The normal East Indiaman at this time displaced 499 tons (to avoid the necessity of carrying a chaplain, which was obligatory by law for every ship of 500 tons and over), and carried 26 guns. Anticipating the Great Commoner's strategy of concentrating upon the Atlantic and the American seaboard which made it necessary for East-Indiamen to look after their own protection, the *Pitt* had been designed to combine the functions of warship and merchantman. She displaced 600 tons and carried 50 guns. See *Despatches to Madras*, Vol. I, pp. 849–50, 23 December 1757.

[6] A snow was a small two-masted vessel, with square sails on both masts and a fore-and-aft gaff-sail. It closely resembled a brig, but it had an extra mast alongside the mainmast, which allowed the gaff-sail to be hoisted independently of the main.

The *Success* had been captured from the French, and Dalrymple stated that it was purchased by Wilson on his advice. When Wilson reached Canton in 1759, the super-cargoes bought it and used it for Flint's abortive mission which would help to reconnoitre the route ahead of the *Pitt*. Thus prepared, Wilson took the *Pitt* to China. His course from Batavia carried him by way of the south coast of Celebes and the north-west coast of New Guinea into the Pacific, after which he reached Macao by passing to the east of the Philippines. The return voyage was made by the same route, the *Pitt* having sailed, in both cases, against the prevailing monsoon.[7] Wilson was back in the Thames on 26 April 1760, six months earlier than was expected, and a grateful Court of Directors rewarded him with a commemorative gold medal.[8]

This voyage fired the imagination of Alexander Dalrymple. As he studied the map of the East Indies, he realized that Wilson's new route circled round the southern fringe of that island world from which other Europeans had for so long been excluded by the tight Dutch monopoly. Staring at the chart, he could not but notice that right in the centre of the archipelago lay a group of islands in the Sulu Sea which were in no way subject either to the Spaniards or to the Dutch. In the light of Wilson's voyage he realized that these islands could be reached at any season of the year. His mind was already filled with ambitious schemes to expand the trade of the East India Company. These islands now appeared to offer a perfect means of re-establishing British trade in the East Indies. They lay in a sort of no-man's land between Manila and Batavia and were well suited to attract the native traders, in particular the Bugis of Celebes.[9] Furthermore, Chinese junks were in the habit of visit-

---

to Tiensin, with his letter to the Emperor, which was to lead to the setting up of the Cohong. See A. Dalrymple *Passages to and from China*, p. 2, and *Oriental Repertory*, Vol. 2, pp. 319–20.

[7] H. B. Morse, *The Chronicles of the East India Company trading to China, 1635–1834*, Oxford, 1929, Vol. V, pp. 71 and 74–5.

[8] Sir H. E. A. Cotton and Sir C. G. H. Fawcett, *East-Indiamen: The East India Company's Maritime Service*, London, 1949, p. 110–11.

[9] cf. the Dutch posts in the Pescadores (1622) and Formosa (1624–62) and the British settlement in P° Condore (1702–5). Above all, Batavia was the example.

The Bugis, from Celebes, had reacted to the Dutch capture of Macassar, in 1669, by developing a thriving maritime trade throughout the eastern islands, and were universally recognized as being the most able and energetic merchants in this region, after the Chinese.

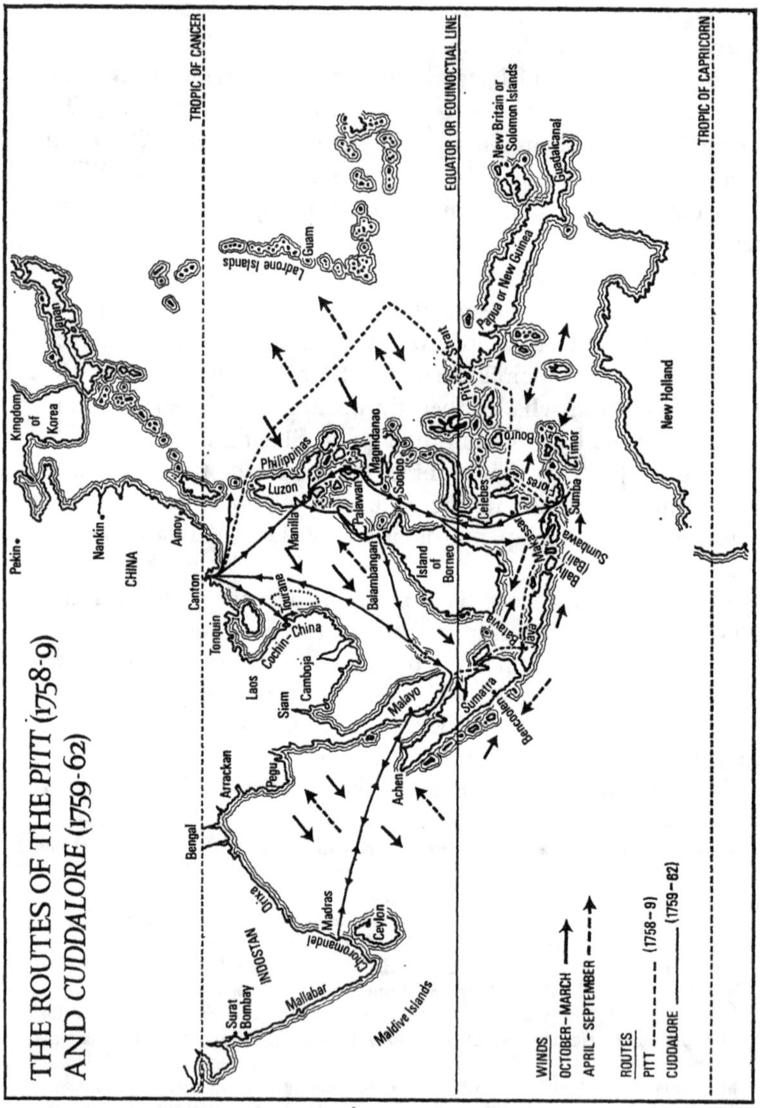

THESE ROUTES HAVE BEEN SUPERIMPOSED ON A SKETCH MAP DRAWN BY ALEXANDER DALRYMPLE IN 1768, WITH THE PREVAILING WINDS AND SOME PLACE NAMES ADDED

ing Sulu,[10] while it would only need a small deviation of course to bring East-Indiamen bound for Canton to these islands. By bringing together native and Chinese traders at a British settlement in these seas, Dalrymple realized that he could initiate a new system of trading with the Chinese. A British settlement in the Sulu archipelago would overcome the human barrier to Anglo-Chinese trade, exemplified by Chinese officialdom in Canton, in the same way that Wilson's new route circumvented the physical barrier of the monsoons. A successful outcome to this experiment promised to open up a new era in Anglo-Chinese trade.

These thoughts were interrupted by the French siege of Madras under Lally, which began in the middle of December 1758 and continued until 17 February 1759. Yet even this interlude helped to further the scheme, for during the siege a certain William Roberts, who had been a supercargo on ships sailing to Manila, was killed by a shell. After his death his effects were put up for sale, and among them were found some Spanish histories of the Philippines. These were bought and studied by Dalrymple.[11]

Here he learnt that the Sulu Archipelago had once been the centre of a flourishing trade with China and Japan, the Moluccas, Malacca, Siam, Cambodia and Borneo. With the arrival of the Spaniards in the Philippines, however, a decline

10 The Chinese were conservative and did not like experimenting with new routes. Despite their possession of the compass, they were 'incapable of long voyages, without a chain of land for their guide'. See A. Dalrymple, *Plan for establishing the Commerce of this Kingdom . . .*, p. 16.

11 Dalrymple did not specify these histories in his Memoirs, but from other references it appears that they included:

Antonio de Morga, *Sucesos de las Isles Filipinas*, Mexico, 1609.

* *Chronica de San Gregorio* (*Manila*?), 1738.

Fr. Francisco Colin, *Labor Evangelica . . .*, Madrid, 1663.

Fr. Murillo Velarde, *Historia de la Provincia de Filipinas de la Compania de Jesus*, Manila, 1749.

* This work is not mentioned in the extensive bibliography of E. H. Blair and J. A. Robertson, *The Philippine Islands 1493–1898*, Vol. LIII, Cleveland, 1908, but there are references to Antonio de San Gregorio who was a missionary in the Islands from 1639–61.

The British were not officially allowed to engage in the trade to Manila, in which Roberts had been employed, but sometimes did so under 'Moorish' colours.

had set in, and repeated attempts had been made to subdue Mindanao and Sulu.[12] The Spaniards had never fully succeeded in these efforts, and from the beginning of the seventeenth century the islanders had begun to retaliate by making the piratical raids on the Spanish settlements, a state of affairs that had continued ever since.

After 1737, the Sultan of Sulu and his advisers had attempted to make peace with the Spaniards, and had even allowed the Jesuits to erect a church and fort on the island. The result, however, was the outbreak of a rebellion led by Bantilan, a claimant to the sultanate, and the sultan himself, Alimud Din I,[13] was forced to leave the island. In 1749 he had gone to Manila to seek help, where the Spaniards had received him and baptized him a Christian, re-naming him King Ferdinand. In 1751 they had tried to restore him to his throne, as a means of putting a stop to the increasingly frequent raids from Sulu. This proved to be a fiasco, however, for when Alimud Din had reached Samboangan, the Spanish fortress and port on Mindanao, he had opened a secret correspondence with the independent native sultan of that island. This had been discovered by the Spanish governor, who became even more suspicious when he noticed that an embassy of Sulu islanders, who had arrived to welcome their sultan, were all armed. The Governor immediately seized the entire embassy, and having arrested Alimud Din as well, sent him back to Manila as a prisoner. As a result, a new war broke out between the Sulu islanders and the Spaniards, and it was said that the year 1753 had been 'the bloodiest in the history of Moro piracy', with the sea-rovers showing more than ordinary cruelty.[14]

Something of all this must have been learnt by the English at Madras through their surreptitious trading links with Manila. In these circumstances they could anticipate a welcome from the islanders, who would see in their presence a possible protec-

[12] For early conditions in the Sulu Archipelago, see De Morga (ed. E. J. Stanley), *The Philippine Islands*, Hakluyt Society, London, 1868, pp. 22–3, 137, 190–3, 336 et seq., 361 et seq.

[13] For an account of this sultan's reign, see H. de la Costa, *Asia and the Philippines*, Manila, 1967, pp. 81–114.

[14] N. M. Saleeby, *The History of Sulu*, Manila, 1908, pp. 179–85.

tion from their enemies. Moreover, if goodwill and forebearance were shown, it was possible that the Spaniards would agree to a British settlement in time, since the traders of both nations had a common interest in the suppression of piracy in these seas. With a return of peace, prosperity on the old scale might be restored to the Sulu Archipelago. Moreover, the Spaniards had no legal grounds for complaint, since the history of Sulu showed that the island had never been fully subdued by them.

Dalrymple had discussed his ideas with the Governor, and Pigot had been much impressed. Yet he was concerned when his protégé made it clear that he wanted to lead this enterprise in person, beginning with a voyage of discovery in the wake of the *Pitt*. This was a bold resolution, but Pigot, feeling that it was not in the young man's best interests, tried to dissuade him. At this time Dalrymple, at the age of twenty-one, was due to succeed Dupré as Secretary of Fort St George within a matter of weeks. After a few years he would have been in line to become a Member of Council, and then the Chief of a subordinate settlement; even an eventual appointment to a Governorship was a possibility. This was an attractive career for the younger son of a distinguished but somewhat impoverished family. To go on this voyage meant the sacrifice of all these opportunities; if the enterprise was successful, the rewards might be great, but the older man was far more aware than Dalrymple of the formidable nature of the undertaking. He realized that if this chance of the Secretaryship was now turned down, it might never recur. Despite all warnings, however, Dalrymple remained characteristically adamant in his determination, so Pigot eventually gave way, reluctantly promising to give him the leadership of any expedition that might be undertaken.

For this task the Presidency had at its disposal the *Cuddalore* snow, under the command of Captain George Baker. There was difficulty in provisioning this vessel, however, for Madras, in the aftermath of the siege, could not provide the necessary supplies. The obvious solution was to send the *Cuddalore* to Calcutta, and this was what Pigot proposed to do. But Dalrymple feared that this might easily lead to delay, and even to a cancellation of his present orders, for once he arrived at Calcutta he would come under the control of Clive, who was the President there. In view of the political problems facing Clive on the morrow of the Battle of Plassey, it was not unlikely that he would want this vessel for other urgent business, and it was for this reason that Dalrymple was able to persuade the Governor to allow him to take the *Cuddalore* to Canton for its provisions.[15] Madras could supply a cargo, however, and this would certainly be necessary, since the ship would be sailing through seas unknown to regular British traders, where provisions would have to be purchased by barter. But since the *Cuddalore* was proceeding under secret orders, it did not seem proper to get the Council to provide this cargo, so Pigot did this at his own expense, and in order to safeguard himself from the charge of using this expedition for private gain, he made Dalrymple a present of any profits that might accrue from three-quarters of the small cargo, the remaining quarter having been made over to Captain Baker.[16]

At Madras, on her way to China, was the *Winchelsea* East-Indiaman under the command of the Hon. Thomas Howe, the younger brother of the Admiral.[17] Before dinner one evening, when both were the Governor's guests, Howe invited Dalrymple to travel to Malacca as a passenger on board the *Winchelsea*, and the offer was immediately accepted, with important consequences. In the first place, Howe, who was an experienced mariner, gave his young friend his first instruction in navigation and seamanship, and Dalrymple's later skill owed much to this excellent grounding. Secondly, this voyage provided an opportunity to discuss what might happen in the East Indies if Spain became involved in the present war on France's side, for another

[15] *European Magazine*, Vol. 42, p. 327.

[16] This cargo consisted of blue cloth, beads, cutlery, etc. Some of these articles were expended to obtain provisions. The rest were bartered at Sulu for goods fit for the China market.

[17] *European Magazine*, Vol. 42, p. 328. In an undated letter from Quebec, James Dalrymple informed Sir David (i.e. Lord Hailes): 'In a letter I have wrote to Colonel Howe I have desired him to thank his brother Tom for his civilities to Sandy [the family nickname for Alexander]; I understand by my Mother's letter that you were to do the same thing, but I thought there was no harm in repeating it.' Nat. Lbry. of Scotland, *Newhailes Archives*, MS. 122. Both Sir David and James Dalrymple had been at Eton, where they probably knew the elder Howe brothers.

passenger aboard the *Winchelsea* was Colonel Draper, homeward-bound to recuperate from his exertions during the recent siege of Madras. Whether they took this opportunity is not recorded, but it is certain that Howe made extracts from Dalrymple's copy of the *Chronica de San Gregorio* (1738 edition), which were later used to supply background information during the British attack on Manila in 1762, where Draper was in command.

Meanwhile, the *Cuddalore* had slipped away from Madras on 16 April 1759, under the command of George Baker. Five days earlier the Governor had obtained his Council's agreement to the despatch of this vessel on a secret service under the charge of Alexander Dalrymple. But Pigot knew that he was exceeding his authority in this matter, for the Secret Committee had only empowered him to employ a vessel on such secret services as were considered necessary for the security of the Company's China ships. This may be why it was more than a year before he reported the voyage to the Secret Committee, and that even then he only told that part of the story which fitted in with these directions. Thus it was stated that Dalrymple was 'to attempt to discover a new route to China through the Molucca Islands and New Guinea, that the China ships may avoid the danger in time of war of going through the Straits of Malacca'.[18]

When Malacca was reached Dalrymple quitted the *Winchelsea* and embarked in the *Cuddalore*, of which he took charge,

[18] Pigot later informed his Council that he was empowered by the Secret Committee of the Court of Directors to employ a vessel on such secret services as he might think necessary for the security of the Company's China ships – see *Fort St George Public Consultations, Range 240,* Vol. 20, pp. 136–8, 2 March 1762.

The *Cuddalore*'s departure is recorded, Ibid., Vol. 17, f. 66.

The orders for this voyage have not been discovered, nor has the Journal been found. The orders for his second voyage in the *London* have frequently been quoted in this context – *vide* V. T. Harlow, *The Founding of the Second British Empire* Vol. 1, p. 73n. This confusion has been caused by an alteration, made years ago, to the document in *Home Miscellaneous Series,* Vol. 771, pp. 5–12, where the date 9 June 1762 has wrongly been changed to 9 June 1760.

Pigot's reference to his orders to the *Cuddalore* are in *Memoranda of the Committee of Correspondence,* Vol. 18, Letter to Secret Committee, 31 July 1760.

though Captain George Baker, under his general supervision, retained control of the navigation and management of the vessel.[19] For the next five months the *Cuddalore* was to remain under their dual control, and though the two men remained friends for life, it was this experience 'that a divided command was incompatible with the public service' which persuaded Dalrymple to turn down the proposal for a similar arrangement in the *Endeavour* in 1768.

Macao was reached on 3 July 1759, and here they found the *Winchelsea* and her consort in the river. They had planned to get their supplies from the ships arriving from Europe rather than from ashore, to avoid the financial burden of having to pay measurage duties. The *Winchelsea*, however, which had left England with the *Pitt* at the beginning of 1758, could not spare any provisions after her long voyage, and the *Cuddalore* was obliged to await the arrival of fresh ships from Europe. Dalrymple therefore decided to put the time to good use by examining the islands to the north of the Philippines, which were on the last stage of the new route to China that he had intended to survey, and the *Cuddalore* left Macao on 27 July. She returned there on 13 October, when difficulties with the Portuguese authorities were experienced for the first time, and as Captain Baker resigned his command on 24 November, Dalrymple had to cope with these on his own.

The trouble had arisen from the desertion of seven crew members during the vessel's earlier stay at Macao from 3 to 27 July, followed by the disappearance of a further two men since the ship's recent return to port. The Portuguese had refused to return these men to the *Cuddalore*. Dalrymple therefore tried to persuade the Chinese to assert their authority over the Portuguese, and threatened that he would return to Madras for help if his grievances were not remedied. Finding that Anson's old Chinese pilot had accompanied the Mandarin on board, Dalrymple

[19] In the eighteenth century it was still possible for the captain of a vessel not to be an expert seaman, e.g. Bougainville. This was not unusual in Elizabethan times – see John Masefield's Introduction (p. xvi) to *Hakluyt's Voyages*, Vol. 1, London, 1927.

assured the latter that the Governor of Fort St George had twelve ships of the same size as Anson's *Centurion* at his disposal, and would not rest until he had recovered these men, even if that necessitated an attack on Macao. When the Mandarin commented that Macao was Chinese, not Portuguese, and that the Europeans must fight their wars in Europe and not bring them to China, Dalrymple observed that where the Portuguese flag flew could only be considered as a Portuguese settlement, and that he would feel it a 'Glory and Happiness' to be employed in punishing these people. His persistence was at last rewarded when the Chinese authorities produced the missing men on 10 April 1760, but six valuable months had been lost.[20]

Anxious to make the best use of his time, yet prevented from carrying out his survey of the East Indies by the imminent onset of the south-west monsoon, Dalrymple now decided to visit Tourane. This would allow him to get a close look at Cochin China, in which he had become interested since reading Bowyear's Journal. Here again, however, he experienced trouble with some Portuguese merchants. He had sent two men ashore in the longboat, but they had failed to return. When he searched for them he found the boat but not the crew, but he eventually traced the latter to a Portuguese ship at anchor in Tourane Bay. After trying to get satisfaction for two days without result, he decided that the time had come to use force, so he manoeuvred the *Cuddalore* into position and opened fire. The two vessels then exchanged shots for half-an-hour, before the Portuguese struck their colours and agreed to return the men. This incident curtailed his visit, for it was reported that the local authorities had sent for some galleys. The *Cuddalore* therefore left Tourane on the 15 June 1760, and followed the coast southwards as far as Cape Cecir, now known as Cape Padaran, until a shortage of supplies forced a return to China.[21] So ended this visit to Cochin China, the brevity of which must have sorely disappointed Dalrymple. Nevertheless, he had penetrated where few English ships of that time had sailed, and he had seen for him-

20 Public Record Office, *Egremont Papers*, 30/47, Vol. 20/1.

21 Ibid. He found it impossible to obtain supplies from the local people.

self the natural strength and excellence of the peninsula and harbour of Tourane, which he was not to forget.

On both the outward and return voyages, the *Cuddalore* passed along the coast of Hainan. Since English visitors were exceedingly rare Dalrymple was most careful not to arouse the suspicions of the local inhabitants, but he paid close attention to all he saw, including the firearms used by the soldiers, and he noted that the local people did not seem to be on the friendliest terms with the Chinese. He later forwarded his observations to William Pitt, in a letter which he sent direct to that Minister, as he thought that information about Hainan might 'possibly be of some Use should the Legislature in Britain deem the behaviour of the Chinese a Motive for Hostilities', a remark which reflects the exasperation then prevailing among European merchants at Canton.[22]

The *Cuddalore*'s return to China was not well received by the local officials. On 10 September 1760 the Mandarins sent the Security Merchants to the factory at Canton to express their surprise at finding that the vessel carried more men than before. They were told that she had only returned for repairs, that several more men had been shipped at Macao, and that she awaited permission to enter the river without paying port charges, since she carried no merchandise. But only after great difficulty was this permission obtained.[23] Dalrymple had to use the good offices of the commander of some war boats which were in company with him, 'a very sensible old man', he commented, 'with whom I frequently drank tea, in his Galley'. Dalrymple argued that the Chinese always afforded assistance to vessels in distress, and threatened to go to some other province if he failed to be satisfied. In view of Flint's visit to Tiensin in

[22] Public Record Office, *Egremont Papers*, 30/47, Vol. 20/1. This letter was to earn him a reprimand from the Court of Directors, who had noted with concern that there was a growing habit for their servants to correspond directly with Ministers; Clive was a particular culprit. In Dalrymple's case they ascribed it to excessive youthful zeal.

The hostility of the local inhabitants of Hainan towards the Chinese was exhibited when some of his men went ashore, armed with cutlasses. They 'were, by signs, invited to cut off the heads of the Chinese, whose backs were turned'.

[23] I.O. Lbry., *Factory Records; China*, Vol. 20, 11 September 1760.

the preceding year, this was a shrewd move and resulted in the *Cuddalore* being allowed to proceed up-river to Whampoa without being measured. The Chinese remained in a most suspicious frame of mind, however, and carefully inspected a cask of beads for suspected hidden arms. They also mistook the longboat's copper water-pump for a gun, until they were given a practical demonstration.[24]

Nearly eighteen months had now passed since the departure from Madras, yet no progress had been made with the projected survey. The delays had largely been caused by the obstructive tactics of Chinese and Portuguese officials, which were, in turn, a reflection of the critical state of Anglo-Chinese relations at Canton. The *Cuddalore* had, in fact, arrived in China at an unpropitious moment. Now Dalrymple's plans were to be further frustrated as a result of wartime developments.

In Sumatra the French had gained control of the whole of the south-west coast, and had expelled the British from their settlements there. They had followed up this success by posting a squadron of frigates in the Sunda Strait, where they waited to intercept the East-Indiamen now due to return from China.[25] The Committee of Supercargoes at Canton had heard of this, and the presence of the *Cuddalore* provided them with an excellent opportuntiy of sending the five East-Indiamen, now waiting to begin their return voyage to England, by a new and untried passage. As these large ships threaded their way through unknown and reef-strewn waters, the snow would act as their scout and guide.

The supercargoes intended these ships to sail by way of the west coast of the Philippines, the Sulu Sea and Macassar Strait to Sumbawa, and thence through the Strait of Sapy to the Indian Ocean and so back to Europe. When they asked Dalrymple to co-operate he immediately agreed to do so, and happily he had in his possession some copies of Dutch charts of Celebes. Thomas Howe had made these copies from originals obtained by Wilson during his voyage in the *Pitt*. Howe had undertaken this weari-

[24] I.O. Lbry., *Factory Records; China*, Vol. 20, 17 July 1760.

[25] See H. Wallis (ed.), *Carteret's Voyage round the World, 1766–69*, Hakluyt Society, Cambridge, 1965, Vol. 1, p. 211n.

some task to help Dalrymple in his voyage, and these charts were now to prove invaluable.[26]

The ships weighed anchor on 30 December 1760, and for the first week of their passage to Luzon they were buffeted by gales. Once Manila Point had been reached, the *Cuddalore* led the way through the various straits, the larger ships reducing sail so that the snow could remain in the van. At night Dalrymple made it his practice to keep a man in the chains, heaving the hand-lead, to give warning of any bank of soundings which were generally found to be steep-to.[27]

Mindanao was reached in a gale on 19 January 1761, and the next morning the *Griffin* ran aground. As it was found impossible to refloat her she had to be abandoned, while the remaining ships carried on to Sulu, where they stayed for five days.[28] Here, at last, Dalrymple found himself at the island which lay at the heart of his whole revolutionary scheme, and he must have experienced intense satisfaction at finding himself in this exceptionally beautiful place. But time was pressing, and he kept his thoughts to himself. His immediate task was to conclude a provisional trading agreement with the sultan; only later did he discover that he should have included the leading datus[29] as well, without whose support no agreement would be binding. It is from his letter to the Secret Committee, in which he described this agreement, that we know that Sulu must have figured in his original instructions, for he stated that 'by touching at Sooloo the consequences expected were obtained'. It is evident that he

26 A. Dalrymple, 'Memoir Concerning the Eastern Islands', 8 December 1796, Nat. Lbry. of Scotland, *Melville Papers*, MS. 1068, f. 72.

27 A. Dalrymple, *General Remarks for the Use of those who have not been accustomed to navigate unfrequented seas*, London, 1806, p. 2.

28 From 25–30 January 1761. The details of this passage have been obtained from the logs of the ships in this convoy, which are in the India Office Library. The ships concerned were the *Griffin*, *Pocock*, *Valentine*, *Suffolk* and *Oxford*.

29 The datus were the local 'noblemen'. See *European Magazine*, Vol. 42, p. 328, where Dalrymple explains the island's government was a 'mixed monarchy'. Although there was a Council where the principal nobility and popular leaders ('Orankies') met, the executive authority rested with a few hereditary officers, including the Sultan, a datu and an oranky. Decisions necessitated an agreement of two of the above, of whom the oranky, as the people's representative, must always be one.

made the utmost use of the short time at his disposal, for in addition to his 'Copy of the Articles of commerce and friendship agreed on with the Sultan of Sooloo, which however rest', he added, 'with the Company to approve or reject', he was also able to send back a long and detailed 'Memoir of Sooloo'.[30]

Much had been accomplished in this brief visit, but now the convoy had to move on. So, after leaving Sulu at the end of January, the ships slowly felt their way down the Strait of Macassar, keeping near the eastern shores of Borneo until they were at last able to sail across to the island of Sumbawa, where they arrived on 29 February 1761. There they remained for a few days before continuing on their way, and they were, wrote Dalrymple, 'the first English ships that ever passed [through] the Strait of Sapy, so far as I know'.

Dalrymple was now on his own once more, and he had to decide on his future course of action. His original instructions seem to have given him a two-fold mission involving the close inspection of the Pitt's Passage, and the task of establishing contact with the Sultan of Sulu. Two years had elapsed since his departure from Madras, and it would be hard to justify an absence exceeding one more year; yet this was insufficient time in which to complete his original programme. Faced with this problem of priorities, he decided to consolidate the relationship already established with the Sultan of Sulu. But since the monsoon would not shift for another two months he decided to make use of the intervening weeks by carrying out local surveys of parts of the north coast of Sumbawa and of the south coast of Flores. This was probably the first British survey of the latter island ever attempted. This work occupied him from February to April 1761.[31]

As soon as conditions permitted, he sailed north towards Sulu

[30] For fuller details, see Chapter III. The letter to the Secret Committee was written from the Strait of Sapy and despatched with the returning East Indiamen, together with Dalrymple's letter to Pitt.

In his Memoirs, *European Magazine,* Vol. 42, p. 327, Dalrymple described this voyage as one of 'general observation, although it had a particular destination' (presumably Sulu).

[31] See A. Dalrymple, *Journal of the Schooner Cuddalore through the Strait of Sapy, and on the South Coast of Mang-e-rye (i.e. Flores), in February, March and April 1761*, London, 1793.

once more, visiting the Dutch fort at Macassar on the way. The appearance of an armed British vessel was most unwelcome to the Dutch, however, for their hold on this area was precarious and they were worried by a civil war which was then raging between the native rulers of Goa and Bony. Their concern was not unjustified, for the ruler of Goa tried hard to get in touch with Dalrymple, and was only prevented from doing so by the Dutch precautions, which included a refusal to allow the Scot to step ashore, all necessary provisions being sent out by boat. More boorish was their failure to answer the *Cuddalore*'s salute on her arrival. Dalrymple was infuriated by this behaviour, which was a foretaste of the treatment that was to anger Carteret when he visited this port on his circumnavigation. Dalrymple was glad to continue on his way to Sulu, where he was able to have his recent treaty with the sultan ratified by the datus, in accordance with custom.

His next port of call was Samboangan,[32] the Spanish fortress on Mindanao. Here Dalrymple had the good fortune to make the acquaintance of Don Manuel Galves, the Governor, who was also a keen and able hydrographer, and this common interest created a bond of sympathy between the two men. The old Governor, who was in the last year of his life, made no attempt to keep his knowledge of these waters a secret, but provided Dalrymple with all the information that he could, and also gave him an introduction to his brother in Manila, with a request that the latter should hand over some of Don Correa's charts and memoirs of the Philippines. It is remarkable that a Spanish official should have been so generous to one who was planning to extend British trade to these islands. This attitude seems to have been due, not only to the mellowness and detachment of old age, but also to local ignorance that an Anglo-Spanish war was imminent.

Armed with Don Galves's letter of introduction, Dalrymple now made his way to Manila. Here he found the Spaniards less openhanded, which he attributed to the suspicions engendered by an English renegade, one Norton Nichols, who was living at Manila. This lack of trust was intensified when the Spaniards

[32] The modern Zamboanga.

observed that Dalrymple took every opportunity to carry out a survey of the Bay in which he was anchored. This had been his common practice during the whole voyage, much of which had been through waters seldom visited by English ships, but the Spaniards were unused to such hydrographical zeal and considered it sinister. There is no reason to believe that Dalrymple's survey was primarily motivated by military considerations, but after the attack on Manila in 1762 many Spaniards were to believe that their Governor, Archbishop Rojo, had been a simpleton and had provided the wily Scot with the information that had led to their downfall. Dalrymple declared that it was quite untrue that the archbishop had given him the use of a book, in which were plans of all their forts, and an account of the islands. 'That I saw on his table such a Book is true,' he continued, 'but he never put it in my power to make a copy of any part of its contents; and I was sailed from Madras before the accounts of the Spanish war arrived there, nor did I hear of that event till after Manila was invested.' He had had no further communication with any of the English at Manila, he pointed out, 'till long after it was taken'.[33]

The voyage of the *Cuddalore* was now drawing to a close, and it only remained to make use of the return passage to carry out some useful surveys. Thus Dalrymple made soundings all along the western coast of Palawan in December 1761, this being a shallow and treacherous passage entirely unknown to the British, but which the Company's ships would have to frequent if a new trading settlement was established in the Sulu Archipelago. He also carried out a preliminary survey of the Anamba and Natuna Islands in the South China Sea, but lamented that he had been seriously handicapped in this work by the loss of his longboat.

33 A. Dalrymple, *General Collection of Charts*, London, 1783, pp. 81–2. For an example of the Spanish attitude, see E. H. Blair and J. A. Robertson, *The Philippine Islands, 1493–1898*, Cleveland, 1903–9, Vol. 49, pp. 284–7. Here Don Simon de Ande y Salazar referred to the 'close correspondence' between the archbishop and Dalrymple, who refused to allow on board the guard sent from the fort. Dalrymple dined at the palace, which he carefully examined, as he did the beach and powder factory.

The archbishop, overwhelmed by events, died on 30 January 1764, and was buried by the British with full military honours.

The *Cuddalore* arrived back at Madras on 28 January 1762, after an absence of nearly three years, and on 2 March Pigot gave a report on the voyage to his Council. He explained that the 'want of stores and other unavoidable accidents' had prevented 'the principal object' of the voyage from being attempted.[34] He then told them of Dalrymple's agreement 'with the chief People of Sooloo, whereby they engage, in consideration of a stipulated cargo to be delivered them, to return goods, in lieu thereof proper for the China Market, which shall produce 300 per cent on the value of the Coast[35] cargo, or in default to make good the deficiency, and all the surplus gain to be on their account'.[36]

At the outset of his voyage Dalrymple had expressed the belief that the East India Company could renew its trade with the Eastern Islands, and extend it beyond its former limits. As a result of his faith and enterprise the authorities at Madras were now prepared to make the experiment. But this new-found enthusiasm was not confined to the merchants. Kempenfelt was equally impressed, and his comments were more telling since they came from a detached and disinterested observer of high intelligence. 'Mr Pigot was very happy in his choice of this young Gentleman for such a Service,' he wrote, 'as he is a person of a Good Education Quick parts and Talents naturally adapted for such an Employ. His Observations have been far from superficial. He has penetrated deep in his Enquirys, and directed them to such Objects as most concerns the interests of the Company to know. He is now going amongst these Islands in the *Royal George* with a Cargo to commence the Establishment of a Trade, which may in time prove the Source of great profit to the Company.'[37] Such praise from a man of Kempenfelt's calibre was

34 This was probably said 'for the record'. It was impossible to consider the commercial venture as being 'for the security of the Company's China ships'; therefore it could not be openly proclaimed as the 'principal object' of the voyage.

35 i.e., the cargo from the Coromandel Coast.

36 *Fort St George Public Consultations,* Range 240, Vol. 20, pp. 136–8. For details of this treaty, see Chapter III.

37 Original, dated 1 April 1762, in *Pocock Papers* at Nat. Mar. Museum, Greenwich, General Correspondence 1761–2, POC/20, MS. 9956.

well worth having, and this was not the last time that Dalrymple was to benefit from it.

The cruise of the *Cuddalore* had been an event of great significance. For the first time a British vessel had carefully reconnoitred the Eastern Islands, where it had opened up new channels for commerce. The trading venture at Sulu, though not a commercial success in itself, pointed the way to the later settlements at Penang, Singapore and in North Borneo. The voyage had provided Alexander Dalrymple with that grounding in navigation, seamanship and surveying which was to enable him to become the first great hydrographer in British history. Moreover, when taken together, the voyages of the *Pitt* and *Cuddalore* began a new era in the East India Company's trade with China. East-Indiamen could now reach Canton at any season of the year, and in times of war they would never again need to be at the mercy of an enemy commanding the Straits of Sunda and Malacca. All in all, this voyage had been a remarkable achievement for a young man in his early twenties, who, at its start, had had no other experience of the sea than the voyage out to India, as a passenger, six years before.

CHAPTER III

The Beginning of the Sulu Enterprise

WHILE the cruise of the *Cuddalore* had been designed to investigate the prospects for British trade in the East Indies, it had also served to impress upon Dalrymple the unsatisfactory conditions prevailing at Canton. For months he had been a close observer of the scene, and had himself been at cross-purposes with Chinese and Portuguese officials. The situation was worse than he had anticipated, which made him consider his Sulu enterprise in a new light. Any British settlement in the Sulu Seas, apart from its other merits, would have to prove capable of solving the problems of the China trade.

These problems stemmed from the self-sufficiency of China. From the days of Rome, Europeans had wanted to trade with the Celestial Empire. To the silks of Cathay, so desired of old, they had now added a rapidly growing taste for tea, while the cult of 'chinoiserie' was creating important new markets for porcelain, lacquered cabinets and other similar luxuries. But their own manufacturers had little to offer in return. As far back as the mid-seventeenth century it had been noted that 'many years have passed since . . . the English, Spaniards, Portuguese and Hollanders, have with indefatigable endeavours persevered towards the acquiring a free and unmolested trade in China. Yet . . . their whole undertakings have proved little better than a labour in vain; for the Chinese finding themselves in the subsistence of their own product; and too strictly observing an ancient Law prohibiting the admission of any strangers into their Country, except such only as bringing Tributes from the adjacent Borders paid Homage to their Emperor as Supreme Lord of the World . . . or else Foreign Ambassadors . . . have shut out and abhorred all correspondence abroad'.[1] This attitude was to

[1] I.O. Lbry., *China Miscellaneous*, Vol. 7., quoting Ogilby, 'Foreign Embassies to China', London, 1656.

persist throughout the eighteenth century. In 1736, after ten years of missionary work in Peking, du Halde observed that 'as the inhabitants find within themselves everything necessary for the conveniences and delight of life, so, wanting no Foreign assistance, they have always affected a shyness to the commerce of strangers. Their ignorance of distant countries flattered them with the fond Persuasion that they were Masters of the whole world, that they inhabited the greatest tract of it, and that whatever was not China was barbarous'.[2] At the close of the century, the Emperor Chien Lung told Lord Macartney that 'Strange and costly objects do not interest me. As your Ambassador can see for himself we possess all things. I set no value on strange objects and ingenious, and have no use for your country's manufactures.'[3]

The harsh fact was that the Chinese were chiefly interested in their trade with neighbouring islands and states, a commerce helped by the fact that wherever they did business they tended to leave behind colonies of their fellow-countrymen. David Scott, the future Chairman of the East India Company, writing to Henry Dundas on 8 December 1794, pointed out the significance of this. 'Previous to the peace of 1763,' he noted, 'by connivance with the Mandarins 100 to 150 Large and 1,000 to 1,500 small vessels left the Ports of China for Cochin China, Cambodia, Siam, Malay Peninsula, Sumatra, Java, Borneo, Celebes, Spice Islands, Sooloo and Philippines and other of the Numerous Islands therewith connected. However insignificant the place to which they traded there they left their Countrymen . . . (who) have gradually established numerous colonys which give them all the advantages which other Nations obtain from Commercial treatys supported by an immense armed force. . . . These colonys both aid and create Trade by adhering to their own Customs.'

[2] Ibid.

[3] M. Greenberg, *British Trade and the Opening of China, 1800–42*, Cambridge, 1951, pp. 4–7.

The author drives home the point by showing that from 1710–59 English exports to the East consisted of £26,833,614 in treasure, and only £9,248,306 in goods. He points out that in the majority of seasons only one-tenth of a ship's stock was in goods, and silver had been known to account for 98 per cent of the cargo.

The writer was uncertain whether this was done by design, or was the result of chance, but no system seemed so well calculated for increasing the consumption of manufactures. It was profitable even though the vessels concerned were unarmed, their only defence being boiling water 'which on a naked assailant from a low prow is often effective'. He observed that the chief Chinese exports were china-ware, silks and raw silk, dye stuffs and drugs, and that in exchange they obtained diamonds, pearls, gold, ivory, ebony, agal agal,[4] sandal wood, spices, tin, pepper, rattans, sago, birds' nests and other items useful for catering, dyeing and lacquering.[5]

European competitors had had varying degrees of success in their efforts to force their way into the Chinese market. The Portuguese had been established at Macao for more than two centuries. The Spaniards carried on a profitable trade between Manila and the mainland by means of Chinese merchants. The British and Dutch, however, had been less fortunate, since their early efforts to trade with China had coincided with the decay of the Ming dynasty and with the long civil war that eventually culminated in the triumph of the Manchus. Thus the Dutch had been driven away from their bases, first on the Pescadores and then on Formosa, until they had come to rely on the Chinese junks visiting Batavia for their commercial links with China. The first permanent English factory in Canton had been established as a result of the *Macclesfield*'s arrival there in 1699, fourteen years after an Imperial decree had declared all the ports of China open to foreign trade.[6] In due course, Canton came to be considered the most convenient port, and with the British withdrawal from Amoy and Chusan,[7] Macao and Canton became the only ports specialising in the European trade.[8]

4 An edible seaweed.

5 John Rylands Library, Manchester, *Melville Papers*, Vol. 927, f. 68.

6 Chong Su See, *The Foreign Trade of China*, New York, 1919, pp. 41–4, pp. 50 et seq.

E. H. Pritchard 'The struggle for control of the China trade during the eighteenth century', *Pacific Historical Review*, Vol. 3, p. 280.

7 In 1707 and 1710 respectively.

8 E. H. Pritchard, 'The Crucial Years of early Anglo-Chinese Relations, 1750–1800', *Research Studies of the State College of Washington*, Vol. 4 (nos. 3 and 4), 1936, pp. 114–15. Writing to Sir Joseph Banks, Alexander

As this trade grew during the eighteenth century, the basic conflict between the Europeans and Chinese became ever more manifest. The Chinese feared, with good reason, that contact with foreigners might undermine the stability of their society. More fundamental was the differing status accorded to the merchant in the two cultures. In Europe he was honoured and was on the way towards achieving political mastery; in China he was despised, and in politics counted for nothing. A direct collision between these two viewpoints was therefore inevitable whenever the Europeans arrived to do business, and though diplomatic missions visited Peking from time to time to seek more favourable conditions, they were generally unsuccessful.[9]

Having become predominant in the China trade, the British had to give the lead in expressing the growing discontent of foreign merchants with the restrictions placed upon them at Canton.[10] In 1753 they drew up a petition in Chinese, demanding better conditions and facilities, greater protection and direct access to the Emperor.[11] When this failed, Frederick Pigou, Thomas Fitzhugh, James Flint and Mason Horner conferred with Père Hallerstein, a Portuguese from Peking, who advised them to explain their grievances in a private audience with the Hoppo.[12] In the summer of 1754, therefore, Flint, who spoke Chinese, tried to obtain such an interview, and when this failed

Dalrymple observed that 'the Company cannot, properly speaking, be said to have had a factory at Amoy. The Super Cargoes went and returned with the ships, and those who remained, were only permitted to remain for expected ships' – letter dated 22 August 1803, Botanical Library, Natural History Museum, London, *Sir Joseph Banks Correspondence,* Vol. XIV.

9 See G. F. Hudson, *Europe and China*, London, 1931, pp. 14–16 and 265–6.

10 It has been calculated that between 1720–64, 311 British ships visited Canton compared with 341 foreign ships – Pritchard, *Pacific Historical Review*, Vol. 3, pp. 285–7. V. T. Harlow, *The Founding of the Second British Empire,* Vol. 1, p. 65 considered that until 1745 the English trade at Canton hardly equalled that of the French and Dutch, but that afterwards it was almost as much as that of all the others combined.

For examples of the increased hindrances being placed upon European trade, see Peter Auber, *China . . .*, London, 1834, Chapters 4 and 5, and Chong Su See, op. cit., pp. 50 et seq.

11 For details see Pritchard, *The Crucial Years . . .*, p. 123.

12 'The Commissioner whose duty it is to oversee foreign commerce. He is always appointed from the Imperial Household' – Auber, op. cit., p. 126.

the Viceroy was approached. Some improvement was promised, and in the case of complaints the English were to be allowed direct access to the Viceroy.

Meanwhile Pigou, who was the East India Company's merchant with the longest experience of conditions at Canton, had returned to England where he prepared a paper suggesting improvements in the management of the trade. He considered that the Company ought to have merchants permanently resident at Canton, since such men would 'have an interest in the Country, which now, hardly one Supra-Cargoe has, every new man follows his own conceits, and takes but little trouble to avoid growing evils, which can only embarrass him a few months'. Permanent residents would get to know China in a way impossible for the supercargoes who only visited Canton once every two or three years, when they were often too busy to make any useful observations. These men ought to be provided with between £100,000 and £200,000 to purchase 'all the cheap good teas, that remain with the Merchants, when the ships are sailed for Europe'. They could also place contracts for the teas, silk and chinaware needed for the ensuing season.[13]

Pigou suggested, too, that the time had come for another embassy to Peking, which should seek to procure the same privileges for other nations as for the British. Apart from asking for the remittance of the 'present' of 1950 taels[14] per ship, he should also seek leave for the Company's vessels to trade at any of the Emperor's ports, since competition would make the mandarins at Canton more obliging.[15]

13 A. Dalrymple (ed.), 'Remarks on the trade at Canton' by F. Pigou, *Oriental Repertory*, Vol. II, London, 1794, pp. 301–3. Dalrymple described Pigou (Pt. 2, p. iii) as the man to whom the Company were 'in good measure, indebted for the alterations, which took place in the management of their affairs in China, after his ultimate return from Canton to England in 1757'. For an account of the inefficient system prevailing before that time, where there was no co-ordination between the activities of the various supercargoes, who were 'as much distinct from each other as they were from the Agents of Foreign Companys', see Ibid., p. 317.

14 In China payments were made by weight rather than by the number of coins. The tael was the standard of value.

15 Ibid., pp. 311–16 and 323. Dalrymple told Banks that the last of the Company's ships to use Amoy had been the *Duke of Cambridge* in 1713,

When Pigou got back to Canton in 1755, however, he found that as a result of some unrest, including trouble between English and French crews, a series of edicts had been issued, confirming and tightening up the existing regulations, and giving the Hong merchants a strict monopoly. For its part, the Company was putting some of Pigou's suggestions into effect. A General Council of all their supercargoes was set up, with the senior Chief as Resident for conducting the whole of the Company's trade at Canton.[16] Meanwhile, Madras was informed that the Directors had consigned the ship *Earl of Holderness* to Harrison, Thomas Fitzhugh and James Flint 'who have our Direction to use their endeavours to open and establish a Trade at Limpao or Chusan in China.[17] This voyage was most successful, but a repeat attempt in 1757 was not, and an Imperial Edict of that year insisted that any foreign vessels entering the above two ports would have to surrender their arms, ammunition and sails, and pay double duties.[18]

Finding their protests unavailing, the supercargoes decided to send a petition to Peking. For this purpose they bought the *Success* snow from Commodore Wilson, and on 13 June 1759 they despatched her to Ningpo under the direction of James Flint.[19] Not only was he to request permission to trade at that port, but he was also instructed to place on record the merchants' complaints at Canton, and to ask that they should be forwarded to Peking. Meeting with a blank refusal at Ningpo, Flint journeyed on to Tientsin, where he persuaded the local officials to forward his paper to the capital.[20] The only result, however, was that he was banished to Macao for three years, as a punishment for ignoring the Emperor's decree by going to Ningpo.

when the port had been abandoned because of increased impositions, though he believed that the Country ships had continued to use it until a later date. *Banks Correspondence*, ut supra.

16 I.O. Lbry., *Factory Records*; *China*, Vol. 20, 21 August 1790.

17 Committee of Correspondence, *Dispatches to Madras*, Vol. 1, p. 294, para. 31, 29 November 1754.

18 E. H. Pritchard, *The Crucial Years . . .*, p. 128.

19 This was only some three weeks before the arrival of the *Cuddalore*. Thus Dalrymple was a close spectator of what followed, which influenced his report to William Pitt, mentioned in Chapter II.

20 Pritchard, op. cit., p. 130.

In addition, he was ordered to return to England at the end of his sentence, and was advised never to visit China again.[21]

Another problem that was causing concern was the difficulty of financing the trade with China. Unless the East India Company could greatly increase its exports to Canton, it had no option but to rely upon heavy shipments of silver to finance its operations, but this made it vulnerable to the attacks of the manufacturing interests in England, who accused the Company of fecklessly spending the wealth that they were laboriously creating. The favourite currency in the Chinese ports was the Mexican silver dollar,[22] and these dollars were drawn to London either by direct exports of British manufactures through Spanish ports, or indirectly through the West Indian and European trades. This silver was also obtained through the illicit traffic

[21] Auber, op. cit., pp. 172–3.

In his letter to Banks, Dalrymple suggested that the Chinese anger was partly due to a misunderstanding, for 'the Super Cargoes, in their Memorial sent up to the Emperor at Peking in 1759, had said, that if Impositions at Canton were continued, they would at last be driven to do what they had done at Amoy: meaning to relinquish the Trade, for they did not know that any violence had been committed at Amoy'. But Dalrymple noted that Campbell, in his edition of Harris's Collection, told of a ship which 'suffered great impositions at Amoy, bore them all very patiently, without even a Complaint, till they had finished their business, and got their guns on board again, for the Chinese took the guns out of the ships that went to Amoy. When the ship had got her guns on board again, she seized a valuable Japan Junk in the Port to recompense them for their losses and kept her by force against a squadron of war boats, which the Chinese Government of Amoy sent out to rescue her'. Thus the supercargoes' 'expression gave great offence as it was construed to be a threat'. *Banks Correspondence*, ut supra.

[22] This had come about because nearly all the trade between Spain and the Philippines passed through Mexico. The Spaniards in Mexico and Peru could only buy the goods they wanted from Manila with silver, since that was the only produce for which there was an Asiatic market. The Asiatic goods required by Spain were shipped from the Chinese mainland to Manila, and were paid for by the Mexican silver dollars – see G. F. Hudson, *Europe and China*, pp. 240–1.

Wm. Coxe, in *Account of the Russian Discoveries*, London, 1780, p. 233, stated that 'no specie is current amongst [the Chinese] except bullion. The Chinese have no gold or silver coin. These metals are always paid in bullion – (i.e., by the Russians) – . . . As gold is very scarce in China, silver is the great vehicle of commerce'.

H. B. Morse in 'The Supercargo in the China Trade', *English Historical Review*, Vol. 36 (1921), p. 201, listed the five coins most commonly used in the China trade in the early eighteenth century.

which British and Dutch merchants carried on with Manila under the colours of native princes. In exchange for the manufactures and other products required by the Spaniards, these trades obtained a proportion of the silver brought over by the annual galleons from Acapulco to Manila.[23] Nevertheless, the supply of silver was often short of requirements and caused much anxiety.

A further way of dealing with this difficulty was to accumulate funds at Canton by encouraging the 'country trade'. This was the commerce that was carried on, both by natives and by Europeans licensed by the East India Company, not only between the various ports in India itself, but also between India, the Eastern Archipelago and Canton. These 'country' ships brought the produce of India and the Eastern Islands for which there was a ready market in China. In marked contrast to the experience of the East India Company, whose ships brought European manufactures for which there was no eager demand, the country trade showed a favourable balance to India.[24] Because the country merchants were not allowed to compete with the Company's ships by carrying such cargoes as tea, they had difficulty in remitting the funds that flowed in from this trade. The practice had therefore grown up whereby these merchants paid specie into the Company's treasury at Canton in return for Bills on the Court of Directors in London.[25]

Yet these were only palliatives. If the charter of the East India Company was to be safeguarded,[26] the Company's trade would have to be put on a healthier basis. This implied an increase of British exports to the Orient, especially of woollen goods. The northern provinces of China were an exceptionally promising

[23] V. T. Harlow, op. cit., Vol. 1, p. 65.

[24] Wm. Milburn, *Oriental Commerce*, London, 1813, Vol. II, p. 483. He calculated that there was a surplus of Indian exports over Chinese imports averaging a value of £1½ million p.a. by the early nineteenth century.

[25] Greenberg, op. cit., p. 12.

[26] The dangerous dependence of the Company upon Spanish silver was emphasized, first on the occasion of the British attack on Manila, and then during the War of American Independence. The Spanish market for dollars was closed from 1779–85, which helped to create an alarming gap between British exports to, and imports from, China. See Greenberg, op. cit., p. 8.

market for woollens,[27] but so long as all foreign trade had to pass through Canton, where it was at the mercy of the Emperor's officials, these remote regions could not be reached.

Dalrymple believed that his Sulu scheme could provide an answer to all these problems. If it was put into operation, the China trade would no longer be at the mercy of the Emperor's corrupt officials at Canton. Friction would therefore be avoided in the future. British manufactures would gain access to the northern provinces of China, while by participating in the profitable country trade between India, the Eastern Archipelago and China the East India Company would overcome its financial problems. A successful outcome to the Sulu experiment would thus result in a great increase in the commerce and profitability of the East India Company.

When Dalrymple returned to Madras in January 1762, at the end of his cruise in the *Cuddalore*, he carried with him the preliminary treaty which he had signed with the Sultan of Sulu. He also brought back the detailed notes which he had made about the islands in the Sulu Archipelago, including all that he had been able to find out about northern Borneo from the Sulu islanders.

The treaty,[28] whose main features he had already explained to Pitt in his letter of 26 February 1761, had originally been signed by himself and the reigning sultan on 28 January 1761, during his first brief visit to Sulu. It had been confirmed by the sultan and the datus when he had revisited the island in September. Then, on his visit to Manila, he had persuaded the captive sultan, Alimud Din I ('Allamodin'), to counter-sign it on 20 November 1761.

By this treaty, the English were to be allowed to choose a site for a factory and gardens on the island, with the right to buy more land for plantations if they so wished. Chinese settlers were to be permitted to join this settlement as 'subjects only to the English'. The East India Company was to be given the exclu-

27 In this connexion Dalrymple drew attention to Parke's dedication to Thos. Cavendish, in his 1588 translation of Juan Conzalez de Mendosa's *The History of the Great and Mighty Kingdom of China*. See the Hakluyt Society's edition of this, published in London in 1854.

28 The original copies, in Malay and English, signed and sealed, are in the I.O. Lbry., *Home Miscellaneous Series*, Vol. 629, pp. 455–62.

sion privilege of free trade to all parts of the sultan's dominions. No other Europeans would be allowed to trade in this area, nor would other British merchants be allowed in without the permission of the Chief of this proposed new English settlement. A Declaration of Contraband was made whereby arms and ammunition could only be sold to the sultan, while the introduction of opium to the island was prohibited altogether. Dalrymple's stand on this point is noteworthy, particularly at so early a period. 'What is very remarkable and much to their Honour,' he wrote, 'is that the Destructive Delight of the Malays as well as of the Moors in general, Ophium, is in no Estimation amongst them and never used. I thought it but just that this should be made a Contraband Commodity tho' the Sultan said it might be imported to vend to the Bugguese. But the hazard of corrupting the Sooloos seemed a sufficient Reason to forego any Pecuniary Consideration of this Nature.'[29]

On the question of defence Dalrymple, with some astuteness, was careful not to overplay his hand. The sultan claimed that he wanted peace with the Spaniards, since 'guarding against them prevented him from reducing to obedience the Borneans and opposing the Magindanaos'.[30] He also expressed a desire for English friendship, though he confessed that he had never heard of these people visiting Sulu before. But when he declared a readiness to relinquish any of his dominions to the latter, Dalrymple was wary and treated this as a test of his real intentions. He therefore decided not to ask for the right to build a fort 'as the request might have raised Jealousy at present', though he was confident that at a later stage 'Leave may doubtless be obtained'.[31]

29 P.R.O., *Egremont Papers*, 30/47, Vol. 20/1, Dalrymple, 'Memoir of the Sooloogaman Dominions and Commerce', 26 February 1761.

30 Magindanao was the old form for Mindanao.

31 After his return to Madras in January 1762, Dalrymple wrote a 'Memoir of Sooloo' which is preserved in the *Orme Mss.*, Vol. 67, f. 32, pp. 97 et seq. A copy of this Memoir, with an accompanying letter, was sent to an unknown addressee – (Orme himself had returned to Europe) – at Fort William, where it was received on 12 April 1762, (Ibid., p. 107). Later, on his way to Manila in the *Neptune* in 1763, Dalrymple described his plan in full in a memoir which is in the *Factory Records, Borneo*, p. 58. This was the version which he published in 1769 in his pamphlet *Plan for extending the Commerce of this Kingdom* . . .

When the Governor and Council at Fort St George came to consider his scheme in detail, they were helped by the information that Dalrymple had been able to glean during his voyage. His first care had been to learn the precise extent of the Sultan of Sulu's empire. This had not been easy to define, but he understood that the sultan claimed dominion not only over the whole of the Sulu archipelago, but also over 'almost one half of Borneo' – a great exaggeration – as well as over a 'great part of Paragoa or Palawan'.

Within this empire the northern part of Borneo was the most extensive and significant territory. Dalrymple had not yet visited Borneo, so that he had been forced to rely upon the Sulu islanders for his information. He had been told of that same lake which the Dutch historian Valentyn had shown on his map, and in which Europeans were to believe for many years to come. It was thought to lie close to the great mountain of Keenabalu ('Keeny Balloo'), and over one hundred considerable rivers were said to flow from this lake into the sea on all sides of the island. These rivers were expected to prove a valuable means of transporting the produce of the interior to the coast. The most important of them was said to be the river Kaely,[32] and the sultan of the lands watered by this river, which had many islands at its mouth, was on good terms with Sulu, to many of whose leaders he was related, and would undoubtedly welcome the English. A million people were said to inhabit the interior of Borneo, and there dwelt the 'Idaan'.[33]

32 Presumably the modern R. Kelai.

33 Dalrymple described the Idaan as 'Gentiles equally rude and desirous of instruction.... They have a savage opinion that their future Interest depends on the murder of the human species assuring themselves they whom they kill in this world shall attend them as slaves in the next world.' Yet they looked upon the Mahometans with whom they came in contact as superior beings who had a knowledge which they themselves lacked. Dalrymple suggested that Jesuit missionaries should be encouraged by the British to work in these regions, since they already operated throughout the greater part of the Philippines and so would afford a vent for 'the produce of these islands, which cannot safely be carried to Manila'. To forestall the outraged criticism that he anticipated from this daring proposal that the British should support Roman Catholic priests, he assured his readers that 'Commerce and the light of Science will infallibly dispel the Clouds of Superstition'. *Factory Records; Borneo*, f. 57, para. 24.

Dalrymple had also paid careful attention to the political conditions in this area. Celebes, where the situation was critical, was on friendly terms with Sulu. So, for the moment, was Mindanao, whose people were at war with the Spaniards.[34] Borneo Proper was at peace with Sulu, but here relations were not good, for an embassy from Sulu had quite recently been murdered in this sultanate.[35] There was, indeed, a history of rivalry between the two, for Borneo Proper had once ruled over an empire which had included the Sulu Archipelago and the Philippines. This empire had slowly been whittled away. First the Spaniards had stripped the sultan of some of his territory, then in the course of the eighteenth century he had had to cede to Sulu 'that part which lyes to the Eastward of Keemanees with Palawan and all the other Islands'. Over Palawan and Balabec, however, there were conflicting claims between the Spaniards and the Sultan of Sulu, though Dalrymple considered that the Spanish claims were ill-founded. 'The Spaniards pretend to a cession of Palawan . . . and Balabec from Sooloo in 1705 before the Sooloos had any pretensions to either,' he wrote, 'and another cession from Borneo in 1752', which was long after Sulu had taken them over.[36]

As he had sailed through these waters in the *Cuddalore*, Dalrymple had also taken the opportunity to study the conditions for trade. He had not been favourably impressed by the prevailing situation in the Sulu Archipelago where, in contrast to the flourishing commerce of which he had read in the old Spanish histories, trade had become stagnant. A number of factors were to blame for this. The Sultan of Sulu had discouraged merchants by levying high duties. The Spaniards in the Philippines had concentrated on the religious work of their missions and on putting an end to the piratical raids mounted by Sulu and Mindanao, so that their commercial activities had been largely confined to the annual galleons which plied between

34 In their war with the Spaniards, the Mindanao islanders fitted out 317 fighting vessels in 1761, some armed with artillery. Dalrymple told of many thousands of men, women and children being captured in this way, brought to Sulu for sale, and then taken by the Bugis to Batavia, etc.

35 Borneo Proper was present-day Brunei.

36 *Orme Mss.*, Vol. 67, f. 32: 'Memoir of Sooloo'.

Manila and Acapulco. In these difficult conditions the Bugis had chosen Pasir,[37] outside the Sulu Sea, as the centre for their extensive commerce, and the only ships that visited the Sulu Archipelago regularly were the few vessels which arrived from India 'under false colours' and Chinese junks, mostly from Amoy.[38]

Dalrymple was confident that this stagnation could be changed into a thriving commerce, but the first need was to find a suitable site for an emporium. An exact position had not yet been chosen, but it was already clear that the ideal site would be in the strategic gap between North Borneo and Palawan. While lying within the dominions of the Sultan of Sulu, and so within the region covered by the treaty, it was sufficiently far away from Sulu to be free from too close a surveillance by the Sultan, and it would also be clear of those seas where piracy was becoming an increasing hazard, year by year.

As he explained in his 1769 pamphlet, where his scheme was fully elaborated, with this area as the centre, a circle could be drawn 2,000 miles in diameter, whose circumference would touch the coast of China and the eastern, southern and western extremities of 'Oriental Polynesia'.[39] This would form the principal trading area, and from the centre of this circle Korea, Japan, the east coast of India and the north coast of Australia ('New Holland')[40] were all equidistant. The full significance of this gap between North Borneo and Palawan was appreciated when the map was closely studied and it was observed how this imaginary circle was divided into two parts by an island chain composed of Borneo, Palawan, the Calamianes and the Philippines; the only way of reaching the islands to the east of this chain in the period of one monsoon was by way of this gap.

[37] Pasir is on the east coast of Borneo in 2° S., looking across to Celebes on the far side of the Strait of Macassar, with the 'Little Paternosters' in the middle of that strait.

[38] *Egremont Papers*, 30/47, Vol. 20/1.

[39] i.e., the East Indies.

[40] In addition to the regional names – Australasia, Polynesia, Magellanica – introduced by de Brosses, whose book *Terres Australes* is mentioned in Chapter V, Dalrymple added the name Australia, but by this he meant the area to the east of South America and to the south of the Atlantic. Magellanica went out of use because there was no continent in that quarter, while M. Flinders transferred Dalrymple's Australia, which would otherwise have suffered similar oblivion, to New Holland.

If an emporium was established in this central position, an end would be seen to the prevailing stagnation, and trade would be drawn from all parts. Woollens and other manufactured goods and metals would come from Britain.[41] From India would flow in those sub-standard cotton piece goods for which there had previously been no market. An indirect benefit from this would be a raising of the standards of the cotton goods produced in India, for under the existing system the East India Company contracted with Indian factors for goods to be delivered, of specified lengths and breadths, at a fixed price, and the Company had to pay money in advance to these people.[42] When these goods had been made, they were brought to the Company's warehouses, where those that were inferior in quality, or failed to meet the measurements laid down, were either rejected or bought at a lower price. The man whose goods were rejected was then free to seek an alternative market for them, and since he had already had the use of the money paid in advance, he could afford to sell these 'rejects' at a cheap price. There was always a ready market for such goods in the Eastern Archipelago where the islanders were not concerned about standard measurements. The Dutch were therefore prepared to buy sub-standard goods, at full price if necessary, and so long as this market was available to him, it paid the native manufacturer to have his work rejected by the Company's agents. All would be changed, however, if the English had their own settlement in the Sulu Archipelago, for then they, too, would have a ready market for sub-standard goods, and by paying a lower price for them, they could bring pressure to bear on the native manufacturer to make certain that his goods matched up to the specified standards.

While an eastern settlement would thus provide a market for

[41] The East India Company was always under pressure to find new outlets for woollen goods, for which there was only a very limited market in India.

'There is not a man in this Kingdom,' wrote Dalrymple, 'so ignorant as not to know, that the greatest of all national objects is to extend the Consumption of our woollen manufactures.' *Plan for Extending the Commerce . . .*, p. 7.

[42] This was necessary because of the prevailing poverty, which prevented the native from accumulating the required capital to maintain himself and his family while he was producing these goods.

British and Indian manufactures, from these islands would come those products for which there was always a ready market in China–birds' nests, agal agal, pearls, camphor, sandal wood, gold-pepper, and so on. These would soon draw Chinese merchants, who in return would bring the teas, silks and porcelain so highly prized in Europe. That this was no idle dream Dalrymple was able to show, by telling how, when he was at Sulu in August 1761, 'the Chinese from Amoy offered to contract to deliver there, three junk cargoes of tea, by the middle of April following, and ten or more in September'.[43] Sulu was already a port of call for these junks, and so was Borneo Proper, so that these seas were well known to them, a most important consideration in opening a new settlement for trade.[44] Once Chinese junks had been persuaded to come, Dalrymple hoped that they would take back with them British woollens for the northern provinces, a market hitherto untapped because of the high duties levied at Canton and on the overland journey from that port.

The success of the proposed settlement entirely depended on attracting both the Chinese and the Bugis, who between them commanded the trade among the Eastern Islands. But if these peoples were to be persuaded to come, the British would have to offer the product most in demand – opium. Dalrymple was alive to the evils of this drug, as was shown by his insistence that it should not be introduced to the island of Sulu, but as a realistic merchant he had to face the fact that it would be impossible to set up an emporium which failed to sell it, for, as he pointed out, 'In almost all the eastern parts, ophium is considered as a necessary of life.' The Dutch were selling adulterated opium at high prices in the islands. Therefore, if the British offered the best opium from Bengal at the same price as the Dutch were

[43] A. Dalrymple, *Plan for extending the Commerce of this Kingdom, and of the East-India Company*, London, 1769, p. 16.

[44] From his own experience he had noted how 'the Chinese navigators are very sorry navigators incapable of long voyages, without a chain of land for their guide; but the line of Formosa, Luzon and Palawan is this guide for their coasters from Amoy and the more northern ports'. *Factory Records, Borneo*, f. 58, 'Enquiry into the most advantageous place for a Capital to the Oriental Polynesia'.

asking, they would immediately draw the commerce of these islands to the British port.

Such a settlement would also allow the British to participate in the spice trade, since cloves, cinnamon and pepper were expected to flourish in the Sulu Islands. Excellent clove-bark could be obtained from 'Malloodoo Bay' in Borneo, but nutmegs would be a problem. The Bugis had promised that they would try to find some plants, but were not prepared to guarantee success.[45]

Dalrymple placed great emphasis on the need to persuade Chinese immigrants to live at this settlement, and the importance which he attached to this foreshadowed the views of David Scott, already noted at the beginning of this chapter. He pointed out how the usual argument urged against colonies, that they drained the mother country of its inhabitants, could not be used against colonies formed by immigrant foreigners. He had no doubt that there would be many Chinese who would be most anxious to come, and they would prove a great vent for manufactures. But the home authorities would have to realize that the Chinese would need to be treated in a different way from the American colonists. The Chinese must be allowed to bring their skills and trades with them, for however justifiable the limitations placed on the Americans might be, such regulations could not be applied to colonists on the other side of the world. The great distances involved would prevent their manufactures from being any sort of threat to those of the mother country.[46]

It was also expected that more distant markets could be reached from Sulu, including Malaya, Siam, Cambodia, and Cochin China to the west, the remoter parts of China, Korea and Japan to the north, and New Guinea and New Holland to the south. Korea, which he believed to be as large as France, was well populated according to all reports, yet no European trade was carried on with that country, though the Koreans had active commercial relations with the Chinese. About New Guinea he had received information from a 'very sensible old man' who had described seven voyages which he had made to that area

[45] Dalrymple, op. cit., p. 8. See also his letter to Wm. Pitt. The Bugis had assured him that cloves would prove no problem.

[46] Dalrymple, op. cit., pp. 96–7.

in search of sea-slug. This trader had told of the cloves and nutmegs to be found on the island of Salawatty ('Sallywatty'), which was also visited by traders from Ternate, while birds' nests, tortoise-shell and pearl-oysters were to be obtained from Waygiou nearby. But he warned Dalrymple that the natives on these two islands, which were well populated, were treacherous. For information about New Holland Dalrymple had turned to the Bugis, and here there was some confusion. There is no need to question the ability of these enterprising traders to reach waters which had been sailed by the Dutch, and it may be recalled that Matthew Flinders, at the beginning of the nineteenth century, was to find traces of trading when he surveyed this coast, but when the Bugis described New Holland as a land that yielded gold, and the natives as being Mahometans and 'well inclined to commerce', we are left wondering whether this was a misunderstanding, or whether they were referring to islands to the north. Dalrymple added the comment that 'this must be referred to the northern part, which seems to be what Marco Polo calls Lochac: he says it is very rich and great, producing plenty of Brazil-wood, and much gold. . . . Geographers ascribe to the Portuguese in early times the discovery of a country in this quarter named Lucat, yielding gold'.[47]

The Governor and Council of Fort St George met to consider this imaginative and highly original plan on 22 March 1762, and to help them in their deliberations there was a letter from Dalrymple himself, who stressed the need for early action. 'It is necessary,' he explained, 'a considerable part of the goods arrive early at Xolo[48] to encourage the Persons concerned in collecting their Quotas, lest from a Despondency they should leave off, or even dispose of what they had collected to the Chinese.' The only ship immediately available was the *Royal George*, which could carry only half the cargo contracted for. It was much more profitable to use a large ship, as port charges were very little different whatever the size, and therefore would be a very big drain on the profits in the case of a small ship. However, since delay would jeopardize the whole undertaking, he suggested that the *Royal George* should be sent to Sulu as soon as possible and

[47] Dalrymple, op. cit., pp. 92–4. [48] i.e., Sulu.

it could be followed by one of the Company's ships in due course.[49]

The Council having agreed to this proposition, Pigot then explained the position and prospects to the Directors, in a General Letter dated 17 April 1762.[50] After commending the great pains which had been taken by Dalrymple, and the ability he had displayed, Pigot stressed that it would be unwise to expect immediate success in this sort of new undertaking. But there were great possibilities ahead. 'The Plan before us,' he wrote, 'is in the first step plain and simple but presents a field of vast extent for the Improvement of your commerce. The great success which has attended your military operations in India has acquired you such a reputation in all parts that if the extending your trade into new branches be a desirable object, perhaps a more favourable crisis may never again offer.' He believed there was no need to worry over the legal position, since the Treaty of Münster had forbidden the Dutch to frequent places possessed by the Spaniards in the East Indies, and by the Treaty of Madrid (May 1667) the British had undertaken to be bound by a like limitation. But these treaties applied only to places actually possessed by the Spaniards, and did not prohibit the English from acquiring possessions in the Eastern Isles, or from trading there.

Pigot explained that the plan was to send the *Royal George*, under Dalrymple's direction, to Sulu with as much of the contracted cargo as could be got together by the end of the month, and she would be followed either by the *Fox* or by the *Osterly* en route for China. Although Dalrymple would endeavour to fill the *Royal George* at Sulu with a return cargo suitable for the European market, the principal object at this stage was to get the trade established rather than to secure an immediate profit. Pigot expressed his confidence in Dalrymple's fitness for leading

49 *Home Miscellaneous Series*, Vol. 771, pp. 27–34. Dalrymple to Governor and Council, 22 March 1762. This letter disposes of the charge that Dalrymple altered the original arrangement as he wanted personal command, which he could only get by choosing a smaller vessel. Few historical characters have been so consistently subjected to hostile criticism based largely on preconceived notions.

50 Ibid. pp. 35–47.

this undertaking by describing him as 'a man of capacity, integrity and unwearied application'.

A certain Mr Kelsall[51] had already been appointed as his assistant, but Dalrymple asked for the addition of a second, who could help him in making a much-needed chart of these eastern waters. To begin with he tried to persuade a Mr Hirst, who had observed the transit of Venus in 1761, by assuring him that 'nothing but another Transit could afford him greater occasion [of doing a public service] than such a Voyage were it only with determining with Astronomical Exactness the situation of the several Places in that ill-described Quarter'. Failing in this, he was lucky enough to get hold of James Rennell, who was later to win great distinction for himself, but was at that time a young twenty-year-old officer in the Royal Navy, serving on board HMS *Grafton* under Captain Hyde Parker.[52] It is to the journal which Rennell kept that we are indebted for our knowledge of this second voyage to Sulu.[53]

There was a change of plan towards the end of April when the *London* packet arrived from England, and it was decided to use this vessel rather than the *Royal George*. The *London* would take half the goods scheduled for Sulu, and the rest would be sent on the first Indiaman which should arrive. A cargo worth £6,000 was put on board the packet, consisting of European and Indian piece goods, and some 'ironry'. Dalrymple had promised to bring such a cargo by the autumn of 1762, and in return his trading partners at Sulu had 'promised to reserve all their goods, which consist of Birds' nest, Pearl, War, Cowries, etc. . . . and till the time of his arrival to exclude the Chinese from their trade, as they commonly sent several large junks there every year'. By

[51] He became a Member of Council in Bengal when Dalrymple was still struggling to get his scheme launched.

[52] Parker was a life-long friend of Dalrymple, became an Admiral and was the father of Nelson's colleague at the Battle of Copenhagen. He was lost in the *Cato* in 1782–3. Rennell later transferred to the army under Clive, and, as a Major, became the Surveyor-General of Bengal. His map of 'Hindostan' was particularly praised. He and Dalrymple remained firm friends and often dined together at the Royal Society Club. Rennell was appointed one of his executors by Dalrymple.

[53] A copy of this Journal is in the British Museum, *Add. Mss. 19,299*. The original was listed in Quaritch's catalogue, item no. 707, in 1952.

early June the *London*'s cargo was loaded, and on 9 June Pigot gave Dalrymple his final instructions.[54] These orders, described as 'improper for public view', told Dalrymple 'to be particular in [his] observation of every nature' and, if expedient, to have a careful look at the harbour of the Nicobars, as he passed. He was also told that 'It is a point which requires serious consideration where to find the place more free from inconveniences and best situated; you will do well therefore to examine as particularly as possible the north end of Borneo and the port of Banguey'. Once at Sulu he was to conclude, if possible, a provisional treaty with the Bugis, disclaiming everything contrary to any treaties which might subsist between them and other Europeans, and endeavouring to get them to bring spice plants. The absolute cession of some suitable spot to the British would be very beneficial.

On the following day the *London* left Madras and headed for the Nicobars, where it was intended 'to put ashore some sheep to breed, there being none in any of those Islands'. After a careful survey of the harbour they carried on to Malacca, where Dalrymple refused to salute the fort, in retaliation for his treatment at Macassar the previous year, which, as Rennell observed, 'occasioned a very warm dispute between Captain Dalrymple and the Dutch ChaBanda.[55]

When they reached the northern end of Borneo and approached that gap of whose importance he had written in his Plan, they were in waters which were new to Dalrymple and to everyone else on board, an area full of dangerous reefs for which

54 *Home Miscellaneous Series*, Vol. 771, pp. 5–12, where the alteration of the date from 9 June 1762 to 9 June 1760 can be seen very clearly. The copyist himself thought that these orders referred to the *Cuddalore*, for in preparing this volume of documents relating to the Sulu enterprise he placed them at the beginning with these introductory words: 'It appears by Letter from Governor Pigot dated 31 July 1760, that the Cuddalore Schooner had been employed by him on secret services under the conduct of Mr Dalrymple. The Governor's Instructions to Mr Dalrymple were as follows. . . .'' That these orders really referred to the second voyage is confirmed by Dalrymple's letter to the Court of Directors dated 30 October 1769 where he specifically mentions his orders of 9 June 1762 – Ibid., pp. 189 et seq.

55 Copy of *Rennell's Journal*, *Add. Mss. 19,299*, p. 17, Shahbandar is the Malay term for harbour master, an office that is still functioning at the mouth of every Malay river.

there was no adequate chart, since the whole of the north-west coast of Borneo along which they were sailing was unknown to European ships at that time. During his previous visit to Sulu, however, Dalrymple had managed to get some information from a pilot, and 'with these directions he constructed a chart or rather a sketch of the Streight of Balabac together with the coast of Borneo, from Borneo Bay to the North point of the Islands. This chart which with regard to particulars might be considered as no Chart at all, was all the direction he had for his Navigation; as all the Spanish draughts disagreed so widely that no manner of dependance was to be placed on them, and indeed we afterwards found that they were rejected with great reason, for probably no draughts were ever made that so much deserved the epithet of chimerical as the Spanish ones of the Streights and Neighbourhood of Balabac'.[56] Thus they felt their way through this dangerous passage, with no other aid than a map constructed from the memory of an aged native pilot, who 'was more than ninety years old'. This old man's ideas of the coast had been obtained from 'cursory views', and the compass he had used had been a Chinese one, 'graduated in a different manner from ours', which he had found difficult to reconcile with the British one. 'He was quite ignorant of our method of describing distance by equal parts so could only express them by comparing them with others that were known to both. And lastly he was forced to speak through an interpreter by whose deficiency we have since found that his account suffered extremely. However the chart agreed so well that Mr Dalrymple was under no difficulty of finding his situation on the Coast', and though the distances were well out, they were 'well proportioned to one another in general. His chief errors were the bearings and distances of Cajayan Sooloo from Balabac, and the depths of water in Albai Harbour'.[57]

The island of Balambangan, strategically situated between Borneo and Palawan, soon became the centre of their attention,

[56] Copy of *Rennell's Journal, Add. Mss. 19,299*, p. 3.

[57] Copy of *Rennell's Journal, Add. Mss. 19,299*, pp. 21–2. Rennell observed that if they knew all the disadvantages under which this sketch map had been constructed, 'I doubt not but the generality of people will readily laugh at the notion of such a draught'.

and they started exploring the coast. They first inspected a bay on the east coast of the island, and after making soundings from the ship's boat, Dalrymple returned to the *London*, weighed anchor and proceeded towards the bay, with a boat on each bow, and a man at the masthead. He normally took on this latter duty himself, but being tired he sent another man up, who saw the discoloured water but did not call out, so that they 'came at once on a little rocky Bank of 11 feet, but having very smooth water we got over without striking, though we were then supposed to draw more than 11 foot'. Soundings made in the southern harbour revealed several coral banks, but there was not time to chart them with any accuracy. They went ashore 'to measure Bases and lay down the situation of the neighbouring Islands', and while they were doing this they found a 'Banguey Boat lately come from Sooloo, with information, later found false, of Spanish men-of-war at Sooloo';[58] this may have been some garbled account of a visiting Spanish ship, in connexion with the peace embassies which both the Sultans of Mindanao and Sulu sent to Manila in 1762, as a result of which Archbishop Rojo showed great attention to the imprisoned former Sultan of Sulu, 'Don Fernando I' (as they styled Alimud Din I), and had even agreed that he and his son, Prince Israel, should be allowed to return to the island that year.[59]

When the *London*'s voyage had been planned, one of the rendezvous fixed for the East-Indiaman, which was to follow with the main portion of the cargo, had been the large bay formed by Banguey, Balambangan and the North part of Borneo. To help this ship find its way, Dalrymple set up a flag on an islet in this bay, and near the flag was deposited a letter containing directions and the latest intelligence. They also left behind one of their Lascars to supply the ship with further information.[60]

Before continuing his journey to Sulu, Dalrymple took this opportunity to make an agreement with the local Bornean chiefs

[58] Copy of *Rennell's Journal, Add. Mss. 19,299*, pp. 27–8.

[59] E. H. Blair & J. A. Robertson, *The Philippine Islands 1493–1898*, Vol. XLIX, pp. 182–86, 'Rojo's Narrative'.

[60] *Rennell's Journal*, pp. 26–8.

at Abai and Tam-Passook.[61] By this new agreement, which he called the Treaty of Bira Birapan, and which was concluded on 26 July 1762, the two chiefs undertook to 'grant freely and absolutely unto the said Company the Island Usocan – commanding the mouth of the harbour – and the part of Borneo to the southward of Abai River called Bira Bira with what more land the English may want hereafter for Plantations of Pepper and other use'. No other Europeans were to be allowed to enter this country, nor were other Englishmen to be allowed there without the Company's leave. All people living within the English territories were to be subject to their jurisdiction.[62]

Having thus obtained the agreement of the local chiefs, Dalrymple now sailed on to Sulu where he arrived in mid-August, but here he learnt of some ominous developments since his last visit. In the first place, a smallpox epidemic had been raging on the island, and it was now discovered that this had carried off twenty of the people most deeply concerned with the 1761 agreement. Moreover, fearing lest they might catch the disease, many of the rest had scattered, so that it was impossible to make contact with them, and they had had no opportunity of honouring the promises which they had originally made. Secondly, Bandahara, the chief datu and the man on whom Dalrymple placed the most reliance, was dead.[63] The original agreement had specified that the English were to do business with him alone, and he had given Dalrymple on his own account an Indent 'to almost half the amount of the whole cargo'. Another difficulty had arisen over their late arrival, partly due to their having been weather-bound for a week at Balambangan,

[61] P.R.O., *Egremont Papers*, 30/47, Vol. 20/1, dated 26 February 1761. Here Dalrymple described Tam-Passook as a province containing *c.* 20,000 people. Abai was its very fine harbour.

[62] The original English copy of the treaty is in the I.O. Lbry., *Home Miscellaneous Series*, Vol. 629, pp. 463–5. Here they received their first news of the smallpox epidemic on Sulu.

[63] Poisoning had been developed into a fine art on these islands, and there was reason to believe that that had caused Bandahara's death. He had recently opposed the reigning sultan's oppression of the Chinese. The sultan was jealous of this datu who, remarked Dalrymple, 'was taken ill . . . all his hair dropped off . . . a former Competitor of the Sultan died under the same extraordinary Circumstances'. Cf. Bendahara, a Malay chief minister.

for on their arrival at Sulu they discovered that a large Chinese junk was on the point of sailing, and it had been their aim to arrive early enough to prevent the goods assembled for them from being sold, instead, to the Chinese. Obviously it was unreasonable to expect the people of Sulu to take any risks in their trade with the English until the latter had demonstrated that they were in earnest and could be relied upon to honour their bargains. The final setback came with the non-arrival of the *Royal Captain*, the Indiaman which had been dispatched from Fort St George with the remainder of the cargo on 3 August 1762, for Captain Tanner had been unable to find his way to Sulu, and so had gone on to Canton. Dalrymple therefore had to make new arrangements, whereby 'the Sooloos engaged to receive the *London*'s cargo amounting to 21,800 Dollars at Cent for cent and to discharge their account at stated times in moietys: One of 20,000 Dollars to be paid in Birds' Nest, Sago, Wax and Cowries. Another of like sum in Birds' Nest, Sago, Teepys and Sharks Fins. . . . This sum faithfully discharged, they were also, should the *Royal Captain*'s cargo arrive, to have it, at Cent for cent on the Coast Invoice and were to deliver it for Goods to be carried to China at their Risk and sold for their Account . . .'[64]

Having done his best to secure satisfactory terms, Dalrymple determined to make full use of this opportunity to complete his survey. On his first visit he had done enough to enable him to complete a general chart of the islands. Rennell described how Dalrymple had previously landed 'and measured Bases to determine the positions of the neighbouring Islands and in order to compleat his work he now brought with him two good Telescopes and a Time-keeper to determine the Longitude of Sooloo by eclipses of Jupiter's Satellites; and a Land Quadrant for the Latitudes: an apparatus which I believe few People would have provided (chiefly at their own expence) who were not certain of receiving a pecuniary reward.

'He had besides measuring a base on the north side of Sooloo

[64] *Fort St George Public Consultation* of 12 April 1763, Vol. 21, pp. 154–7. Joint letter from Dalrymple and Kelsall, Ibid., pp. 141–54. See also *Miscellaneous Letters Received*, Vol. 47, p. 135, 26 November 1765.

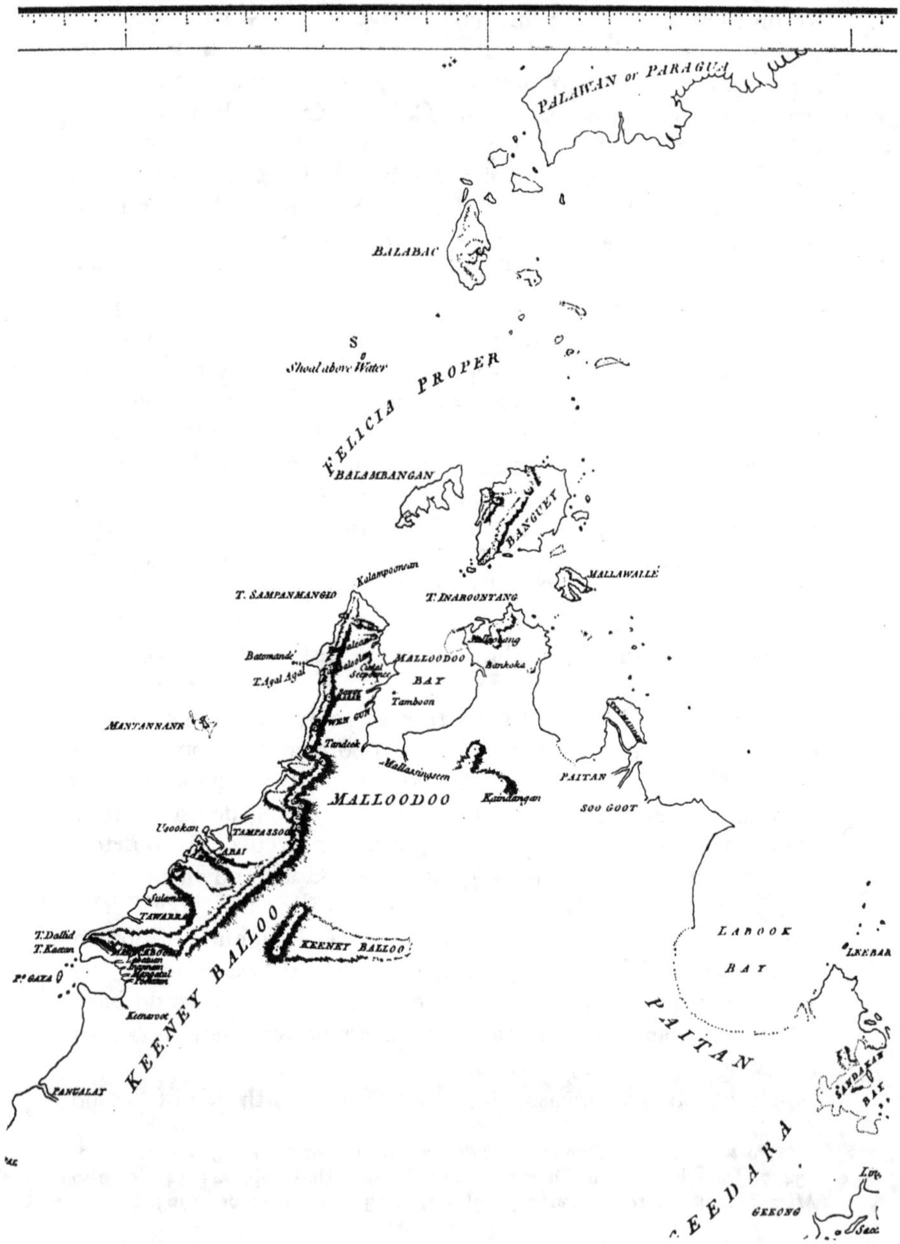

NORTH BORNEO

PART OF ALEXANDER DALRYMPLE'S 'CHART OF FELICIA AND PLAN OF THE ISLAND OF BALAMBANGAN' (1770)

been on the tops of some of the Hills from whence an extensive prospect can be obtained; by this means he determined the situation of several of the North-West Islands, for as these islands are low they can easily be seen over one another'.[65] He is said to have charted some eighty islands during this visit.

The final duty which he had to perform was to obtain a cession of the site he had chosen for a settlement – the island of Balambangan. This cession is said to have taken place on 12 September 1762, and Dalrymple told how he had persuaded the Sultan Bantilan to hold a Council of all the Sulu chiefs, at which the cession of the island was requested, and agreed to.[66]

The smallpox epidemic, Bandahara's death and the impending change of government with the expected return of the old Sultan from Manila, had all combined to introduce a state of nervous tension on the island, and the recurring hostilities with the Spaniards had made the Sulu islanders suspicious of all Europeans. The Sultan, too, was causing difficulties. He had not been a party to the original commercial agreement, and he did his best to stir up opposition to the new one. Neither Dalrymple nor Rennell was impressed by him as a person, the former referring to him as 'that old fox', while Rennell described his idleness and lack of concern for the welfare of his subjects, his lack of dignity and authority, and his untrustworthiness, stating that he would 'pimp for, or cheat any man living'. Moreover, relations were probably not improved by a rebellion on the island, led by a native of Manila who had formerly been a servant of Dalrymple. This man, who had gathered a following of 2,000 people, had run away from Dalrymple's service on his previous visit and now claimed to be Prince Israel, the old Sultan's son. The islanders became so suspicious that, as Rennell recalled, 'upon our attempting to drive a few small Palisadoes round our tents to preserve our moveables, the Town was immediately alarmed with the report of making a Fortification; and this opinion was probably corroborated by the mistake of Mr

[65] *Rennell's Journal*, p. 63.

[66] The original cession has not been located, but it is referred to in the Treaty of 19 September 1763, and in Dalrymple's letter to the Court of Directors dated 30 October 1769 in *Home Miscellaneous Series*, Vol. 771, p. 189.

7—AD * *

Dalrymple's reflecting Telescope for a small Cannon'.[67] In early October events took an uglier turn when 'Two or Three of the Principal People of Sooloo having taken umbrage at the behaviour of the others in purchasing our Goods thought proper to insult and threaten them. . . . One of these people having contributed towards fitting up our house insisted upon having the materials returned which happened to be part of the Palisadoes. The other party offered him payment for them but he refused it and insisted upon pulling them down. This occasioned all the armed men of the other Party to assemble in a body before the house which stood in a square near the mouth of the River'. Since Dalrymple's party numbered only twelve – six Europeans and six armed 'Caffries'[68] – they naturally felt alarmed, but the affair petered out in Gilbertian fashion, for after the men had spent some fifteen minutes 'strutting and parading . . . with the clattering of their wooden targets and their lances', the situation was saved by the appearance of a troop of women who came to act as mediators, after which 'the Warriors dispersed to our no small satisfaction'.[69]

The time had come to return to Madras, but as conditions at Sulu were so disturbed they decided to get their supplies from the Spanish fortress at Samboangan, on Mindanao, where Dalrymple had become so friendly with the Governor during his cruise in the *Cuddalore*. True to character, Dalrymple had not allowed his other preoccupations and worries to stop him from trying to learn all that he could, and he had asked 'one of the Imans or Priests' to get him a history of the island, but, as he wryly remarked in a marginal note to Rennell's log, 'the delivery of this was delayed by the priest until the moment of departure, and when he returned to Sooloo and had an opportunity of getting some of his Sooloo Friends to examine it, instead of the

[67] *Rennell's Journal*, pp. 40–41.

[68] In his 1806 pamphlet on Pirates (pp. 29–30n), Dalrymple remarked that this was 'the name given in India to the woolly headed Negros, several of whom are Portuguese slaves at Makau, brought from Timor: it is a corruption of an Arabic word "Caffer", an Infidel, given to the African negros by the Arabs, but extended by the English to all the woolly headed race'.

[69] *Rennell's Journal*, p. 65.

Sooloo History it was found to be a Transcription of some Arabian Fables'!

They had left Sulu and were on their way to Samboangan, when on 21 November 1762 they met a Spanish ship and were told that war had broken out between their two countries. This news prompted Dalrymple to draw up a scheme for exploiting the war by seizing from the Spaniards the Southern Philippines – a plan in which he specifically did not envisage an attack on Manila;[70] but unknown to them all, Manila had already been attacked.

From the first it had been obvious that both the Spaniards and the Dutch would be concerned over the establishment of a British settlement in this area. The Dutch had no legal grounds for any pretensions here, but with the Spaniards it was a different matter. History showed that they had never succeeded in subduing Sulu for any appreciable period, and the Sultan of Sulu claimed dominion over an empire, but it was hard to define the extent either of the Spanish claim or of the Sulu dominions. In his letter to Pitt, on 26 February 1761,[71] Dalrymple had frankly stated that it was 'very difficult to determine the limits of this Empire as several Places mentioned in the Spanish Histories are not to be found in their Draughts and tho' the names of others are inserted their situation and Description are very erroneous'. He knew, however, that the Spaniards had never given up their ambition to conquer Sulu, and he may have heard of their 1753 expedition to take possession of Palawan. On that occasion the Spanish commander had 'made a careful and exact survey of the islands of Palawan and Balabak', but along all the coasts had found only mangrove swamps, reefs and inhabitants who were always hostile. Nevertheless, he had taken possession of the land, claiming to have done so 'with due solemnity (and) with the express knowledge and consent of the inhabitants'.[72] As Dalrymple had remarked in his 'Memoir of Sooloo', written seven months

70 Dalrymple, 'Plan of an Expedition for the Conquest of the Southern Philippines', dated 23 November 1762, B.M., *Add. Mss. 19,298*.

71 Dalrymple 'Memoir of the Sooloogannan Dominions and Commerce', *Egremont Papers*, ut supra.

72 Quoted by N. M. Saleeby, *History of Sulu*, Manila, 1908, p. 209. The Spanish claim was based on a cession by the 'King of Bruney'.

earlier, 'That so rich a Jewel will become an object of Envy is beyond doubt and therefore It is reasonable to suppose every Measure be taken by our Rivals to Supplant Us'.[73] He had hoped that it might be possible to establish a settlement in this Archipelago by peaceful means, but now that war had broken out he thought that the British should seize this new opportunity.

Dalrymple realized that some would oppose military action against the Spaniards in the Philippines on the grounds that it would jeopardise the supply of silver, at present obtained by the British through the 'very lucrative commerce . . . carried on from India to Manila under sanction of Moorish Colours'. He believed that the danger was exaggerated, since this silver was the produce of the trade between Manila and America; without Manila, America would open her arms to any who could import the produce of India[74] and China, and though he did not propose the capture of Manila itself, the possession of the southern islands would be a great restraint on the Spaniards in that capital. To be justified, however, a conquest must either meet the expense of its attainment by being retained, or it must be of sufficient value to induce the enemy to make important concessions at the peace talks for its recovery. Since the chief motive of the Spaniards for maintaining these islands was their religious zeal, he believed it was quite possible that in return for permitting the Missions to operate in this area, 'Manila itself might then be ceded and Perhaps Valuable Commercial Priviledges granted also to us. Even if they did not react in this way, they could not afford to have so large a part of their Dominions severed from Manila, particularly as they already suffered severely from the Inroads of the Moors', and this must be an important point in any peace negotiations.

To emphasize the value of these islands, he enumerated their products and estimated their population as amounting to approximately 350,000. Their present lack of commercial value he attributed entirely to the indolence and bad government of the Spaniards. The defences were not formidable, being designed

[73] *Orme Mss.*, Vol. 67, f. 32.

[74] Dalrymple tended to include the East Indies in the term 'India', reserving 'Hindostan' for the Indian mainland.

against native rather than European enemies, and he suggested that the forces necessary need not amount to more than 'a Europe ship', one or more smaller vessels equipped for war, and a detachment of fifty Europeans and some Sepoys. After taking on board her cargo at Sulu, the ship would proceed to Sambo-angan, whose reduction would be a matter of course. Then Missamis[75] must be taken, since its capture would give access to the Illanon, the native inhabitants of the interior. Finally, the island of Zebu to the north of Mindanao must be seized. Since the island of Bohol, the eastern neighbour of Zebu, was believed to be already in revolt, this should be sufficient. The essence of Dalrymple's Plan was to gain the maximum advantage from the minimum military effort, such as would be well within the Company's own resources.

On returning to Sulu, Dalrymple and his companions learnt of the capture of Manila. This news reached them on 24 December 1762, and it immediately had a most beneficial effect upon the islanders, who had esteemed the Spaniards as 'the most powerful and warlike people in the world'. On loading their return cargo, the *London*'s crew 'could not help remarking that the Inhabitants of Sooloo wore a much more pacific aspect than usual: in all probability this was occasioned by the news of our being in possession of Manila.'[76] In these easier conditions, and with a favourable north-east wind now blowing, they were impatient to be off, and so no time was lost in taking on their cargo of forty tons of cowries, and some sago, wax, mother-of-pearl, and red and yellow woods for dyes, a cargo 'proper for the China market'.

On the return voyage to Madras Dalrymple took the opportunity, on 23 January 1763, of landing on, and taking formal possession of, the island of Balambangan.

[75] Misamis is on the north coast of Mindanao.
[76] *Rennell's Journal*, p. 75.

CHAPTER IV

The Settlement at Balambangan

WHEN Dalrymple reached Madras again, in March 1763, there was considerable disappointment, the greater because hopes had been pitched so high. The risks were clearly bigger than had been foreseen, and it was decided that no further action could be taken by the Governor-in-Council until new instructions had been received from England.[1] This, in turn, placed Dalrymple in an awkward position. In order to undertake this venture four years earlier, he had stepped aside from promotion to the Secretaryship, so that his place on the promotion-ladder had now been filled. Furthermore, Governor George Pigot, who had been his staunchest supporter throughout, was soon due to retire to England and there was no reason to anticipate the same far-sighted and enthusiastic backing in the future. In these circumstances, Dalrymple decided that his best move would be to return to England himself, so that he could explain his scheme in person to the Court of Directors. Pigot, however, though sympathizing with his motives, pointed out that this would create a dangerous precedent. He therefore suggested that Dalrymple should go through the formality of resigning, as he was certain that whatever their decision, the Court of Directors would fully understand this action, and that he would have no difficulty in being re-instated when the time came. Dalrymple accordingly followed this advice.

On 27 June 1763 he received formal permission to return to England, and a week later he left as a passenger in the *Neptune* for Canton, with orders to call at Sulu en route, where he was to settle the accounts of the previous year's voyage. Once more, however, the fates were unkind to the enterprise. The first difficulty was the slow progress of the *Neptune*, which did not reach

[1] *Home Miscellaneous Series,* Vol. 771, pp. 55–7.

Malacca until 4 August. At Malacca Dalrymple found the *London*, and he reported to Madras that he intended taking her along to Sulu as well, as she might not only be useful to the *Neptune* but would also give him the opportunity of sending advices to Manila, which was now under British occupation.[2]

After this tedious start, they did not reach Sulu until 7 September, where they learnt of a further misfortune which would make it well-nigh impossible to collect the Company's debt. The agreement signed in Sulu the previous season had insisted that when the *Royal Captain*'s cargo arrived, the goods 'should be received at 100 per cent on the Coast price by the Sooloos, who were to pay for [the cargo] in gruff goods[3] to be transported to Canton on their risk and disposed of there for their account and all exceedings of the Sooloo price to be remitted to them ...'. The whole purpose of this arrangement had been to ensure that the islanders would receive a further consignment of goods, on which they might make a handsome profit, only after they had paid their outstanding debts. It was now learnt that the *Royal Captain*'s cargo had been forwarded from Canton to Manila, and the British authorities there had immediately sent it to Sulu, where the goods had been divided 'amongst the different people'. As the islanders now had all the goods in their hands, they were bound only by their word to pay their debts, and it was impossible to feel any optimism in this matter.[4] Nor had the *Neptune*'s slow passage helped, for now it was essential that they should leave after a very short visit, as otherwise they would be in danger of losing their passage through the change of the monsoon.

While at Sulu, Dalrymple met the Chinese commander of a vessel from Batavia, whom he had previously come across in Sulu in 1761. This man had come back 'as much a spy as to settle accounts', and had brought a letter from the Governor-General at Batavia to the Sultan, proposing a Treaty of Friendship with the Dutch. Dalrymple had been assured by the Suluans

[2] *Home Miscellaneous Series*, Vol. 22, p. 148.

[3] Gruff goods were those that were bulky.

[4] *Factory Records; Borneo*, f. 57, Dalrymple to Secret Committee, Manila, 7 February 1764.

that a polite refusal would be returned, and was in any case confident that the treaty he had negotiated excluded the Dutch from any legal intervention. Meanwhile he had endeavoured to keep on the best of terms with this Chinese commander, since the latter was a great expert on the trade of the eastern archipelago and would readily settle, Dalrymple believed, at any British settlement in these seas.

Since his previous visit there had been a change of government on the island, for Bantilan was now dead and had been succeeded, as *de facto* sultan, by his son, Alimudin II. Prince Israel, the son of the exiled sultan, was also on the island. Because of Dutch intrigues, Dalrymple decided that the cession of Balambangan, which he had already obtained from the previous sultan, needed to be buttressed by a further cession of South Palawan and North Borneo, and so he made an agreement to that effect with Alimudin II on 19 September 1763.[5]

Her short stay meant that the *Neptune* had had to leave behind a large part of the cargo that had been collected for her, and when she sailed on 19 September 1763, Dalrymple decided to go by way of Manila, so that he could report in person to Dawsonne Drake, the Deputy Governor,[6] and his Council.

Manila was reached on 6 October, and here he found that the British authorities had signed a new agreement with the exiled sultan which, as Drake stressed, was intended to reinforce the treaty already concluded by Dalrymple. This new agreement

[5] *Home Miscellaneous Series*, Vol. 99, pp. 263–4. The Spanish original is in *Home Miscellaneous Series*, Vol. 629, pp. 479–81. E. A. Julian, in her thesis, declares that this Spanish copy is quite unintelligible. Dalrymple explained that the original and the Spanish translation were delivered to him sealed up, just as the *Neptune* was leaving on 19 September, and it was only when he opened it to show it to the exiled sultan at Manila that he found it to be considerably different to what he had expected. In the Spanish version his request for South Palawan and the North end of Borneo with all the intermediate islands was implied, but not 'clearly expressed'. Furthermore, the people signing it were not those properly in authority. He had therefore forwarded from Manila only the Malay version, retaining the Spanish one himself.

[6] Dawsonne Drake had been a Member of Council at Fort St George at the time of the *Cuddalore*'s return in January 1762, and so was fully conversant with the history of the venture.

had been dated 23 February 1763,[7] but it had promptly drawn a protest from Archbishop Rojo, who had surrendered Manila to the British, and who claimed that he had already obtained a treaty himself from the sultan which cut right across the British claims. Dalrymple saw the details of this treaty and found that the old sultan had expressly promised Sulu, Basilan, Palawan and all the towns on Borneo to the Spaniards. 'The Sultan alledged,' he wrote 'this was more than he had really granted . . . however he acknowledged enough to make me think some measures necessary to supersede the Spanish Pretensions.' Because Drake's treaty implied recognition, it was impossible for the British to say that any agreement signed by the old sultan was unconstitutional and invalid. However, Dalrymple persuaded the sultan to surrender his copy of Drake's treaty, and he advised that the Company should now simply expunge it from their records. In addition, he had persuaded the sultan 'that a Convention of the Estates should declare by a Public Act that no Treaty concluded by him in his absence should be in force . . . and that his acceding to this Edict should be insisted on previous to his assuming the Government'.[8]

This incident naturally made the English wonder whether the old sultan was to be trusted. Dalrymple felt that proper allowance must be made for the fact that he had been slighted by the British, and that no warm attachment to their cause could be expected from him. Moreover, this exile was naturally not prepared to expose himself unnecessarily to the enmity of the Spaniards, whose prisoner he had been for so long, and Dalrymple himself had 'always recommended to him to keep on a plausible footing with the Spaniards'. There was no doubt, however, that he had a 'violent disposition', and the most hopeful arrangement therefore seemed to be a delegation of authority to Sarapodin, his eldest son by a concubine, who would rule in his name 'the Borneo Dominions' and Palawan. As Dalrymple pointed out, this solution would win for the British the friendship of a man 'of

[7] *Home Miscellaneous Series*, Vol. 629, pp. 467–9 and *Factory Records; Borneo*, f. 56.

[8] *Factory Records; Borneo*, f. 57, Dalrymple to Secret Committee, 7 February 1764.

very great Capacity, Moderation and Application . . . (and) of great Integrity', while for Sarapodin, the establishment of a successful British settlement within his dominions would soon make him the most considerable prince in the East. For their part, it was essential that the Company should appoint a man who would readily co-operate with a native prince; Dalrymple suggested that the Hon. Thomas Howe would be an admirable choice, under whom, if the Company thought fit, he himself would be most happy to serve.

It was apparent that the future of Dalrymple's scheme was now in the balance. In Madras, Palk was about to succeed Pigot as Governor, and it was uncertain what support could be anticipated from him and his Council. The attitude of the present Court of Directors in London had not yet been made known. In Manila, Dawsonne Drake and his Council were having little success in dealing with the Spanish opposition, and the personal authority of Drake himself was in question. With so much uncertainty, it was essential that the restoration of the old sultan to his Sulu dominions should not be mishandled. Dalrymple had already been worried about Drake's activities, which were causing concern to the local Chinese and might dissuade them, he feared, from settling at any new British establishment.[9] Four days after his arrival at Manila he therefore wrote to Fort St George to announce his intention of returning to Sulu.[10]

The handing over of Manila to the Spaniards under the terms of the Treaty of Paris was complicated by disputes which had broken out between Drake and his Council, culminating in Drake's resignation before the ceremony was completed. Dalrymple was requested to take over this office himself. This he felt bound to do, though, as he said, he looked upon the office and the occasion as equally disagreeable.

The British party finally left Manila on 16 April 1764, and reached Sulu on 19 May. Within a fortnight the British fleet was on its way again, but the *London* and a galley remained at the island under Dalrymple's command. Indeed, the authorities

[9] *Factory Records; Borneo,* f. 57, Dalrymple to Secret Committee, 7 February 1764.

[10] *Home Miscellaneous Series,* Vol. 771, pp. 79–81, para. 88.

at Madras were alarmed when they were told 'by private hands' that nine or ten sampans were also with him, with between one and two thousand Chinese, and that he also had a military force of 120 native soldiers, complete with artillery and military stores. It was naturally feared at Fort St George that he was about to take matters into his own hands, and to establish his settlement without authority.[11] Whatever the temptation, he made no effort to do this.

In the meantime, he had received a promise from Madras that a ship would be dispatched to Sulu that season, and on 18 June he sent the *London* to wait for the expected vessel at Balambangan, he himself following in the galley on 3 July. He continued in the region of that island until the beginning of September, but when no ship appeared he decided that he must return to Sulu and load the *London* for China. This was a great disappointment. If these first essays at trade had been successful, the argument for establishing a settlement would have been very strong, but at first he had suffered from sheer ill-luck, and now he had been left unsupported by a lukewarm Council at Madras. The behaviour of the authorities at Fort St George was all the more reprehensible since not only did they send the ship direct to Canton, instead of via Sulu as promised, but she carried with her a letter from the Court of Directors which, if it had been received by Dalrymple in time, might have altered the whole outcome of this interesting experiment.[12]

In this letter the Directors underlined all the difficulties and dangers of such a project, and stressed the lack of civilization 'of the generality of the Malays', who were treacherous people to trade with, and had, indeed, killed some of Dalrymple's own men, 'yet we are satisfied you entertained the Project with a view to advance our Interest and to lay a plan for future benefits to Us, and the enlarging our Trade where we have as yet scarce any Knowledge or footing, and therefore though we do not at

[11] *Madras Military and Secret Consultations*, Range 251, Vol. 51, 1 October 1764.

[12] *European Magazine*, Vol. 42 (1802), p. 324. Dalrymple recalled that he had spent the weeks of waiting at Balambangan in planting 'cocoa-nut' and fruit trees.

present . . . approve of making a settlement, yet We recommend that you do continue to keep up the Intercourse of Trade there . . .'. This letter had commended Dalrymple's conduct; a second, written two months later, added that although it was not their intention to incur the considerable expense of a settlement, 'we had no Intentions to prevent a Residence'. So the Directors ordered that 'if you find a Residence at Xolo is feasible, that Mr Dalrymple be appointed our Resident there if he chooses it; with one or two Covenant Servants to assist him . . . by a Residence there opportunities may be had of exploring those Parts, and striking out some advantages very beneficial to the Company, and from what we have observed of Mr Dalrymple's conduct in this affair, we make no doubt of his acquitting himself in the said Station to our Satisfaction . . .'; in particular, more information was required of Borneo and the adjacent islands.[13] Dalrymple would have been the perfect choice for these tasks, and such an appointment might have altered the whole direction of British enterprise in the East; on the other hand, this would have prevented his return to England, and without his presence in London and his writings on the problems of the South Pacific, it is doubtful whether Cook's first two voyages would have followed the pattern they did.

After he had sent the *London* to Balambangan, and before he had followed in the galley, Dalrymple had been occupied in restoring the old sultan to authority in Sulu. Having successfully accomplished this, he then turned to the question of the lands in which the British were interested. 'The Sultan and the People who form the Government of Sooloo made a cession by way of Sale to the Company of the Northern part of Borneo from Towson Abai in abt. 6° on the N.E. side to Keemanees on the west in abt. $5\frac{1}{2}$° N.Lat. with all the islands to the Northward of Borneo comprehending part of Palawan. . . . The Island Balabac etc. And in this cession there was a stipulation that the Company might appoint one of the Sultan's sons or Relations to the administration of these Districts. Accordingly I gave Dato Sarapodin a Commission to govern them for the Company which

[13] *Madras Despatches*, Vol. 2, 9 March and 13 May 1763, pp. 623–8 and 739–41.

was ratified under the Sultan's hand and seal.'[14] After he had returned to Sulu at the end of his vain wait off Balambangan, Dalrymple consolidated the British position by negotiating with this new government a treaty similar to the one which he had concluded in 1761, whereby the Sultan and people of Sulu permitted the English to purchase ground for a factory and garden and acknowledged the right of Chinese to settle under the jurisdiction of the English, while the latter were to have the exclusive right of free trade in the Sultan's dominions.[15]

Having done all that was possible, Dalrymple now left Sulu for the last time, and proceeded to Canton, and so to England, which was reached on 10 July 1765.

On his arrival home he found that conditions were no longer favourable to his scheme. The instructions suggesting a residency at Sulu had been sent when Laurence Sulivan had 'gained the ascendancy in the direction', but Dalrymple now found a battle raging over the whole question of the Company's future, with Clive and Sulivan the chief protagonists. Little attention to his plan could therefore be expected for some time to come.[16] Nor was any encouragement to be looked for from Fort St George, where the earlier optimism had given way to a mood of resigned withdrawal. 'We are sorry,' wrote the Council on 18 October 1765, 'after so much pains have been taken by Mr Dalrymple supported as far as we could prudently answer for, that his Expectation of the advantages resulting from this Commerce should be totally disappointed. . . . With respect to the cession of Territories . . . whatever these Grants may be it does not appear to us they will ever answer to the Company.'[17] Despite their present preoccupations, the Company's Directors in London

[14] *Miscellaneous Letters Received,* Vol. 47, f. 135, Dalrymple to Directors, 26 November 1765. The cession itself is to be found in *Home Miscellaneous Series,* Vol. 629, pp. 488–9 and is dated 2 July 1764; in his 'Memoirs' Dalrymple gives the date as 29 June 1764 – *European Magazine,* Vol. 42, p. 324.

[15] *Home Miscellaneous Series,* Vol. 629, pp. 495–501, dated 28 September 1764.

[16] See L. S. Sutherland, *The East India Company in Eighteenth Century Politics,* Chapters 5 and 6.

[17] *Home Miscellaneous Series,* Vol. 771, pp. 91–5, para. 40. General Letter from Fort St George, 18 October 1765.

were disconcerted by this attitude, however, and on 19 February 1766 told Madras that even if the debts incurred were, as seemed likely, irrecoverable, 'we do not infer . . . that the Trade with those Islands is incapable of being rendered Lucrative'; no rights were to be renounced, nor opportunities of friendship with the islanders to be lost, 'yet this is not the proper time to assert our pretensions . . .'[18].

For a time the scheme hung fire. Dalrymple devoted himself to the study of Pacific exploration, while the Directors concentrated on domestic problems which threatened to undermine the stability of the Company. The latest crisis had begun in April 1766, when the Directors received a despatch from Clive, who advised them to expect a surplus of over £1,650,000 p.a. from the territorial revenues of Bengal, Bihar and Orissa.[19] This was to prove a great exaggeration, but the damage was done. Clive, who had assumed the diwani[20] on behalf of his employers, believed that this would result in a striking increase in the wealth of the East India Company, and this was a widely held view. The inevitable result was a speculative boom in East India Stock, which resulted in a powerful demand for higher dividends.[21]

[18] Ibid., pp. 99–104.

[19] V. T. Harlow, *The Founding of the Second British Empire*, Vol. II, p. 43. It has been calculated that the total surplus revenue from all the East India Company's settlements (including Bencoolen) for the whole period 1776–84 only totalled £3,877,000. C. J. Hamilton, *The Trade Relations between England and India*, p. 146.

[20] 'The office and power of the King's Dewan . . . in former times was "the collecting of all the revenues, and, after defraying the expences of the army, and allowing a sufficient fund for the support of the Nizamaut, to remit the remainder to Dehly". This . . . is not the office we wish to execute . . . experience convinces us, how unfit an Englishman is to conduct the collection of the revenues, and follow the subtle native through all his arts, to conceal the real value of his country, and to perplex and elude the payments. We therefore entirely approve of your preserving the ancient form of Government, in the upholding the dignity of the Subah. We conceive the office of Dewan should be exercised only in superintending the collections, and disposal of the revenues. . . .' Court of Directors to Select Committee in Bengal, 17 May 1766. Quoted in H. Verelst, *A View of the English Government in Bengal*, Appendix, p. 136.

[21] Sutherland, op. cit., pp. 138 et seq. East India Stock, whose value before the receipt of Clive's despatch was 164, rose to a maximum of 273 in 1767. Those interests demanding higher dividends founded the *East India Examiner* to voice their views; the Directors tried to answer with the *East India Observer*.

The market 'bulls' asserted that there was 'a moral certainty' that a 15 per cent dividend was feasible.[22] It was useless for the Directors to point out that the Bengal revenues could only be transferred to England by a large increase in the goods exported from Bengal or by taking over the burden of supplying the other Asiatic settlements with bullion. These pleas were overridden, and in November 1766 the dividend was raised from 6 per cent to 10 per cent, which still left the speculators far from satisfied.

In these circumstances the Directors were ready to consider any proposals that promised a way out of their difficulties. The election of Thomas Rous and Thomas Saunders as Chairman and Deputy Chairman in the spring of 1767 provided a propitious moment for a new approach, as Saunders had become a personal friend of Dalrymple in the years that had elapsed since 1753, when the one had been Governor, and the other a newly-arrived Writer, at Fort St George. The interest of the Court of Directors was evident when on 30 September 1767 it referred to a joint Committee of Correspondence and Treasury the consideration of the most effectual measures for extending the trade of the Company. In this context one of the Directors, unknown to Dalrymple, obtained a copy of his Plan and made extracts from it. Then, in February and March 1768, the two committees began a series of meetings to consider it in detail.[23]

At these meetings Robert Gregory, the recognized authority on the trade of Bengal,[24] showed himself an enthusiastic supporter of this scheme, which faced up to the 'difficulty of remitting home the Bengal revenue, without ruining the Country'. This could not be done in specie, of which there was a grave shortage in Bengal at that time. As Burke's Committee Report of 1783 stated, 'to send it in silver was subject to two manifest

22 *East India Examiner*, Vol. VIII (8 October 1766), p. 47. See, also, Ibid., Vol. III, pp. 15–18.

23 This was the very time when Hawke was opposing Dalrymple's appointment to the command of the *Endeavour*, and the latter's refusal to go on that expedition in any other capacity must have been influenced, to some extent, by this promising alternative.

24 See Sutherland, op. cit., p. 288n. He was a Director and MP and had aspirations to the Chairmanship of the Company.

inconveniences. First, the country would be exhausted of its circulating medium; second, to send silver into Europe would be to send it from the best to the worst market. It was necessary therefore to turn the Company's revenue into its commerce'.[25] This was precisely what Dalrymple's Plan proposed, though London was not to be the destination of that commerce. 'If the production and manufactures of Bengal can be carried to some port to the eastward, and disposed of for goods fit for the China market,' wrote Dalrymple, 'then the exportation of money from Bengal will, at least in part, be avoided, and the returns thither from the eastward . . . will occasion a constant circulation without impoverishment.'[26]

The combined Committee concluded that a settlement at Balambangan would be most advantageous, but it would be prudent to start operations 'very privately and cautiously', so that they could gauge more accurately the probable extent of the trade, the security of property in this area, and the likelihood of interference from European neighbours, most particularly from the Dutch. They would also have to decide 'whether Government should be apprized of the plan before any steps are taken towards executing it'. If they were to be in a position to send out orders by the ships of the next season, now was the time to consider these matters.[27] Thus Dalrymple was asked to submit 'the general heads of an expedition to Balambangan', and in less than a fortnight he did so, outlining his ideas on the objects immediately in view, and emphasizing the need to provide adequate monetary resources in the first stages, until the native merchants developed sufficient confidence to allow trade to develop by barter. He expressed his personal preference for carrying on this trade, in the first instance, from an armed ship rather than from a fort on shore.[28] On 7 July the Committee agreed to go ahead with the scheme, and a message was sent to

[25] Quoted by Hamilton, op. cit., p. 139.

[26] A. Dalrymple, *A Plan for extending the commerce of this kingdom. . . .* pp. 3 et seq.

[27] *Home Miscellaneous Series,* Vol. 771, pp. 115–46. Committees of Correspondence 26 February, 1, 8 and 22 March 1768.

[28] *Factory Records; Borneo,* f. 18, 26 April and 8 May 1768.

Scotland, where Dalrymple was visiting his family and friends, informing him of this decision and of the plan to purchase a ship, with a request that he should return to London.[29]

It may seem strange that, at the very moment when events at last seemed to be going his way, the seeds were sown of the conflict that was to cost Dalrymple the leadership of this expedition, and even his place in the Company's service. Yet, whatever views may be held as to his judgment, it is impossible not to respect his attitude. Having spent so many months in the Sulu Archipelago, he had no illusions as to the magnitude of the task to be accomplished. An English settlement in that area would have to contend with islanders of uncertain temper, with a growing threat of piracy, and with opposition and intrigues from both Spanish and Dutch neighbours. Success would bring great rewards, but would only be won through unremitting effort, and it was essential that careful thought should be given to the basis on which this new settlement was to be established. Dalrymple felt that the Committee was not paying sufficient attention to these important matters. As he explained, the post would be one of 'much danger and inquietude. I thought it was candid, before they advanced too far, to have these preliminaries settled . . . although it was a point I had much at heart, it was not a job; and I was in that temper of mind, that I would rather have returned to Madrass [sic], in the common line, than have gone to Balambangan in a mode not entirely agreeable to myself'. In view of the difficulties which he would have to face, he wanted a reward commensurate with the risks. A less scrupulous man would have waited until the preparations were so far advanced that it would have been difficult to have refused his demands, or would have looked for his reward from private trade, but that was not Dalrymple's way.

Thus, when the Committee of Correspondence met on 3 August 1768, its members were in a quandary. On the one hand they had heard encouraging evidence from Robert Gregory, who estimated that an eastern settlement which could absorb the

[29] Dalrymple, *An Account of what has passed between the India Directors and Alexander Dalrymple*, London, 1768, pp. 11–12. *Correspondence Reports*, Vol. 8, 7 July 1768.

Bengal investment would yield, in four or five years, an annual profit of £100,000.[30] On the other, they had been presented by Dalrymple with a paper outlining the terms on which he would serve, and they were shocked; their reaction confirmed his suspicion that they had given little thought to this aspect of the enterprise. He had already told them, in his paper in May, that he did not consider a Council to be wise in an infant settlement. 'The only instance of a new Establishment within my memory', he wrote, 'was Negrais[31] where there was no Council. I could never think of going unless I was to have the carrying my own Plan into Execution.' He now explained that he wanted the command of the ship and the choice of the men who were to go on the expedition. Above all, he wanted sufficient prospects for the future. 'If I am fixed at Balambangan to my own satisfaction,' he wrote, 'I mean to devote my whole life to promote the success of that establishment, and shall look upon it as my home.' In return for such a commitment he asked for substantial rewards. The Company should grant him an annuity, transferable for another life; he should be allowed to engage in the pearl fishery; he should have a commission on all cargoes bought and sold at Balambangan; if he should die in the Company's service and leave any children unprovided for, the Company should give each of them a pension of £100 p.a. In return, he undertook to accept no presents in money, and to keep an account of any other gifts; if these conditions were unacceptable, he asked to be returned to Madras.[32]

In insisting that the Chief must not rely on private trade for his reward, Dalrymple pointed out that in such commerce the object must be to buy cheap and sell dear. This was in direct

[30] The 'Investment' signified the goods purchased by the Company in the East, primarily for the European market. As early as 1757 the practice began of sending silver from Bengal to China to purchase the teas, etc. intended for Europe. The amount so sent averaged *c.* £100,000 p.a. – see Hamilton, op. cit., p. 138. By absorbing Bengal's produce and converting it into goods fit for the China market, Balambangan promised to end this annual export of silver from Bengal.

[31] See Chapter I, pp. 8–10.

[32] Dalrymple, *An Account . . .*, pp. 16–26. *Factory Records; Borneo*, f. 46, 3 August 1768.

conflict to the overall interest of such a settlement,[33] which must draw in strangers from every quarter by giving good prices for their commodities, and by selling to them cheaply such goods as they required. He added this revealing comment by way of self-analysis: 'I know my own temper to be such, that whatever I pursue must be with the whole mind; if I take up the pursuit of money, it is likely that desire will absorb every other idea.'

The Directors were deeply disappointed. One of them told Dalrymple of the warm zeal that there had been for the scheme, but that there now seemed to have entered into it 'motives of interest', and that 'there appeared a general repugnance and disgust at the idea of an expedition so wide from their ideas . . . an independence for life . . . leaves the impression of the possibility of that security, being an inducement to relax from your endeavours . . . it hurts every way, and must not be thought of . . .'.[34] In these views the Directors misjudged their man, but in the year 1768 their attitude was understandable. The battle over Clive's *jagir*, and speculation in the Company's shares, had embroiled them all in party politics. With feeling running high in the country over the wealth of the returning 'nabobs', and over the Company's role in the affairs of Bengal, the Directors were naturally anxious not to create a fresh target for their enemies to aim at. There was, of course, a fundamental difference; apart from the small annuity he was asking for, whatever wealth would come to Dalrymple through these proposals could only come through a flourishing trade at Balambangan. His wealth would be earned through the creation of wealth.[35] He could also point

33 cf. Adam Smith, *The Wealth of Nations*, Dent & Sons, Everyman Edition, 1962, Vol. II, p. 134. 'It is the interest of the East India Company, considered as sovereigns, that the European goods which are carried to their Indian dominions should be sold there as cheap as possible. But the reverse of this is their interest as merchants.' It is noteworthy that Dalrymple and Adam Smith were well acquainted with one another as early as 1766.

34 Dalrymple, *An Account* . . . , pp. 28–9.

35 When he again offered to take over the management of this settlement in 1774, Dalrymple recalled that the Directors had originally objected that his 'share of the profits at Balambangan might be more than Lord Clive's Jaguire; I am not sanguine enough to expect that this would happen in many years, but I have the satisfaction to consider that (supposing the share only 1/10) it could happen by no other means than the Company's receiving

out with some justification that not only was he promising to commit his whole career to this one project, but he had already sacrificed much on its behalf. Had he stuck to his Secretarial post at Fort St George in 1759, he would have been a great deal better off financially than he now was. Only the generosity of his old patron George Pigot had kept him solvent. He pointed out that Kelsall, his assistant on his second voyage to Sulu, was now a Member of Council at Bengal. Not many men could claim, at this time, to have left India poorer than they arrived, but he was able to do so, and no one could suggest that that was through incompetence.

Rous and Saunders had been succeeded by Boulton and Sir George Colebrooke, and the new Chairman frankly admitted to Dalrymple that he had been worried about implementing the scheme from the first, and thought that much more consideration was needed than had so far been given. The two men remained on friendly terms during the ensuing conflict, but as the weeks passed it was becoming increasingly clear that through a lack of vigorous leadership the matter was going to be shelved. As early as 24 August the Chairman was stating that it was now too late to put the scheme into execution that season, and it was at this same meeting that Dalrymple first suggested publishing his Plan with the clear intention of bringing pressure to bear on the Directors.[36]

In an attempt to keep the scheme alive, Dalrymple met the Chairman and his Deputy in the following month and explained that his terms had only been intended as a guide to his wishes, but that if it was felt that the success of the Plan depended upon himself, which he 'had not so high an opinion' of his own consequence as to think, then 'no pecuniary considerations' would

---

from Balambangan . . . a clear profit of 10 per cent on their whole Capital'. *Miscellaneous Letters Received*, Vol. 58, f. 299, Dalrymple to Directors, 9 December 1774.

36 With the affairs of the Company in a critical state, this was no idle threat. See Sutherland, op. cit., Chapter VII. Pigot was a MP and was about to take an active part in the Company's affairs once more. The Dalrymple family were also known to the Johnstones, and although the former in no sense belonged to the Johnstone faction in party or Company politics, the Directors must have feared the possibility of such an alliance.

prevent him from executing it.[37] He was assured that the expedition had been postponed, not dropped, and the Correspondence Committee had, in fact, already suggested that the President of Madras should be instructed to send a vessel to take possession of Balambangan 'and to pursue all necessary measures for opening a Trade to the Eastern Archipelago'.[38]

Determined to keep up the pressure, on 5 October Dalrymple informed the Directors that it was his intention to publish his Plan, adding, ingenuously, that 'should any objections against such a publication occur to you, it will be a favour to communicate them'. Two days later the Committee asked him to attend, and he was simply told that 'all publication was improper'. The Chairman, courteous as always, told him that he must do what he thought right, but Robert Jones added: 'What you do shall be at your peril'.[39] To Dalrymple this was insufferable, and he erupted, bringing the meeting to a disorderly end.

For some time thereafter, relations remained strained, but preparations continued, and on 26 October 1768, at the request of the Committee, Dalrymple surrendered the papers in his possession relating to the Sulu venture,[40] mentioning that if they found another person for the enterprise, 'I promise to afford him all the information in my power'. At the same time, clearly believing that he might now be dropped, he asked for a reward for his past services, for, as he reminded them, 'notwithstanding my warmth of temper, it was me [sic] who opened the intercourse, and obtained many important grants for the Company in a quarter of the world whereto perhaps no other had extended his ideas'. Meanwhile, before publishing his Plan, he had decided to publish an account of what had passed between himself and the Directors, so that any who saw good reason why

37 Dalrymple, *An Account . . .*, pp. 56–7.

38 *Correspondence Reports*, Vol. 8, 11 August 1768.

39 Jones was a MP and was Lord Sandwich's supporter in the Direction. See Sutherland, op. cit., pp. 124–5. Dalrymple, *An Account . . .*, pp. 78–9.

40 *Miscellanies*, Vol. 17, pp. 444 and 453. *NB.* the list includes Pigot's 1759 Instructions for the *Cuddalore* which now seem to have disappeared. *Factory Records; Borneo*, f. 54.
Dalrymple, *An Account . . .*, p. 96.

the Plan should not be published would have a chance of informing him in good time.

With the necessary documentation in their hands, the Committee decided that the time had come to acquaint the Government of their intentions. It is probable that their decision was forced on them by the impending publication of Dalrymple's pamphlet, after which there could be no pretence to secrecy. A letter asking for the King's protection and support for this undertaking[41] was therefore sent to Viscount Weymouth[42] on 28 October 1768. It described the fourfold aims of the settlement as:

'To divert the Chinese Trade into this Channel, by procuring a Resort of Chinese to settle at Balambangan, and engaging the Chinese Junks to visit and dispose of their Cargoes there.

'To extend the Sale of the Manufactures of Great Britain to Cochin China and the Northern Provinces of China, and receive from thence many of those Commodities, which can now only be obtained from Canton at very high prices.

'To open a Market for the Consumption of the Manufactures of Bengal, and by adding to the Balance of Trade in favour of Bengal to encrease the circulating Specie in the Bengal Provinces.[43]

'And finally to extend the Company's Trade into the unfrequented parts of Asia.'[44]

While awaiting a reply, on 4 November orders were sent by Express Overland to Bombay, warning the authorities there 'to prepare with all expedition, one of your armed vessels to be dispatched as soon as possible to take possession of [Balambangan] in the name of the King of Great Britain, and of the East India Company, by virtue of a Grant from the Sultan of Xolo . . .'. The 'utmost dispatch' and 'profound secrecy' were to be observed, 'that no other Power may penetrate to traverse the design'. The vessel sent was to remain at the island until relieved, and 'no umbrage' was to be given to the Neighbouring Powers;

41 *Correspondence Reports*, Vol. 8, 27 October 1768.

42 Secretary of State for the Northern Department.

43 The reasons for this shortage are discussed in some detail in Hamilton, op. cit., Chapter VI, 'Economic Disorders in India, 1765–93'.

44 *Factory Records; China*, Vol. 19, Directors to Lord Weymouth, 28 October 1768.

it was also desired, doubtless in view of the four years that had now elapsed, that an attempt should be made to get the cession of Balambangan confirmed, and the 'earliest intelligence of . . . success' was to be sent 'by an overland Packet in Cypher, or the first ship'. Madras was also informed of these moves.[45]

When Lord Weymouth replied, he noted that the King was 'extremely surprised' to be asked for his protection for a measure about which he had never been consulted, and to hear that the Company had seized an Island 'without the least information of any other Right . . . except that of Utility'.[46] In their reply, the Directors could only apologize for their 'oversight' in not keeping the King informed. Nevertheless, they were able to show that they had acted within the limits of the Charter, and they gave their reasons for believing that neither the Spaniards nor the Dutch had any legal grounds for objecting to the action which the East India Company had taken.[47]

The Ministry found it difficult to come to a decision, but on 29 March 1769 Weymouth told the Company that their claims, if not watertight, at least appeared to be plausible, and that Sir John Lindsay had therefore been ordered to give the undertaking his full support.[48]

45 *Home Miscellaneous Series*, Vol. 99, pp. 259–61, 4 November 1768, Enclosure A. Ibid., Vol. 101, pp. 95–98, 11 November 1768.

When the Deputy Chairman told Dalrymple, on 5 September, that Madras was to be ordered to send a vessel, the latter pointed out that Madras had no such vessels. Therefore this letter explained that 'for expediting this plan . . . we have directed it to be entered upon from Bombay, where a proper vessel may be sooner found for this purpose than on your Coast; but . . . we intend to place the management of the Undertaking under your Inspection'.

46 Harlow, op. cit., Vol. 1, p. 86 quoting *Home Miscellaneous Series*, Vol. 771, pp. 127–31, Weymouth to Chairs, 24 November 1768.

47 *Home Miscellaneous Series*, Vol. 99, Chairs to Weymouth, 16 December 1768. Enclosed with this letter were the despatch to Bombay, 4 November 1768; a translation of the Sultan of Sulu's cession of Banguey, dated 19 September 1763; the Sultan of Sulu's cession of Balambangan and adjoining areas, 2 July 1766. Dalrymple was scornful to note that the Directors had carelessly described Balambangan as lying 'considerably *Eastward* of the Philippines'.

48 Harlow, op. cit., Vol. 1, p. 87. Sir John Lindsay was the Crown's representative in India, Ibid. Vol. II, pp. 50–51. *NB.* that Dalrymple had written to Weymouth to refute the Spanish claims. *Home Miscellaneous Series*, Vol. 100, pp. 177–9, 1 May 1769.

A year had been lost, but preparations were renewed in the summer, and on 20 June 1769 the Court of Directors ordered the Committee of Shipping to procure a vessel and to appoint a commander and officers, while the Committee of Correspondence was to nominate leaders for the expedition. Furthermore, the latter committee agreed unanimously that a gratuity of £5,000 should be paid to Dalrymple in recognition of his 'important and very valuable services'.[49] A letter to Madras explained that the dispatch of Commissioners to India, who were to direct the operations of the several Presidencies to one uniform plan, and the support of the Royal Navy, made this a most favourable opportunity to try out the new scheme.[50] Meanwhile, an experienced captain in the Company's maritime service, who was on leave in Edinburgh, was asked for his views and, in reply, expressed the opinion that Balambangan would soon rival Batavia if the Governor of the new settlement avoided the error, common in such circumstances, of being 'in too great a hurry to get Rich'.[51]

At this stage, however, the events of the previous year were largely repeated, since neither side had changed its position. Dalrymple again proposed that he should have a commission on all goods bought and sold at Balambangan, and that at the end of three years he should be given £8,000, which was the equivalent of an annuity of £500 p.a., if his private fortune acquired in the expedition did not already amount to that sum. The Committee was prepared to allow him a commission on all the trade, and was ready to concede the principle of the gratuity, though it would not agree in advance to the amount that he had specified. There was deadlock, however, over the degree of authority which the new Chief was to enjoy. The Committee was determined that there should be a Council, while Dalrymple was adamant that he must have the sole management of the expedi-

49 *Home Miscellaneous Series,* Vol. 771, p. 147. The gratuity represented the exact amount that Dalrymple would have earned had he remained at Madras as Secretary from 1759–69.

50 Ibid. Vol. 101, p. 98, 30 June 1769.

51 *Miscellaneous Letters Received,* Vol. 52, pp. 228–9, Thos. Forrest to Sir G. Colebrooke, 31 July 1769.

tion, while pledging himself for all damages, public and private, that might result from any improper conduct on his part.

His belief that the Chief should have these wide powers was not unreasonable. Balambangan was far from the nearest British settlement, had jealous European rivals on either flank, and was situated in an area where piracy was rife, and where there was no stable local government. The Directors, however, would not compromise, and further correspondence from Dalrymple was ignored.[52]

Dalrymple now tried to find some way of breaking the deadlock to prevent the loss of yet another year. One suggestion which he made was that the Plan should be submitted to a committee of men with experience of the Company's affairs in the East, and for this he proposed George Dudley, Thomas Saunders, Henry Savage, Hon. Thomas Howe, Robert Orme and Thomas Fitzhugh.[53] This was a highly competent body of men, but since at least four of them were his personal friends the idea was unlikely to meet with approval. At the same time, Dalrymple was again suggesting that he would publish his Plan.[54] The response of the Court of Directors was curt; as the plan was now under their own consideration, it would be 'highly improper' to submit it to any such committee, and its publication would be 'greatly prejudicial' to the interests of the country in general, and of the Company in particular.[55]

Yet the scheme was not moribund, for as a result of the earlier orders sent to India, two ketches and a schooner had been despatched from Bombay to the Sulu Archipelago, and at the very moment when Dalrymple was declaring his intention of 'laying open his great discoveries which for certain interested motives

[52] *Home Miscellaneous Series*, Vol. 771, pp. 163–4, Dalrymple to Directors, 24 August 1769.

Ibid., p. 180 Dalrymple to Directors, 22 September 1769.

Ibid., pp. 205–8, Dalrymple to Directors, 30 October 1769. Here he stressed the dangers of delay.

[53] Dudley had been Deputy, then Chairman, 1765–6. Saunders was Deputy Chairman 1767–8. Fitzhugh was an expert on the China trade. *Home Miscellaneous Series*, Vol. 771, pp. 234–6.

[54] In 1768 he had only published his introductory pamphlet *An Account of what has passed . . .*

[55] *Miscellanies*, Vol. 18, p. 345, letter dated 13 December 1769.

(had) not been prosecuted by the Directors',[56] Captain Savage Trotter, moored off Balambangan, was preparing a report on the situation as he found it, and of the new treaty which he had obtained in consequence of the Company's orders.[57] Meanwhile, the Directors at home had been informed by their expert advisers that there were no legal reasons why they should not proceed with this undertaking, but that the attitude of the King's Ministers should be ascertained before any further steps were taken. The Chairman and his Deputy therefore wrote to Lord Weymouth on 10 February 1770, submitting this legal advice and expressing a wish to proceed as speedily as possible with the enterprise, provided they could be assured of Ministerial support.[58]

The price that had to be paid for earlier indecision became apparent in the early months of 1770 as the Falkland Islands crisis developed. Until this had been resolved Lord Weymouth had to be careful to give the Spaniards no further grounds for complaint, yet he did not wish to discourage this experiment. He therefore saw the Chairman and Deputy Chairman of the Company in private, and 'after some Conversation it was agreed that it should be considered as if nothing had passed and that no notice should be taken of the Letter'.[59] A month later the Chairman and his Deputy were again asking Lord Weymouth, whether, in view of the Directors' desire to proceed expeditiously, he had any objections to a settlement being established on Balambangan.[60] Within a week Weymouth had received another letter, this time from Dalrymple, who was fretting at the thought that yet another season was about to be missed. The latter was now confident that he had convinced the Company of the value

56 *Gentleman's Magazine*, Vol. XXXIX, p. 607.

57 This report, dated 20 December 1769, reached England six months later. In concluding his treaty, Trotter had made the same mistake that Dalrymple had done on his first visit to Sulu, when only the Sultan had signed, which invalidated the treaty.

58 *Home Miscellaneous Series*, Vol. 102, pp. 17–18.

59 For an account of the Falklands crisis, see Harlow, op. cit., Vol. 1, pp. 22–32. See also pp. 88–9. The letter to which Weymouth was referring was that from the Chairs dated 10 February 1770.

60 *Home Miscellaneous Series*, Vol. 202, p. 18. Chairs to Weymouth, 20 March 1770.

of his Plan, but he was not so sure that either the Company or the Government realized the dangers of delay. He pointed out that within a few days the last ships for Bombay would have left, and it was imperative that a decision should be reached before then so that the necessary orders could be sent to India.[61]

It was Dalrymple's revelation that the Directors considered the plan to be at a standstill, pending a reply from the Minister, which infuriated Weymouth. He asked for an immediate explanation,[62] but the Company seems to have been at a loss to reply and could only plead a misunderstanding; they would now proceed, they added, as if their last two letters had never been written.[63] Thus, with the Government's role now clarified, the Committee of Correspondence was instructed to resume its preparations.

When Savage Trotter's report from Balambangan was received in June, it was handed on to Dalrymple for his comments. Trotter had found that Sultan Alimud Din I, who had been brought back from Manila to Sulu in 1764 by Dalrymple, was still in power, and was 'extremely solicitous to have a settlement of the English . . . in some part of his Dominions, as a Balance against the power of either the Dutch or Spaniards'.[64] There was one feature in Trotter's report which Dalrymple considered to be particularly dangerous, for Trotter had promised protection to the Sultans of Sulu and Mindanao against the Spaniards. Dalrymple had always taken the view that European disputes should be settled by the European powers on their own, and it had been Trotter's type of policy which 'drew the old Sultan of Bantam into a war, which lost him his Crown, and the Company their Commerce in his Dominions'.[65]

61 *Home Miscellaneous Series*, Vol. 102, pp. 71–4.

62 Ibid., Vol. 102, pp. 75–9, Weymouth to Chairs, 29 March 1770.

63 Ibid. Vol. 771, pp. 262–5.

64 Ibid. Vol. 102, pp. 337–60.

65 *Miscellaneous Letters Received*, Vol. 53, f. 17, Dalrymple to Directors, 26 June 1770. Also Ibid., f. 170, (same date) wherein he advised the Company to begin preparing a variety of specimens of British manufactures. The goods which would prove suitable for this market would not be the same as were sent to other parts of India, and this was something that could not be left until the last moment.

With the arrival of summer, battle was joined for the third year in succession over the powers and rewards appropriate to the leadership of this settlement. In a long letter to the Directors, Dalrymple revived the idea, first suggested by him six years earlier, that the Hon. Thomas Howe should be associated with the settlement, for, as he put it, Howe's 'known coolness of Temper must surely be thought by the Directors the very thing they want to qualify my supposed warmth of Temper'. But he still remained opposed to the idea of a Council. The Directors had argued that the object of a Council was not to act as a check upon his authority, but in case of a dispute with a foreign Power, when no Ministry could be happy if all authority lay in one man's hands. Dalrymple argued that in such cases 'nobody in the Company had final authority'.[66]

He returned to the subject of financial reward in his letter of 3 August 1770, and as his views have much bearing on what happened later when his plan was put into execution under different leadership, they are worth quoting. He began by observing that his original patrimony as a younger brother was small, and that the expenses and disbursements in his eastern voyages which could not be brought to account were very considerable. While still in India, he had received £1,200 from Pigot to help him, and was poorer when he left the East than if he had never been in the Company's service. His last five years in England had also been expensive, though his tastes were inextravagant. 'I am very sensible,' he continued, 'that a Chief of Balambangan by little dirty jobs and by preying on the people committed to his charge may put in his own pocket half of the Company's disbursements. I doubt not a man "doing as other men have done" may make a very ample fortune. . . .' He pointed out how well his contemporaries and juniors had done financially, and with good reason feared that while all the labour of establishing Balambangan would be his, another would reap the reward. He reminded the Directors that 'Queen Elizabeth wisely gave Rawleigh an office equiavlent to £10,000 p.a., and to Rawleigh England is indebted for her American Plantations'.[67]

[66] *Home Miscellaneous Series*, Vol. 771, 17 July 1770, pp. 267–82.
[67] Ibid., pp. 287–301.

The suggestion of sending out Thomas Howe was taken up by the Directors, and on 22 August 1770, after seeing the Chairman, his Deputy and the Committee of Correspondence, Howe offered his services. Having been asked to state his proposed terms, Howe countered by submitting twelve questions, the answers to which would show more clearly what his duties would be.[68] The Committee therefore called in Howe and Dalrymple and read out the answers; it was stressed that these were provisional and could be amended, but they proved a disappointment, and after considering them for a few days, Howe withdrew his offer to serve. In doing so, he expressed his mortification at finding the powers proposed for him too confined, for he had hoped for a more ambitious plan wherein he could have contributed 'to put an Establishment at Balambangan, in so prosperous and stable a situation as would have . . . laid the foundation of a great and permanent Extension of the Company's Commerce. . . .'[69]

This was probably the moment when Dalrymple lost faith in the scheme, even though he continued in charge for the time being. For not only had Howe withdrawn, but he himself was to be saddled with the Council against which he had fought for so long.[70] With the purchase of the *Britannia* on 5 September 1770 the enterprise was at last proceeding in earnest, but during the winter months petty, querulous arguments showed an unhappy spirit now prevailing between Dalrymple and the Directors. For this he was much to blame in the final stages, and it must be assumed that after his long and lonely struggle to get his Plan launched, his disappointment at the terms on which it was proceeding was acute, and that he felt no confidence in success being achieved on this limited scale. However understandable his dissatisfaction, a more co-operative attitude on his part might have saved the whole enterprise, with incalculable results.

The break came in March 1771, beginning with a dispute

68 *Correspondence Reports*, Vol. 9, pp. 237–8.

69 *Home Miscellaneous Series*, Vol. 771, pp. 313–20.

70 The Chief was to receive £1,000 p.a. and a commission of 5 per cent on the settlement's trade. The Senior Council member would receive £400 p.a. and 3 per cent and the Junior Council member £300 p.a. and 2 per cent. There would also be two Factors.

over the appointment of a factor, about which Dalrymple had not been consulted, or even informed, and culminating with the Directors' refusal to pay him any salary until after he had arrived at Balambangan, despite the work he had been doing in preparing for the expedition for the last six months. His vigorous protests finally resulted in his dismissal on 21 March 1771.[71]

This ended Dalrymple's immediate connection with the expedition, though he was asked for assistance on occasion. He refused the request of the Secretary to hand over a letter of introduction to the 'Maharaja at Borneo' because, while he himself was too well-known to the Suluans to be suspected by them, anyone else who tried to open up relations with Borneo Proper,[72] whose people were on bad terms with the Sulu islanders, was bound to cause trouble. But he responded to the Secretary's further request for the pamphlet on his Plan, by presenting the Company with six copies.

It would be irrelevant to recount the subsequent failure of this enterprise under John Herbert, who had been chosen to succeed Dalrymple as the Chief of the settlement, but one feature of Herbert's instructions must be stressed. These instructions introduced for the first time to the East Indies the free-port system which had been operating in the Caribbean since 1766. This distinction, which is almost invariably attributed to Penang, belongs in fact to Balambangan. One does not know whether Dalrymple was directly responsible for getting this free-port system inserted in the instructions, but it is likely enough, for he was a personal friend of Adam Smith, just as he was a strong supporter of Light's experiment at Penang. Admittedly this freedom of trade was to be only a 'temporary indulgence to promote as great intercourse as can be affected with all the ports and people to the Eastward', and that thereafter 'some moderate contribution towards the expenses . . . [of] protection and security' was to be exacted. Nevertheless 'to excite as great a resort as possible of shipping to Balambangan', the port was to be 'entirely free and open to the Vessels of all Nations and the Merchandize to be imported and exported . . . [was] not [to] be subject to

71 *Home Miscellaneous Series*, Vol. 771, pp. 341–55.
72 Borneo Proper was modern Brunei.

duties of any kind'.[73] These instructions reinforce the impression that had the Balambangan scheme been launched under the personal leadership of Alexander Dalrymple, it would have become a famous landmark in the history of South-East Asia.

Herbert's appointment, however, proved a foolish one, as he did not have the required personal qualities and was at Bencoolen at the time of his appointment, which made it impossible to give him adequate instructions. Moreover, he let it be known that his own preference for such an emporium would have been Rhio rather than Balambangan, and it is always unwise to appoint a man to lead an enterprise in which he does not believe. The spirit in which the expedition was carried out was well demonstrated by the leisurely outward voyage of the *Britannia*, which left Madras in August 1772, but only reached Balambangan in December 1773.[74]

Herbert's régime has been described as 'a riot of fraud and peculation',[75] and when his settlement was attacked and destroyed by a party of Sulu islanders on 26 February 1775, in suspicious circumstances, the experiment had cost the Company approximately £170,000.[76] Thus in fourteen months Herbert and his Council had brought to destruction the fruit of Dalrymple's

[73] India Office Library, *Bombay Dispatches*, 12 June 1771, paras. 28/29 pp. 38 et seq. The free-port system was also on a temporary basis at Penang in the first instance, and Raffles visualized a similar temporary arrangement at Singapore.

[74] This slow voyage was in stark contrast to Dalrymple's consistent emphasis on the necessity for speed. His own estimate had been a voyage of six to eight months – see *Home Miscellaneous Series*, Vol. 771, pp. 213–22.

[75] Harlow, op. cit., Vol. 1, p. 93. He tells the story of Herbert's settlement on pp. 92–7. The 'dirty little jobs' about which Dalrymple had warned were soon in evidence.

[76] Harlow, op. cit., Vol. 1, p. 96. On 1 December 1774 – see *Annual Register* – the Chairman told the General Court of Proprietors that it was intended to appoint a Supervisor for Balambangan, at a salary of £6,000 p.a. On 9 December Dalrymple offered to take over the settlement on his original terms.

See *Miscellaneous Letters Received*, Vol. 61, f. 119, for an eye-witness account of the final attack. It is worth recalling that Dalrymple had recommended a ship as 'a much greater protection to a new establishment than any fort'. He had intended to use forty soldiers 'against an Indian enemy. I do not mean to make any Provision against a European Power' – *Home Miscellaneous Series*, Vol. 771, p. 226, dated 10 January 1770.

labours over a period of as many years. Nevertheless, the Sulu enterprise had pointed the way, and at Penang, Singapore and Malacca a conscious effort was made in later years to put into execution some of Dalrymple's ideas.[77]

During the nineteenth century the British became increasingly aware of the need for a settlement in the regions chosen by Dalrymple. With the impressive growth of the China trade, they were alarmed at that long stretch of sea-way between Singapore and China, where their ships had no protection from Malay and Chinese pirates, or a haven wherein to shelter from periodic typhoons.[78] The ever-increasing piracy in eastern waters was a symptom of the power-vacuum that followed in the wake of declining Dutch and Spanish sea-power. Dalrymple had been alive to the dependence of commerce upon sea-power and had wished to see his countrymen adopt the policy of the Dutch, who had built up their position in eastern waters 'by a proper exertion of the Naval Power', backed up by the assistance of the native islanders. He had visualized a British policy of co-operation with all the islands to the east, and had remarked that 'they who have heard of the Ladrone proas will easily conceive how excellent these would become when instructed by the English'.[79] Moreover, he considered that he had chosen a position well adapted for the exercise of naval power. With picturesque exaggeration he described the northern harbour of Balambangan as being capacious enough, despite some shoals, to contain 'all the

[77] See *Personal Records*, Vol. XII, pp. 215 et seq.: 'The importance of Prince of Wales Island [i.e. Penang], tho' now brought forward as a naval arsenal, has long been acknowledged in a Commercial View, and as likely to bring into our hands a great part of the lucrative and extensive trade with the Eastern Islands, which has hitherto been carried on by the Dutch from Batavia and Malacca. With the intention of participating in this trade an attempt was made to form a settlement on the Island of Balambangan . . . great advantages have uniformly been looked for, from the Company possessing a permanent establishment in, or on the way to, the Eastern Seas.' The Governor-General had stressed that a mart for the sale of opium to the eastward would provide the treasury at Canton with a supply of bullion.

[78] G. S. Graham, *The Politics of Naval Supremacy*, Cambridge, 1965, pp. 49–60.

[79] P.R.O., *Egremont Papers*, 30/47 Vol. 20/1, 'Memoir of the Sooloogannan Dominions and Commerce', 26 February 1761.

navy of England in good soundings',[80] while the Sound and Bay of Maloodoo, off North Borneo, was 'scarcely to be paralleled'.[81] Had his scheme been tried and found practicable, not the least of its advantages would have been the checking of piracy in eastern waters.

In the mid-nineteenth century British interest in North Borneo revived and was not confined to the protection of a vital trade route. It was 'Rajah' James Brooke who stated that 'with a little energy British influence could easily be extended from Borneo through the Sulu Archipelago and as far as New Guinea . . . Great Britain could obtain nominal sovereignty over a vast stretch of Territory which would be clear of the Dutch on the one hand, and the Spaniards on the other'.[82] Thus three-quarters of a century after their conception, Dalrymple's ideas were again motivating Britain's eastern policy.

80 Dalrymple, *A Plan for Extending the Commerce . . .*, p. 20.

81 Ibid., p. 12. Malloodoo Bay was the modern Marudu Bay. *NB.* the treaty of 19 September 1763 specified that Balambangan should be "a Place of Trade, and for building and repairing Ships'.

82 G. W. Irwin, *British and Dutch Policy in Borneo, 1809–88* (unpublished Ph.D. thesis, Cambridge), p. 148, quoting Spencer St John 'Rajah' Brooke, p. 62. Since published – *Nineteenth-century Borneo: a study in diplomatic Rivalry*, The Hague, 1955. Reprinted Singapore, 1967, p. 88.

It is noteworthy that in 1849 Dalrymple's 'Essay towards an account of Sulu' was reprinted in Vol. III of the *Journal of the Indian Archipelago*, in view of 'the interest which at present attaches to Sulu'. This same volume also included an appraisal by a member of a French mission to China, (quoted by an American who was certain that a European colony would be the result), which judged the Sulu Islands to be 'well adapted for a European colony. In fact, there do not appear to be any islands of the East Indies of equal importance'.

CHAPTER V

The Great Southern Continent

'I DID not expect to have found myself mentioned by name in the work which you have just published,' Dalrymple informed Dr Hawkesworth in 1773; 'I concluded that the same influence which prevented me from going in the *Endeavour* . . . would impose silence concerning the merit of every attempt of mine to throw light on former discoveries in the South Seas, and I thought that attempt could not be mentioned without a certain degree of approbation which is due to every performance intended for the publick information, however ill that performance may be executed; in this, however, I was mistaken, since I find myself attacked by implication as having misrepresented the Spanish and Dutch voyages to support my own ill-grounded conjectures; you have indeed passed over in silence whatever you thought could do me any credit.'

The revival of interest, in the mid-eighteenth century, in Terra Australis Incognita did not originate with Alexander Dalrymple, nor did he inaugurate the British search for it in the period following the Seven Years' War. His belief in the Great Southern Continent was largely based on traditional arguments. But by following these arguments to their logical conclusion he was able to transform the abstract theories of his predecessors and contemporaries into a land-mass of specified size and location. This was a contribution of the greatest significance, for the truth of ancient theories could now be put to the test by undertaking the exploration of clearly defined areas. That this task was primarily undertaken by British seamen was due to Dalrymple more than to any other man; the discoveries of Captain Cook were the outcome of the theorisings and scholarship of Alexander Dalrymple. It was understandable, therefore, that the latter should be angered by the 'illiberal imputations' of Hawkesworth, who had depicted his contribution as being confined to the creation of ill-founded hypotheses that it had been the destiny of Captain Cook to destroy. The passage of time has justified Dalrymple's resentment, for subsequent historians have commonly adopted Hawkesworth's opinions, thus inflicting lasting damage on Dalrymple's reputation.

The concept of establishing British trading settlements in the South Pacific did not come into existence in the eighteenth century, for this had been a motive behind the Elizabethan attempts to enter the South Seas by the Straits of Magellan.[1] But the eighteenth century saw a revival of interest in the Pacific, which began with the writings of William Dampier and was kept alive by privateering expeditions[2] and by Anson's voyage round the world. Furthermore, during the Seven Years' War the British established a naval supremacy which made it impossible thereafter for any other nation to thwart their designs in that ocean.

A reflection of this renewed enthusiasm for exploration and expansion was the exceptional popularity attained by the various Collections of Voyages published at this time.[3] These tomes appealed to a wide reading public, and even in the library of Edward Gibbon, according to Pinkerton the geographer, they held pride of place. The new edition of Harris's Collection, edited by John Campbell in 1744–8, was of particular importance, and evinced the enthusiasm that was aroused by the triumphal return of Commodore Anson. The British, Campbell urged,

[1] V. T. Harlow, *The Founding of the Second British Empire, 1763–93*, Vol. 1, London, 1952, pp. 13–15.

[2] These included Dampier, 1703–7; Woodes Rogers (accompanied by Dampier), 1708–11; Shelvocke (and Clipperton), 1719–22.

[3] Some of the most important Collections during this period included:

M. Thevénot, *Relations de divers voyages curieux*, Paris 1663–72.

A. and J. Churchill, *A Collection of Voyages and Travels*, 4 Vols., London, 1704 (Vols. 5 and 6, 1732).

John Harris, *Navigantium atque Itinerantium Bibliotheca*, 2 Vols., London, 1705.

John Campbell, Ibid. 'carefully revised, with large additions'. 2 Vols., London, 1744–8.

See E. Lynam (ed.), *Richard Hakluyt and His Successors*, Hakluyt Society, London, 1946, Chapter III, 'English Collections of Voyages and Travels', by G. R. Crone and R. A. Skelton, who point out (pp. 88–9) that merchants were subscribing to these volumes in a substantial way by the middle of the century.

must seize their new opportunities. 'We want not Capacity,' he wrote, 'we want not Power, but we want Will . . . let us deserve, and we shall succeed . . . If we search, we shall find; if we knock, it will be opened.'[4]

The chronicler of Anson's voyage had encouraged this call for action by suggesting that great discoveries were yet to be made in the South Pacific. Schouten, he pointed out, had found proas[5] similar to those in the Ladrone Islands far out in the Pacific. This could only be explained 'by supposing that there is a range of islands, near enough to each other to be capable of accidental communication, which is extended from the Ladrones thither'. All who had crossed the Pacific in a southern latitude had met with several very small islands, which implied that the Ladrones might be 'only a part of an extensive Chain of Islands, spreading themselves to the Southward, towards the unknown boundaries of the Pacific Ocean . . . reaching from Japan, perhaps to the unknown Southern Continent'.[6]

Men had disputed over the possible existence of this Southern Continent for many centuries. In the sixteenth century Mercator and Ortelius had given their powerful support to the notion of Terra Australia Incognita, but in the eighteenth century professional geographers were divided in their views. The fourth edition of the well-known Geography of Varenius talked of a continent that stretched 'to the Streights of Le Maire, whence the Shore is perhaps continued to New-Holland, where the Lantchidol Sea is received into a Gulph on the other side whereof is New Guinea, which (very probably) is contiguous to the Shores of the Streights of Le Maire'.[7] Herman Moll believed that there was 'a vast tract of land' in these regions.[8] Emmanuel

4 Campbell, op. cit., Vol. 1, p. ii.

5 The long Malay sailing canoes.

6 R. Walter, *A Voyage Round the World in the Years 1740–44*, London, 1748, pp. 343–4.

7 B. Varenius, *A Complete System of Geography* (4th ed.), London, 1765, pp. 177–8. The Lantchidol Sea was 'a bay between New Holland and New Guinea; two Peninsulas of the South Continent', p. 172.

8 H. Moll, *Atlas Geographus*, Vol. 5, London, 1717, Chapter 1, 'Terra Australis Incognita'.

See also J. N. L. Baker, *The History of Geography: collected Papers of J N. L. Baker*, Oxford, 1963, p. 186.

Bowen, the royal geographer, was, on the other hand, more cautious. He thought it 'very probable, that New Guiney, New Holland, Van Diemen's Land, and the Land of the Holy Ghost . . .[9] make all together one great Continent, separated from New Zealand by a Streight', but confessed that 'what countries there may be, nearer the South Pole, or round it, is intirely unknown . . . it is still uncertain whether there be any Land, or only open Sea, from the 56th degree of S. Lat., all round, quite to the pole'.[10]

John Campbell firmly believed in a Southern Continent. 'It must lie,' he pointed out, 'between the Country of New Zealand . . . and the Country which was seen by Captain Sharpe and Mr Wafer in the South Seas.'[11] He acknowledged that 'many wise and knowing People' considered it 'a chimera, fit only to take up the empty Brains of wild Projectors', but he argued that 'these sort of Hasty Conclusions are extremely fatal to Science in general, and to the Art of Navigation in particular'. As he reminded his readers, 'there is wanting to the Eye a Southern Continent'. Evidence for its existence was inevitably slight, nevertheless he believed it to be favourable. 'We have numberless Voyages to the East Indies, and a great many round the Globe,' he wrote, 'yet we have few, very few, thro' that Ocean, in which the Continent is supposed to lie; and these Voyages, serve all, in some measure, to confirm this Opinion; because in every one of these Voyages, some Land or other was discovered, either Continent or Island. Now, it is Certain, that Islands, great and small, are seldom, if ever, at a very great Distance from a Continent; and therefore, where there are many Islands, it is at least a very probable Sign, that there is some Continent not far from them.'[12] He went on to suggest the wealth that was awaiting

[9] This referred to Quiros's discovery of 'the great land, which they called Austrialia del Espiritu Santo', where they had arrived on 1 May 1606 in the large Bay of St Philip and St James. This was the northernmost island of the New Hebrides, still known as Espiritu Santo.

[10] E. Bowen, *A complete System of Geography*, Vol. II, London, 1747, pp. 777 et seq.

[11] Campbell, op. cit., Vol. 1, p. 331.

[12] Ibid., pp. 270–1.

exploitation. 'The Discovery of all new Lands,' he observed, 'has a natural Tendency to the Increase of Commerce.' It was almost certain that any lands discovered in this area would be 'really as rich and plentiful, as any Countries on the Face of the Globe, without exception', for they would all lie within the 'fifth Climate'[13] which was 'according to the Laws of Nature, the most fertile, as well as the most wholesome'. Campbell considered it strange that no European potentate 'ever seriously undertook the conquest' of these southern lands, however little was known about them. He supposed that this was due to the expense. 'The great Point,' he proclaimed, 'is to be the first Discoverer, the lawful Lord and Proprietor of this new Trade; which must very soon render the Power possessed of it, if properly managed, the most considerable Maritime Power in Europe.'[14]

One of the conclusions which Anson had drawn from his circumnavigation was that if the British wished to take a serious interest in the Pacific, they would have to secure bases on either side of the continent of South America, and for this he proposed either 'Pepys Island'[15] or the Falklands in the South Atlantic, as well as Juan Fernandez in the Pacific. Moreover, he was soon in a position to put these plans into effect, since he was appointed to the Admiralty staff in 1745. But though, after four years, plans were afoot to search for Pepys Island, to explore the Falkland Islands, and to carry out a voyage of discovery in the vast South Sea, the whole scheme had to be given up because of Spanish diplomatic pressure.[16] This did not mean, however, that the British had abandoned their pretensions to the Falkland Islands, which would soon become the focal point for an international crisis.

Across the Channel, Frenchmen were also beginning to respond to the challenge of the Pacific, a reminder that this was

[13] According to the usage of the time, that meant the area between 30°47′ and 36°30′.

[14] Campbell, op. cit., Vol. 1, p. 271.

[15] This non-existent island was reputed to have been discovered by Cowley between latitudes 47° and 48° S., some eighty leagues from the continent and stretching as far as 53° S.

[16] R. E. Gallacher (ed.), *Byron's Journal of his Circumnavigation, 1764–66*, Hakluyt Society, Cambridge, 1964, pp. xxxvii–xxxviii.

yet another field for rivalry in the Anglo-French struggle for commercial and imperial supremacy in the eighteenth century. But whereas British protagonists for the existence of a Southern Continent largely based their case on theoretical foundations, the reputed discovery made by Binot Paulmyer de Gonneville was the starting point for French endeavour.

Gonneville had left Normandy in command of the *Espoir* in 1503, and after visiting the Canaries and Cape Verde, he had apparently crossed the Equator on a south-south-westerly heading, until he had been driven off course by a violent gale when in the latitude of the Cape of Good Hope. In January 1504 he had then sighted land, where for the following six months he and his crew had lived on friendly terms with the natives, one of whom accompanied them on their return voyage. This was Esomeric, the son of a local ruler. Back in the English Channel, the Frenchmen had been attacked by an English pirate, and had lost their ship and its papers. Many of the crew, however, survived, including Esomeric, and in an effort to get redress from the English, Gonneville made a statement to the naval authorities, an authenticated copy of which has survived.[17] The memory of this voyage remained alive, but the document gave no clue as to where this discovery was to be placed, and later interpretations were to include South America, Madagascar, and even 'Australasia' to the south of the Moluccas.[18]

It was Pierre de Maupertius, the mathematician and astronomer, who had first stimulated French interest in a Southern Continent in a letter to Frederick the Great of Prussia 'sur le progres des sciences'. In pointing out those parts of the southern hemisphere which had not yet been explored, he had stressed that it was most improbable that this vast portion of the globe was occupied only by water, since capes and coasts had been reported from time to time by different explorers. The discovery of a Southern Continent would be valuable from the viewpoints both of commerce and of science, since the separation of such a

[17] J. Dunmore, *French Explorers in the Pacific*, Vol. 1, *The Eighteenth Century*, Oxford, 1965, pp. 1–7.

[18] Ibid., p. 48. This was de Brosses's belief.

land-mass from all others would necessarily reveal 'many things of different kinds absolutely unknown to us'.[19]

This letter had been read to the Literary Society of Dijon in May 1752, and Charles de Brosses had been much impressed by it. The Society was an influential one, and as President of the Burgundian Parlement, de Brosses was both a literary and public figure of importance. He decided to develop Maupertius' ideas in a memoir, and Buffon, the naturalist, suggested that this memoir should also be expanded, with the idea of encouraging French exploration in the Pacific as a conscious response to the growth of British sea power.[20] Further evidence of the growing French interest in these regions was provided by the *Gentleman's Magazine*, which in 1763 published a 'Theory of the Antarctic Regions' by the French geographer Buache.[21]

The *Histoire des Navigations aux Terres Australes* by de Brosses was the pioneer study of the Pacific Ocean. De Brosses claimed that the discovery of Terra Australis could prove the most noble and rewarding enterprise that any man could undertake. The Old World would be enriched by the commerce of a New. 'What comparison is there,' he asked, 'betwixt such an acquisition and that of a poor little province, ravaged and desolated, with the utter ruin of many thousand families', which tragedy would cost far more than the discovery he was calling for.[22] He also emphasized that in these distant parts of the world commerce, and not conquest, should be the principal aim. For this purpose it would only be necessary to have a few well-placed

19 Charles de Brosses, *Histoire des Navigations aux Terres Australes*, Vol. 1, Paris, 1756, pp. 1–4.

John Callander made a free translation of this work, entitled *Terra Australis Cognita* (Edinburgh 1766), in which he twisted the arguments in favour of an exploration of the Southern regions to support British, instead of French, action. He did not name de Brosses, but merely acknowledged his indebtedness – a considerable understatement – to the 'ingenious author of Histoire des Navigations', or simply to 'the French author'. For some reason, de Brosses's name is similarly omitted from the French copy of the original work seen by the present writer.

20 Dunmore, op. cit., pp. 44–6.

21 *Gentleman's Magazine*, Vol. XXXIII, January 1763, pp. 32–6. This included a 'Chart of the Antarctic Polar Circle, with the Countries adjoining'.

22 de Brosses, op. cit., Vol. 1, p. 5; Callander, op. cit., Vol. 1, p. 4.

colonies, supported by some good forts, since the surest way of keeping savage peoples in order was to make them realize that they would always wish to exchange their own products for those of the Europeans.[23]

It was de Brosses's misfortune that this work was published at the very moment when his country was embarking on a war that was to strip her of her Canadian and Indian empires, and was to give the British the command of the seas. It was the latter, therefore, who were in the best position to benefit from his theories. Nevertheless, Bougainville was one Frenchman who had carefully read this book, and it inspired him to a course of action that was intended to recompense his country for her recent devastating losses. He dreamed that out of the disasters of the Seven Years' War there should arise, phoenix-like, a new French Empire in the Pacific. Bougainville realized the strategic significance of that ocean, and he knew that the British were becoming aware of it, too; the first essential, therefore, was to bar their way by taking possession of the Falkland Islands.[24] It was with this intention that he planted a French colony in the islands in January 1764, having first obtained the backing of the French Court, and seven months later this occupation was publicly proclaimed.

The British reaction was prompt, and on 17 June 1764 the Hon. John Byron received Secret Instructions[25] to make a reconnaissance of the Falkland Islands and of the South Atlantic, including a search for Pepys's Island, after which he was to enter the Pacific and to inspect the coast of New Albion. By January 1765 Byron was carrying out his survey of the Falklands, and in June the master of his supply ship was reporting to Lord Egmont, the First Lord, with a letter describing this work. On 20 July Egmont sent Byron's charts and surveys to the Duke of Grafton, the Secretary of State for the Northern Department, and on that very day a decision was reached to form a British settlement in the Islands, the result being the despatch of Captain John McBride, who landed on West Falklands Island in January 1766.[26]

23 de Brosses, op. cit., Vol. 1, p. 18.
24 Dunmore, op. cit., pp. 58–9.
25 Gallagher, op. cit., pp. 3–9.
26 Ibid., pp. xxxix–xlii.

In the midst of all this activity, Alexander Dalrymple had returned to England in July 1765. He was now twenty-eight years old, with twelve years' experience of India and the Far East behind him, nearly half of that time having been spent in East Indian waters. When he reached London he soon realized that this was an unfavourable moment in which to pursue his Sulu venture, but it was equally obvious that the exploration of the Pacific was commanding widespread attention. Apart from the interest that it was arousing in French and British circles, similar reports were being received from far afield. When he himself had first visited Manila in 1761, he had learnt that the Jesuits there were 'possessed of a fund of 123,000 dollars,[27] for prosecuting discoveries and establishing settlements in those parts laying to the Southward of the Moluccas', where it was known that land existed, 'but whether continent or island no discoveries yet have reached far enough to determine'.[28] There were also reports that the Dutch were sending out a small, well-manned fleet to undertake discoveries in the South Seas, for which experienced pilots and draughtsmen had been engaged.[29] Even the Prussians were showing an interest, though perforce only academic, with Count de Redern reading a paper in Berlin on the Southern Continent, wherein he sought to collate all previous discoveries and observations.[30]

Dalrymple realized that the British would have to act vigorously and quickly if they were to take the lead in the exploration of the Pacific. As it happened, he had been making a close historical study of this subject from the moment of his first arrival in India, where he had refused to be deterred either 'by the disposition of his companions, or the want of books'. If we can judge by an Inventory of the Library at Fort St George as it was in the year 1729, the selection of books was indeed meagre, since the works of Hakluyt and Thevénot then represented the

27 approx. £30,750.

28 *European Magazine,* Vol. 42, p. 322. In his letter to Pitt (1761), Dalrymple referred to 'New Guinea and the unexplored, not undiscovered, Southern Regions'.

29 *Scots Magazine,* Vol. 28, report dated 11 June 1766.

30 *Monthly Review,* 1770 (Part 2), 'The History of the Royal Academy of Sciences and Belles-Lettres at Berlin for . . . 1765 . . .'.

entire literature available on this subject. It was therefore a fortunate moment for him when Robert Orme arrived to join the Council at Fort St George. Orme, who was later to win literary distinction with his famous *History of the Military Transactions of the British Nation in Indostan*, quickly spotted the intelligence and zeal of this young writer and gave him permission to make full use of his own private library.[31] It was there that Dalrymple came across an account of the voyage of Bouvet.[32] This French explorer had attempted to follow the track once sailed by Gonneville, and his voyage had resulted in the discovery of the steep, snow-covered land which Bouvet had named Cape Circumcision, under the impression that it formed a headland of the great Southern Continent, rather than the island which it really was. Because he did not understand the French language – how he must have cursed those wasted weeks in the French Academy in Edinburgh – Dalrymple was forced to translate this work, word by word, with the aid of a dictionary. He now realized that in Bouvet he had found a kindred spirit, for the Frenchman, when a lad of sixteen, had formed an ambition to explore that immense void around the south pole about which geographers knew nothing. Dalrymple, too, who was not much older, had found in the search for a great Southern Continent that cause for which he was seeking, a task not unworthy of his heroes of old, Columbus and Magellan.

To understand what this task entailed, it was necessary to study what had already been achieved by earlier explorers, but Dalrymple, 'for want of lights to follow', found this a difficult subject to master. However, Lally's siege of Madras provided him with moments of enforced idleness, during which he sketched out a collection of voyages of discovery in the South Pacific, a task made easier by the Spanish Histories of the Philippines that he acquired at the sale of the effects of the deceased William Roberts. Later he was able to amplify these materials with others

[31] *European Magazine*, Vol. 42, pp. 325–6.

[32] See Dunmore, op. cit., pp. 197–201 for an account of this voyage. Dalrymple may have been reading a short abstract of the voyage which appeared in *Les Journaux Trevoux*, printed at Paris in 1740, or he may have seen its reproduction in de Brosses's work, if a copy had reached Madras by this time.

which he picked up during his voyages between 1759–64, when 'he acquired, amongst the Spaniards, some very valuable papers, and intimations from Spanish writers, many of whose works he also procured'. He had no opportunity to arrange these materials while he was in the East, but he was already visualizing some large-scale literary work, as is shown by a letter which his eldest brother wrote to James Boswell at this time. Describing Alexander as 'a more romantic person than our modern cold times have produced', Lord Hailes noted how, after he had been 'bred a merchant upon dry land, he has become an able navigator, and if he lives will be an author voluminous and vast. He has sent me', continued Hailes, 'a sketch of a work in six volumes in Folio, in which he wishes to be a sharer "tho he cannot, as he says, undertake ye whole".'[33]

His reputation as an authority on Pacific voyages preceded him to England, for Kempenfelt had returned, after the British capture of Manila in 1762, with the Admiral's despatches. The Earl of Egmont was then the First Lord of the Admiralty, and when Kempenfelt called, he found the Earl, as Dalrymple put it, 'intent on prosecuting discoveries in the South Seas'. Egmont 'applied to Kempenfelt for information on the subject: that gallant officer, with the liberality so distinguishable in his character, instead of recommending himself to the attention of the First Lord . . . by the information he had received from Alexander Dalrymple, without any reserve or confidential communication, but merely in conversation, told the Earl of Egmont, that all he knew on the subject he had learned from a Gentleman, who was expected home, offering to introduce him to his Lordship when he arrived. The Earl of Egmont desired him to do so; and Captain Kempenfelt called upon Alexander Dalrymple after his return to England, and informed him of the Earl of Egmont's desire to see him; which Alexander Dalrymple declined, as Lord (then Sir George) Pigot and the Earl of Egmont were at variance".[34] This cannot have helped in his later dealings

[33] Quoted by R. H. Carnie in *Lord Hailes – a Study,* unpublished Ph.D. thesis in the University Library, St Andrews, p. 14, quoting from Yale MSS., letter dated 13 February 1763.

[34] *European Magazine,* Vol. 42, p. 324. This may have been a political feud, for Pigot became a MP and soon attached himself to the Rockingham faction.

with the Admiralty, but he was not a man to forget past and present favours.

The two expeditions that were organized by Egmont did nothing to lessen confidence in the existence of a great Southern Continent. When Byron had disregarded his orders and had made a direct crossing of the Pacific, he may have hoped, as a modern study has suggested, to rediscover the Solomon Islands.[35] His track had taken him around the northern rim of the Tuamotu Archipelago, and as he had sailed past that group he had supposed that the loss of the great swell, and the southward flight of 'vast Flocks of Birds' were convincing evidence of the existence of land in that quarter. 'Had not the winds failed me in the higher Latitudes,' he wrote, 'I make no doubt but I should have fell in with it, and in all probability made the discovery of the S° Continent.' He also argued that the existence of these well-populated islands in the middle of this vast ocean could only be accounted for by supposing that there was 'a Chain of Islands reaching to the Continent'.[36]

Byron had returned to England on 7 May 1766, and arrangements for a second expedition had immediately been put in hand. This was to be under the command of Captain Wallis in the *Dolphin*, with Captain Carteret as his second-in-command. It was known to be 'Captain Byron's positive opinion' that the Southern Continent was not far southward of 'King George's Islands'.[37] There was no question that Egmont was now openly aiming at a discovery of that Continent, and the orders for the new voyage stated that there was 'reason to believe that Land or Islands of Great Extent, hitherto unvisited by any European Power may be found in the Southern Hemisphere between Cape Horn and New Zealand, in Latitudes convenient for Navigation, and in Climates adapted to the produce of Commodities useful in Commerce'.[38] These orders had been issued after Egmont had

[35] Gallagher, op. cit., pp. liii–lviii. [36] Ibid., p. 105.

[37] i.e., Takapoto and Takaroa, on the north-west fringe of the Tuamotu's – see Andrew Sharp, *The Discovery of the Pacific Islands*, Oxford, 1960, p. 102.

[38] G. Robertson (ed. H. Carrington), *The Discovery of Tahiti . . .*, Hakluyt Society, London, 1948, p. xxii.

had a conference with the King, in which he had emphasized the importance of the Falkland Islands and of the Straits of Magellan for the prosecution of voyages of discovery in the South Pacific. He had wanted quick action to follow the return of Byron, 'before a war with France or Spain, or the jealousy of those two powers should oblige Great Britain to part with the possession of the Falkland Islands or otherwise interrupt the attempts of Great Britain in that part of the World', and the King had been 'graciously pleased to authorize this second expedition to be undertaken, in hopes of finding a continent of great extent never yet explored or seen between the Streights of Magellan and New Zealand'.[39]

Wallis and Carteret were separated after passing through these Straits, so that the *Dolphin* was alone as she approached Tahiti, which was a new discovery. As she neared the island on 17 June 1767, the ship's master recalled how they 'saw the Appearance of a very high Land to the Southward'. Thus, when they left the island six months later, he was surprised that Wallis had decided to follow a westerly heading, instead of sailing southwards where he had often expressed his hope of finding 'a mutch More Extencive Country'. This present westerly course meant that 'the Southern High Mountains and their Boundarys was now left to be discovered by those who may come after us'. Robertson remained convinced that there was a Southern Continent, and he believed that a 'large fleet of vessels that Came round the S.W. point of Port Royal Bay Came from that Country'.[40]

In the meantime, Thomas Hornsby, the Professor of Astronomy at Oxford, read a paper to the Royal Society in 1765, relating to the forthcoming transit of Venus. He explained that

[39] Ibid., p. xxvii. Egmont resigned at about the time that this expedition departed. He had been disturbed by a report received on the 26 June 1766, that the French intended to use the Falklands as a base from which to discover 'Les Terres Australes'. Failing to carry his colleagues with him, he resigned in mid-August, and was succeeded by Sir Charles Saunders. See H. Wallis (ed.), *Carteret's Voyage Round the World*, Cambridge, 1965, Vol. 1, p. 12 and note and p. 15.

[40] Robertson, op. cit., pp. xxviii–xxix. The 'high mountains' were apparently clouds on the southern horizon.

for technical reasons it would be desirable to make observations from the Pacific, and he reviewed the reported discoveries of Quiros and Mendana in an effort to decide where it would be best to site the observers. He also mentioned in passing, that it would be 'a worthy object of attention to a commercial nation to make a settlement in the great Pacific Ocean'.[41] On 5 June 1766 the Council of the Royal Society considered the matter, and it was 'Resolved by ballot unanimously, that one or more astronomical observers be now sought out and engaged to observe the next Transit of Venus....'[42] In the following month the Earl of Morton P.R.S. got in touch with the Admiralty to supply them with a list 'of some places in the Southern Hemisphere for observing the transit of Venus on the 3 June 1769 ... and desiring their Lordships to give directions to the officers of such of His Majesty's ships as shall be sent into the Southern Hemisphere, to take observations and make remarks'; on 15 August 1766 the Admiralty confirmed that this would be done.[43]

Dalrymple wished to take an active part in the exploration of the Pacific, and 'to recommend himself to this employment, so much wished for', he was now working on his new historical collection of all the discoveries yet made in the South Seas.[44] When this work was completed, it was to enable him to combine in his own generation the roles of a Richard Hakluyt and a John Dee. Whereas the majority of the eighteenth century collections of voyages were varied and cosmopolitan in their approach, Dalrymple, like Hakluyt before him, wished his own to serve a specific purpose. Thus, as the Elizabethan, in the 1590s, had concentrated on the newly opened trade with the Orient, Dalrymple intended to focus his readers' attention on the quest of the

41 See *Philosophical Transactions* (abridged), Vol. XII, (1763–9), London, 1809, pp. 265–74. See also H. Woolf, *The Transits of Venus; a study of eighteenth century science*, Princeton, 1959, and J. C. Beaglehole (ed.), *The Journals of Captain Cook*, Hakluyt Society, Cambridge, 1955, Vol. I, pp. lxxiv–lxxxiii.

42 *Council Minutes of the Royal Society*, Vol. 5 (1763–8).

43 Adm. 2/540, p. 144.

44 A. Dalrymple, *An Account of the Discoveries made in the South Pacifick Ocean Previous to 1764*, London, 1769 (printed 1767), pp. viii–ix.

Southern Continent. Of both it may be said with equal truth that they sought 'the advancement of national greatness by means of trade'.[45]

Writing both as historian and cosmographer, Dalrymple originally planned to publish his work in two parts. The first would consist of an historical collection of voyages to that part of the South Pacific where the Southern Continent could be expected to lie, while the second part would include a geographical description of the discoveries already made, a critical examination of the routes followed by previous explorers, and the reasons why he believed in the existence of this continent. For a number of reasons, however, he decided to reverse the order of publication. If the work was to serve as a testimony to his own fitness for this task, which was his intention, there must be no delay in its appearance, yet he was still in search of further materials for his historical collection. The result was his *Account of the Discoveries made in the South Pacific Ocean, previous to 1764*, of which he had copies printed in 1767, though it was not published until 1769, having been purposely held back until the return of Bougainville.

Because his great object was the discovery of a Southern Continent, Dalrymple confined his attention to that part of the South Pacific which lay between America and the intersection of Schouten's track by that of Tasman, the only area where there was sufficient space for so extensive a land-mass. Within this space he devoted the major portion of his book to a geographical description of all the places which had hitherto been discovered in the course of the two centuries which separated the voyages of Magellan and Roggewein. This was accompanied by a map in which he sought to reconstruct the routes followed by the various expeditions, while in the margins of his account he gave, where possible, the latitudes and longitudes of the various discoveries, with a warning to his readers that in the absence of astronomical

[45] For Hakluyt, see the article on him by J. A. Williamson in *Richard Hakluyt and his Successors*, Hakluyt Society, London, 1946, Chapter 1. For his concentration on the Orient, see pp. 14 and 39.

A. Dalrymple, *An Historical Collection of the Several Voyages and Discoveries in the South Pacifick Ocean*, London, 1770, Vol. 1, pp. vii–viii.

observations he was far from imagining that these positions attained 'a minute precision'.[46]

In his theoretical arguments in favour of the existence of a Southern Continent, which occupied the final sixteen pages of this first volume, Dalrymple largely relied upon the traditional proposition that a Continent was 'wanting on the South of the Equator, to counterpoise the land on the North'. De Brosses had laid great stress on this, and had asked his readers to consider the effect of so great a quantity of land in the Northern hemisphere, with apparently so little in the South, bearing in mind 'that the weight of earth is, to that of sea-water, nearly as five to three'. On our globe's 'most enlarged surface under the Equator', wrote de Brosses, 'there is a mass of earth, extending about 120 degrees, separated only by the Atlantick Ocean, and a mass of water, extending about 240 degrees, intermixed only with a few islands. To this inequality of weight may, perhaps, be attributed the rotation of the earth upon its axis by the Equator, which motion being once impressed on the machine, is perpetuated continually *in vacuo*. If this conjecture has any foundation, we might suppose that, the inequality of weight being much greater betwixt the Artick and Antarctick hemispheres than it is from one third of the Equator to the other two thirds, the rotation of the globe should be rather by the Poles than by the Equator, were there not, in the Antarctick hemisphere some vast tract of unknown land to counterbalance that in the Artick'.[47]

Dalrymple's contribution to this argument was to work out in detail the size and location of the continent that this theory postulated. He showed that within the tropics the ratio of land to water, north and south of the Equator, was in approximate balance. But when the measurement was made from the Tropics of Cancer and Capricorn to latitudes 50° N. and S. respectively, this near balance was no longer in evidence, for whereas in the northern hemisphere almost equal quantities of land and water

[46] It has to be remembered that the eighteenth century geographer was further handicapped by knowing nothing of the position or velocity of the ocean currents in the Pacific, and, unlike his modern successors, he was unable to base his conclusions on a comparative study of later reports and descriptions.

[47] J. Callander, *Terra Australis Cognita*, Edinburgh, 1766, Vol. 1, pp. 8–9.

had been discovered, in the equivalent regions of the southern hemisphere very little land had so far been revealed. If it was supposed that the empty spaces were all water, this would mean that there would be eight times as much water as there was land. To retain the concept of a globe in balance, it was natural to assume that there were 'in the southern hemisphere, hitherto totally undiscovered, valuable and extensive countries, in that climate best adapted for the conveniency of man, and where, in the northern hemisphere, we find the best peopled countries'. Beyond these limits, too little was known to make possible any valuable comparison, and in such regions the climate was in any case likely to be too severe to be useful to man.[48]

The largest portion of any such Southern Continent would have to be in the South Pacific, since the tracks followed by Halley and Bouvet left only a small area available in the South Atlantic. Even if the latter consisted entirely of land, Dalrymple calculated that 3,640 square degrees of continent must still be awaiting discovery if the counterpoise theory was correct. He now used his knowledge of previous voyages of discovery to show where there was space available to contain this extensive land-mass. After utilizing all the area left to the south of the Indian Ocean and to the west of New Zealand, he concluded that 'the space unknown in the Pacifick Ocean, from the Tropick to 50° S. must be nearly all land'.[49]

Dalrymple also contributed a new argument of his own in favour of a Southern Continent, based on his twelve years' experience of the monsoon winds in India and the East Indies. 'The tropical regions in wide oceans,' he pointed out, 'have a constant easterly wind; but where there are extensive chains of land, these winds not only become in general less steady, but are interrupted, during some months of the year, by a westerly wind.'

[48] Dalrymple, *An Account of the Discoveries* . . . , pp. 90–2. He calculated that within the tropics there were 2,470 square degrees of land in the north to 2,420 square degrees in the south, and 5,810 square degrees of water in the north to 5,860 in the south. From the Tropic of Cancer to 50° N. he calculated that there were 4,880 square degrees of land to 4,840 of water. But from the Tropic of Capricorn to 50° S. there were only 1,060 square degrees of land, so far discovered, to the 8,660 square degrees that must be water, if no land was found.

[49] Dalrymple, op. cit., p. 94.

He argued that if there was a continent or extensive range of land in the regions suggested, monsoon winds would develop; otherwise, the easterly winds would remain constant. On his own admission, however, there were 'in the voyages thro' the Pacifick Ocean . . . few instances related of the winds', so that this ingenious argument was unconvincing.[50]

As evidence of actual sightings of the continent he referred to three voyages. First there was 'the discovery of Juan Fernandes, who in the passage from Lima to Chili, having stood to the westward a certain distance for the advantage of a fair wind, steered south till he discovered land, which he supposed to be the Southern Continent, as he saw on the coast the mouths of very large rivers. . . . The country was very fertile and agreeable, and appeared much better and richer than Peru. . . . It was inhabited by white people . . . very well disposed, and cloathed with very fine cloths'.[51] He also mentioned the voyage of Theodore Gerrards in 1599, who was carried by a gale into 64° S. after passing through the Straits of Magellan, where he saw a mountainous country covered with snow. Finally, in 1624 the *Orange*[52] was said to have seen 'this Continent twice, in the passage from Cape Horne to Juan Fernandes, once in 50° South, and again in . . . 41° South'.

For the probable character of this continent, Dalrymple turned to the voyage of Roggewein.[53] Even before the latter had discovered Easter Island he had seen signs of land which suggested that the continent was not far away, but it was the island itself which gave 'some idea of the Continent adjoining: no voyage hitherto performed, points out so strongly the original of the

[50] Ibid., pp. 96–100. As evidence of westerly winds in the South Pacific, he drew attention to the *Chronica de la Provincia de S. Gregorio de las Philipinas,* which introduced a quotation from Quiros 'speaking of appointing one of the galleons to Peru from Manila. . . . "For the route and voyage is I know much easier and shorter than from Manila to New-Spain", which can only be if there are westerly winds in the South Pacifick Ocean'.

[51] Ibid., pp. 100–1.

[52] Ibid., p. 102. The *Orange* was part of the Nassau fleet which was under the command of Jacob l'Heremite – see Burney's *Chronological History*, Vol. III, chapter 1, for an account of this fleet. It was typical of the many inaccuracies in Hawkeworth's work that l'Heremite should have been credited with this sighting, which was not the case, since the *Orange* had become separated from the rest of the fleet.

[53] Ibid., p. 103.

Peruvian manners and religion. That country from whence Mango Capac[54] introduced arts, laws, manufactures, and all the comforts of civilized life, cannot fail of amply rewarding the fortunate people who shall bestow letters instead of quippos[55] and iron in place of more awkward substitutes'.

The authority for Juan Fernandes' supposed discovery of the Southern Continent was a Memorial which had been drawn up by Dr Juan Luis Arias for presentation to King Philip IV of Spain.[56] Dalrymple had come across the Arias Memorial 'in a very curious collection of original papers, in two volumes, taken from the archives of Spain'. He had purchased these two important volumes, which contained both manuscript and printed material, and which had once belonged to the library of 'the celebrated Colbert, the French Minister', from a bookseller in Covent Garden, after his return to England in 1765.[57] Dalrymple

[54] He was the first of the Incas. Pedro Sarmiento de Gamboa, in his *History of the Incas* (completed in 1572), claimed that he reigned for a century and died in A.D. 665, at the age of 144 – see Sir C. Markham (ed.), *Sarmiento's History of the Incas*, Hakluyt Society, Cambridge, 1907, pp. 60–2 and 194.

[55] A quipu was the ancient Peruvian substitute for writing, whereby various coloured threads and knots were used. It is interesting to note this eighteenth century notion of a link between Easter Island and Peru, presaging Thor Heyerdahl's theories, though in reverse.

[56] Arias was a friend of Quiros. For background information on this memorial, see Celsus Kelly (ed.), *La Austrialia del Espiritu Santo*, Hakluyt Society, Cambridge, 1966, Vol. 1, pp. 129–33. Dalrymple published the Spanish original of the Arias Memorial in Edinburgh in 1773, during his dispute with Hawkesworth, and translated part of it in his second letter to the same. Sir C. Markham (ed.), in *The Voyages of Pedro Fernandez de Quiros, 1595–1606*, Hakluyt Society, London, 1904, Vol. II, Appendix VIII, pp. 517–36 also gives a translation of the complete Memorial.

[57] Dalrymple, *An Account of the Discoveries . . .*, p. xxvii, and *Catalogue of the Authors who have written on Rio de la Plata, Paraguay and Chaco*, London, 1806, p. 16. Matthew Flinders, who knew him, stated that Dalrymple obtained Torres' letter at Manila in 1762, but this was incorrect. Dalrymple obtained various unspecified Spanish documents during his visits to Manila in 1761 and 1763–4, including some Spanish histories of the Philippines, in which references to Torres' letter may well have appeared. But the Arias Memorial provided him with his first important account of Torres's voyage. He did not come across Torres's letter itself until after 1790, for in that year, in his reply to Buache's Memoir, he stated that he was assured that the original letter was then 'still in Spain'. Later he obtained the letter, his translation of which appeared in Volume II of Burney's *Chronological History* in 1806, pp. 467–78.

displayed an uncritical confidence in the Arias Memorial, for its untrustworthy features had not yet been revealed by voyages of discovery. In reality it was a curious blend of fact and fiction, but its discoverer not unnaturally placed as much credence in Juan Fernandes' supposed Continent as he did in Torres' Strait, which this document again brought to the attention of a forgetful world. Thus Dalrymple entered them both on his map.

When he had completed this work, Dalrymple attempted to win influential support in his bid for the leadership of a new expedition to the Pacific. He therefore wrote to the Earl of Shelburne, the Secretary of State for the Southern Department[58] in the new Chatham Ministry. As an excuse for making this direct approach he expressed his desire to obtain official approval before publishing his compilation of discoveries from the original writers, 'lest this general information should have any improper consequences to the Government'. But he confessed that this was not the sole purpose of his letter. 'Having had five years' experience in voyages of this kind,' he wrote, 'thro' seas unknown, and amongst people with whom we have no intercourse, I presume to think myself qualified to be usefully employed in such an undertaking. At the same time, I am not insensible, notwithstanding the instances of Dampier, Halley, etc, how foreign to rules of office it is, to form the most distant expectations, that a person may be employed in the publick Service by Sea, who has no rank in the Navy.'[59] According to Kippis, his aim was to obtain a brevet commission,[60] which was just the arrangement under which Bougainville was sailing around the world in command of a French naval vessel.

Shelburne was interested and wished to find out more about Dalrymple. Indeed, years later the latter recalled that Shelburne had 'expressed a strong desire to employ him on these discoveries,

[58] Apart from being responsible for Home and Irish affairs, this Department also dealt with correspondence connected with Western Europe, India and the colonies.

[59] P.R.O., *Chatham Papers*, 30/48, Vol. 31, f. 11, letter dated 24 November 1766. Though in the Chatham Papers, it seems certain that this was the letter which Dalrymple stated, in his Memoirs, that he had written to Shelburne at this time. It had probably been forwarded to Chatham for information.

[60] A. Kippis, *Life of Captain Cook*, London, 1788, pp. 15–16.

at the same time expressing his regret that he was not acquainted with Alexander Dalrymple when Captain Wallis was sent'.[61] Now it chanced that Adam Smith had returned to England from his continental tour with the Duke of Buccleugh in November 1766, and Dalrymple had been introduced to him by his eldest brother, Lord Hailes. They met both in Edinburgh and in London, where Adam Smith was working throughout the winter months in the British Museum. He was studying colonial administration, which broght him into contact with Shelburne, who was thus able to ask him for information about his new friend. As a result, Adam Smith wrote a letter to Shelburne on 12 February 1767:

'I send you Quiros's memorial, presented to Philip the Second, after his return from his voyage, translated from the Spanish in which it is published in Purchas,' he wrote. 'The voyage itself is long, obscure and difficult to be understood, except by those who are particularly acquainted with the geography and navigation of those countries, and on looking over a great number of Dalrymple's papers I imagined this is what you would best like to see.

'He is besides just finishing a geographical account of all the discoveries that have yet been made in the South Seas from the West Coast of America to Tasman's discoveries. If your Lordship will give him leave, he would be glad to read this to you himself, and show you on his map the geographical ascertainment of the situation of each island. I have seen it; it is extremely short . . . whether this may be convenient to your Lordship I know not; whether this continent exists or not may perhaps be uncertain; but supposing it does exist, I am very certain you will never find a man fitter for discovering it, or more determined to hazard everything in order to discover it.

'The terms he would ask are, first, the absolute command of the ship with the naming of all the officers, in order that he may have people who both have confidence in him and in whom he has confidence; and secondly, that in case he should lose his ship by the common course of accident before he gets into the South

[61] *European Magazine*, Vol. 42, p. 325. This was written within the lifetime of the statesman, who had by then become the Marquis of Lansdowne.

Sea, that the Government will undertake to give him another. These are all the terms he would insist upon.

'The ship properest for such an expedition, he says, would be an old fifty-gun ship without her guns. He does not, however, insist upon this as *a sine qua non*, but will go in any ship with a hundred to a thousand tons. He wishes to have but one ship with a good many boats. Most expeditions of this kind have miscarried from one ship's being obliged to wait for the other, or losing time in looking out for the other.'[62]

This ambition to lead an expedition to the South Pacific was not the act of outrageous presumption that some writers have suggested. In many respects Dalrymple was exceptionally well qualified for the task. He was acknowledged by all to be an expert navigator, and few professional seamen, even when they had spent a lifetime at sea, could match his ability in surveying and cartography. Admittedly his own experience had been limited to five years at sea, but much can be learnt in that time, and his schooling had been in unknown and reef-strewn eastern waters which provided an admirable training for the conditions that could be expected in the South Seas. It is worth recalling, too, that he had far more practical experience than had Bougainville who was just beginning the circumnavigation that has remained a notable voyage in French maritime history.[63] Dalrymple expected to make up for his lack of experience in managing a ship on a long ocean voyage by having under his command a skilled ship's master, a practice common in Eliza-

62 This letter is quoted in the unpublished and unfinished *Life of Alexander Dalrymple* by A. Hugh Carrington, which also contains the information respecting the connexion between Adam Smith and Shelburne, and the manner in which Dalrymple became acquainted with Adam Smith. The manuscript has been deposited with the Alexander Turnbull Library, Wellington, New Zealand. The original letter is in the Shelburne Correspondence in Bowood House, Wilts.

63 For Bougainville's voyage, see Dunmore, op. cit., pp. 57–113. After his return to England in 1765, Dalrymple opened a correspondence with de Brosses, which continued until the Frenchman's death. But when the latter informed Dalrymple of Bougainville's impending departure on his voyage of discovery, this correspondence was momentarily suspended, as Dalrymple feared it might 'facilitate the enterprises of a rival State'. It was renewed as soon as Bougainville had departed – See A. C. Taylor, *Le Président de Brosses et L'Australie*, Paris, 1937, p. 157.

bethan times and one that still survived.[64] His unsurpassed knowledge of previous discoveries in the South Pacific was likely to prove most advantageous. Moreover, if the voyage was to be made under the auspices of the Royal Society his chances were far from hopeless, since the Society's President was the Earl of Morton, who was himself an Edinburgh man. The Earl knew the Dalrymples from nearby Musselburgh. Furthermore, as Kippis pointed out, this was a time 'when economy was much talked of' and when it was desired to keep down all expenses. Kippis described the Earl as being 'as frugal a man as ever came out of Scotland'; in any expedition that the Society might organize under his leadership, the aim would be to get 'a person appointed to the command of the ship who was qualified to make the observation, and willing to accept that command as a satisfaction for doing it'.[65] In such circumstances, Dalrymple would be the ideal choice.

The Royal Society was already making active preparations to observe the forthcoming transit of Venus. Dalrymple had attended his first meeting of the Society on 20 March 1766, and he was again present on 19 February 1767 as the guest of Dr Morton, one of the two Secretaries. On 2 July 1767 his paper 'On the formation of Islands' was presented by Dr Morton at another session. He had thus become known to important officials of the Royal Society by the time that its Council met on 12 November 1767, when it was decided to set up a committee 'to consider of the places proper to observe the ensuing transit of Venus, and the method, the persons fit, and other particulars'. This Committee meeting was on 17 November, when it was decided to send two observers to Fort Churchill in Hudson's Bay, and two 'to such places of the South Seas, as shall be proper for the purpose, and at which they shall find it practicable to establish themselves for making the Observations; and that the Government be applied to, to furnish a ship to attend the Observers upon this Business . . . Proper persons thought of at present for making the Observations, are Mr Bradley, Messieurs

[64] See John Masefield's Introduction to *Hakluyt's Voyages*, London, etc. 1927, p. xvi.

[65] Kippis, op. cit., pp. 15–16.

Mason and Dixon, Mr Dunn, Mr Greene, and Mr Dymond, and Mr Dalrymple. The last will be a proper person to send to the South Seas, having a particular Turn for Discoveries, and being an able Navigator, and well skilled in Observation'.[66]

At the next meeting, on 3 December 1767, the Committee turned its attention to the leadership of the proposed expedition to the Pacific, and it was suggested that Captain Campbell, who was one of the Committee's members, 'if he pleases to go . . . or some such lover of Astronomy (a Captain of a man of war) would be a proper Person to command the Ship, which goes to the South Seas'. Meanwhile, Maskelyne, the Astronomer Royal, had seen the various candidates mentioned, as well as William Wales, whom he himself had added to the list. Dalrymple and Dunn, in addition to Wales, had expressed their willingness 'to engage in this Business'. The Secretary was therefore instructed to invite those concerned to attend the Council meeting on 18 December.[67]

It is not clear how Captain Campbell reacted to the above proposition,[68] but there was no ambiguity about Dalrymple's position, for when he wrote to Dr Morton to express his pleasure on receiving 'the favourable Intentions of the Council of the Royal Society', he took pains to forestall any misunderstanding about his attitude. 'It may be necessary to observe,' he wrote, 'that I can have no thoughts of undertaking the Voyage as a Passenger going out to make the Observation or on any other footing than that of having the management of the Ship intended for the service. . . .'[69]

Up to this point the Royal Society had confined its attention to the forthcoming transit of Venus, and its only interest in the Pacific had been in the choice of a suitable location for making these astronomical observations. While Dalrymple fully appreciated the significance of that event, however, and would have paid the closest attention to it, he could not have contemplated an expedition which would have gone into the middle of the

66 *Minutes of the Council of the Royal Society of London,* Vol. 5.

67 Ibid.

68 *N.B.* that on 14 January 1768 Dalrymple attended a meeting of the Royal Society as the guest of Captain Campbell.

69 *Royal Society Miscellaneous Mss.,* Vol. III, f.14, Alexander Dalrymple to Dr Morton, 7 December 1767.

unexplored South Pacific, only to confine its activities to astronomical observations. In his view, the exploration of the South Seas would have to be a part of this undertaking, and on such an expedition he could not conceivably have been content to remain a mere bystander. Even a return to Madras would have promised greater opportunities than three years spent as an astronomical observer. Furthermore, he must have been aware that the Directors of the East India Company, of which his old Governor and friend, Thomas Saunders, was now the Deputy Chairman, were showing a renewed interest in his Sulu scheme. If that plan was put into operation he had every reason to anticipate a rewarding and challenging future. It was understandable, therefore, that he would only agree to undertake this present task on the most favourable terms.

On 18 December 1767 Dalrymple, Dymond, Dunn, Green and Wales duly attended the Council, and each specified the conditions on which he was prepared to go. Further meetings were held to carry on with the preparations, and then, on 15 February 1768, it was agreed to submit a Memorial to the King, wherein it was stated that 'the passage of the planet Venus over the Disk of the Sun, which will happen on 3 June, in the year 1769 is a phenomenon that must, if the same be accurately observed in proper places, contribute greatly to the Improvement of Astronomy, on which Navigation so much depends'. After mentioning the preparations that several other great European powers were making to carry out the necessary observations, the Memorial reminded the King that 'the like appearances, after the 3 June 1769 will not happen for more than 100 years'. The expenses, exclusive of the ships needed, were expected to amount to £4,000, which the Royal Society was in no condition to provide, and the matter was therefore submitted to His Majesty's royal consideration 'with all Humility'. Five weeks later, on 24 March 1768, the President was able to inform the Council of the Royal Society that the King had agreed to make the above sum of £4,000 available to meet these expenses.[70]

[70] *Minutes of the Council of the Royal Society,* Vol. 5. This memo. recalled that it was an Englishman, Jeremiah Horroe, who had been 'the first person since the Creation of the World who calculated the passage of that

On 29 February 1768, Shelburne told the Admiralty that it was the King's decision that a suitable vessel should be provided by the Royal Navy.[71] Therefore, on 5 March 1768 the Admiralty requested the Navy Board 'to propose a proper vessel to be fitted for this service',[72] and three days later the latter body suggested the *Tryal* sloop, but pointed out that she was in Deptford Dock for repairs and could not be ready before the end of May, 'and there is no vessel at home', they added, 'to be depended on for so long a voyage that can be sooner fitted'.[73] On 10 March the Admiralty advised the Navy Board that this would cause too much delay, and asked them to investigate the suitability of the *Rose*. The Royal Society was still expecting Dalrymple to lead this expedition, and on that same evening the President entertained him as his guest at a dinner at the Royal Society Club.[74] The Navy Board's report on the *Rose* was ready by 21 March. This document expressed doubts about that vessel's ability to carry sufficient quantities of provisions for such a long voyage, and it was suggested that a cat-built vessel, such as could be purchased in the Thames, might be suitable. The Admiralty immediately agreed to this proposal, and two days later the Navy Board was arranging for a survey to be made of the *Valentine* and the *Earl of Pembroke*.[75]

---

planet over the Sun's Disc' in 1639. It would therefore be a dishonour if the British, 'justly celebrated in the learned world', neglected the present opportunity. It was because the necessary preparations had not been made in good time that 'the passage of the Planet, in . . . 1761 was not observed in some places from whence the greatest Advantage might have redounded to the Improvement of Astronomy'. After reciting the various stations where it was proposed to place observers, the Memorial noted 'that a Correct Set of Observations made in a Southern Latitude, would be of greater importance than many of those made in the Northern, but the observers concerned ought to leave 'early in this Spring'.

71 Hugh Carrington, *Life of Captain Cook*, London, 1939, p. 51.

72 See C. Knight, 'H. M. Bark *Endeavour*', *Mariner's Mirror*, Vol. XIX, 1933, pp. 292–302.

J. C. Beaglehole (ed.), *The Journals of Captain Cook*, Hakluyt Society, Vol. 1, Cambridge, 1955, pp. cxxiii et seq.

National Maritime Museum ADM/A/2605. P.R.O., adm.2/541.

73 Nat. Mar. Mus., ADM/B/180. P.R.O., Adm. 106/2199.

74 Dinner Registers of the Royal Society Club. Dalrymple had first dined at the Club on 7 January 1768, as the guest of William Russell.

75 Nat. Mar. Mus., ADM/A/2605. P.R.O., Adm. 3/75.

There has always been some confusion as to who was responsible for the choice of the *Endeavour*, arising from Kippis' statement that Palliser and Cook together chose this ship. This statement was said to have been made on Palliser's authority, but it seems to have been due either to a lapse of memory or to a misunderstanding, for Cook had not yet been suggested for the command. There appears to be no good reason to doubt Dalrymple's claim, which he not only made in his letter to Hawkesworth, but repeated thirty years later in his Memoirs, that the recommendation was largely his. According to his own account, after he had been appointed by the Royal Society to observe the transit of Venus from the Pacific, 'the Admiralty approving of his being employed for this service, as well as for prosecuting discoveries in that quarter, Alexander Dalrymple accompanied the Surveyor of the Navy to examine two vessels that were thought fit for the purpose. The one he approved was accordingly purchased'.[76] Two days after the survey the *Earl of Pembroke*, later renamed *Endeavour*, was procured.[77]

Only at this stage did it become obvious that the Royal Society and the Royal Navy differed over the question of command. This misunderstanding came into the open when the Council of the Royal Society met on 3 April to hear about the purchase of this ship, for in their letter the Lords Commissioners of the Admiralty had asked 'to be informed of the number and quality of the persons intended to be sent to make the said observations' and to be advised as to the instructions that should be given to the commander of the vessel. The Council undertook to prepare these instructions and notified the Admiralty that two observers would be sent out, but at the same time its members heard from their President 'that he had recommended Mr Dalrymple to the Lords of the Admiralty for the command of a vessel . . . but had

[76] *European Magazine*, Vol. 42, 325. He was the Royal Society's choice as commander, and the Navy Board was selecting a vessel at the express desire of the King, who had agreed to help the Society in this manner. A cat-built bark was rigged like a snow, and was the very type of vessel that Dalrymple would have chosen, in view of his own experience in the *Cuddalore*. Moreover, with all his faults he was a strictly honourable man who was not in the habit of making false statements.

[77] ADM/B/180 and Adm. 106/2199.

been informed by their Lordships that such appointment would be entirely repugnant to the regulations of the Navy'.[78] Deadlock ensued, for Dalrymple refused to consider going out merely as an observer. Furthermore, in his Memoirs he stated that offers were made 'that the instructions for the voyage should be entrusted to him, and the Officer commanding the vessel be positively ordered to follow his opinion, on the compliance with which his promotion was to depend', but that he had declined this offer since he knew, from his own experience in the *Cuddalore*, 'that a divided command was incompatible with the public service in such voyages'.[79] The Council, finding that he would only go if he could be granted the 'free command', therefore decided to make a new appointment at a future meeting.

On 5 May 1768 Cook appeared before the Council of the Royal Society and 'accepted the Employment'. Sympathy seems to have been felt for Dalrymple, who had dined as a guest at the Royal Society Club on 28 April and twice more during the summer, and who was also taken to one of the Society's meetings. With the voyage itself, however, he had no further connexion, except that he 'withheld no information in his power to give'. This information included his book and chart, which he had printed but did not publish until after Bougainville's return. The fact that he gave this book to Banks is sometimes considered as further evidence of his supposed hostility towards Cook, but this is surely to misinterpret the meaning which this expedition had for contemporaries. It was a scientific undertaking which was being organized by the Royal Society, and the senior representative of that Society on board the *Endeavour* was Joseph Banks F.R.S.; even after its return it was frequently referred to as Banks's expedition.

In presenting these materials to Banks, with the chart which showed Torres's track along the south coast of New Guinea, Dalrymple told him about the Arias Memorial which was the authority for his chart. This Memorial recorded the decision of Torres, 'with the consent of his companions, to continue the discovery', after they had been separated from Quiros. 'Being pre-

78 *Minutes of the Council of the Royal Society*, Vol. 5.
79 *European Magazine*, Vol. 42, ut supra.

vented by stress of weather from making circuit of the land of the Baia, to see whether it were an island or mainland, as they had imagined,' wrote Arias, 'and finding himself in great straits in 21° S., to which high latitude he had persevered in sailing in about a SW direction . . . he put back to the NW and NE up to 14°, in which he sighted a very extensive coast, which he took for that of New Guadalcanal; from thence he sailed westwards, having constantly on the right hand the coast of another very great land, which he continued coasting, according to his own reckoning, more than 600 leagues, having it still to the right hand (in which course may be understood to be comprehended New Guadalacanal and New Guinea). Along the same coast he discovered a great diversity of islands . . . he continued his voyage on to Bachan and Ternate, and from thence to Manilla. . . .'[80] When Cook sailed through Torres Strait in the *Endeavour*, he had this information at his disposal. The Robert de Vaugondy map in Charles de Brosses's work also showed this strait, and it has been suggested that this map was probably based on the Dutch edition of the Neptune François, published in Amsterdam in 1700, where the results of Torres's voyage were clearly shown.[81] Otherwise, knowledge of Torres's discovery had been largely forgotten by the mid-eighteenth century, and it was Dalrymple's discovery and publication of the Arias Memorial, and his later acquisition and translation of Torres's original letter, which Burney was to publish in 1806, that restored this knowledge to the world.[82]

Now that he could take no further part in the expedition to

[80] Sir C. Markham, *The Voyages of Pedro Fernandez de Quiros, 1595 to 1606*, Hakluyt Society, London, 1904, Vol. II, pp. 525–6.

[81] H. Wallis, *The Exploration of the South Sea, 1519 to 1644*, D. Phil. thesis, Oxon, 1953, pp. 332–4. In his Letter to Dr Hawkesworth (p. 29) Dalrymple wrote: 'Altho' you are pleased to pass it over in silence Torres' track, which I had laid down in my Chart from Arias's memorial, determined the *Endeavour* to pass between New Holland and New Guinea; there were great differences of opinion on the subject; Captain Cook insisted, on the authority of Pingré, that Torres had passed to the northward of New Guinea, Mr Banks maintained that he had kept it on his right hand; the Track in my chart decided the point: and Mr Banks, the very first time I saw him after his return to England, quoted the words of Arias's memorial, which he could only have got from me'.

[82] Burney, op. cit., Vol. II, pp. 467–78.

the Pacific, Dalrymple determined to complete his *Historical Collection of the Several Voyages and Discoveries in the South Pacific Ocean*. His purpose was to help in 'establishing an Intercourse with a Southern Continent', and this was to be a collection of those Spanish and Dutch voyages to the Pacific which were relevant to the discovery of that mysterious land. To ensure that the meaning of the original writers was not obscured or misrepresented, he planned to give a literal translation though, as he put it himself, 'I am not insensible that the undress and uncouth sound of a literal translation is enough to frighten all readers except the very few who take up a book merely for information; but it was to these few I have devoted my labours'.[83]

The work was to be in two volumes, the first being devoted to the Spanish explorers, and the second to the Dutch, to which he decided to add his own experiences of the Sulu pearl fishery, not only for its own interest, but also for its bearing on Quiros's voyage. He also included a paper on the probable location of the Solomon Islands.

In his Introduction he developed his ideas on the advantages of discovering a Southern Continent. He drew attention to the benefits which had been derived from the progress of science and of commerce, for 'by an intercourse with distant countries, and the view of man under all the variety of circumstance and climate, if the intellectual endowments of the human species have not been extended, their common rights, at least, have been almost every where promoted, and established in some countries, in which, before this era, the people were mere slaves to an ignorant race of nobles'.[84]

To those who objected that this country already had too many possessions he answered 'that there can be no object more interesting to a maritime and commercial state, than discovery of New Lands, to invigorate the hand of industry, by opening new vents for manufactures, and by a New Trade to encrease the active wealth and naval power of the country'.[85] Former discoveries had disclosed that 'not only many large islands, and small ones

[83] Dalrymple, *Historical Collection* . . . , Vol. I, p. x.
[84] Ibid., p. xvii. [85] Ibid., Vol. I, p. xxi.

without number, swarming with people, are scattered over the South Pacific Ocean, but that it is more than probable another Continent will be found there, extending from 30° S. towards the Pole ... countries so well situated, so extensive, and so full of civilized inhabitants, must afford a very beneficial commerce: so that considered, either from the advantages immediately to be derived from thence, or as a barrier to secure the trade of the East-Indies, the examination of the countries situated in the South Pacifick Ocean, seemed to be an object of great consequence to the East-India Company, within the limits of whose exclusive charter these countries lye ... but the East-India Company are too much engaged in territorial dominion to think of commerce and discovery'.[86]

Some argued that colonies drained the mother-country of her people, and that as these colonies grew stronger they would inevitably demand their independence. Dalrymple disagreed. 'If colonies are aiming at independence,' he wrote, 'the only means of preventing these intentions, and of securing the power and prosperity of the mother-country, must be by extending its commerce to distant nations who can have no connexion with those discontented colonies.' The Americans were at present exploiting the over-riding importance of their trade to Britain. If new lands were discovered, the American colonies would lose their decisive importance and 'would be unable to compel this country to a precipitate concession', while the mother-country herself 'being less dependent would be less jealous'. He hastened to add that he meant no general condemnation of the American colonists. 'The common rights of humanity,' he declared, 'entitle them to represent their grievances ... the first step of tyranny is to shut the ear against the complaints: the last to shut the mouth of the complainant.'[87]

Dalrymple was advocating exploration in the interests of increasing trade. The Spaniards were not the people to emulate, for they had subjected Columbus's new continent to pillage and conquest, whereas the humane policy of trading 'with the potent and populous empires of Mexico and Peru' would have brought them far greater wealth in the end. The British should aim at

86 Ibid., pp. xxv–xxvi.

87 Ibid. Vol. I, pp. xxvi–xxvii.

'discoveries not merely of the figure of the lands; not with a view of colonizing; not with a view of conquest; but of an amicable intercourse for mutual benefit'.[88]

As he was writing this Introduction to his *Historical Collection* in October 1769, the work of exploration was going on apace. Cook was approaching New Zealand for the first time, while de Surville, outward-bound from Pondicherry, was sailing towards the long-lost Solomon Islands from the north-west, this island group having been previously sighted, though not recognized, by Bougainville, who had completed his circumnavigation some six months earlier. In this revival of exploratory endeavour, Dalrymple was anxious that his countrymen should play a worthy part. The situation demanded, he said, 'immediate attention from every Englishman, for it may be very justly said, the being of the British Empire rests on our insular situation, and powerful navy.... Our navy, undoubtedly, is superior to all others at present, because our colonies are so. But if other nations are negligently permitted to extend their navigation to remote parts, and to gain such an accession of commerce and power as the discovery of a New World would afford . . . we may then indeed cry, "Time was – but time is past . . ."'.[89]

Anxious to awaken the British to their great opportunities, and to arouse in them that sense of urgency that the times demanded, he now fell a victim to his own propaganda and wrote one rash paragraph that not only lessened his immediate credibility, but was to lay him open to undeserved derision in the future. To demonstrate the size and location of the Southern Continent postulated by the counterpoise theory was one thing, but to calculate its probable population and trade was to invite ridicule. 'The number of inhabitants in the Southern Continent,' he wrote, 'is probably more than 50 millions.' He believed, with exaggerated precision, that the distance between the eastern and western extremities of this continent would amount to 5,323 statute miles, 'a greater extent', as he pointed out, 'than the

[88] Ibid., Vol. 1, p. xxviii.

[89] Ibid., p. xxx. Nor could it be overlooked that the French were making their own preparations to observe the transit of Venus. For this purpose, Pingré, the librarian of the French Academy of Sciences, had drawn up a Memoir—see H. Woolf, *Transits of Venus . . .*, pp. 150 et seq.

whole civilized part of Asia, from Turkey to the eastern extremity of China. There is at present no trade from Europe thither', he concluded, 'though the scraps from this table would be sufficient to maintain the power, dominion, and sovereignty of Britain, by employing all its manufacturers and ships'.[90]

The first volume of the *Historical Collection*, devoted to the Spanish voyages, was published in 1770, and on 8 November of that year a group headed by Benjamin Franklin proposed Dalrymple's nomination as a Fellow of the Royal Society, the Certificate describing him as 'A Gentleman well versed in Mathematical and Geographical Knowledge and translator of Voyages to the South Seas and other Places from Spanish'. He was elected on 14 February 1771, in time to hear Cook's letter from Batavia read to members on 30 May. Later that year, on 21 November 1771, Dalrymple attended the meeting at which James Cook was the guest of Maskelyne, who 'delivered at the Table' various manuscripts including 'The Journals of their late astronomer Mr Charles Green', and a manuscript folio 'Observations made by appointment of the Royal Society at King George's Island and in the South Sea by Mr Charles Green . . . Captain Cook . . . and others from 13 April to 5 July of the same year'.[91]

It was the question of the Southern Continent, however, that most closely concerned Dalrymple. Here the voyage had been inconclusive, though it had lopped off important sections of this supposed land, thus undermining confidence in the counterpoise theory. Cook himself had urged that another voyage was needed to settle the question. The widespread importance attached to this matter had been dramatically demonstrated by the recent Falkland Islands crisis,[92] for it was the possible existence of a

[90] Ibid., Vol. 1, pp. xxviii–xxix. It has to be remembered that this work was intended to be a work of propaganda, so that a degree of imaginative exaggeration was to be expected. As Sir Isaiah Berlin recently remarked (*Sunday Times*, 6 November 1966, p. 41), 'No great doctrine of originality or power in human affairs appears to me ever to have got into the common consciousness of men unless it was to some extent over-stated.' A work devoted to pure scholarship would have been unlikely to stir men into action in this quest for a Southern Continent.

[91] *Journal of the Royal Society*, Vol. XXVII (1771–74). The *Endeavour* had anchored in the Downs, at the end of her voyage, on 12 July 1771.

[92] For an account of this crisis, see Harlow, op. cit., Vol. 1, pp. 22–32.

Southern Continent which gave these islands their significance. They would remain a potential danger to peace until the reality of the Southern Continent had either been established or disproved.

Furthermore, the British could not ignore the increasing activity of the French and Spaniards in the Pacific. Jean-François-Marie de Surville, after re-discovering the Solomon Islands without realizing that he had done so, had just missed meeting the *Endeavour* in northern New Zealand. He had then crossed the Pacific in that latitude and had reached the Peruvian coast, near Callao, on 7 April 1770. This had roused the Spaniards to action, and in October 1770 Don Felipe Gonzalez had sailed on the voyage which was to lead him to the re-discovery of Easter Island, from which he returned in March 1771. Seven months later Marion du Fresne left France to take back to Tahiti Ahu-toru, the native whom Bougainville had brought to France. After repatriating his passenger, Marion was instructed to seek the Southern Continent once found by Gonneville. Yet another French explorer who was active at this time was Kerguelen, who left France in May 1771 in search of Gonneville's Land and the Southern Continent, which he intended to seek to the south of the Indian Ocean.[93]

In view of this foreign competition, Dalrymple had chosen a favourable moment in which to publish his *Historical Collection*, and the French and German editions that followed bore witness to its powerful impact. In 1771 the Admiralty asked the Council of the Royal Society to draw up instructions for a new expedition under Captain Cook, and in accordance with the normal practice a committee 'of the most eminent Fellows of the Society cognizant of the subjects concerned' was set up by the Council to carry out this task.[94]

Soon after the *Endeavour*'s return, Dalrymple and Benjamin Franklin were among 'a company of men of liberal sentiments'

[93] J. Dunmore, *French Explorers in the Pacific*, Vol. 1, pp. 114–65 (de Surville), pp. 165–95 (du Fresne), and pp. 196–249 (Kerguelen).

[94] *The Records of the Royal Society of London*, London, 1940, pp. 46–7. C. R. Weld, *History of the Royal Society*, London, 1848, Vol. II, p. 54. It is to be presumed that Dalrymple was either a member of this Committee, or was consulted by it as an expert witness.

who were discussing the voyage and the discoveries that had been made. The conversation turned to the lack of corn, fowls and of all quadrupeds other than dogs which had been revealed in New Zealand, and it was suggested that an expedition should be organized to make good these deficiencies. Franklin, who warmly supported the idea, suggested that the British had a moral obligation to do this, since their own riches and comforts had come from abroad, their country having 'produced originally nothing but sloes'. It would also be far-sighted policy, since civilized men would provide a better market than savages. Dalrymple stated that he would be prepared to take command of the vessel on such an expedition, and he and Franklin were entrusted with organizing the enterprise and raising money by an appeal for public subscriptions. Dalrymple estimated that the scheme would cost £15,000,[95] but the appeal failed and nothing more was heard of the plan.

Captain Cook set out on his second voyage on 13 July 1772, and five days later Dalrymple was writing to Lord North to propose a voyage of discovery in the South Atlantic. Stressing the need to increase the country's commerce, population and navigation, he explained that it was his intention to undertake the voyage at his own expense. His purpose in approaching Lord North was to ensure that the voyage would not have international repercussions, for the dangerous Falkland Islands crisis was still fresh in the memory. His intention was to search for the 'very large pleasant island' which La Roche had reported seeing in 45° S. in the year 1675.[96] On 24 July 1772 he asked for an interview with Lord North, which took place on 15 August. But this marked the end of the scheme, for Lord North talked much more about the Balambangan venture than he did about this new project, about which he said that he could make no decision until he had discussed the matter with his colleagues. Dalrymple heard no more about it.[97]

95 *Plan by Dr Franklin and Mr Dalrymple for benefitting distant unprovided Countries*, 29 August 1771.

96 For a discussion about the identity of this land, see Beaglehole, op. cit., Vol. II, p. 617, n2, and Burney, op. cit., Vol. III, pp. 395–403.

97 A. Dalrymple, *Collection of Voyages in the South Atlantick*, London, 1775, Introduction.

The influence of Dalrymple's *Historical Collection* on the conduct of Cook's second voyage has been dealt with at length in Professor J. C. Beaglehole's masterly edition of the *Journals of Captain James Cook*, and while it would be superfluous to enter into details of it here, it is worth quoting the following passage: 'These two volumes of 1770–71 certainly went the voyage, and they could never have had a more devoted reader. As a compendium of documents in a field which Dalrymple . . . had taken peculiarly to himself, they were invaluable. They presented the earlier discoveries as a series which could be checked, with enough detail to make identification possible.' Beaglehole describes Cook as making his tour with this 'guide-book always in his hand', so that beneath Cook's 'incorruptible gaze much might expand into a new clarity, but something might fade away . . . Dalrymple . . . had collected a great deal that turned out to be fact, and the dissipation of Juan Fernandez' land is balanced by the solidifying of Quiros's Bay of St Philip and St James'.[98]

Cook's second voyage had demonstrated beyond doubt that the great Southern Continent of ancient tradition did not exist. How Dalrymple adapted his theories to this new evidence is not known, but it is very possible that a clue is to be found in the writings of Sir George Staunton. On 28 June 1787, six weeks after the first convicts had left Portsmouth for Botany Bay, Sir George dined at the Royal Society Club as the guest of Alexander Dalrymple. The convict settlement was therefore a probable topic of conversation. A few years later Sir George accompanied Lord Macartney on his mission to China and wrote the official

98 Beaglehole, op. cit., Vol. II, p. lxxxix. Nor was the outcome of this voyage, great as that was, the only advantage reaped from the labours that had gone into the production of this *Historical Collection*, James Burney, whose *Chronological History* is one of the classic works on the exploration of the Pacific handsomely acknowledged the help that he had received. 'To Mr Dalrymple', he wrote, 'I have been greatly indebted for assistance. From his large collection of scarce Spanish books, I have been furnished with several original accounts of Spanish discoveries, which I had no other means of procuring. Much labour has likewise been saved me by his *Historical Collection* . . . , a work which, besides giving a clear outline of the subject, has been extremely useful as an index to direct me to original information. It has, indeed, been my Vade Mecum.' Burney, op. cit., Vol. 1, pp. ix–x. Burney had not only served in Cook's last two voyages, but had also sailed under Captain Hugh Dalrymple, Alexander's elder brother.

account of that embassy. On its outward passage the expedition visited Tristan da Cunha, which Dalrymple had suggested as an alternative site for a convict settlement. Here Staunton mused on the old counterpoise theory of a great Southern Continent, and in view of his dinner with Dalrymple, when this island group was much in his host's mind, it may well be that he was expressing Dalrymple's modified version of the theory. The islands of Tristan da Cunha, wrote Staunton, were 'situated in that part of the southern hemisphere, in the neighbourhood of which a continent, to balance the quantity of land in the northern hemisphere, was once expected to be found; but where it has since been discovered that there is none. Of what extent, however, the bases of those islands are under the sea, cannot he ascertained; or whether they may, or may not, be sufficient to make up for the defect of land appearing above water. Navigators report, that to the eastward of them are other small islands, differing not much in latitude, such as Gough and Alvarez Islands, and the Marsonines; as well as extensive shoals, lying due south of the most southerly point of Africa, and extending easterly several degrees. That all these together form a chain, some of subaqueous, and some of super-aqueous mountains; but all connected by their roots, is perhaps, a conjecture less improbable, than that they should separately arise, like tall columns, from the vast abyss'.[99]

In place of the old Southern Continent, whose existence they had disproved, Cook's first two voyages had unveiled New Zealand and the eastern seaboard of Australia. Thus at the very time when the American colonists were bringing the first British Empire to ruin, two new lands had been revealed that were eminently suited to white settlement. The opportunity was at hand to achieve triumph out of disaster. But by a strange twist of

[99] Sir G. Staunton, *An Authentic Account of an Embassy from the King of Great Britain to the Emperor of China*, London, 1797, Vol. 1, pp. 201–2. At that time these islands were still uninhabited, though Staunton was impressed by their potential value. His 'Marsonines' were presumably the illusory Marseveen which appear to have had their origin in sightings of icebergs – see Beaglehole, op. cit., p. 647n, where he mentions that Halley showed them, but that Dalrymple, in his *Memoir of a Chart of the Southern Ocean*, was unconvinced of their reality.

fate it was Alexander Dalrymple, to whom these discoveries owed so much, who now did his utmost to prevent their exploitation. For though this was the true Terra Australis, it was not the Great Southern Continent of his dreams. The fifty million civilized people with whom the British could trade had shrunk to a scattering of the most primitive peoples on earth. There was a danger, in the aftermath of the American Revolution, that the British would miss their great new opportunity by succumbing to a mood of deep disillusion. At this critical hour Dalrymple could only suggest a policy of despair, as his vision, for once, had failed him.

The British first paid serious attention to Australia's potentialities in connection with the convict problem. On the eve of the American Declaration of Independence at least a thousand convicts were being shipped to America each year, so that the closing of this outlet caused a crisis in the penal system. It was to meet this emergency that the British government introduced the Hulks Bill in 1776. This was only intended as a temporary solution and in 1779 the matter again came up for consideration.[100] A House of Commons Committee then considered the whole problem of the transportation of felons, and Sir Joseph Banks was one of those consulted by this committee. He expressed the opinion that the thinly populated Botany Bay in New Holland, with its mild climate and adequate soil, was best suited for this purpose, and he suggested that Britain would gain from such a settlement by having new outlets for her trade, and for the employment of her shipping. The committee accepted his advice.[101]

Another to draw early attention to the potentialities of Australia was J. M. Matra, who had sailed on Cook's first two voyages. He wrote to Banks in July 1783, stating that he had 'heard a rumour of two plans for a settlement in the South Seas; one of them for New South Wales to be immediately under your direction, in which Sir George Young, Lord Sandwich, Lord Mul-

[100] Eris O'Brien, *The Foundation of Australia*, Sydney, 1950 (2nd edition), pp. 89 et seq.

[101] E. Smith, *The Life of Sir Joseph Banks*, London and New York, 1911, pp. 213–4. *Common Journals*, Vol. 37 (1778–80), col. 311.

grave, Mr Colman and several others are concerned', and he expressed an ardent wish to join in this venture. A month later he published *A Proposal for establishing a Settlement in New South Wales*, which he advocated as a means of compensating for the loss of the American colonies, and of offering a haven wherein the American Loyalists could mend their broken fortunes. In this scheme he also included suggestions for trading with China, for using this new continent as a base from which to exploit the fur trade on the north-west coast of America, for trading with the Moluccas and for cultivating the flax plant. The fall of the Fox-North coalition government caused some delay, but the new Pitt Ministry took up this matter, and after Matra had been interviewed by Lord Sydney in April 1784, the scheme was modified to include a provision for the transportation of convicts.[102]

In April 1785 a House of Commons committee was set up under the chairmanship of Lord Beauchamp to suggest a site for a convict settlement. Matra and Banks proposed New Holland, but the committee was unconvinced about the commercial possibilities of that area and recommended that West Africa should be investigated. This was done by the Admiralty sloop *Nautilus* in August 1785, but its report was unfavourable.

It was against this background that the East India Company asked Dalrymple for his reactions to the proposal to establish a settlement on Norfolk Island 'to supply India with Cordage and with Masts, for want of which the Maritime Force employed in India has been often reduced to distress'. He sent his reply on 13 July 1785, and he afterwards expanded this and a subsequent letter into his pamphlet entitled *A Serious Admonition to the Publick on the intended Thief-Colony at Botany Bay*.

Two considerations determined Dalrymple's attitude. From a long-term point of view he believed that any attempt to colonize this vast, thinly-populated land would inevitably lead, in time, to another War of Independence on the American model. His

[102] Smith, op. cit., pp. 214–5.
Historical Records of New South Wales, Vol. 1, Part 2 (1783–92), Sydney, 1892, pp. xxiii et seq.
Historical Studies, Australia and New Zealand, Vol. 9, No. 35, p. 224 (November 1960), in article by M. Clark, 'The Choice of Botany Bay'.

more immediate fear was that a colony in New South Wales would prove incompatible with the maintenance of the East India Company's monopoly. He knew that important members of the new Administration in England disliked this monopoly, and that decisions had been taken, or were in contemplation that year, which would infringe it,[103] but he himself was convinced that it was essential for the success of the Company's trade. This was particularly true of the Eastern Islands, in which he had a close personal interest. 'The India trade cannot be protected by Treaties, and regulated by Consuls,' he pointed out, 'but must be carried on in armed vessels, and, consequently, requires the stability and discretion of a well-regulated Company, to protect the Commerce, and prevent the Trader, on the other hand, from becoming his own Judge and Avenger.'[104] If the Company's monopoly was not maintained in this area, he feared that native piracy might become even more dangerous. As he wrote a few years later, 'the Governments in the Islands . . . are not such as afford a Security to the Merchants. The Vessels that do carry on a Trade to the Eastern Islands, may be said to carry it, sword in hand, and the frequent instances of Vessels being cut off, has made that trade very precarious. As Arms and Ammunition would find a ready Vent, the danger would be greatly increased by an open Trade; for the Indian pirates are very numerous and only want Arms and Ammunition to command, to become formidable'.[105] This was a valid argument that drew attention to a serious problem.

Because he had devoted so much energy to the task of re-establishing the Company's trade with the Eastern Islands, he

103 e.g. the agreement allowing Etches and his partners to operate the fur-trade between the north-west coast of American and Japan, etc., and that permitting Samuel Enderby and his associates in the Southern Whale Fishery to operate within the limits of the East India Company's area of exclusive trade.

104 Alexander Dalrymple (ed. G. Mackanesss), *A Serious Admonition to the Public on the Intended Thief Colony at Botany Bay* (original edition London, 1786), Sydney, 1943.

105 A. Dalrymple, *A Fragment on the India Trade (written 1791)*, London, 1797, p. 12. He also argued that it would prove impracticable to maintain the Company's monopoly in such an area in isolation; that monopoly had to be kept intact.

was now blinded to the great opportunities that were waiting to be seized in 'New Holland'. He knew that some of his close friends had different views, including Sir Joseph Banks who foresaw 'the future prospect of Empires and Dominions that cannot be disappointed', and the probability that England might 'revive in New South Wales when it is sunk in Europe'.[106] But with his attention concentrated upon the Eastern Archipelago, where the Company was about to renew its efforts to re-establish its trade, Dalrymple mustered every argument that he could think of to prevent this experiment of an Australian colony from being attempted, including the suggestion that the British had no legal right to Eastern Australia, which had first been discovered by unknown Europeans in the sixteenth century, and explored by the Dutch at the beginning of the eighteenth century.[107]

Dalrymple's own proposed solution to the convict problem was to suggest Tristan da Cunha as an alternative to Botany Bay. He argued that the prevention of crime was more important than its punishment which served only to deter criminals. At Botany Bay criminals would have 'every object of comfort and ambition', which would encourage rather than deter crime. At Tristan da Cunha they could easily be supplied from the Cape of Good Hope, and visiting whalers could also bring them essential supplies in exchange for the oil which the colonists could collect. Moreover, 'the situation of Tristan da Cunha makes all guard unnecessary, and they ought to be left to themselves without arms, and with such small Boats as could not go off the Coast'. They could soon become self-sufficient, since they could grow potatoes, and get plenty of food from the abundance of sea-lions, penguins, and similar creatures. The island was too remote to

106 G. Mackaness, *Sir Joseph Banks: his relations with Australia*, Sydney, 1936, p. 44.

107 He based these assertions on his recent discovery of the Dauphin Map, and on the report by Nicolas Struyck. See Burney, op. cit., Vol. IV, p. 450. He admitted that he did not believe in this argument himself, but in view of 'the many dangerous consequences to be dreaded from this Thievish Plan he would not be sorry if it should be given up from apprehensions that were groundless, since real danger could not influence Ministers to desist'. His own advice was that the British should only attempt to colonize parts of Australia if other nations made the attempt, 'but never till then'.

make escape possible, and in time this settlement might become useful to visiting ships.[108]

Fortunately, Dalrymple's views did not prevail. In June 1786, after a prison-hulk riot at Plymouth, the Cabinet considered possible locations in the West Indies, Canada and West Africa, without coming to a decision.[109] But on 18 August 1786, Lord Sydney at last drew up the heads of a plan 'for effectually disposing of convicts, and rendering their transportation reciprocally beneficial both to themselves and to the State, by the establishment of a colony in New South Wales'.[110]

The search for a Southern Continent resulted in the mapping of the Pacific. It was the good fortune of Captain Cook to play the major role in this work, and his great achievements have had their due reward. It should never be forgotten, however, that it was largely due to the labours of Alexander Dalrymple that this was a British undertaking. His great influence and his election as a Fellow of the Royal Society are evidence that his theories were acceptable to the scientific authorities of his day. As he himself observed, 'errors may lead to the truth, but when all men's notions are ground in one mill, they serve no purpose of investigation or discovery'. For his indispensable part in this great work, from which his countrymen have continued to reap incalculable benefits, his name should be held in high regard.

108 This letter, included in his pamphlet, was written on 1 September 1786.

109 *Historical Studies, Australia and New Zealand*, ut supra.

110 V. Harlow and F. Madden, *British Colonial Developments, 1774–1834*, Oxford, 1953, p. 435. Nevertheless, some attention was paid to the warnings of Dalrymple and those who thought likewise. Ships from Botany Bay were forbidden to trade with the 'Settlements of our East India Company, as well as the coast of China, and the Islands situated in that part of the world' – *Historical Records, Australia and New Zealand*, Vol. 2, No. 8, pp. 256 et seq.

CHAPTER VI

The British in the East Indies, 1761-1805

(i) *1761–84. Mindanao and Celebes*

THE disaster that had overtaken Herbert's settlement on Balambangan did not terminate the East India Company's ambitions to establish an emporium in the Eastern Islands. In the first place, Dalrymple's theories had become official policy and the Company was now alive to 'the infinite Emolument the vicinity to China and the Exclusive Vent of Cotton Cloths in the Eastern Islands would yield'.[1] Furthermore, this seemed a favourable moment in which to pursue an expansionist policy in this area, at a time when the growth of the Company's maritime forces was in sharp contrast to the decline of Dutch and Spanish sea-power.[2]

The Sulu Archipelago had been chosen for Dalrymple's initial experiment not only because of its intrinsic merits, but also because it lay outside the Dutch and Spanish spheres of influence. After the setback at Balambangan, however, the East India Company began to develop a more aggressive attitude by taking an interest in the large islands of Celebes and Mindanao, where their Dutch and Spanish rivals possessed isolated bases without having brought either island under control.

Commodore Wilson's voyage in the *Pitt* had forewarned the Dutch that their English rivals were beginning to intrude in waters from which they had long been excluded. The reaction of the Dutch had been sharp, so that when the *Warwick* returned from China by the eastern passage in 1761 she was boarded near the Moluccas by a Dutch official from Tidore, who declared

I am grateful to the *Journal of Pacific History* for permission to reproduce parts of my article 'Alexander Dalrymple and New Guinea' in Chapters VI and IX.

[1] A. Dalrymple, 'Memoir of Sooloo', 1762, *Orme Mss*, Vol. 67, f. 32, p. 97.

[2] P. J. Blok (translations by O. A. Bierstadt), *History of the People of the Netherlands*, New York and London, 1912, Part V, p. 146.

that English vessels were not allowed to sail through these seas, since they were a Dutch preserve. Soon afterwards the Dutch authorities at Batavia heard rumours that the East India Company was planning a settlement on the island of Salawatty, off the coast of New Guinea.[3] They decided to destroy this and to try to end the English Company's use of the new route to China. They therefore organized an expedition early in 1762, which was instructed to extirpate any English settlement on Salawatty and then to 'cruize all along the coast of Papos, to set on fire all the Vessels they might meet with on that coast, to make no Prisoners, to be as Auxiliaries to the Kings of Tidore and Ternate in doing this, and effectually to root out and destroy all Interlopers'.[4] It was clear that the Dutch would not lightly relinquish what remained of their power; nevertheless, the confidence of their British rivals was growing all the time.

The Sulu enterprise, by which Dalrymple hoped to extend British influence throughout the Eastern Archipelago,[5] was an instance of this confidence. With the outbreak of the Anglo-Spanish war in 1762 he even recommended the seizure of the Southern Philippines, which would have brought Mindanao within the British orbit.[6] In the event, the British attacked Manila and left the Southern Philippines alone, but from this time onwards they took an increasing interest both in Mindanao and Celebes, and lost no opportunity to glean intelligence about both these islands.

The islanders of Mindanao were themselves eager for an English alliance against their Spanish neighbours, and on 2 March 1763 Dawsonne Drake and his Council were reporting

[3] The voyages of the *Pitt* and the *Cuddalore* may have given rise to this story, for after leaving Sumbawa the latter had headed eastwards for Flores. The Dutch would probably have heard, in addition, confused rumours of an intended settlement (i.e., Sulu).

[4] Secret Committee to the Earl of Halifax, 16 January 1764, *Home Miscellaneous Series*, Vol. 97, f. 3, p. 9. This enclosed what purported to be a copy of the Secret Resolution of the Batavian Council, which the English had 'found means to procure'. There is another copy in *Dutch Records* – A, Vol. XVIII.

[5] In his 'Memoir of Sooloo' Dalrymple estimated the population of the Sulu empire at *c.* 300,000 people, with a further million in 'allied' territories (i.e., islands not under Dutch or Spanish control).

[6] For an outline of this plan, see Chapter III.

to London that an ambassador, from the 'King of Mindanao' was expressing his master's desire 'to cultivate a Friendship with the English and allow them to settle upon any part of the Island that would be most convenient to them'. The Directors were cautious but interested, and told their servants at Madras to consider whether a Residency there would be feasible, and could be effected without endangering 'our prudent Amity with the Spaniards'.[7]

It was Captain Thomas Forrest who provided the Company with its fullest information about Mindanao. He had been recruited by Herbert to help with the founding of the Balambangan settlement, and his adventurous voyage through the Eastern Islands in a small native craft was the one bright feature in the sorry story of that venture. His voyage had a twofold purpose. In the first place, he was to attempt to acquire the cinnamon, cloves, nutmegs, pepper and clove bark which Dalrymple had suggested could be cultivated on Balambangan, and in the second place he was to undertake a voyage of discovery in seas very little known to the English. His return route brought him to Mindanao in 1775, where he was obliged to stay for several months until the change of monsoon should allow his return to Balambangan. This gave him plenty of time for observation, and he described how the Spaniards, apart from their main base at Samboangan, controlled the west, north and north-east coasts, where they had planted Christians from the Philippines,[8] while the independent Illanos[9] ruled the large bay in the centre of the south coast, as well as the great lake and part of the interior. Forrest's main concern was to find a site where the East India Company could, if it wished, establish a fort and warehouses, for which he felt that an island near the mainland, with a good harbour, would be most suitable. Bunwoot Island, off the Mindanao River and thus near the capital, answered these needs, and the Sultan and his brother, Rajah

[7] *Madras Despatches*, Vol. II, 31 December 1763. See also *Factory Records; Borneo*, f. 57, Dalrymple to Secret Committee, 7 February 1764, where he suggested that the British and Spaniards should 'mutually Guaranty the Protection of the other's Dominions and Allies from all Intruders', since a restoration of peace was in the interests of both parties.

[8] Known as Bisaya.

[9] The Illanos were feudal sultans.

Moodo, divining his wishes, made him an offer of it, and nine days later the grant was signed and sealed.[10]

Three months earlier the Sultan had written a letter to King George III, wherein he had noted that whereas the Spaniards intermeddled with the island's religion, and the Dutch usurped dominion and sovereignty, the English confined their attention to trade. That was why he was anxious for an English alliance and was willing to give the East India Company 'any Island wherever they may chuse to settle in my Country, where they may build a Fort and entertain Soldiers as many as they please . . . Opposite any such Island . . . I will give them 1000 Fathoms in Length upon the Sea Coast and 1000 Fathoms inland'. He would enter into offensive and defensive treaties with the Company, and if the English fought the Spaniards or the Dutch he would join in with them. 'There are many Islands . . . to the Southward in Meanges', he added, 'to the East there is Yap; Islands not yet properly discovered and known, I will give any of those Islands to the Company. . . .'[11]

The East India Company was equally interested in the Island of Celebes. In 1759 a short geographical and historical description of the island had appeared in the *Universal Modern History*. The writer of this article had asserted that the people of Celebes were particularly brave and hard to conquer, and this opinion was soon supported by Dalrymple and other observers. The article also argued that Celebes had important commercial attractions, since it was not only in close proximity to 'the great island of Borneo, abounding in gold, diamonds, pepper and other rich commodities', but also had the Spice Islands and the Philippines as close neighbours, while even Siam, Cambodia, Cochin-China and China were all within three hundred leagues. Because of this favourable geographical position a 'prodigious trade' was carried on at all the 'great towns of the coast'.[12]

Shortly after the publication of this description Dalrymple was in a position to give a first-hand account of conditions on the

[10] Thomas Forrest, *A Voyage to New Guinea . . .*, London, 1779, pp. 249–50.

[11] *Home Miscellaneous Series*, Vol. 134, pp. 77–8 (duplicates on pp. 73–4 and in Vol. 128, pp. 496–7.

[12] *Universal Modern History*, London, 1759, Vol. 9, pp. 334–6.

island, for in the early summer of 1761 he visited the port of Macassar. Here he found a tense situation. The two principal native states in Celebes were Bony and Goa. The prince of Bony was an unwilling ally of the Dutch, for one of his predecessors had had to flee to Batavia in the seventeenth century, which had given the Dutch an opportunity to establish themselves in Celebes in return for the aid which they had given him. But the prince of Bony and his people resented the price which they had had to pay for this aid, since they were still expected to provide the Dutch, each year, with large quantities of rice. It was known that the Dutch position was weak, for in the whole of Celebes there were said to be only about one thousand Europeans, and these were separated from each other by immense distances. Only at Macassar were they in a strong position, for there the powerful Fort Rotterdam was garrisoned by about five hundred soldiers. Yet Dalrymple found that even these men were 'destitute of shoes and stockings, even when on board the Guard Vessels, and probably ill-used from their acknowledged inclination to desert', and he was told that a Dutchman could not go half-a-mile from the Fort 'without the utmost hazard of his life'. Thus it was no surprise to find the island in a state of revolt at the time of his arrival. The trouble had broken out in Bony and it was believed that the ruler of Goa, though ostensibly neutral, had nevertheless suggested the formation against the Dutch of a general alliance of all the native princes on Celebes, including his rival the prince of Bony.

When the 'King of Goa' had heard of the arrival of English vessels in the area he had immediately sensed the appearance of possible new allies against the Dutch. This was an unexpected development, for before the arrival of the convoy of East-Indiamen at Sulu in January 1761, escorted by Dalrymple in the *Cuddalore*, no English ships had ever been known to visit that island. A report of their arrival had been brought back by a Noquedah[13] from Goa, who had happened to be in Sulu at the time. The King of Goa had immediately sent a representative to Sumbawa to try to intercept the English ships, for that was known to be their next port-of-call, but he had missed

[13] i.e., the captain of a native vessel.

them. When the *Cuddalore* had visited Macassar on her way back to Sulu in the early summer the King of Goa had again tried to make contact with Dalrymple, but he had failed because of the precautions which the Dutch had taken to isolate the English vessel. Knowing how far away were the English settlements, the King had therefore reluctantly come to the conclusion that the chance of an English alliance had now been lost, and so had decided to seek the help of the Spaniards instead. An ambassador was thereupon despatched to Manila.

On its way to Manila this embassy visited Sulu on 18 August 1762, and it chanced that Dalrymple, now on board the *London,* was also there at the time. The ambassador therefore sent some of his men over to the *London* to explain to Dalrymple that though he was now instructed to try to persuade the Spaniards to renew their alliance with Goa, his people also strongly desired an alliance with the English. Dalrymple replied that this was the wish of his own countrymen, too, though they were 'cautious of interfering with any other Europeans'. He told them that he was authorized to conclude an alliance if they were free from engagements with others, but if they were under a treaty with any other Europeans he must not stipulate anything contrary to the treaties subsisting between Britain and the countries concerned. In answer, wrote Dalrymple, 'they declared they were under no engagements with the Dutch . . . (but) they had antiently a Treaty with the Spaniards[14] whereby they were bound to yield each other mutual assistance'.

Dalrymple therefore promised to 'conclude a Friendship' if the Spaniards rejected the proposed alliance, mentioning that the one condition that the East India Company would insist upon would be a grant of Kayela, where he was assured that there was an excellent harbour, with permission to build a fort there. The ambassador from Goa now began to visit Dalrymple in person, and at these conferences the two men drew up proposed Articles of Friendship and Commerce.[15] In 1763, however, Dalrymple, while at Manila, learnt that these negotiations had

14 'which the historians of the Philippines place in the year 1618', wrote Dalrymple.

15 National Library of Scotland, *Melville Papers,* MS. 1068, ff. 79–80.

been brought to nought because the ambassador and all his party had been killed by pirates from Mindanao. At the same time he learnt that the insurrection in Celebes had ended indecisively, though it had had the effect of ending the long rivalry between Goa and Bony.[16]

Although his negotiations had thus been undone, Dalrymple had gathered a good deal of information about Celebes. It seemed that the King of Goa had once exerted authority not only over the whole island of Celebes, but also over an empire that had included Tidore, the Moluccas, Ceram, Amboina, Banda, Timor, Flores, Sumbawa and other islands. When Europeans first reached the East Indies this empire was already in decline, but Dalrymple argued that its erstwhile existence made nonsense of the 'Antient Dutch Pretensions grounded on the cession of the King of Ternaté'. As an indication of the civilization attained by this kingdom, he mentioned that Navarette had visited Macassar in 1658 and had found that this ruler possessed a considerable library, including some European books and maps.[17] He noted that Celebes was more important for its commerce than for its own productions, for the Bugis traded at all places as far as the Malayan peninsula to the west,[18] and New Holland and New Guinea to the east. Their vessels were superior to any others in that area, and they now always used compasses, though not charts 'in which they are inferior to the Chinese; but they have a great aptness in understanding them, when they can obtain any from Europeans'.[19]

Further information about Celebes came from Carteret who had wintered there during his circumnavigation. When this became known after his return to England in 1769, the Chairman and Deputy-Chairman of the East India Company requested from Lord Weymouth 'fresh information of that and the adjac-

[16] A. Dalrymple, 'Memoirs of Celebes', Fort St George, April 1763. *Home Miscellaneous Series*, Vol. 795, pp. 33–47.

[17] Navarette was a Spanish missionary who was sent from the Philippines to China. Dalrymple was told that these European books still survived. He was intrigued by the islanders' writing, which was distinct from the Malayan script.

[18] He mentioned Quedah as being the farthest they went to the west.

[19] *Home Miscellaneous Series*, Vol. 795, pp. 33–47.

ent Islands [which might] greatly conduce to the Improvement of the Navigation, and the opening new and extensive Channels of Commerce in those parts'.[20] As a result of this request Carteret met Laurence Sulivan and gave him a full account of his experiences in Celebes.[21] Like Dalrymple he had arrived at a time of unrest, which had obliged the Dutch to try to prevent the local princes from making contact with the Englishmen. Nevertheless, one of these princes, the 'King of Wadjo', managed to get a message delivered to Carteret, asking for an English alliance in return for facilities to establish a settlement on his coast.

This growing knowledge of conditions on Mindanao and Celebes was complemented by much new information regarding the islands to the east of the Moluccas, stretching away as far as New Guinea. This intelligence was brought back by Captain Thomas Forrest after his voyage in the *Tartar*, which culminated in his visit to Mindanao, as already described. Forrest left Balambangan in this little native vessel in the year 1774.[22] The *Tartar* had first made for Sulu, whence, heading south-eastwards, she had passed close to Ternate and Tidore. After coasting along Batjan she had altered course towards the east and so had reached New Guinea. Forrest had continued along this coast until he came to Dorey Harbour in Geelvink's Bay, where he had found nutmeg trees which the natives assured him were plentiful. They seemed unaware of their value, though they fully appreciated the commercial importance of their other products, such as plantain, coconuts, pineapple and breadfruit. The articles most in demand with these natives were various items of ironmongery. Forrest discovered that the Dutch would not allow the natives of Ternate or Tidore to trade here, for fear that they might deal in nutmegs, but the Chinese came, armed with passes from the Sultan of Tidore and flying Dutch colours.[23]

20 Ibid., Vol. 100, p. 499, 31 August 1769.

21 *Carteret's Voyage Round the World* (ed. H. Wallis), Hakluyt Society, Cambridge, Vol. 1, 1965, p. 92.

22 This native craft had been chosen to avoid suspicion when it passed close to Dutch-controlled islands. It had the added advantage that it was small enough to be rowed and was of shallow draught. To maintain his disguise, Forrest only took two Europeans with him to act as mate and gunner. The rest were Filipinos, Moluccans and Lascars.

23 Forrest, op. cit., p. 106.

On leaving Dorey Forrest had headed northwards, and on the way he had found the well-populated island of Geby, strategically situated in the middle of Gillolo Passage. Off its north-west end there was another island behind which, he was told, some French ships had lately lain and had obtained 'many nutmegs and clove plants, which they carried to their islands of Bourbon and Mauritius . . . (and) since . . . to the Seychelles, and some . . . even . . . to the West Indies'.[24] He had then carried on to Mindanao, where he arrived on 12 May 1775, and a week later he had received confirmation that Balambangan had been sacked by some Sulu islanders, and that the survivors had retired to Borneo.

With the destruction of the Balambangan settlement it was necessary to find a new site for an emporium, since the East India Company was now fully determined to re-establish its trade in the Eastern Islands. Forrest's voyage fitted in with these plans, for he had touched at islands that lay outside the limits of effective Dutch control, and these were the very islands whose trade Dalrymple had hoped to attract to Balambangan. In seeking a site for a new settlement it was natural that the Directors thought first of Mindanao and Celebes, which had been so much in their minds in recent years, and the outbreak of the American War of Independence appeared to offer an unprecedented opportunity to establish settlements in one or both of these islands. For the American war, like the Seven Years' War before it, soon became a struggle between the European powers for supremacy in the competition for overseas expansion, and it was not long before Britain found herself at war with both her Dutch and Spanish rivals. In 1779 the Spaniards, in a bid to recover Gibraltar and Minorca, had joined the French in the war against Britain, and in December 1780 the Dutch determination to join the Armed Neutrality brought about a British declaration of war.

[24] Ibid., p. 155. See also Auguste Toussaint (trans. J. Guicharnaud), *History of the Indian Ocean*, London, 1966, p. 180. He states that Pierre Poivre first collected cloves and nutmegs here in 1755, taking them back to Mauritius. He returned in 1767, and in 1770–1 sent a further two expeditions. For an account of the Dutch method of enforcing their monopoly, see Forrest, op. cit., pp. 32–3.

Among those who saw in this crisis an opportunity to establish British settlements in Mindanao were two naval officers who had taken part in the expedition against Manila in 1762, Admiral Sir Hyde Parker[25] and Captain William Brereton. In the Introduction to his *Account of the Philippine Islands,* the manuscript of which he had shown to his friend Alexander Dalrymple, Sir Hyde Parker expressed the view that the selfish incompetence of the British authorities at Manila after the capture of that city had made a mockery of the sacrifices of the soldiers and sailors in the 1762 campaign, Nevertheless, Mindanao still provided hope for the future. Writing within three years of Herbert's fiasco at Balambangan, the Admiral advocated a revival of Dalrymple's scheme, but with Mindanao replacing Balambangan. 'A good port in the China Seas is much wanted,' he wrote, 'and would be attended with the highest advantages to our Commerce. Among the great number of Islands situated in these Seas there is none perhaps more worthy of our attention than this of Mindanao. The possession of a well fortified Harbour on it would infallibily bring with it and Secure to us a participation of the Spice Trade. . . It cannot be doubted I think but that the near neighbourhood of an English port to the Moluccas will inevitably draw to it a considerable part of their productions in spite of the vigilance or precautions of the Dutch.' Only in one respect did his views differ sharply from those of his Scottish friend, for whereas Dalrymple was invariably a doughty champion of the East India Company's monopoly,[26] Parker, in pointing out how a British settlement in these seas could help in the extension of trade by new discoveries, opined that such action was 'incompatible with the confined views or spirit of a trading company and not to be thought on unless the shackles which at present fetter our Commerce were knocked off'.[27]

For his part, Captain Brereton recalled how he had been left 'charged with the King's affairs at Manila' in 1762. There he had been visited by an ambassador from Mindanao, dressed

[25] He was the father of Nelson's reluctant colleague.

[26] In deference to public opinion Dalrymple carefully avoided the term itself.

[27] B.M., *Add. Mss.* 19, 295, ff. 2–8.

in 'sumptuous ornaments and attire', who had come to express his master's desire for an English alliance. The rupture with Spain now allowed the British to establish themselves in this island, whose possession would not only provide them with 'great quantities of gold', but 'would open to the India Company a vast field of commerce amongst those Eastern Islands, and render His Majesty's new discoveries of benefit to the nation'. The conclusion of his letter showed how Dalrymple's theories had now become orthodox doctrine, for Brereton stressed that spices could be grown on Mindanao, and that 'Encouraging and enlarging this Commerce would enable the India Company to purchase their Cargoes in China without draining this Country and India of their specie'. The Company would also have 'great opportunities of vending infinite quantities of coarse goods'.[28]

As it happened, decisions had already been taken in that direction, for after the Cabinet had decided, on 3 August 1780, to invade South America by way of India,[29] the Directors of the East India Company had agreed to co-operate on the understanding that the plan should be extended to include the seizure of Mindanao and Celebes. To help the Directors to formulate their plans, it was convenient that Captain Thomas Forrest was on leave in England.[30] After further consideration, however, it was considered that priority should be given to an attack upon the Cape of Good Hope, in order to safeguard the trade route to India. But when this expedition to the Cape was at last put in motion, it was mishandled by its commander, Commodore George Johnstone, who allowed himself to be surprised and

28 Nat. Mar. Mus., transcripts of the *Sandwich Papers*, San/T/7, Brereton to Sandwich, 14 November 1780.

29 In October 1779 Sir John Dalrymple, having proposed an attack on South America, discussed this in London with Sir Joseph Banks who pointed out that Cook's discovery of the Sandwich Islands facilitated such an operation.

See also V. T. Harlow, *Founding of the Second British Empire*, Vol. 1, pp. 104 et seq.

30 He was in London by 1 February 1779 and was doubtless the 'Mr Forrest' whom Alexander Dalrymple entertained at the Royal Society Club on 2 March 1780. He was almost certainly the 'T.F.' who annotated Dalrymple's *Account of Celebes*, presumably in preparation for the abortive 1780 expedition.

forestalled by a French squadron under de Suffren.[31] Thus the Cape remained inviolate, and Britain's trade to the Orient continued to be burdened with consequential costs of protection for a further fifteen years.

An opportunity to attack the Spanish and Dutch bases on Mindanao and Celebes did not recur. Nevertheless, the American War was disastrous for the Dutch, whose East India Company lost its factories on the mainland of India and saw its communications with the homeland severed by the British. This caused its storehouses at Batavia to overflow with goods which the home authorities would not permit it to sell on the open market, so that the Batavian government found itself chronically short of money. The Dutch East India Company never recovered from the effects of this war,[32] and the Dutch representatives at the peace talks were therefore in a weak position. With French help they did manage to prevent the British from acquiring the Cape of Good Hope and Trincomali, but they were forced to concede the British demand for free navigation in the eastern seas. The latter asserted this right not only to safeguard their East India Company's shipping routes to China, but also to establish the right to trade with any of the Eastern Islands that were not in Dutch possession. To the Dutch, however, this represented a grave threat, for their spice monopoly relied upon trading agreements with the native princes, and these agreements would inevitably be jeopardized by granting this concession.[33]

(ii) *1784–92. An enforced interlude*

Despite its success at the peace talks the East India Company found itself in a difficult position in the aftermath of the American War. It was being subjected to attacks and criticism from many quarters, to which the most convincing answer would have been an expansion of its trade, particularly in the Eastern Islands. Yet this was a policy which it was prevented from pursuing for several years because it would have embarrassed the

31 Harlow, op. cit., pp. 106 et seq.

32 B. H. M. Vlekke, *The Story of the Dutch East Indies*, Cambridge, Mass., 1946, pp. 116–26. Blok, op. cit., pp. 186 et seq., and p. 323.

33 N. Tarling *Anglo-Dutch Rivalry in the Malay World, 1780–1824*, Sydney, 1962, pp. 9 et seq. Harlow, op. cit., pp. 384–93.

Government's foreign policy, and since the establishment of the Board of Control in 1784 the Company's Directors were obliged to pay the closest attention to the views of the Administration.

The growing volume of criticism of the Company included attacks from industry. The East India Company had always been vulnerable to criticism of its export record, because wool, which for so long had been Britain's major export, was particularly difficult to sell in either India or Canton. Nor did these provide easy markets for other manufactured goods. The Company therefore had to rely upon large exports of silver for its purchases, which laid it open to the charge that it was draining the country of its currency. Others attacked it because of its monopoly of the eastern trade.[34]

The weight of these attacks was made more telling by the backing they received from Adam Smith, whose *Wealth of Nations* was first published in 1776. He argued that a monopoly could only be justified for a limited period in the initial stages of a trade, after which it should be 'laid open to all the subjects of the state'. He also attacked the East India Company's sovereign powers in India, which he held to be incompatible with its mercantile interests.[35] The Directors of the East India Company took these criticisms seriously, for both the Younger Pitt, the new prime minister, and Henry Dundas, who was in effective charge of the Board of Control, were known to be much influenced by the teaching of Adam Smith.[36] Now that the Company's sovereign powers in India had been brought under governmental control by the establishment of the Board of Control in 1784, there was every danger that Pitt and Dundas might follow their master's advice still further by terminating the Company's monopoly.

34 T. S. Ashton, *An Economic History of England: the 18th century*, London, 1955, pp. 160–1. From the admittedly suspect statistics of the period it seems that the Company accounted for 20 per cent of the country's imports, but only 10 per cent of its exports. For attacks on the Company's monopoly from industry, see C. H. Philips, *The East India Company 1784–1834*, Manchester, 1940, p. 75.

35 Adam Smith, *The Wealth of Nations*, London (J. M. Dent, Everyman's Edition), Vol. 2, 1962, pp. 134 and 241.

36 Dundas did not become President of the Board of Control until 1793, but he was a leading influence in its deliberations from the first.

The East India Company could not stifle these criticisms by expanding its trade in the Eastern Islands, however, since the Government was anxious not to alienate the Dutch. It was realized that the United Provinces were no longer in a position to follow an independent foreign policy, and as a result, an Anglo-French diplomatic war had developed for the allegiance of the Dutch people. It was still uncertain whether the future would prove to lie with the Stadtholder, whose traditional policy was one of alignment with the British, or with the so-called 'Patriots' and their allies, whose sympathies lay with the French. The significance of this conflict for the safety of Britain's trade with China needed no emphasis.

At first it was the French who were successful, for in 1785 they were able to conclude an alliance with the Dutch. This caused the British ambassador at the Hague in 1786 to begin the process of creating a party in Holland which was opposed to French influence.[37] As tension mounted in the following year the Prussians, backed by the British, intervened on the Stadtholder's behalf.

In this situation Henry Dundas and W. W. Grenville attempted to fashion an eastern policy which would enable the British to remain on good terms with the Dutch and thus hold French influence at bay. Dundas did not believe that an Anglo-Dutch conflict of interests was inevitable, since the prime concern of the British was to preserve their empire in India, whereas that of the Dutch was to uphold their monopoly of the spice trade. At first he considered that this could be achieved without sacrificing the ambitions of the East India Company. 'When talking of Trincomalé and the navigation of the Eastern Seas,' he told Grenville, 'you write as if the possession of these was incompatible with the interest of the Dutch on account of the spice trade . . . I do not see how there is any inconsistency between their having the exclusive spice trade, and yet our having Trincomalé . . . and . . . a free navigation in the Eastern seas for the purposes of our China trade, and likewise for the purpose of opening new markets both for our Indian and European manu-

[37] Tarling, op. cit., pp. 16–17.

factures . . .'[38] But when he drew up a Memorandum one month later, entitled 'Considerations on the Subject of a Treaty between Great Britain and Holland, relative to their Interests in India', he had modified these views, and now thought that in the interests of peace the East India Company should be ready to abandon 'the navigation, and intended settlement, in one of the Eastern Islands', though it should not renounce its rights to either in case there was a deterioration in Anglo-Dutch relations. To safeguard Dutch purchases of textiles for their East Indian trade, he considered that Negapatam should be returned to them. To compensate for these important concessions, the Dutch should permit the British to use all their 'Harbours and Ports for the purposes of Navigation, or naval refreshment', with particular reference to the Cape and Trincomali. To make up for a withdrawal from the eastern seas, he also wished to see the British acquire a port at Riau.[39]

This line of thinking prevented the East India Company from pursuing an expansionist policy in the Eastern Archipelago for the time being. Only in the Strait of Malacca, which commanded the set-route from the mainland of India to that island world, could it seek to attain its aims. At Riau it was forestalled by the Dutch, but it managed to establish a settlement at Penang. In 1792, however, the end of the Anglo-Dutch negotiations was at hand, when the British ambassador presented the Pensionary of Zealand with what he termed 'an ultimate ultimatum',[40] by which time the East India Company had already resumed its reconnaissance of the Eastern Islands.

(iii) *1792–1805. The Eastern Islands at large*

Alexander Dalrymple always considered that the Company's monopoly was essential in the Eastern trade, and he was worried by the concessions which had been wrung from the Company by the Parliamentary Act of 1786 'for the Encouragement of the

[38] V. T. Harlow and F. Madden, *British Colonial Developments 1774–1834*, Oxford, 1953, p. 15, Dundas to Grenville, 2 September 1787. Grenville was Vice-President of the Committee for Trade, and a member of the Board of Control.

[39] Nat. Lbry. of Scotland, *Melville Papers*, MS. 1068, ff. 20–37.

[40] Tarling, op. cit., pp. 43–51. Harlow, op. cit., Vol. 2, pp. 329–65.

Southern Whale Fishery'. [41] He was critical of the Directors for agreeing to an Act of Parliament which 'permitted the Fishers to navigate as far East of the Cape of Good Hope as . . . 50°E and as far North as the Equator . . . because under this pretext, Vessels may resort to a Port of Rendezvous to which the Indian vessels of all descriptions may go; and thereby these ships, pretended to be Fishers, may carry cargoes for India, and receive other cargoes of Indian produce, to smuggle into Europe'.[42]

Dalrymple believed that the East India Company was 'more competent to extend the Commerce to effect than any Chance Adventurers' and he placed great hopes on the voyage of 'Discovery and Survey amongst the Eastern Islands' for which orders had been despatched to Bombay on 23 March 1790. This called for a new survey of the coast of New Guinea and was the first move by the East India Company towards a resumption of its expansionist policy in the Eastern Islands. But a return to this forward policy had been foreshadowed as early as 1786 when the Court of Directors had told Lord Cornwallis that 'the great importance of the China trade, the necessity of extending by commercial means the resources for our investment from that country, as well as the good policy of awing the Dutch to prevent a rupture with them, or in case of its taking place, to be able to avail ourselves of it advantageously, to break effectually their spice monopoly, make us look with sanguine expectations to the benefit of an establishment somewhere near the Pitts

[41] Harlow, op. cit., Vol. 2, London 1964, p. 305. It is worth noting that Dalrymple knew Adam Smith well and described him as 'a man of much investigation, knowledge and sagacity; with a heart overflowing with benevolence and sociability', but he doubted his judgement as 'he was strongly tinctured with French Philosophy and Systime. . . . The opinions of such a man, or of any man, are not to be admitted as infallible dogmas; but to be fairly weighed, before they are adopted' – Dalrymple, *Thoughts of an Old Man of independent Mind, though dependent Fortune*, London, 1800, p. 4.

For the arguments in favour of preventing the trade to the East Indies from becoming a free trade, see Dalrymple, *A Fragment on the India Trade*, London, 1797, p. 3. This was the published version of his 'Memorandum on Trade to the South Seas and the North-West Coast of America', dated 23 February 1791, for which see Harlow and Madden, op. cit., pp. 36–40.

[42] Ibid., p. 39. For these geographical limits, cf. Harlow, op. cit., Vol. 2, p. 307.

Straits, which by the judicious choice of an harbour for shelter and refreshment, for our ships which may make that passage, as well as for promoting the most important operations in case of future war, will effectually answer those purposes'.[43]

The inspiration for this new policy had come from the wrecking of the *Antelope* packet on her return from Macao in 1783. As it was mid-summer, she had been returning by way of the Eastern Passage so as to avoid the south-west monsoon, but Captain Henry Wilson had chosen too easterly a track and the *Antelope* had struck on one of the Palau Islands. Captain Wilson and all his crew had got safely ashore, where they were well treated by Abba Thulle, the 'king' of the island. After a few months they had been able to build themselves a new vessel in which to return to China, and so to England, accompanied by the king's son, Lee Boo. The latter had become a great favourite with London society, but unhappily he had contracted small-pox from which he had died.[44] Dalrymple and the Directors of the East India Company had seen in this personal tragedy the opportunity to combine a humanitarian mission to the islands, to bring news of the prince's death, with the execution of an important survey as the preliminary to the possible establishment of a new eastern settlement. Up to this time the Directors had still been wondering 'whether it might be advisable to avail ourselves of the good disposition of the people of Magindino [i.e. Mindanao] towards us, either by carrying on a trade on the part of the Company, or encouraging discreet individuals to open that trade for their own profit. . . '[45] but henceforth they began to concentrate their attention upon the islands in the neighbourhood of New Guinea.

No time was lost in beginning the new survey,[46] and on 24 August 1790 John McCluer left Bombay in the *Panther*, soon

43 Harlow and Madden, op. cit., p. 54.

44 See George Keate, *An Account of the Pelew Islands* . . . , London, 1788, for a full account of this episode.

45 Harlow and Madden, ut supra.

46 The orders for the survey are to be found in *Bombay Despatches*, Vol. 11, pp. 130–58, dated 25 March 1790. See Chapter 9 for an account of the survey. It is noteworthy that these orders went out exactly one week after Dalrymple had replied to Buache's Memoir concerning the location of the

to be followed by the *Endeavour*. McCluer reached the Palaus on 21 January 1791, where he broke the news of Lee Boo's death to the king. Afterwards he handed over presents, to which the king responded by granting the British the island of Cooroorah, where McCluer laid the foundation-stone of a fort.

McCluer now made his way to New Guinea on a voyage that was to open up some interesting new opportunities for the East India Company. His first task was to carry out the important survey of the north-west coast of New Guinea which was to reveal the existence of McCluer's Inlet. In the course of this survey he also made the important discovery that the Banda nutmeg grew near the coast, and when he went to Bencoolen for fresh supplies at the end of the year, the news of this important find went with him.

After re-stocking and repairing his two vessels, McCluer returned to the Palau Islands by way of Sulu, and here he found a most promising political situation, for the present sultan was none other than the Sarapodin whom Dalrymple, thirty years earlier, had wished to see appointed ruler of Balambangan and 'Felicia Proper'. An 'old Radjah' assured McCluer that Sarapodin was a strong friend of the East India Company and had played no part in the sacking of Herbert's settlement on Balambangan. He also found that Dalrymple was still remembered with admiration and affection, and he himself was treated with 'all the civility in their power' while he took on a full cargo of seed, grain and cattle. When, at last, he was ready to leave, the Sultan himself entrusted McCluer with a letter to the Government in Bengal 'begging the Company to renew their former friendship, and enter an alliance with him', while his son also wrote a personal letter to Dalrymple.[47] Similar reports of this desire for friendly relations with the English came a little later

Solomon Islands. This may have been a mere coincidence, but it is possible that he feared future French claims which might conflict with British interests in this area.

47 Nat. Lbry. of Scotland, *Melville Papers*, MS. 1068, ff. 56–65, McCluer to Dalrymple, 23 January 1793, with enclosed letter from Muhammed Alimudien to Dalrymple dated Sulu, 30 November 1792. See also my 'Alexander Dalrymple and New Guinea', *Journal of Pacific History*, Vol. IV (1969), pp. 83–104.

from the *Albion*, which visited Sulu on 27 June 1795. On that occasion the ship's purser noted how they met with every possible attention from the natives and were graciously received by the Sultan, who expressed 'his earnest desire to be useful to any of the Honourable Company's Ships that might hereafter touch there'.[48]

When Dalrymple received McCluer's report, he felt that the succession of his old friend Sarapodin as Sultan of Sulu provided the Company with a great opportunity to re-establish a trading settlement in that area. The requirements of national policy were no longer an obstacle, for with the outbreak of the French Revolutionary Wars in 1793 it became inevitable that the course of Dutch politics would be decided henceforth by the fortunes of war. Dalrymple therefore sent extracts of McCluer's letter to Dundas, and argued that 'so favourable an opportunity of establishing an Interest in the Eastern Islands is not likely again to offer,' since the Company could now negotiate with 'a Man of the greatest worth and honour I have known in any Country; and of very distinguished abilities'. To explain the situation more fully, he asked Dundas to arrange for 'a few minutes conversation'.[49]

Having thus re-opened relations with Sulu, McCluer continued on his way to the Palau Islands where he arrived on 20th January 1793. He now considered that he had completed his mission and felt free to gratify a desire that he had harboured for the past two years. In an entry in his Journal on 2 February 1791 he had described these islands as 'a perfect paradise' where he could happily have spent the rest of his life. Now he took the 'unprecedented step' of handing over his command to Wedgeborough,[50] so the *Panther* returned to Bombay without

[48] Ibid., MS. 1069, f. 122.

[49] Nat. Lbry. of Australia, Canberra, MS. 43/14, A. Dalrymple to Henry Dundas, 3 February 1794. For the political background in Sulu, see N. M. Saleeby, *History of Sulu,* p. 211. For French interest in Sulu, and Louis XV's letter to the sultan, dated 14 December 1770, see *Home Miscellaneous Series,* Vol. 107, f. 29. For reports of Spanish intrigues, Ibid., Vol. 116, pp. 663–5.

[50] Keate, op. cit., Supplement. It was eloquent testimony of McCluer's reputation that the Directors informed Bombay on 13 January 1794 that they yielded most willingly 'to your recommendation and permit of Captain McCluer's name being continued on the strength of the Marine during his

him, and as the *Endeavour* had already sailed for Macao, he was left on his own with the islanders.

In the meantime John Hayes, a fellow officer in the Bombay Marine, had heard about McCluer's discovery of the Banda nutmeg on New Guinea and had formed a syndicate to exploit the situation.[51] The *Duke of Clarence* and the *Duchess* were fitted out for the voyage from Calcutta to New Guinea, and though contrary winds forced him to take the long route around the south of Australia, Hayes eventually reached Dorey Harbour in Geelvink's Bay, on the north coast of New Guinea. Here he had a friendly reception from the natives, and found nutmegs, cloves and the beautiful birds of paradise.

Lacking sufficient resources to continue on his own, he decided that he would have to return to Calcutta, where he hoped to persuade the Bengal Government to take over this new territory. But he also wished to make the best use of what had already been accomplished, so he left the *Duchess* at Dorey to establish a trading post there. He himself went first to Macao where he had an unexpected meeting with McCluer who, after fifteen months on the Palau Islands, had decided to return to the service of the East India Company. Leaving the islands in a native craft with a crew of six, McCluer had made a remarkable nineteen-day voyage to Macao without compass or other navigational aids, and with only Captain Wilson's map to guide him. At Macao he had bought a vessel in which he planned to return to Bombay by way of the Palau Islands. It was at this stage that he had his chance meeting with Hayes, who told him of the colony that he had planted in New Guinea, and of its dire need of provisions.[52] McCluer thereupon agreed to go to New Guinea with the necessary stores, after he had re-visited the Palaus.

---

stay in the Pellew Islands'. McCluer took pains to dissociate his officers from his decision which he knew would be considered an 'act of insanity'. He hoped to 'benefit my country by enlightening the minds of these noble islanders'.

51 *Australian Encyclopaedia*, Sydney, 1958, Vol. 4, pp. 449–50. It seems very doubtful whether Hayes and McCluer met in Calcutta, as stated. Ida Lee, *Commodore Sir John Hayes*, London, 1912, p. 10, observes that this fruit always fetched high prices in the Indian and Chinese markets.

52 Ida Lee, op. cit., p. 134.

McCluer left Macao on 24 July 1794, and after depositing some horses, fruit trees and rice at the Palau Islands he continued on his way to New Guinea. His arrival at Dorey Harbour[53] was to prove more significant than either he or Hayes could have foreseen, for while he was there an ambassador arrived from the east coast of Ceram with proposals that promised to provide the East India Company with the very opportunity to establish a base on or near New Guinea which the Directors had recommended to Cornwallis in 1786. The ambassador had been sent by a native prince named Nuku, who claimed to be the rightful ruler of 'Papuoa' and of all the neighbouring islands unoccupied by the Dutch, including Geby. He invited the English to come to his Kingdom in Ceram, and complained of the long neglect which their countrymen had shown to his family, whom Captain Thomas Forrest, in their name, had promised to protect against the Dutch.

When McCluer wrote to Dalrymple about this embassy from Nuku, he urged that it would be folly for the East India Company to give up what had already been achieved. If the British did not persevere, the present friendship of the natives would turn to hatred. He believed that a 'very grand Commercial field might be opened, for not only the produce of the Moluccas but of the Sooloo Seas and the Philipinas including the whole in the same voyage'. But he did not consider that Dorey Harbour was a suitable site from which to carry on this commerce, since it was both unhealthy and out of the way. He recommended either Batanta or Geby, which had 'one of the finest harbours in the world'. He visualized a commercial system being established whereby three or four small vessels would be 'constantly on the flight at all Seasons of the year collecting their Trade', by utilising the contrary monsoons on either side of the Equator.[54]

[53] Despite its unhealthy climate, the colonists had named it 'Restoration Bay'. McCluer noted that this Bay, in lat. 2° 24′ S., was 'only 4 hours' walk from where I was in the *Panther* [on the opposite coast, in McCluer's Inlet] and some of the natives knew me again'.

[54] Nat. Lbry. of Scotland, *Melville Papers*, MS. 1068, f. 86, McCluer to Dalrymple, Fort Marlborough (Bencoolen), 16 May 1795.

The islands over which Nuku claimed sovereignty included Waygiou, Batanta, Salawatty, the Mysol group, and all the chain of islands down to the Aru group, as well as the eastern part of Ceram and the island of Geby.

When Dalrymple forwarded this letter to the Secret Committee, he reminded them of the advantages that the East India Company would derive from a Settlement in the Eastern Islands, which would provide both a market for inferior Indian cottons and also 'the Vent of the produce of the Eastern Islands to the Chinese'. He still considered that Balambangan would prove the best site of all, but he was prepared to give full support to this new scheme, and agreed with McCluer that Geby, with its excellent harbour and healthy climate, would be a good choice.

To help them in their deliberations, Dalrymple also furnished the Directors with a memorandum outlining the story of Nuku's rise to power, since he was a key figure in the whole scheme. Dalrymple recalled that Forrest, during his voyage in the *Tartar* galley in 1774, had 'by some chance conveyance transmitted a letter to the Sultan of Teedoré'. The Dutch at Ternate had heard about this, and when they had found themselves at war with the English, during the American War of Independence, they had felt it necessary to tighten their hold over Tidore, which was so important for the preservation of their spice monopoly. In about 1782 they had therefore seized the Sultan of Tidore, in order to replace him with a puppet of their own choice, and the deposed sultan had been removed to Batavia, where he had apparently died. Three of his sons, however, had escaped to Ceram, where one of them – Nuku – had set up a new government. In 1783 Nuku had given a striking proof of his desire for English friendship when he had learnt of a mishap that had befallen the *Northumberland* Indiaman. Captain Rees had sent some of his men ashore on the south coast of New Guinea to fetch water, but hostile natives had seized the boat, and all its occupants had either been captured or killed. Hearing of this, Nuku had sent twenty-four proas to New Guinea to secure the release of the survivors, and they were then taken to Bencoolen accompanied by an ambassador who was instructed to negotiate a treaty with the English. The authorities at Bencoolen had sent his envoy on to Bengal where he had arrived in May 1785. In due course the Bengal Government had arranged for Captain Thomas Forrest to take him back to Ceram, but owing to the receipt of a false report that the sultan had been deposed by the Dutch, Captain Forrest had left his charge at Bencoolen.[55]

McCluer's voyages amongst the Eastern Islands had thus provided the East India Company with an opportunity to establish a trading settlement either in the Sulu Archipelago or at Geby. Indeed, there was a case for trying them both, since they were situated on the two major alternative routes to Canton. However, before either plan could be attempted the whole political situation was altered by a dramatic turn of events in the Netherlands which forced the Stadtholder to flee from his own country and to seek refuge in England in January 1795. French control of the United Provinces would imperil Britain's whole eastern trade, so it was essential that every advantage should be taken of the Prince of Orange's presence in England. He was therefore persuaded to 'send addresses to all the colonies of the State, that they admit in each of them the troops and ships which his Britannic Majesty shall be pleased to send thither, with a view to preventing the French from making themselves Masters thereof, and as being the Troops and Vessels of a Power in friendship and alliance with their High Mightinesses', after receiving from King George III himself the 'strongest assurances that all the colonies or ships of which he [i.e., George III] should take possession should be restored at the Peace'. The Prince asked the officers on the spot to judge for themselves whether this was not a wiser policy than to resist at all costs and thus allow the British to capture these posts by force, when they would be under no obligation to return them.[56]

In the event, the Cape of Good Hope surrendered, after a show of force, in September 1795, Trincomali having done so the month before. In October 1795 the authorities at Madras sent an expedition to the Moluccas, and by the following March both Amboina and Banda had yielded. Only on the island of Ternate were the Dutch left unmolested.

The whole question of future British policy in the East

[55] Nat. Lbry. of Scotland, *Melville Papers*, MS. 1068, ff. 93–6, Dalrymple to Secret Committee, 21 December 1795. After writing to Dalrymple, McCluer vanished from the scene, being lost at sea – see C. R. Markham, *A Memoir on the Indian Surveys* (2nd. ed.), London, 1878, p. 5 for outline account.

[56] Tarling, op. cit., pp. 51–3.

Indies was now in the balance and in December 1796 Dalrymple submitted two memoirs on the subject for the Company's consideration. He knew that the Dutch settlements in the East Indies would have to be returned at the Peace, but he wanted to see Britain's present military advantages exploited to the full.

His first Memoir dealt with the Eastern Islands as a whole. These, he argued, were primarily important to the East India Company because of their value to the China trade. Certainly the opportunity should be taken to collect the best plants of nutmegs and cloves in Banda and Amboina, even if spices were not so important as they had once been.[57] But the China trade, he wrote, 'is of much greater importance to us, than to any other Nation of Europe, as well from our great consumption of Tea, as from our National Exports of Woollens, Tin, Lead and Copper; if to these we add the Commodities of the Eastern Islands, obtained by English Manufactures, and by the refuse of the Investment, in India, for Europe, by which Picked Goods only would be offered at the Company's sales at home I conceive the Prosperity of the East India Company's Commerce would be established on the surest foundation . . .'

He therefore proposed that 'Settlements for the Eastern Intercourse should be fixed in places lying in the course of Navigation to China, where the Natural Strength of Situation will require but very few Europeans . . . and but a few Sepoys, from India, to render them secure against any Country Enemy, or chance European Cruizers'. As suitable sites he suggested one near the Straits of Allas or Sapy; one on New Guinea, near the 'Portuguese Strait' if that was found navigable; one at Geby 'which appears a very fit situation for planting the cloves from Amboina, and the nutmegs from Banda'; one at Tourane; and the capital settlement should be at Balambangan. Only experience would show, he added, 'whether any would be requisite between Balambangan and P° Pinang in the Strait of Malacca'.[58]

57 A view shared by Lieut. S. Dalrymple who, writing from Amboina in December 1797, noted that 'the clove and nutmeg plants are now pretty generally circulated throughout India' – J. R. Lbry., *Melville Papers*, Vol. 677, f. 537.

58 He may have been thinking of Riau or Singapore. He had carefully read, and commended, Captain Alexander Hamilton's *A New Account of*

Thus Dalrymple wanted to see the restoration of the Dutch East Indian bases counter-balanced by a return to his original plan of a settlement at Balambangan, with the East India Company's right of free navigation through the islands ensured by the establishment of strategically-sited bases to command the main routes used by East Indiamen on their way to and from Canton.

His second Memoir was devoted entirely to Celebes, the island in which the East India Company had long taken a particular interest. Dalrymple considered that the British should take the present opportunity to capture it, as this would be an effective way of dealing with the shortage of military recruits in India. This problem had been brought to his attention by Andrew Ross, an old friend living in Madras. Ross had told him that the shortage was due to the 'very great depopulation of the Country, South and North, due to war and famine in India. Ross thought that it was bad policy to recruit soldiers in India 'whilst there are such immense tracts of Jungle and other waste lands (and a great part, doubtless, every way capable of Cultivation)'. He believed that the answer lay in securing the necessary recruits for the Sepoy battalions from the Eastern Islands, and he had therefore sent copies of his Memoir to both Dalrymple and David Scott, hoping that they would discuss the matter together.[59]

This scheme appealed to Dalrymple, who considered that the Eastern Islands were particularly well suited to raising recruits because of their feudal form of government. Such a policy would have the added advantage of freeing the Company from total dependence on 'the natives of Hindustan, who have interests of their own, independent of ours, and who are liable to be corrupted by the Indian Powers'. Celebes alone could pro-

the East Indies, Edinburgh, 1727, on p. 98, of which Hamilton recalled that in 1703 'I called at Johore in my way to China . . . and [the King] made me a present of the island of Sincapure, but I told him it could be of no use to a Private Person, tho' a proper place for a Company to settle a Colony on, lying in the centre of Trade, and being accommodated with good Rivers, and safe Harbours . . .' See also A. Dalrymple, *Oriental Repertory*, Vol. 1, p. 105, where he specifically states that Hamilton's book 'is well worth attentive perusal'.

59 Nat. Lbry. of Australia, Canberra, MS. 43/16 and 43/16a, Andrew Ross to A. Dalrymple, 3 October 1795.

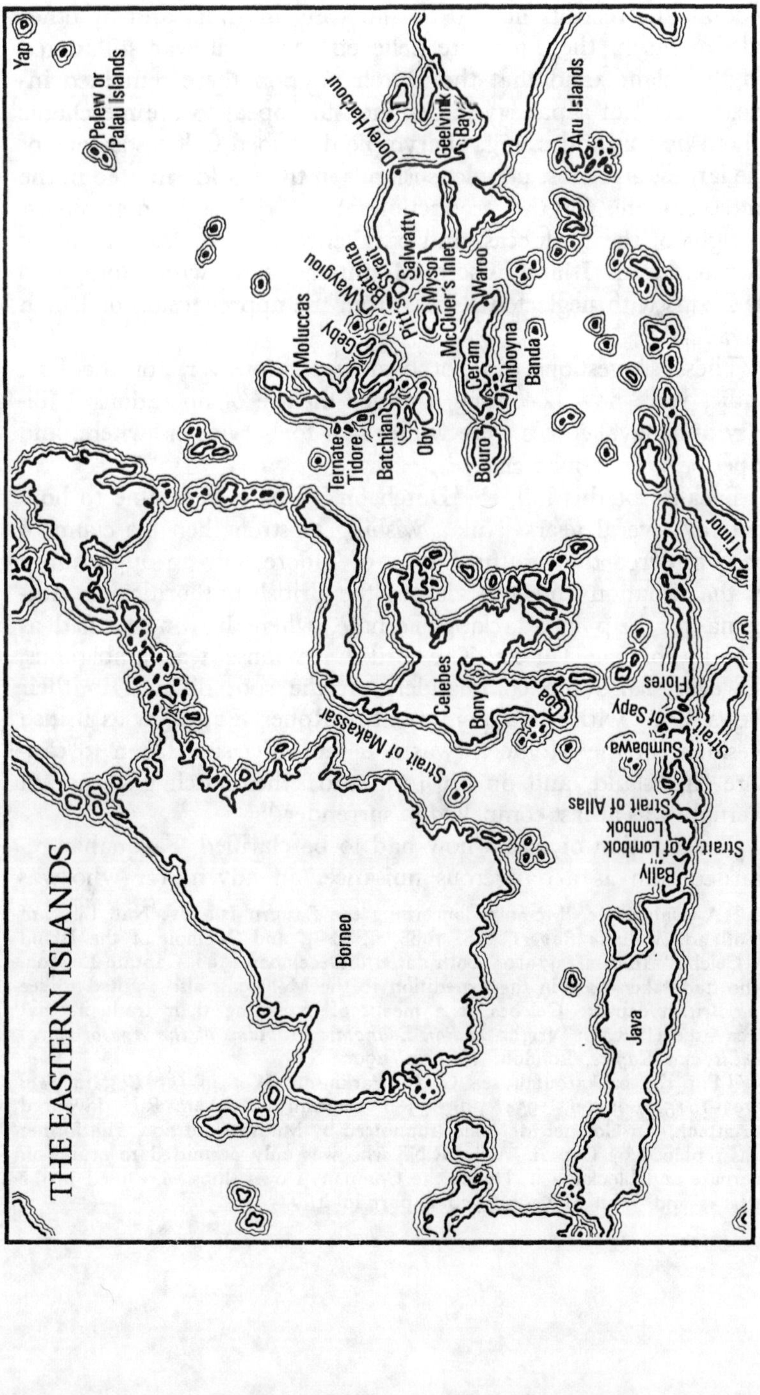

BASED ON A MAP IN WILLIAM MILBURN'S ORIENTAL COMMERCE (1813)

vide all the recruits needed by the army in India and by other settlements in the East. He believed that civil war still raged on the island, and that the Dutch position there remained insecure. And in a panegyric designed to appeal to the merchants whom he was addressing, Dalrymple described Celebes as 'one of the largest and most populous islands in the world, situated in the finest climate, for the production of the richest Spices; almost in sight of the Moluccas, and parallel to Borneo; famous for its diamonds, an Island whose Mountains glow with Gold, and its Plains with neglected Riches from the apprehension of Dutch Invaders'.[60]

These suggestions did not bear fruit, however, for the East Indies were now becoming a minor theatre of operations. Military and naval forces were withdrawn for service elsewhere, and a period of inactivity ensued.

Because of this lull, the Dutch on Ternate were able to hold out for several years. Nuku, wishing to strengthen his claim to be considered the rightful Sultan of Tidore, saw an opportunity in the situation and appealed to the British authorities on Amboina for help in attacking Ternate, where his uncle ruled as an ally of the Dutch. The British response was ambiguous, however, since the commanders on the spot differed in their views. Only with the appointment of Robert Farquhar as British Resident in the Moluccas was a definite decision taken to capture the island, and on 20 June 1801 the Dutch governor of Ternate was at last compelled to surrender.[61]

The position of Nuku now had to be clarified. Farquahar regarded him as a dangerous nuisance, an adventurer who was

60 A. Dalrymple, 'Memoir Concerning the Eastern Islands', Nat. Lbry. of Scotland, *Melville Papers*, MS. 1068, ff. 72–4, and 'Memoir of the Island of Celebes', Ibid., ff. 97–105, both dated 8 December 1796. Captain Lennon, who had taken part in the expedition to the Moluccas, also wanted to see the British capture Celebes as a means of extending their trade in that area – see H. R. C. Wright, *Indian Economic Problems of the Age of Cornwallis and Raffles*, London, 1961, p. 290.

61 For the background, see C. N. Parkinson, *War in the Eastern Seas 1793–1815*, London, 1954, pp. 135–6. Captain Pakenham R.N. favoured an attack, but Colonel McNeale (supported by Madras) did not. The former was replaced by Captain Astle, R.N., who was only permitted to cruise off Ternate and blockade it. Hence the Company's own ships were used in the attack, and John Hayes played a part in it.

at present making piratical attacks on his own, but might in the future be joined by other 'good-for-nothing Rovers and Idlers'. He was therefore unwilling to see Nuku restored to power on Ternate, which might thus become a refuge for deserters, pirates and smugglers, and 'as great a nuisance to the British Malookas, as the Mahratta Possessions to the British Indies'. Dalrymple was concerned at this attitude, which he considered to be both unjust and short-sighted, for he realized that Nuku was the key figure if, as he hoped, the East India Company decided to follow McCluer's advice by establishing a settlement on the island of Geby. It was nonsensical, he wrote, to consider Nuku's hostility to the Dutch as piracy, in the same way that the reference to the Mahrattas implied 'that the Mahrattas were Invaders and the English natives'. Nuku, he urged, should be treated as a friend, who, it should be remembered, had acted with great generosity at the beginning, and, more recently, 'with great justice to the Country Ships' which had traded with his dominions.[62]

Impressed by these observations, the Court of Directors ordered the Madras government to purchase Geby and the adjacent islands from Nuku.[63] In the meantime, Farquhar, who had since

62 Dalrymple took this opportunity to give a fuller account of Nuku's history. It was now known that when the Dutch had taken his father to Batavia, the old sultan had been reproached for his friendship with the English, but had been offered restoration to his throne if he would be content with Tidore alone, and would give the rest of his dominions to the Dutch. He had rejected these terms and had 'found means to write this, under his own hand, to his son Nookoo at Teedoré . . . enjoining Nookoo never to form an alliance with the Dutch, but to cultivate a friendship with the English'. Nookoo had therefore fled from the island, but had been elected sultan of Tidore by his followers in exile, and was generally so recognized on Tidore itself. The Dutch had appointed his cousin as sultan, but the latter had a secret understanding with Nuku, who had withstood years of war with the Dutch, and who, from Waroo on the north-east coast of Ceram, had managed to assert authority over 'the greater part of the ancient Teedoré Dominions'. Thus, argued Dalrymple, the Dutch had lost all claim to any privileges granted by previous sultans of Tidore in those territories over which Nuku now ruled. A. Dalrymple, 'Sultan Nookoo', *Boards Collections*, Vol. 74, Draft no. 1617, which includes Farquhar's Report. Marked 'Examiner's Office' 31 March 1801'. See also S. G. Robinson, *English Expeditions to the Dutch East Indies during the Revolutionary and Napoleonic Wars*, unpublished. MA thesis, London, 1933. pp. 131 et. seq.

63 Tarling, op. cit., p. 60.

been replaced for exceeding his authority, had obtained the island of Obi from the Sultan of Batjan, but his successor, Colonel Oliver, found Nuku unwilling to part with Geby and Fau. In any case, the Madras government felt that the East India company's legal claims to all three, even supposing that Nuku could be persuaded to sell, would be highly questionable. Wellesley, the Governor-General, supported this view, for by October 1802 he had received the definitive peace terms agreed upon at Amiens, which specified 'the unreserved and unqualified restitution' of the Dutch possessions in the Moluccas, with all the powers and privileges attached. In his view this precluded him from acquiring Geby and the adjacent islands.

Nevertheless, Wellesley fully accepted the importance of this archipelago to the British, and decided to return to Dalrymple's original plan by re-occupying Balambangan. He stressed the island's war-time role, not only in providing shelter and provisions on the route to China, but in offering a base for military and naval operations, as well as a post for gaining intelligence of enemy movements. His description of the island's commercial advantages might have been written by Dalrymple himself. It was Farquhar who was chosen to re-establish a British settlement on this island in October 1803. But with the renewal of the Anglo-French war, Wellesley found his resources stretched to the limit in India itself; he could not contemplate military action in the East Indies as well, and Balambangan, isolated and unfortified, would have been indefensible. The settlement was therefore finally withdrawn in November 1805.[64]

Thus ended forty years of continuous effort by the East India Company to re-establish itself in the East Indian trade. In 1802 the views of Dundas had prevailed, and by a deliberate act of policy the British Government had decided that these waters should be avoided by ships of the East India Company in times of peace. But the Treaty of Amiens had ushered in a truce and not a peace, so that this decision must be judged to have been premature, and the battle for the islands soon had to be fought all over again. With the downfall of Napoleon, however, the same policy prevailed, and the British once more withdrew.

64 Ibid., pp. 60–62.

There was, therefore, no immediate tangible reward for all the activity of these past years. Yet the vision remained, and if bases within the archipelago were to be denied, then the trade must be drawn to carefully sited posts in the vicinity. The solution was eventually to be found in Penang, Malacca, Singapore and North Borneo. These, and not the abandoned, uninhabited and almost forgotten island of Balambangan, were the true fruits of Alexander Dalrymple's labours.[65]

[65] For a description of the memo sent by Raffles to Canning in 1816 suggesting possible sites for a trading post, including W. Borneo, see R. Coupland, *Raffles 1781–1826*, Oxford, 1926, pp. 79–81. It is noteworthy that Raffles began his career as a clerk in India House where Dalrymple had his Hydrographic Office, so it is not unlikely that the two men met. Their views on the best way to trade in the archipelago were notably similar. For a description of present-day Balambangan see K. G. Tregonning, *North Borneo*, London, 1960, p. 187.

CHAPTER VII

The Kingdom of Cochin China

WHEN Alexander Dalrymple studied the old records of the East India Company at Fort St George, between the years 1757–9, he became almost as interested in Cochin China as in the Eastern Islands. Both areas seemed to offer exceptional opportunities for an expansion of British commerce. As he himself explained, his studies had been 'in quest to explore and compleat "A View of the Countries Adjacent to Pegu" ' and his labours had been rewarded when he had chanced to come across 'a letter to the King of Cochin China with Instructions to a person bound thither regarding the measures to be pursued in endeavouring to obtain a settlement there'. He had immediately become curious as to the outcome of this earlier attempt to expand British trade, and had begun to search for further information. He had 'met with many disappointments from Books being wanting and from the confusion of those still remaining', but at last he had been fortunate enough to discover the Journal of Thomas Bowyear.[1]

Bowyear had been despatched by Nathaniel Higginson, the President at Fort St George, in 1696, in an effort to open a British factory at Faifo, but his mission had failed. Nevertheless, he had been approached by ambassadors from Cambodia who had 'endeavoured to persuade him to open a Trade with their Country, assuring him he would be free from the imposts and difficulties met with in Cochin China'. Bowyear had been favourably impressed, and had considered that there were good prospects of finding a market for woollen goods, but, to Dalrymple's surprise, this suggestion had never been put to the test.

Dalrymple had viewed this country for himself in 1760, during his voyage in the *Cuddalore*, and though his experiences

[1] India Office Library, *Orme Mss.*, Vol. XIX, f. 2, pp. 23–5.

there had suggested that the time was not yet ripe for further action, nevertheless he had been greatly impressed by the natural advantages of Tourane. Here was a harbour which could easily be rendered impregnable, since it was 'formed by a High Peninsula, connected to the Continent by a long low Isthmus'. Furthermore, the peninsula was large enough 'for all necessary cultivation and habitation'. He was confident that Chinese junks of all sizes would always be prepared to visit this port, since they could 'navigate thither, never being out of sight of Land; and but very little way out of sight of their own coasts'.[2] Another who was voicing his approval of this same harbour, but from the viewpoint of trade with India rather than with China, was Captain Thomas Forrest, who observed that there was 'a great demand at Turon . . . for the muslins and cottons of Bengal, and there sugar is exceedingly cheap. Turon is an excellent harbour, at the mouth of a spacious river. A factory there might answer'.[3]

An opportunity to put this advice to the test came with the unexpected arrival at Calcutta, in February 1778, of two Cochin Chinese Mandarins. Their passage to India as passengers on board the *Rumbold,* a country ship in the China trade, had been due to an accident, for when this ship had visited Tourane, a Portuguese Jesuit named Juan de Loureiro had asked that they might be taken as far as Donai, the southernmost province, whither the King had retreated. The *Rumbold,* however, had been forced far to the southward by the combination of a strong current and a violent gale, and this being the season of the north-east monsoon, it had been found impossible to fight a way back to the coast. The decision had therefore been taken to bring these unexpected guests to Calcutta, whence they could return to their own country on another ship at the appropriate season.[4]

Their arrival at Calcutta aroused great interest, not only

[2] A. Dalrymple, 'Some Notes concerning the trade to China' (June-August 1790), *Oriental Repertory,* Vol. II, London, 1794, pp. 321–2.

[3] Thomas Forrest, *A Voyage from Calcutta to the Margui Archipelago,* London, 1792, p. vi.

[4] Alastair Lamb, *British Missions to Cochin China, 1778–1822.* Journal of the Malay Branch of the Royal Asiatic Society, Vol. XXXIV, Parts 3 and 4 (nos. 195–6), Kuala Lumpur, 1961, pp. 26–7.

amongst the British, but also at Chandernagore where the French Chief, Chevalier, tried to get in touch with de Loureiro, to find out what the English were planning to do. The Portuguese missionary did, in fact, visit Chandernagore, and suggested that the French should make use of Bernardo Moniz, a Portuguese merchant who had come with him from Cochin China. The British got to hear of these discussions, which could not have come as any surprise since the French had never lost interest in this area. Indeed, as recently as 1775 Vergennes, after calling attention to the new British settlement at Balambangan, had suggested that only Cochin China had 'escaped the eyes of the English. But can we delude ourselves', he had asked, 'into believing that they will delay in penetrating here? If they decide to come before us, we will be excluded forever. We will lose an important [foothold] in [that] part of Asia which would make us masters, capable of intercepting the English [trade with China] in time of war.... If they were to establish themselves here, they would regard us as their vassals upon every Asiatic coast'.[5]

Warren Hastings determined to make use of this present opportunity. In arranging for the return of the Mandarins to Cochin China, he would, at the same time, try to obtain new trading privileges. As he explained to the Directors, this commerce would provide a new market for such European commodities as 'iron, lead, copper, cutlery, glassware and broad cloth, together with various manufactures of Bengal to the Cochin Chinese, but more particularly to the Chinese junks, and the procuring returns in gold, silver, pepper, cinnamon, cassia, elephants' teeth, aquila wood.... The Company have always had in view', he had continued, 'the encouragement of a trade with the Chinese junks, this was Mr Dalrymple's object when he proposed the settlement at Balambangan....'[6] He explained that his own proposal was confined to sending a single man as a resident in Cochin China, where he was told

[5] Thomas E. Ennis, *French Policy and Developments in Indochina*, Chicago, 1936, p. 25. The words in brackets have been substituted from Lamb, op. cit., p. 8.

[6] Quoted by Lamb, op. cit., pp. 15–16, from the Bengal General Consultations, 30 March 1778.

that '70 or 80 junks resort to the single port of Turon in one season and that the trade is the chief support of the town of Macao'. He also stressed Tourane's valuable geographical situation, close to Canton, the Philippines and the Eastern Archipelago, and bordering on Siam and Malacca to the westward.

Hastings' arguments carried the day and Charles Chapman was appointed on 9 April 1778.[7] The political conditions of the country, however, prevented this mission from achieving anything, and the outbreak of the Anglo-French struggle during the War of Independence soon absorbed all the energies of both countries elsewhere.

In the past, various European nations had traded with Cochin China, the Portuguese having chosen Faifo as the site for a factory as early as 1535. In the seventeenth century the Dutch, English and French had also become interested, when a civil war between Tonkin in the north and Annam in the south had created a demand for European firearms, but when a truce was arranged in 1672 this demand for weapons disappeared, and by the end of the seventeenth century the Portuguese were once more in sole command of this trade. For in times of peace there was as little demand here, as there was in China, for European manufactures.[8]

The French were the first to plan a return to Cochin China. Dupleix established agents at Tourane to carry on a business there on his private account, and O'Friell, his nephew, inspected that Bay. Pierre Poivre, who was in Paris in 1750, had also been there and recommended Tourane as an admirable commercial centre which could easily be fortified.[9]

Poivre had, in fact, just returned from a two-year mission to Cochin China, where his efforts to obtain trading concessions had been frustrated by the the opposition of local government officials. In 1765, however, a new situation developed with the

[7] Ibid., p. 17.

[8] Lamb, op. cit., p. 5. Joseph Buttinger, *The Small Dragon: a political history of Vietnam*, New York, 1958, pp. 200–8. Arrowsmith's Atlas of 1813 showed Cochin China with frontiers very similar to those of present-day South Vietnam, with Tonking to the north.

[9] Buttinger, op. cit., p. 259.

death of the ruler, Vo-Vuong, and the subsequent breakdown of orderly government. A rebellion broke out, led by three brothers from the village of Tay-son, from which the movement took its name. This insurrection gathered strength, and as the authority of the Nguyen rulers in the south evaporated, the Trinh sovereigns in Tonkin found the temptation to renew the old struggle irresistible, despite the peace that had lasted for more than a century. In 1774 they therefore invaded the neighbouring territories and seized the town of Hué, and the civil war now became a three-cornered affair, with the Tay-son rebels and the Trinh invaders fighting for supremacy, and the Nguyen, from their southern strongholds, striving for very survival.[10]

Ever since the Society of Foreign Missions, from its Paris headquarters, had sent out its first priest to Cochin China in 1664, the French had been able to maintain some contact with that country through these missionaries. But the Mission made little progress until a remarkable man, Pigneau de Behaine, arrived on the scene in 1774 as apostolic vicar to Cochin China, Tonkin and Cambodia.[11]

Arriving in Cochin China just before the rebellion broke out, the bishop was provided with a great opportunity which he was quick to exploit. The King realized that this uprising could only be put down with the help of foreign troops, and the bishop promised to go to France to seek this support. It was a well-known feature of French missionary effort that the missionaries themselves looked upon it as part of their function to further the interests of the State by combining commercial and religious activities,[12] and the bishop now demonstrated this by asking that the reward for such French help should be the cession to them of a harbour and some territory. On this understanding he set out for Europe in 1786, taking with him the eight-year-old son of the king, the latter then being in exile in Siam.[13]

[10] Lamb, op. cit., pp. 7–9.

[11] Ennis, op. cit., p. 26. Pigneau de Behaine became Bishop of Adran in 1771, at the age of thirty.

[12] Ibid., p. 13, note 4.

[13] A. Dalrymple, 'Second Memoir on Cochin China' (dated 19–21 March 1803), I.O. Lbry., *Factory Records; China*, Vol. 195, last paper. His first memoir has not been located.

In France the mission received warm acclaim, both from the public and from officialdom, and the bishop, in February 1787, had the opportunity of reporting to Louis XVI and to some of his senior ministers in person. He argued that French military intervention would not only help to circumvent British attempts to drive the French from India altogether, but, by providing a foothold in Cochin China, could also be the means of increasing France's trade with China. The bishop remained in France throughout the spring and summer of 1787 waiting for the government to come to a decision, but this was not an opportune moment to commit France to a military adventure in a far-off land, where the outcome of the war must be uncertain, and any benefits could only materialize in the long-term. The truth was that France's intervention in the American war had brought her severe financial crisis to a head, while diplomatically she had been thrown on to the defensive, so that her alliance with the Dutch was crumbling in the face of mounting British and Prussian intervention in the Low Countries.

The visit of the bishop was well publicized in the French press, and there were further ways in which the British were kept alerted as to possible dangers from French competition in the East. In 1785 a new Compagnie des Indes had been formed, while on 16 February 1787 the supercargoes at Canton were informing their Directors in London of the arrival of a French mission from Pondicherry, under the command of d'Entrecasteaux. It was believed that he not only wished to improve French relations with China, but also hoped to establish a commercial base in Cochin China.[14]

On 28 November 1787 the French government went through the formalities of signing a treaty with the king of Cochin China, whereby the latter, in return for French aid, would cede to the French Crown 'absolute ownership and sovereignty' over Tourane and Pulo Condore,[15] and the French would have

14 E. H. Pritchard, *The Crucial Years of Anglo-Chinese Relations, 1750–1800*. Research Studies, the College of Washington, U.S.A., Vol. IV (Nos. 3 & 4), 1936, p. 218.

15 Both the British and the French showed interest in this group of islands to the south of the Cambodia River. William Dampier recommended Po Condore – see his *New Voyage Round the World* (modern edition, in-

'entire liberty of commerce in all states of the Kingdom of Cochin China, to the exclusion of all other Europeans'. John Barrow, who visited the country as a member of the Macartney embassy to China in 1792–3, remarked that this treaty was 'evidently directed to the building ... of a naval force that should one day overcome our territorial possession in the East', and, writing in 1806, he was by no means certain that the attempt would not be renewed.[16]

Under the terms of this treaty the French government had promised to send to Cochin China four ships with 'twelve hundred infantry, two hundred artillery, and two hundred and fifty Kaffirs', complete with arms and ammunition. What Pigneau did not know, however, was that he had been the victim of a deception, and that the French Foreign Minister, within four days of signing this treaty, had sent incompatible orders to Governor Conway of Pondicherry. In any case, the latter was known to be hostile to French commitments in India, and would certainly be unsympathetic towards any further expansion in Asia, for he believed that France did not possess the necessary resources to defend and maintain such settlements. Now he received secret instructions which empowered him to decide whether Pigneau's expedition to Cochin China should take place immediately, later, or not at all. Thus when the bishop reached Pondicherry in May 1788, he found Conway raising every sort of obstacle to his mission,[17] and no help was forthcoming. According to Dalrymple's information, a force had, in fact, been sent from France, consisting of a fifty-gun ship, ten frigates, several sloops and seven transports carrying between six and seven thousand men, but this had proceeded no further than Mauritius because of Conway's opposition, and, soon afterwards, because of the outbreak of the French Revolution.[18]

---

troduced by Sir A. Grey), London, 1937, pp. 267–8. At the beginning of the eighteenth century the British established a short-lived settlement there – see Captain Alex Hamilton, *A New Account of the East Indies*, Edinburgh, 1727, pp. 205–6. In 1721–2 the French made a careful reconnaissance of the group, but abandoned the idea of settling.

[16] Ennis, op. cit., Appendix A, pp. 194–5.

[17] Buttinger, op. cit., p. 239.

[18] Dalrymple, *Second Memoir*, ut supra.

Despite this opposition Pigneau did everything possible to raise a volunteer force in Pondicherry. This had delayed him for a year, but on 19 June 1789 he was at last able to leave, still accompanied by the young Prince Canh, with two merchantmen and a private army of several hundred volunteers, and this force he now took to Saigon.[19]

With the outbreak of the French Revolution, Dalrymple was hopeful that the time might have arrived for the British to renew their efforts in Cochin China, where the French would probably be forced to abandon their plans. 'It would be very desirable,' he wrote, for the British 'to get possession of Turon.' Writing on the eve of the Macartney mission,[20] one of whose objects was to procure an offshore island on the Chinese coast for a British factory, Dalrymple remarked that such an arrangement would prove unsatisfactory 'because, supposing, what is by no means probable, that the Chinese government would allow an European fixed Establishment in their Country, the Trade would be carried on under the same restrictions as at present, and the vicinity would expose them to effectual obstructions from the Officers of Government; this Objection would operate against Macao, should the course of European politics ever expose the Portuguese Flag to Hostility. Macao is also very strong by natural situation, but the Peninsula is barren, and not fit for cultivation like that of Turon, and the Harbour at Macao will not admit Ships of the largest size'.[21]

After the failure of the Macartney embassy, however, the British were too fully occupied with their campaign against the Dutch East Indies to take any immediate interest in Cochin China, where King Nguyen Anh, aided by his French volunteers, and by the divisions in the ranks of his enemies, was gradually winning control of the country. Yet the king was still anxious to obtain foreign help, and on 13 January 1798 he wrote a letter to the British Governor at Malacca, suggesting that the British should establish friendly relations with his court.

19 Ibid., and Buttinger, op. cit., p. 239.

20 This embassy visited Tourane on its outward voyage, as described by John Barrow, *A Voyage to Cochin China in the Years 1792 and 1793*, London, 1806.

21 Dalrymple, *Oriental Repertory*, Vol. II, p. 322.

A fact, moreover, which could not have escaped attention was that the 'true translation' of this letter was signed by Pigneau himself, which suggested that he was not in sympathy with the French Revolution, or with the war which his countrymen were waging against Great Britain. After the opening courtesies, this letter stated that 'His Majesty having heard that the Governor has under his charge a large supply of Arms and Military stores of all descriptions, and being in great want of these articles, has judged it expedient to depute Mr Olivier... and a Chinese, in His Majesty's Service, to communicate his wishes to the Governor of Malacca... His Majesty informs the Governor that his country is involved in perpetual warfare.... Should the Governor be disposed to send Merchant Ships to His Majesty's Ports, His Majesty, aware of how much depends upon the favourable reception of Strangers, will omit no opportunity of promoting a permanent intercource with the City of Malacca....'[22]

This letter was forwarded, by the hand of Olivier, to Madras for a decision, and on 23 May 1798 Olivier was asked to draw up a list of the articles required. When he complied with this request, four days later, he asked for a speedy reply so that he might sail while the monsoon remained favourable, and added that even if the authorities at Fort St George could not immediately supply the articles on his list because of their own needs, 'there will still be a prospect that a change of circumstances will hereafter enable His Majesty to derive the benefit he looks to in an alliance with your Nation...'. The Governor and his Council were clearly anxious not to offend this emissary, or to lose an opportunity of establishing contacts with this Kingdom, from which they might derive political advantages in the future. Yet they could not spare either military or marine stores, which had become 'so scarce and so dear', but orders were sent to Lieutenant-Colonel Campbell at Malacca to issue as large a quantity of shot as he could spare, for which Olivier had expressed a particular need.

In the following year a certain Mr Berry was reported to have visited Cochin China, arriving at Saigon in April 1799. Here he recorded having seen a large armament of 80,000

[22] I.O. Lbry., *Board's Collections,* Vol. 49, Paper 1109.

men and more than 1,000 vessels in the process of being fitted out. The Englishman had been impressed by the king's skill as a carpenter and by his enthusiasm for ships, and he had given a long and detailed description of this fleet. 'His Majesty,' he wrote, 'observed that we were the first Englishmen he had seen and was inquisitive for our motives for visiting this Country. We were represented to have been induced by mere curiosity and not with Trading Motives. The King paid some high Compliments to the English Nation.'[23]

While these developments appeared to foreshadow better prospects for British trade in Cochin China, conditions were deteriorating in the Chinese Empire, where Ch'ien Lung had abdicated after a reign which had lasted for sixty years. After such a long period of strong rule it was well-nigh inevitable that dissident elements should see their opportunity in the accession of a new and untried ruler. The new emperor, Chia Ch'ing (1796–1820), was soon faced with the first of a series of rebellions, and in 1803 an attempt was made to assassinate him while he was being carried through the streets of Peking in his chair of state. Apart from this growing unrest, the East India Company's officials soon had to contend with the new emperor's policies, including the first Imperial Edict against foreign opium in 1799.[24]

J. W. Drummond, the President of the Select Committee of Supercargoes at Canton,[25] described these new difficulties in a letter home. 'The Insurrections are not quelled,' he wrote,

[23] Dalrymple, *Second Memoir*. He commented that the King's ability to build so formidable a fleet in seven short years was 'a very serious consideration', for 'if the French were to get a footing in that Country they might form a navy not only superior to any maritime Force we have in India but even to enable them to cope with us in every part of the World, and they could with much greater facility invade Bengal from Saygon than from Mauritius'.

[24] M. Greenberg, *British Trade and the Opening of China, 1800–42*, Cambridge, 1951, p. 110, suggests the earliest decree was in 1729. For a copy of the 1799 decree, see H. B. Morse, *The Chronicles of the East India Company trading to China, 1635–1834*, Oxford, 1929, Vol. II, Appendix M, pp. 344–6.

[25] There were usually about twelve supercargoes at Canton, of whom the three or four senior members formed a President and Select Committee. J. W. Drummond later became Lord Strathallan.

'nor does there appear a probability of their subsiding; and the Imperial Treasury is, I believe, at a very low ebb. There has likewise been a persecution of the Christians in the Western Provinces, and a French missionary has been apprehended whilst performing Divine Service, who is, I fear, likely to suffer death; therefore, the boasted support of the Emperor to our faith merits but little credit; nor can we, I think, look forward to any great advantages to be derived from any embassy that could now be sent....' From these circumstances Drummond concluded that the answer lay in a move to new territory. 'There is,' he continued, 'a vast field opened for the formation of a settlement, or for a commercial intercourse, with the King of Cochin China, whose successes against the usurpers of his Throne and Kingdom have lately given him possession of nearly the whole of his dominions; and, from the best authority, I have heard that he is well inclined to solicit support from or listen to any proposals made him on the part of the English. The Extent of Territory he can now call his own is immense, and rich in all the produce of the East; and although no immediate advantages might be reaped... in consequence of the 27 Years Civil War which has existed... still it might prove ultimately beneficial, by offering a place of security to resort to, so close to the Empire of China, and from whence all its produce could be procured by means of Junks, in the event of disturbance of this Government. And it is with that Idea that I have considered the acquisition of Luconia might be of very great national consequence....'[26]

At approximately the time when Drummond wrote that letter, an event was occurring in Europe which brought a new threat to the British position in Canton, for in the summer of 1801 French and Spanish forces invaded Portugal. If the French followed this up with naval attacks upon Portuguese positions in the East, including the seizure of Macao, the British trade route to China would be severed. In these circumstances, the authorities in London decided to forestall the French by sending a naval force to assist the Portuguese to retain Macao. The

[26] Nat. Lbry. of Scotland, *The Melville Papers*, MS. 1069, f. 180, 11 June 1801. Luconia was Luzon in the Philippines.

Select Committee at Canton learnt of this decision on 22 January 1802 and were alarmed, for it was not difficult to foresee an indignant reaction from the Chinese. This naval force arrived in March 1802, but before any attempt had been made to land the troops news was fortunately received of the preliminary Anglo-French peace treaty. The expedition therefore left for India on 2 July 1802. Yet the home authorities were still worried, and when Lord Hobart, on 16 November 1802, ordered the immediate restoration to the Governments of France and Holland of their several possessions in India, he added a warning. There was reason to fear, he stated, that 'the French Government either by intimidation or otherwise may endeavour to obtain possession of the Portuguese settlements in the East Indies, or of Macao, by which the British possessions in India and the security of the commerce of His Majesty's subjects with China would be greatly endangered', and the necessary steps were to be taken to prevent this.[27]

Sensing that the security of Cochin China was now becoming a matter of national concern, Dalrymple once again turned his attention to that kingdom, and in view of the circumstances of the hour he tended to stress the strategic issues that were at stake. In the winter of 1801–2 he therefore submitted his first Memoir on Cochin China to the Court of Directors. This elicited no immediate response,[28] and in the summer of 1802 he wrote to Henry Dundas on this subject, enclosing a newspaper cutting with his letter. This report, he suggested, 'strongly points out the expediency of improving, without delay, the present good disposition of the King of Cochin China, in order to consolidate the peace and Friendship of a Power that might have been so formidable to us, if directed by French Councils'.[29] The paragraph in question was from *The Star* of 23 July 1802

[27] I.O. Lbry., *Factory Records; China. Secret Consultations,* Vol. 2 (1800–5). Lord Hobart was the Secretary of State for the Colonial and War Dept.

[28] This Memoir was laid before the Secret Committee of the East India Company, by the Chairman, on 12 November 1801. It has not been located, but like the second it was inspired by a newspaper report. See *Minutes of the Secret Committee,* Vol. IV (1782–1806).

[29] Nat. Lbry. of Australia, Canberra, MSS. 43/19/20, Dalrymple to H. Dundas, 26 July 1802. Xerox Copy in Cambridge University Library.

which stated that 'The *Dispatch*, Captain Hutchinson, is safely arrived [at Bombay] with a Cargo of Sugar from Cochin-China. The Captain states that the King had issued an Edict, by which free Ingress into all the Ports of Cochin-China had been granted to all English Vessels, with exemption from Port Charges, and duties of every description. This exclusive mark of favour to English Vessels is said to have been principally occasioned by the favourable Impression of the National Character, communicated by some emigrant French officers, and Banished Priests, who had entered into the service of the Government of Cochin-China. The Rebellion which had long existed in that Country continued to oppose some resistance to the regular Authority, but decided advantages had lately been obtained by the Latter, which promised to bring the contest to a speedy termination.'

Dalrymple also took this opportunity to suggest a novel means of promoting British influence and of enlarging the bounds of geographical knowledge. For this he proposed to recruit the talents of the 'many Surgical young men' turned adrift by the signing of the Peace of Amiens. 'It occurs to me,' he wrote, 'that it would be easy to establish a Publick Institution for Surgical Men to be employed in the truely Christian Charities of their Art amongst the Natives of distant Countries. The Instruments for Observation would pass as part of their Medical Aparatus; and by their not interfering in matters of Religion or Government, they would be enabled to acquire much information, without raising suspicions, and exalt the dignity of our Country by so benevolent an Institution.' The expense of providing them with a few simple Instruments for observing latitudes would be slight, 'and if they instructed the Natives in their profession it would extend their own influence very much: a Correspondence might be kept up, not only with our own Settlements, on the allegation of wanting Medicines, but between the different Surgeons. Not only our Political Interests would be promoted and secured by this Institution but much advantage would in time accrue to Science and Natural History, as well as to Commerce.'

Dalrymple wrote his second Memoir in March 1803, when

Anglo-French tension was increasing. At this time reports were being received of 'extraordinary preparations in the Ports of France and Holland', and General Decaen, who had been appointed Captain-General of the French territories in the East in the previous December, was just setting sail with 1,300 troops and six ships under the command of Durand de Linois.[30] The British had also begun to re-arm.

In this document, Dalrymple suggested that this was an opportune moment for a new British initiative in Cochin China, where it appeared that the king was so shocked by what he had heard of the revolutionary excesses in France, including the beheading of Louis XVI, that he could not credit all that he was told. 'Perhaps,' wrote Dalrymple, 'the part that England had acted in the late crisis of Europe may have occasioned that Estimation in which he holds our Nation.' Apart from the above report in *The Star*, further evidence of the king's friendship was to be seen in his treatment of the English ship *Generous Friends*, for after the captain and chief mate had died, he had 'sent Capt. Barisy with some soldiers on board for her protection, to carry her to China and deliver her up to the Owners.'

Dalrymple stressed the significance to Britain of a country lying 'so much in the rout [sic] and neighbourhood of China. . . . Our China Exports in British produce and manufactures are, I am assured, $\frac{3}{4}$ [sic] of the whole amount of the Tea imported into England from China'. It had to be remembered that Napoleon, in unguarded moments, had talked 'of fraternizing China. . . . If there be any Truth in the Report that the French have obtained Macao from Portugal, there will be a clue in the unguarded expression. . . . The possession of Macao by the French would be the ruin of our Trade to China'. If war should break out over this, the king of Cochin China was Britain's natural ally.

Dalrymple agreed that it was difficult to make out a convincing case for Cochin China's immediate trading potential, though Lord Macartney had managed to sell good quantities of woollens during his short stay en route for China, and if the king could be persuaded to clothe his soldiers and sailors in

30 Lamb, op. cit., p. 100.

woollens, 'as we did our seapoys', the market would improve. Of greater immediate significance was the probability that the 'imbecile' Chinese government would 'speedily crumble in pieces, and then our having a stable footing in Cochin China would be of the utmost importance'. There were reports that the king would transfer his capital to Hué, north of Tourane, and leave Saigon. 'In that case, if the Company could obtain the province of Donai[31] on paying annually the present amount of the revenues, it would in a very few years amply reward them in revenue, as multitudes of Chinese, etc. would resort thither to cultivate Rice, Sugar, Pepper etc. if Lands were allotted on easy terms.' But this would entirely depend on developing 'a perfect good understanding' with the king, and that must be the primary object.[32]

The Directors of the East India Company were fully convinced that immediate action was called for, and the Chairman and his Deputy had a meeting on this subject with Lord Castlereagh, the new President of the Board of Control. On 3 April 1803 Castlereagh informed the Chairman that he had now gone into the matter more fully and wanted to impress upon the Company the great importance of developing good relations 'with so growing a Native Power, particularly in its naval resources: placed as it is immediately in the Track of our Trade to China. We cannot watch the conduct of its Government too narrowly'. He therefore wanted an immediate opening of communication with the king of Cochin China, to get the information which might lead later to a more permanent arrangement, and he expressed his personal belief that the French would wish to re-establish themselves in India before they turned their attentions to Cochin China. A week later Castlereagh was signifying his agreement to the immediate despatch of David Lance on such a mission.[33]

For many years Lance had been one of the Committee of Supercargoes at Canton, and was now living in retirement in

31 Donai was the southernmost province, near Saigon. *N.B.* the river Dong Nai which flows into that city.

32 Dalrymple, *Second Memoir*, loc. cit.

33 I.O. Lbry., *Factory Records; China and Japan*, Vol. 20, Castlereagh to Chairman of East India Company, 3 April 1803.

England. He and Dalrymple were friends of long standing, and they must have been working together on this project, for on 13 April 1803 the Secret Committee was considering papers which they had separately submitted, 'it having been for some time in contemplation to depute a Person on the Company's behalf to proceed to Cochin China'. These papers, including 'Draft Instructions for David Lance, Chief Supercargo at Canton', were then submitted to Castlereagh, and returned by him with the Board's approval on 22 April.

David Lance sailed to Cochin China on the *Coutts*, Castlereagh having suggested that an East-Indiaman should be employed 'to impress the Cochin Chinese who were interested in naval affairs'.[34] The *Coutts* arrived in the Bay of St James, south of Saigon, on 5 September 1803, and here she spoke the brig *Eleanor* whose commander, Captain Allan, had left Saigon for Hué, the ancient capital to the north. Lance was advised by Captain Torrin, who was in command of the *Coutts*, that it was too late in the season for them to go to Hué, carry on negotiations there with the king, and then proceed to Canton, for such a course of action would probably result in their missing the passage to China before the change of the monsoon. As Captain Allan was on his way to Hué, Lance therefore decided to entrust him with a letter to the king, explaining the purpose of the mission and the cause of its delay. In the meantime, Captain Allan 'fully confirmed the accounts of the favourable Disposition of the King towards the English and that of their Exemption from all Duties'.

At Canton, Lance informed Drummond and the Select Committee of the orders he had received and stated that 'from Information collected since my arrival here I find every Motion that induced to this Mission before I left Europe considerably strengthened'. But he had also found that his health had been seriously affected by the hot weather experienced on the outward voyage, and he was 'apprehensive of very serious Consequences to it should I now undertake a Voyage which would immediately carry me to a Hot Climate in which I must prob-

[34] A clear reference to Dalrymple's *Second Memoir*, where this subject was treated at length.

ably continue for many Months. I therefore avail myself of the power vested in me by my Instructions to name one of the Supra Cargoes on the spot to execute this Commission. I accordingly nominate Mr John William Roberts. . .'.[35]

Lance provided Roberts with his own instructions, with Dalrymple's two Memoirs which contained 'the history of Cochin China from the commencement of their Revolution down to 1801', as well as with papers communicated by Drummond which carried on that story to the present time. It was anticipated that when the king of Cochin China had not only won back his lost dominions, but had also conquered Tonkin, friction would develop between the empire of China and the kingdom of Cochin China. For in theory the king of Cochin China was 'Feudatory to the Empire of China', yet in practice he had at his command 'a victorious army of 300,000 Men and a Navy hitherto unequalled by any Native Power in the East'.

Unfortunately, the British had not reciprocated the king of Cochin China's gestures of goodwill. On 20 October 1799 the latter had sent duplicate letters to the Governor-General in Bengal and to Tranquebar, seeking 'to reclaim a vessel . . . captured by the *Nonsuch* (Capt. Thomas) and condemned and sold on pretence of wanting some necessary documents'. The lack of attention to his protests had caused 'some diminution' in his regard for the English. Roberts was therefore to make the necessary apologies and to promise redress. If the king asked for aid against his enemies, this would have to be referred to Bengal, but he was to be encouraged in the belief that he would not have to look elsewhere for help. At the same time, he must be made to realize that nothing could induce the British to 'hazard in any degree' their long-standing ties with China.

In Canton it was felt unlikely that the king of Cochin China could be persuaded to offer Donai to the British, as Dalrymple had suggested, but 'he might be induced to give an Establishment on his Coast . . . such [as] . . . the Island of Callao or Campillos

[35] I.O. Lbry., *Secret Consultations, China*, Vol. 268, Lance's Diary, David Lance to Jas. Drummond and the Select Committee, Canton, 6 November 1803.

situated about twenty miles to the S.W. of the Harbour of Turon.... This possession might contribute to extend the Sale of Opium should the Port of Macao no longer be a depot for that article as may be the case in the event of war with Portugal. Chinese Junks from the Provinces of Tchekian and Fokien to the amount of several hundred used to frequent this part of the coast.... As the chief consumption of opium in this Empire is in the provinces, it is most probable that should the Chinese find a constant supply of that article ready for them at this port, a considerable fraction of the consumption of China may be taken from thence without hazard to our trade here or dependence of the vile inhabitants of Macao...'.

The optimism behind the planning of this mission is evident in the statement that Lance had had an interview with Castlereagh a few days before sailing, and that the latter had stated his intention of having a constant Resident in Cochin China, 'should Mr Lance's reception be favourable, of which he entertained little doubt'.

Roberts was reminded that the king was 'the principal and almost the sole merchant of his dominions', so that all commercial discussions must be with him. A 'most beneficial' trade was looked for from this mission, since 'the commerce of Cochin China with the European Nations before the Revolution must have been of considerable extent, as both the French and Dutch Companies sent their ships to Touron, and about a Century ago there was a large vent of woollens at Tonquin'.

These instructions demonstrate the train of thought which guided those who were responsible for this mission. Merchants and statesmen alike feared that the French might attempt to seize Macao. At the same time they were worried lest a war between Cochin China and the empire of China might provide the French with opportunities to infiltrate and to endanger British trade with Canton. To the Governor-General and his Council in Bengal, the exclusion of the French from Cochin China was even more important than developing British trade with that kingdom. For the merchants in Canton, there was the hope that a settlement in Cochin China would prove a means of circumventing the obstacles to trade imposed by

Chinese officialdom, as Dalrymple had suggested years before.[36]

Of the mission itself, little need be said. Roberts reached Tourane on 4 December 1803, only to discover that the king was campaigning on the borders of Tonkin. Twelve days after his arrival, Roberts was visited by two Mandarins. One of these was a Frenchman, Philippe Vannier, who had at one time been a friend of the deceased Bishop of Adran, and who, as an ex-naval officer, had helped the king to build his powerful new navy.[37] From his conversation with these two men, Roberts learned that the king was not expected to return for some time, and it was agreed that his best policy would be to proceed to Bengal and to come back to Tourane in the summer, when he could hope for an interview with Nguyen Anh. The fears felt in Canton that a war with China might break out were strengthened, and Roberts was assured that Nguyen Anh no longer needed foreign aid in his struggle, and would not consider granting any territory or island to the British. Throughout the interview the Englishman found Vannier friendly, but inquisitive as to British intentions, and anxious to impress him with the monarch's power. At the same time, Roberts received information from the supercargoes at Canton that some of the Frenchmen in the king's service were far from friendly towards the British.[38]

After his arrival at Calcutta in February 1804, Roberts submitted a report to Wellesley in which he noted the influential position of the French Mandarins at the king's court, but expressed his confidence that the revolutionary acts of a regicide government had much disturbed that ruler. Roberts believed that most of the Frenchmen concerned were royalist at heart, and would therefore be willing to help the British. He still believed that the Island of Callao could be obtained from the king, if sufficient patience was shown, and regarded this as his principal task.[39] Wellesley, while fully alive to the importance of excluding French influence, was less sanguine, and doubted whether Frenchmen, even when they were royalists, would aid the British, for, as he pointed out to Roberts, 'the cause of

36 Lamb, op. cit., pp. 104–10.

37 Ibid., p. 111 and note.

38 Ibid., pp. 110–13.

39 Ibid., p. 118.

Monarchy in France . . . is not necessarily the cause of Great Britain in India'; even French royalists would not wish to see a diminution of French power abroad.[40]

Roberts was back in Tourane Bay on 22 July 1804, but soon realized that Nguyen Anh was not interested in establishing friendly relations with the British. At first he was at a loss to explain this, but he was later led to believe that Captain Allan, when bringing Lance's letter announcing the mission, had used some unguarded expressions which had given the impression that the British intended to obtain Tourane or some other port. The king had apparently feared that any such establishment might give the British too much power, and might even endanger his own government, and Roberts suspected that these fears had been encouraged by both the French and Portuguese.[41] The course of events in India would have provided them with plenty of convincing evidence. A series of disappointments followed. The king was slow to grant an interview at Hué, and when he did so he would only accept a portion of the presents offered which, despite being represented as a custom of the country, was so unlike anything experienced in other Eastern lands that it was inevitably interpreted as a studied gesture of contempt. Throughout the interview, the king acted in an aloof manner, and made it quite clear that he would not permit a representative of the Company to reside at his court. Moreover, he would only allow British ships to trade at his ports on the same terms as were granted to those of other nations. Roberts' refusal to accept Nguyen Anh's presents put the seal on the mission's failure.[42]

At Canton the supercargoes concluded that the mission had failed because of foreign intrigues, and they were particularly suspicious of M. Dayot. This Frenchman, who was now in the

[40] Ibid., p. 119.

[41] Ibid., p. 146. It was learnt that a Portuguese from Macao had spread rumours that the British meditated an attack, and that he had been so successful in this that when the *Discovery*, a surveying vessel, appeared upon the coast, she was denied refreshments. See J. F. Davis, *China*, Vol. 1, London, 1857, pp. 66–7.

[42] Ibid., pp. 124–41, Roberts' Journal, 22 July – 25 August 1804; pp. 143–8, Roberts' Report to Wellesley.

service of the Spanish Governor of the Philippines, had formerly helped to build up the Cochin Chinese navy. It was known that he had been in Tourane early in 1804, between Roberts' two visits, and had been negotiating for closer commercial relations between the Spanish Philippines and Cochin China.

Interest in this far-away kingdom did not die. 'Can you give me any information concerning Cochin China?' wrote Dalrymple to his friend Captain James Horsburgh, 'I have only found that Mr Roberts's Mission totally failed.'[43] And a few months later the publication of John Barrow's *Voyage to Cochinchina* revived all the old arguments. In truth, however, this land had become a backwater in the French wars, not because the views expressed as to its strategic significance had been wrong, but because the French were in no position to exploit the influence they had gained. The king of Cochin China, having established his independence, did not need to call upon such foreign aid as would have endangered the status quo, and no further British mission was to take place until 1822. Between 1778 and 1822 there were four British missions to Cochin China, each of which as has been pointed out elsewhere, was 'dominated by the vision of Alexander Dalrymple'.[44] Their principal effect was the negative one of keeping French influence at bay, since the king was made to realize that if he welcomed French interests he was likely to provoke English intervention. The British had lost their own great opportunity for a more active role when they had felt unable to respond to, or to follow up, Olivier's visit in 1798.

[43] University of Edinburgh Library, MS. La II, 589, Dalrymple to Horsburgh, 19 September 1805 (Postscript).

[44] Lamb, op. cit., p. 228. These missions were those of Chapman in 1778; Lord Macartney in 1792–3; Lance and Roberts in 1803–4; and Crawford in 1822.

CHAPTER VIII

The Fur-Trade and the Search for a North-West Passage

THE search for a North-West Passage had been a principal objective of British maritime enterprise in Tudor and early Stuart times, and in the eighteenth century this task was taken up anew. As interest in the Pacific Ocean quickened, so was there a greater incentive to find a direct route to it, and Hudson's Bay, with its coastline still known only in part, was a natural starting-point for such a quest.

As a commercial organization the Hudson's Bay Company was only interested in exploration when this promised to benefit its fur-trade. Such was the case when its French competitors began to make spectacular progress inland, for now there was a very real danger that while the Hudson's Bay Company remained confined to its coastal stations the French would gain control of the rest of the continent. If the Company was to retain its leading position in the fur-trade, this was a challenge that had to be met.

The initiative came primarily from Arthur Dobbs in partnership with Captain Christopher Middleton.[1] This is not the place to go into the story of that venture, or of the bitter dispute that subsequently developed between the two men. It is enough to say that while Dobbs retained his faith in the reality of such a passage, Middleton did not, and however barren was the argument in itself, it did serve to focus public attention on this problem, so that in 1745 Parliament was induced to offer a reward of £20,000 for the discovery of a North-West Passage.

[1] E. E. Rich, *History of the Hudson's Bay Company*, Vol. 1, 1670–1763, N.Y., 1961, Chapter XL.

In 1747 Dobbs sent out a further expedition which found the Chesterfield Inlet, but in 1761–2 this had been shown to be an inlet, and not the looked-for Passage. Then in 1771 Samuel Hearne had reached the mouth of the Coppermine River, which he had believed to lie in about 71° 54′ N., and his overland journey had shown that no passage could be looked for to the south of this river-mouth.

Moreover, the search for a North-West Passage was not confined to the east of the continent, for the instructions issued to Captain John Byron for his circumnavigation in 1764, like those drawn up for Drake nearly two centuries earlier, had suggested that it should be sought along the Pacific coast of North America. Furthermore, just as Robert Thorne and William Bourne had written about a route to the Pacific via the North Pole in Tudor times, so was this idea now revived by the Hon. Daines Barrington.[2] On 19 January 1773 Barrington informed the Council of the Royal Society that he had discussed with Lord Sandwich 'the practicability of a Navigation to the North Pole, and by it to the East Indies', and the Council thereupon decided to recommend such a voyage to the Administration.[3]

The result of this initiative was the 1773 polar voyage of Captain Constantine Phipps (later Lord Mulgrave), who sailed up the west coast of Spitzbergen and managed to exceed by several miles the farthest north (80° 23′ N.) reached by Hudson in his historic voyage of 1607, the first directed towards the North Pole.[4]

Finding this route unproductive, the Council turned its attention to the Pacific, and in a meeting on 17 February 1774 Daines Barrington proposed that a voyage of discovery to the northern coasts of the Pacific Ocean should be recommended. Again a letter was sent to Lord Sandwich on the subject, and on 21 April 1774 the Council learnt that a voyage on the lines

[2] Daines Barrington was a member of the Council of the Royal Society. He was a friend of Lord Hailes, and so became acquainted with Alexander Dalrymple to whom he introduced himself in 1770.

[3] *Minutes of the Royal Society*, Vol. 6.

[4] L. P. Kirwan, *A History of Polar Exploration*, Penguin Books, Harmondsworth, England, 1962, pp. 45, 67–8.

proposed would be undertaken 'after the return of Captain Cook in 1775'.[5]

In the meantime, the Russians and the Spaniards had been active on the north-west coast of America. In 1740 Vitus Bering had crossed over to Alaska, thereby inaugurating the Russian fur-trade in that region, and as the traffic developed the Russians occupied the Aleutian Islands. The Spaniards, who had occupied Upper California in 1769, were alarmed at this Russian activity to the north, and on 11 April 1773 the authorities in Madrid ordered the Viceroy to send an expedition to find out how far southwards the Russians had penetrated. After an unsuccessful voyage by Juan Hernandez an expedition took place in 1775, when the *Santiago* under the command of Heceta discovered the mouth of the Columbia River, while the *Sonora,* which had become separated, and on which Maurelle was the pilot, reached 57° N. An account of this expedition appeared in the *London Magazine* for December 1780, and Daines Barrington published Maurelle's narrative in his *Miscellanies* of 1781.[6]

It was to this no-man's land between the Russian and Spanish settlements that Cook was directed on his final voyage. 'Upon your arrival on the coast of New Albion,' he was instructed, 'you are to put into the first convenient port . . . and then to proceed Northward along the coast, as far as the latitude of 65°, or further, if you are not obstructed by lands or ice; taking care not to lose any time in exploring rivers or inlets, or upon any other account, until you get into the aforementioned latitude of 65°. . . . Then you are very carefully to search for, and to explore, such rivers or inlets as may appear to be of a considerable extent, and pointing towards Hudson's or Baffin's Bays; and if, from your own observations, or from . . . information . . . from the natives . . . there shall appear to be . . . even a probabil-

[5] *Minutes of the Royal Society,* Vol. 6.

[6] H. R. Wagner, *The Cartography of the N. W. Coast of America to the Year 1800,* 2 Vols., Berkeley, Calif., 1937, Vol. 1, pp. 162–79. It is Wagner's belief that the Spanish Government had sent a copy of Maurelle's account to the British Government in March 1776, to inform it of the Spanish discoveries on that coast, in view of the rumours circulating concerning the intentions of the forthcoming expedition under the command of Captain Cook.

ity, of a water passage into the aforementioned bays . . . you are . . . to use your utmost endeavours to pass through . . .'[7]

In the carrying out of these instructions, Cook's visit to the north-west coast of America had important results. In the first place, the 'first convenient port' which he chose was Nootka Sound, where sea-otter and other skins were procured from the Indians. Cook noticed that the latter were most anxious that the English should pay another visit, 'and, by way of encouragement, proposed to lay in a good stock of skins'.[8]

When, after Cook's death, the expedition visited Canton on the return journey, these skins proved a highly profitable investment. Captain James King recalled how he had sold his twenty sea-otter skins for some eight hundred Spanish dollars, and his men at Macao had also done well. He estimated that the total amount obtained for the furs in the two ships was not less than £2,000, yet they had got rid of two-thirds of their skins at Kamschatka, since they had considered them to be worn out and had then no idea of their potential value. John Ledyard later recalled that skins, which did not cost the purchaser sixpence sterling, sold in China for one hundred dollars, nor had they obtained one quarter of the skins which they might have done.[9] Even higher prices might have been obtained had they been skilled in bargaining. This experience had induced Captain King to stress the commercial possibilities that had been revealed, and to suggest that with the help of the East India Company much could be accomplished.[10]

This was a pertinent observation, whose significance was soon appreciated by Alexander Dalrymple. He and Sir Joseph Banks had been brought in by the Earl of Sandwich to help the editor, the Right Reverend J. Douglas, and Captain King, the author of the third volume, to prepare the official account of Cook's third voyage for publication. Because of the American war this work did not reach the public until 1784, but Dalrymple

[7] Jas. Cook (ed. Dr Douglas), *A Voyage to the Pacific Ocean*, London, 1785 (2nd edition), Vol. 1, pp. xxxiii et seq. [8] Ibid., Vol. 2, p. 285n.

[9] Jared Sparks, *The Life and Travels of John Ledyard*, London, 1828, pp. 96–7.

[10] Jas. King, *A Voyage to the Pacific Ocean*, London, 1785 (2nd ed.), Vol. 3, p. 435.

had been receiving first-hand reports of the expedition long before that. The ships had arrived back in England in October 1780, and on the 5th of that month, and again on 2 November, Captain King was being entertained to dinner at the Royal Society Club as Dalrymple's guest. Whatever may have been their social relationship, the two men found it hard to work together and had a series of disputes over the maps and illustrations for these volumes.[11] Nevertheless, at this early stage Dalrymple was being apprised of the discoveries that had been made, of the important new branch of commerce that had been opened, and of the vital part that the East India Company ought to play in its exploitation. A seed had been sown in his mind that would one day blossom forth in an imaginative plan to combine the operations of the East India and Hudson's Bay Companies. First, however, more needed to be known about the geography of the North American continent, and Dalrymple's imagination was about to be set alight by a series of dramatic reports that were sent back by the first fur-trading voyages to the north-west coast of America.

In drawing up Cook's Instructions, the Admiralty had deliberately decided to ignore the supposed strait leading into the Western Sea of John de Fuca, between the latitudes of 47° N. and 48° N., and the Archipelago of St Lazarus which Admiral de Fonte was reputed to have discovered between 50° N. and 55° N., for the latter was considered to be a purely imaginary concept, and the former, destitute of any sufficient external evidence, bore 'many striking marks of internal absurdity'.[12] This was why Cook, when he left Nootka Sound and ran into some very heavy weather, made no attempt to keep close to the shore; to have done so, even had the *Resolution* not been leaking, would have been to court disaster. Thus, as far north as 60° N. no real survey of the coast had been made. All that could be said was that 'wherever seen, it presented the appearance of a continuous mountain range'.[13]

[11] B.M. *Egerton Mss*, 2181, f. 107.
[12] J. Cook, *A Voyage to the Pacific Ocean*, Vol. 1, pp. xl–xli.
[13] J. A. Williamson, *Cook and the Opening of the Pacific*, London, 1946, p. 202.

The last point which needs to be noted here, about this voyage, was the belief that Cook's Inlet, in 61° N., was the mouth of a great river.

The official account of Cook's last voyage was on sale in June 1784, and the potentialities of this new branch of the fur-trade soon became public knowledge, not only in Britain, but throughout Europe, America and the Far East. Enterprising men were inevitably tempted to exploit these new opportunities, but first the problem of the East India Company's monopoly had to be faced. Those British merchants who wished to play a part in the trade, but were not in the Company's service, either had to obtain a licence from the East India Company or were forced to carry on a surreptitious trade under foreign colours.

On 29 April 1785 the Court of Directors met to discuss various proposals from groups of merchants who were seeking licences, and on 6 May a decision was announced. Mr Etches and his partners were to be licensed to send two ships for one voyage, and on specified terms, by way of experiment.[14]

There now followed a series of voyages that revived interest in the geography of the north-west coast of America, and, in particular, in the legends of de Fuca and de Fonte. Captain Hanna, in 1785, was the first private merchant to reach that coast, and the 20,600 dollars realised for his 740 skins confirmed the initial optimism, so that other ships soon followed.[15] Captain Hanna was back on the coast in the following year, when he discovered, to the east of Fitzhugh Sound, innumerable islands which appeared 'to extend to a great distance Eastward', as well as signs of a large river.[16]

[14] Harlow & Madden, *British Colonial Developments 1774–1834*, Oxford, 1953, pp. 21–27. Dalrymple viewed this as another unwise concession, like the proposed convict settlement at Botany Bay and the agreement over the whaling interests, forced upon the Company by an Administration too much influenced by the free-trade doctrines of Adam Smith – see his undated (post-1787) paper on *The Fur Trade* in *Home Miscellaneous Series*, Vol. 494, pp. 429–39.

[15] *Monthly Review*, Vol. LXXX, London, 1789, p. 507.

[16] A. Dalrymple, *A Plan for Promoting the Fur Trade, and securing it to this country by uniting the operations of the East-India and Hudson's Bay Companies*, London, 1789, pp. 10–14.

Captain Hanna had been operating from Canton, but the next expedition was carried out from Bombay by the *Captain Cook* and the *Experiment* under the general command of James Strange. The latter was a servant of the East India Company, and enjoyed the powerful backing of David Scott, its future Chairman, who bore the entire expense of this voyage. Strange's instructions described the two principal objects in view as 'in the first Instance, Exploring for the benefits of Navigation and Secondly with a View to Establish a new Channel of Commerce with the North-West Coast of America'. The exploration was intended to include a wide-ranging survey of the American and Asiatic coasts of the Pacific, and, in addition, it was suggested that 'If you could in your Range along the Coast of America, land any of your Crew who choose to turn out Volunteers on the occasion in some Centrical Situation, with a Promise of returning to them again, We conceive it might be attended with singular advantage, as by attaining the Language thus, it might in future prove very useful . . .[17]

Strange reached Nootka in the summer of 1786, where the surgeon Mackay volunteered to remain in accordance with these Instructions, and after collecting 'every rag of fur' available, they left the Sound on 28 July, and four days later discovered and named Scott Islands. Here Strange designated 'Oxenford Bay in honour of my respected friend Sir John Dalrymple', a suggestive remark.[18]

On 4 August they decided to explore an inlet which had excited their curiosity. For 'at least twenty-five miles' this maintained a width of two miles and ran due east and west. From the summit of a nearby mountain Strange saw that the two extreme points towards which they had been steering 'formed the Entrance into a Bay as extensive in Circumference as the eye could reach', at the east end of which was an opening 'two or three leagues wide'. 'It stricks(sic) me,' he wrote, 'that the Inlet in question, is very probably the Strait, said to be Discovered many years ago, by Admiral de Fonte; the Existence of which, Captain Cook in his Narrative, Regrets not being able

[17] *Home Miscellaneous Series*, Vol. 484 (5), pp. 422–7.
[18] Ibid, Vol. 800, p. 89.

to Disprove.'[19] Strange had, in fact, discovered Queen Charlotte Sound.

This journal was received by the Examiner's Office on 1 March 1788, and was doubtless being studied by Alexander Dalrymple, in his Hydrographer's Office in India House, very soon afterwards. Dalrymple's work on Cook's last voyage had given him a close knowledge of all that had previously been discovered about the north-west coast of America. Now he had the report of one who had closely inspected a portion of the coast missed by Cook. Here Strange had discovered that that part which Cook's maps had shown as a straight coastline contained, in reality, many islands, and a passage stretching eastwards, where de Fonte was supposed to have found a strait, with a very extensive bay at the end of it.

Other vessels had been on this coast at the same time, for in 1786 the *Nootka* and the *Sea Otter,* under the command of John Meares, had wintered in Prince William's Sound (the farthest north reached by Strange), where they had suffered greatly, but had made no important discoveries. In 1787, however, there were some notable developments, for in that year the *King George* and *Queen Charlotte,* under Captains Nathaniel Portlock and George Dixon, both of whom had been with Captain Cook on his last voyage, were on the North-West Coast. After discovering Meares in Prince William's Sound and offering somewhat grudging aid,[20] Portlock and Dixon decided to separate. It was resolved that while Portlock remained here and sent a long-boat to discover what could be obtained from Cook's River, Dixon should sail to the south. The two ships would reunite at Nootka Sound in the autumn.

This meant that Dixon would be visiting a coastline which had previously been passed by Captain Cook and the Spaniards. He remembered how Cook, after leaving Nootka Sound, had been unable to sight the coast again until he had reached 55° 20′ N., and so had been unable to inspect the place assigned by geographers to the Strait of Admiral de Fonte, an omission that he

[19] *Home Miscellaneous Series,* Vol. 800, pp. 97–8.

[20] V. T. Harlow, *The Founding of the Second British Empire,* Vol. 2, London, 1964, pp. 433–4.

had regretted even though he had been sceptical of the Strait's existence. Maurelle's account of the earlier Spanish voyage along the same coast had been published by Daines Barrington in his *Miscellanies*, where the Spaniard was quoted as having written: 'We now attempted to find out the Straight of Admiral Fonte, though as yet we had not discovered the Archipelago of St Lazarus, through which he is said to have sailed. With this intent we searched every bay and recess on the coast, and sailed round every headland, lying-to- in the night, that we might not lose sight of this entrance. After these pains taken, and being favoured by a North-West wind, it may be pronounced that no such Straights are to be found'.[21] Dixon's voyage was about to disprove this emphatic Spanish statement; it may have crossed his mind that if they wished to dissuade the British from exploring this coast, the report was well calculated to achieve that end.

Dixon left Prince William's Sound on 14 May 1787 and slowly proceeded down the coast, collecting furs. By 1 July he had reached that part which Cook had been prevented from seeing, and it was now that he found himself abreast of the northern end of a 'very considerable group of islands'. He was, in fact, approaching the group that he named Queen Charlotte Islands. On 28 July he was in the strait to the eastward of them, where the setting of the tide 'from that land which we supposed to be the continent' made him conclude that there was 'a large river setting out from that part of the coast. The river called Los Reys, by de Fonte, is near this place; and though what he says about it is almost incredible, yet, from the above circumstance, it appears very probable, that there are deep inlets into the country . . .'[22]

Clearly this coastline was unlike that described by Maurelle, or depicted in Cook's outline sketch. Dixon himself wrote that 'the situation of these islands . . . evidently shows that they are the Archipelago of St Lazarus, and consequently near the Straight of de Fonte, though further research must be given to his

[21] W. Beresford (introduction by Dixon), *A Voyage Round the World*, London, 1789, pp. xiii, xv–xvi.

[22] Beresford, op. cit., p. 217.

pompous account of the place'.[23] A reviewer also noticed 'a very great resemblance' between the southern parts of the straits separating Queen Charlotte's Islands and the Archipelago of St. Lazarus.[24]

While these discoveries were being made to the north of Nootka Sound, Captain William Barkley, in command of the *Imperial Eagle* and under Austrian colours, sailed out of that harbour on a south-easterly heading. His wife was with him, and she recorded their great astonishment when they 'arrived off a large opening extending to the eastward, the entrance of which appeared to be about four leagues wide, and remained about that width as far as the eye could see . . . which my husband immediately recognised as the long lost strait of Juan de Fuca, and to which he gave the name of the original discoverer'. No further investigation was made of this strait, but the *Imperial Eagle* made for Macao, whence news of this discovery was promptly forwarded to England.[25]

On 8 August 1787 Captain Dixon had fallen in with the *Prince of Wales* (Captain Colnett) and the *Princess Royal* (Captain Duncan) off Nootka Sound. As the *Imperial Eagle* was at that moment collecting furs in the Sound, Dixon suggested that the north-east side of Queen Charlotte's Islands would be the most promising area to try. The two vessels therefore appear to have separated at this stage, Captain Colnett going to the stretch of coast suggested by Dixon, while Duncan went southwards to the Strait of Juan de Fuca.

When Colnett reached Dixon Entrance, he wrote in his log that 'Without a search to investigate, the inland navigation . . . might not improperly be conjectured to run to Hudson's Bay from the Depth of Water, width of channel and tending to the N.E. as far as the eye could reach . .'.[26] At approximately the same time Charles Duncan, off the mouth of the Strait of Juan de Fuca, entered the following in his log, on 15 August

23 Ibid., p. xiii.

24 *Monthly Review,* Vol LXXX, pp. 509–10.

25 G. Williams, *The British Search for the North-West Passage in the 18th century,* London, 1962, p. 218.

26 P.R.O., *Capt. Colnett's log,* Adm. 55/146, p. 233. (The original lacks punctuation.)

1788: 'The Indians of Claaset[27] said that they knew not of any Land to the Eastward: and that it was A'ass toopulse, which signifies a Great Sea; they pointed that the sea ran a great way up, to the Northward; and down to the Southward on the East side, they likewise said, that at a great distance to the Southward, I should find men that had guns. . . .'[28]

Back on the North-West Coast in 1788 was John Meares in the *Felice Adventurer,* accompanied by William Douglas in the *Iphigenia Nubiana.* After calling at Nootka Sound these two separated, Douglas going to Cook's 'River' to work his way down the coast, while Meares went southwards from Nootka. Between them they intended to cover the whole coast between 45° N. and 60° N.

Thus it fell to Meares to investigate the Strait of Juna de Fuca, and he described how his long-boat had been despatched to examine the strait more closely. Before being stopped by hostile Indians it 'had sailed near thirty leagues up the strait, and at that distance from the sea it was about fifteen leagues broad, with a clear horizon stretching to the East for fifteen leagues more'. He and his men had concluded that the end of the strait 'could not be at any great distance from Hudson's Bay'.[29] Douglas, too, was optimistic, for when he returned to Macao he let it be known that 'he was intending to prosecute some discoveries he had made on the North-West Coast of America, which he thinks promises a passage thro'. . .'.[30]

As report after report from these fur-trading vessels referred to islands, deep inlets and possible large rivers, it became evident that the north-west coast of America differed materially from that described by Captain Cook. Though many informed writers

[27] An Indian village close to Cape Claaset, which appears to have been the modern Cape Flattery.

[28] See the legend on the map entitled 'Sketch of the Entrance of the Strait of Juan de Fuca . . . by Charles Duncan', published by A. Dalrymple, 14 January 1790. Dalrymple had Duncan's log in his possession, but now it unfortunately seems to be lost.

[29] J. Meares, *Voyages made in the Years 1788 and 1789,* London, 1790, p. 179.

[30] Nat. Lbry. of Scotland *Melville Papers,* MS. 1069, f. 71, Blankett to Dundas, 8 April 1791. Douglas's log was in Dalrymple's possession when he devised his fur-trade plan.

believed that they contained unlikely and even ridiculous features, it began to seem that there might be some factual basis to the old legends of de Fuca and de Fonte. Alexander Dalrymple, in particular, was quick to see great possibilities in the new discoveries. He knew that British participation in the fur-trade on this coast was jeopardized by two developments. In the first place there was the danger that this coast would be closed to English vessels through the northward expansion of the Spanish settlements and the southward extension of the Russian stations. Furthermore, the Americans, who had just won their independence, might seize control of this branch of the fur-trade. But Dalrymple now realized that if the Pacific coastline contained deep inlets and, as some believed, considerable rivers, it was reasonable to hope that means could be found to convey furs from the interior of Canada to the Pacific. It occurred to Dalrymple that if the East India and Hudson's Bay Companies linked forces, their combined power would overwhelm all outside competition, whether it came from foreign rivals or from independent British merchants.

In the meantime, various adventurous spirits had suggested an overland crossing of the vast Canadian continent. As early as 1765 Major Rogers, who had won fame in the Seven Years' War with the Rangers, and had spent eight years in the 'least known part of North America', expressed 'Moral Certainty' in the existence of a North-West Passage, along which he expected to find water for a great part of the way. In 1772 he submitted a revised plan, in which he foreshadowed the trans-continental route later followed by Lewis and Clarke. Both plans were considered by the Lords Commissioners of Trade and Plantations, who were interested but not sufficiently convinced to give positive support.[31] Shortly afterwards Rogers lent these plans to Jonathan Carver who, in 1778, published his book *Travels through North America in the Years 1766–68*. This work was a best-seller, and it is very possible that a copy of it was seen by the Canadian fur-trader Alexander Henry who, in October 1781, addressed a long letter to Sir Joseph Banks (to whom Carver's book had been dedicated) on 'A Proper Rout, by Land, to cross the great

[31] Williams, op. cit., pp. 172 and 182.

Contenant of America from Quebec to the Westernmost Extremity'.[32]

In 1784 George Dixon had also written to Banks to propose an overland crossing by way of Quebec and the Lakes.[33] Then in 1786 John Ledyard visited London, where his plans for an overland crossing from Nootka to Virginia aroused much interest among some 'gentlemen of science', who included Banks. The ship on which he sailed from Deptford, however, was stopped after Dalrymple, who had supplied charts and other information under the mistaken impression that the vessel was sailing under licence of the East India Company, had learnt of his error and had warned the Company's chairman.[34]

The plan that was taking shape in Dalrymple's mind required a detailed knowledge of the interior of Canada, and this would have to come from the Canadian traders rather than from the Hudson's Bay Company. Among the Canadian traders the most significant figure, in this respect, was Peter Pond. In 1784 Pond was a disgruntled man who felt ill-used by his partners in the North-West Company. He had therefore gone to Washington to seek new employment, taking with him a sketch-map of the North-West which he had drawn up, the first map ever made of that territory.[35] But finding the Americans, in the spring of 1785, too pre-occupied with their immediate post-war problems to show any interest in his schemes, Pond had thereupon returned to Montreal.

This visit to Montreal allowed him to see the first published accounts of Cook's last voyage, with descriptions of the valuable furs of Nootka Sound and of the discovery of Cook's 'River'. If an overland route to the Pacific Ocean could be found, the Canadian traders would be in a peculiarly good position to exploit it, and none of them knew more about the possibility of

[32] *The Banks Letters* (ed. W. R. Dawson), London, 1958, p. 406. (See also p. 204 for a letter from Carver referring to difficulties in publishing his book, the letter being dated 13 August 1778). [33] Ibid., p. 270.

[34] Jared Sparks, op. cit., p. 229. P.R.O. C.O. 77/25 Dalrymple to Michie, 19 August 1786.

[35] M. W. Campbell, *The North-West Company*, Toronto, 1957, p. 47. Pond was an American by birth, which made Dalrymple suspicious of his loyalty.

finding such a route than Peter Pond. A memorial had already been presented to the Governor on 4 October 1784, on behalf of the North-West Company, asking for the exclusive right to the trade of the North-West for the next ten years, in return for which the Company would undertake exploratory surveys of the land extending westwards from Hudson's Bay to the Pacific between latitudes 55° N. and 65° N. On 18 April 1785 Pond sent his own memorial to the Governor, supporting the above petition and enclosing his map, and on 6 June General Hamilton forwarded these two memorials and the map to Lord Sydney, the Home Secretary. Soon after its receipt the map was shown to Dalrymple.[36]

Peter Pond's map was of real value to practising fur-traders, since it showed the routes to be followed to Lake Athabaska, and the relative positions of important rivers, lakes and portages, but its longitudes were wildly out, the western extremity of Lake Athabaska being shown as 132° W. instead of the correct 112° W., thus placing it seven hundred miles too near to the Pacific.[37] At this stage Pond correctly showed the Mackenzie River (to use its modern name) flowing from Great Slave Lake to the Arctic Ocean.

The growing belief that an overland crossing of the continent would prove practicable further encouraged Dalrymple in his plan to combine the operations of the East India and Hudson's Bay Companies. This scheme would give the British the control of the fur trade, for not only would they command the sources of supply, but they would also have the option of marketing their furs in either Asia or Europe, as the state of the market dictated.

Dalrymple was further influenced by the reports which he received of the fur-trade operations of the first two seasons on the North-West Coast. These had clearly demonstrated that some form of regulation was required to prevent this promising trade from being ruined by over-exploitation. Dalrymple had

36 M. S. Wade, *Mackenzie of Canada*, Edinburgh and London, 1927, pp. 289 et seq. For Pond's memo, see H. A. Innis, 'Peter Pond and the Influence of Captain James Cook on exploration in the interior of North America', *Proceedings and Transactions of the Royal Society of Canada*, 3rd Series, Vol. XXII, Ottawa, 1928, pp. 131–41.

37 Williams, op. cit., p. 231.

received from J. H. Cox a list of the furs sold at Canton, and the Spanish dollars realized for them, by all the ships concerned in 1786–7, and from this it appeared that five thousand and six skins had been sold in 1787 alone.[38] If an unlimited number of furs was allowed into Canton, two consequences must follow; the price at Canton would drop sharply, while the price on the North-West Coast would rise, 'and the Adventurers being without mutual communication, the Number of Purchasers on so remote a Coast would be alternatively too great to obtain Cargoes; and too small to take off the furs collected; which would throw the trade infallibly into the hands of the Spaniards at their Settlements; or of the Americans . . .'. If his plan was not adopted, he argued, 'the Americans will certainly beat us out, as they can sail much cheaper than we can; and as it is a branch of Trade that does not require a great Capital.'[39]

In practice, Dalrymple visualized a ship sailing from England to China, and after leaving her outward-bound cargo at Canton, departing again for the north-west coast of America by 1 July, to receive the furs collected there 'by the Hudson's Bay Company's agents'. The ships would remain on that coast until the equinoctial gales were over, and would then return to China which would be reached in December, so that the ships would be ready to return to England in January or February.

If this original and imaginative scheme was to be a practicable proposition, it would be essential to discover extensive inland waterways along which heavily-laden canoes could travel in the manner of the Canadian traders. Dalrymple therefore determined to unravel everything that had been learnt of the geography of these territories. He had been kept well-informed about the discoveries that had been made on the North-West Coast by his various friends at Canton.[40] Thus he had been able

[38] A. Dalrymple, *A Plan for promoting the Fur-Trade, and securing it to this Country, by Uniting the Operations of the East-India and Hudson's Bay Companys*, London, 1789, p. 27

[39] Ibid., p. 31, and Dalrymple, *A Fragment on the India Trade*, London, 1797, pp. 25–6.

[40] They included William and Thomas Fitzhugh, and David Lance, who were old and close friends, as well as John Henry Cox with whom he kept up an active correspondence.

to procure the journals of Captains Hanna and Barkley, as well as those of Meares and Douglas for their expedition of 1788. In addition, both Duncan and Dixon were in London. For the discoveries that had been made on the east coast he was able to turn to Wegg, the Chairman of the Hudson's Bay Company, with whom he dined week after week at the Royal Society Club, and who put at his disposal all the geographical materials in the Company's possession, which Dalrymple found to be 'very copious' and much exceeding his expectations. He had also received the map of the Canadian traders which, though 'extravagantly extending the limits of their Peregrinations, yet, when corrected by Mr Turnor's astronomical observations . . . is of great use'. He had studied the Indian maps, which conveyed 'much information of the Northern parts, where European documents fail'.

In fixing the longitudes of the coasts Dalrymple found himself on much firmer ground. William Wales was able to provide him with accurate positions obtained during his visit to Hudson Bay in 1769 to observe the transit of Venus, while on the west coast the 'late voyages, particularly those of Captains Cook, Hanna, Portlock, Dixon and Barkley [had] ascertained with competent precision the longitudes' of the Pacific coast from 43° N. to 60° N. Taken in conjunction with the Spanish discoveries, this meant that the longitudes of the west coast were now well known from 40° N.

As he studied the various materials concerning the interior of Canada, including Pond's map, Dalrymple became increasingly interested in the reports of 'rivers and lakes for many hundreds of miles to the westwards of Hudson's Bay'. But his first efforts to get the Hudson's Bay Company to send out a qualified surveyor to examine this country met with a disappointing response, the only result being the despatch of a reluctant fifteen-year-old boy from the Grey Coat School, with only the most rudimentary training.[41]

It was Lake Athabaska which caused the greatest confusion. On Pond's map it was named Arabaska, where it had been

[41] R. Glover (ed.), *David Thompson's Narrative,* Champlain Society, Toronto, 1962, pp. 19–20.

displaced so far to the west that it had been located within 150 miles of the Pacific. He had depicted it as being sausage-shaped. Hearne had also shown a lake of somewhat similar shape on his map, which he called Lake Arathapescow, and in view of the similarity of name and shape it was not surprising that Dalrymple and others thought that these were two variants of the same lake. In reality, however, Hearne's Arathapescow was Great Slave Lake, which Pond included on his map, but depicted as being circular in shape.[42]

Working on the assumption that Pond's Arabasca and Hearne's Arathapescow were the same lake, Dalrymple tried to decide its proper location. He compared Hearne's longitudes with those obtained by Philip Turnor, in whose observations he rightly placed great confidence. In the collections of the Hudson's Bay Company he found two maps, by Hearne and Turnor respectively, of the route from Churchill to Cumberland House, and whereas Hearne had made the difference of longitude 13½°, Turnor's astronomical observations showed it to be only 9½°. On this basis Dalrymple decided that he would be safe in reducing Hearne's estimate of the distance from Churchill to Lake Athabaska by one-third. Less justifiably, he cut down his estimate of latitude by the same amount, probably because he knew that Hearne's calculation of latitude on his third journey in 1772 was not to be relied upon. On that occasion Hearne had shown the latitude of the mouth of the Coppermine River to be 72° N., whereas Dalrymple had estimated, with notable accuracy, that it was in about 68° N. Hearne, as he pointed out, had given only one observation for latitude in the whole of his journey from 7 December 1770 to 30 June 1772, though his quadrant had not been destroyed until 6 October 1771. After mentioning that it was not clear from the records whether that quadrant had been replaced or adequately repaired, Dalrymple suggested from this lone observation 'we must suspect some incompetency in the instrument: for Mr Hearne does not seem to have been wanting in assiduity, and Geography is much indebted to him'. Dalrymple had therefore rejected 'with diffi-

42 R. Glover, 'Hudson Bay to the Orient', *The Beaver,* Hudson's Bay Company, Winnipeg, Winter 1960, p. 50. Pond called it simply 'Slave Lake'.

dence' Hearne's lone observation.[43] The latter, though anxious not 'to enter into a dispute with, or incur the displeasure of Mr Dalrymple', was upset by this questioning and tried to defend his account, but the facts were against him. As a modern authority has pointed out, the chief value of Hearne's journal did not really lie in the geographical information that it gave, but in its understanding record of Indian life.[44] Here it needs to be stressed that there is no justification for the oft-repeated statement that Dalrymple had taken his opportunity to make a venomous attack upon Hearne.

During the winter of 1787–8 Philip Turnor was back in England, preparing his maps. He had been working as a surveyor in the Company's service since 1778, and by 1782 he had completed his surveys of the Moose and Albany districts, since when he had been occupied in routine trading activities. By chance, it seems that Samuel Hearne was in England at the same time. Dalrymple met Turnor and was much impressed with the work that the surveyor had already accomplished.[45]

Before it could be affirmed that Dalrymple's plan was practicable, much more knowledge was still required, not only of the interior of Canada but of the North-West Coast and of Hudson's Bay as well. Dalrymple's researches had led him to believe that the western limit of Lake Athabaska must lie in about 114° W. (the real figure being 112° W.), and as he remarked, 'this gives a new face to the Country between Hudson's Bay and the South Sea, and greatly increases the space of undiscovered parts towards the Western Coast of America'.

On the North-West Coast itself, the situation seemed more promising than had originally been visualized, for report after report was suggesting that the lands so far discovered were islands rather than the continent itself. 'If this opinion be well grounded . . . then the distance between the two Seas will be still more reduced; and the Navigation, being carried on through

43 A. Dalrymple, *Memoir of a Map of the Lands around the North Pole*, London, 1789.

44 J. B. Tyrrell (ed.), *Hearne's Journey from Hudson's Bay to the Northern Ocean*, Champlain Society, Toronto, 1911, p. 17.

45 J. B. Tyrrell (ed.), *The Journals of Samuel Hearns and Philip Turnor*, Champlain Society, Toronto, 1934, pp. 60 et seq., and p. 80.

Sounds covered by Islands, abounding with excellent Harbours, will be exposed to little danger when the Coasts are properly surveyed'. Obviously, the farther inland a sea-communication extended from the west coast, the easier it would be to combine the operations of the two companies. 'The Hudson's Bay Company have already Establishments very far inland; Hudson's House . . . is above 530 Geographic Miles to their nearest Settlement in the Bay: the distance remaining to complete the Communication is about 800 Geographic Miles.' Although Turnor had told him that the river to Hudson's House was as easy to navigate as the Thames, and the Indians said that it remained like that farther on, Dalrymple felt that an easier route from Hudson's Bay to the west coast might be found by way of Chesterfield Inlet, or some of the other rivers and inlets from Hudson's Bay, 'connecting with the Arathapescow, Dobaunt and other Lakes'.

He noted how Chesterfield Inlet was 'navigable for more than 200 Geographic Miles; and the greater part by vessels of any size', and assumed that the failure to exploit its commercial advantages was due to the reported aversion 'to any Northern Expeditions' amongst the Hudson's Bay Company's servants on the spot. On the evidence of the Indian maps, and of one 'apparently by a European, though anonymous', the sea, beyond the limits of Captain Middleton's discoveries, continued to the Copper River. 'The evidence Captain Middleton brings of his Frozen Strait,' wrote Dalrymple, 'does not appear to me conclusive; and, as the same effects which were accounted for by it, would be produced by a Communication to the Northward of Repulse Bay, which he supposed shut up Hudson's Bay on the North, I have thought it most eligible to omit Middleton's Frozen Strait, and continue the Coast of Southampton Island as far to the Northward as Fox traced it on the East Side.'[46]

With the evidence of a large number of islands on the west coast, it seemed worth pondering anew the old stories of de Fuca and de Fonte, to which the new discoveries bore so remarkable an affinity. de Fonte's narrative, as Dalrymple recalled,

[46] Dalrymple, *Memoir of a Map of the Lands around the North Pole*, pp. 13–14.

had first appeared in *Memoirs for the Curious* in 1708, and it had been given new prominence when T. Swaine Drage published his *Great Probability of a North-West Passage* in London in 1768.[47] That de Fonte was an historic character seemed confirmed, as Dalrymple noted, by a reference to him in Burgomaster Witsen's *Nord and Ost Tartarye*, published in 1705.

According to the legend, de Fonte was supposed to have discovered, in 1640, a collection of islands off the north-west coast of America which he named the Archipelago of St Lazarus. After sailing for some 260 leagues in crooked channels among these islands, he had then found a river in 53° N. which he had named Rio de Las Reyes. He had journeyed up this river in a north-easterly direction for a further sixty leagues, reaching fresh water about a third of the way up it, until he had come to a tidal lake which he had named Lake Belle. On the south side of this he had found a river, which he had named the Parmentiers. He had worked his way up this river, and after negotiating eight falls he had eventually reached another great lake which he had named Lake de Fonte. This was 160 Leagues long by 60 broad, and lay east-north-east by west-south-west. In it were several large islands, and ten small ones, and the lake was reported to abound with cod and ling. From the east-north-east corner stretched another expanse of water which he called Strait Ronquillo, where he learnt of the presence of a ship, owned by Gibbons, the Major-General of Boston, and navigated by a certain Shapley.

Many had poured scorn on this tale, pointing to the lack of original documents to give it substance, and in 1786 there had been published an English edition of *Voyages and Discoveries*

[47] Dalrymple, *Plan for the Fur-Trade*, pp. 14–17. For an interesting account of the de Fonte legend by a contemporary of Dalrymple, see Jas. Burney, *A Chronological History . . .*, Vol. III, London, 1813, pp. 192–4. He recalls how Witsen's account told of a famous Portuguese seaman named de Fonta, who visited Tierra del Fuego and Staten Land in 1649, which seems to establish him as an historic character. Burney mentions that Dalrymple's final view was that the story was 'a jeu d'esprit of James Pettiver'. A modern discussion of the whole subject can be found in H. R. Wagner 'Apocryphal Voyages to the North-West Coast of America' in *Proceedings of the American Antequarian Society*, Vol. XLI (April 1931), pp. 179–234.

in the North by Dalrymple's erstwhile acquaintance John Reinhold Forster, who suggested[48] that the careful explorations of the Spaniards and of Captain Cook on the west coast, as of Hearne inland, had left no room for the rivers and lakes traversed by de Fonte, or for the Archipelago of St Lazarus. A cautious scholar would have waited for more evidence. Fortunately for modern Canada, Dalrymple, in his quest for urgent action, was prepared to be wrong. He recorded the various criticisms that had been levelled against this legend to undermine confidence in its authenticity, and showed that plausible answers could be found to many of them. He believed that there was sufficient evidence in favour of the tale to warrant its investigation. 'It is so much easier,' he observed, 'to treat with derision than to investigate.' He pointed out that it was 'well ascertained that there were such Persons at Boston, and its neighbourhood, as Major-General Gibbons, who was with Sir Thomas Button, in his Discovery Voyage to Hudson's Bay; and Captain Nicolas Shapley'. He had been assured 'by the celebrated Dr Franklin, from the researches he had made at Boston', that Shapley 'passed under the appellation of Old Nic . . . I shall only add that I have seen at the British Museum a MS chart of part of the coast of New-England by Nic Shapley'.[49] Furthermore, Captains Hanna and Dixon believed that they had found evidence of a great river in 53° N., as well as the Archipelago of St Lazarus.[50]

Encouraged by their discoveries, Dalrymple was inclined to believe in the basic truth of the tale, though he acknowledged that error had crept into it in its present form. Thus he admitted his inclination 'to suppose Lake de Fonte to be Arathapescow Lake; if it was not for the circumstance of Cod and Ling, which implys it to be salt water: the direction and extent of the Arathapescow Lake countenance the supposition: in such case R. Parmentiers would be Arathapescow River'.[51] Doubtless there

[48] J. R. Forster, *Voyages and Discoveries in the North*, London, 1786, pp. 454–5.

[49] Dalrymple, op. cit., pp. 17–22.

[50] In 1786 Hanna, on his return to the North-West in the *Sea Otter*, entered Fitzhugh Sound, which was about 50′ beyond the farthest reached by Dixon.

[51] Ibid., p. 17n.

was much wishful thinking in such deductions, but there was also that imaginative insight that produced such fruitful results. Dalrymple believed that his scheme, if practicable, would give Britain control of the fur-trade, but it required the discovery of extensive water communications, either through the continent, or around its northern coastline. If there was an element of truth behind the de Fonte legend, then there was the promise of such a communication. The fur-trading voyages to the North-West Coast had suggested that the legend was not entirely without foundation. Therefore there was much to be gained by making a thorough survey, to probe to the bottom the suggestion of an apparent connection, by way of rivers and lakes, with New England. However sanguine, there was wisdom, too, in Dalrymple's insistence that this whole problem should be thoroughly investigated, before the trade was irrevocably lost to the Americans and Russians – and with the trade, the possession of the north-west coast of America.

The story of the supposed voyage of Juan de Fuca was of older origin, having been first published by Purchas. It claimed that Michael Lok, once British consul at Aleppo, and an historic character, had met an elderly Greek pilot named de Fuca in Venice, in 1596. De Fuca had told Lok that in 1592 he had been sent by the Viceroy of Mexico to search for the supposed Strait of Anian. Having followed the western coast of America until he was between 47° N. and 48° N., he had found a broad inlet. Entering this inlet, he sailed 'more than twenty days, and found that land trending still sometime N.W. and N.E., and North, and also East and South Eastward, and very much broader sea than was at the said entrance, and that he passed by divers islands in that sailing. And that at the entrance of this said Strait, there is on the North West coast thereof, a great headland or island, with an exceeding high pinnacle, or spired rock, like a pillar thereupon'. On land were some people clad in skins. De Fuca, having reached the 'North Sea', had then returned to Acapulco. In reprinting this account, James Burney thought it inconceivable that the strait which actually exists in this latitude, and, apart from its width, so well corresponds with this account, should have been hit upon by chance in a description first published in 1625.[52] The exaggerations in the story could have originated through its not coming direct from de Fuca himself. Dalrymple was persuaded, by 1789, that de Fuca's Strait had been re-discovered, not only by the pillar spotted by Captain Duncan and appearing on Dalrymple's published version of the latter's chart, but by further news which he had received from his friend the Hon. C. F. Greville. This story had come from the retiring (temporary) Governor-General of India, Sir John Macpherson, who had been told at the Cape of Good Hope that the Spaniards had recently 'found an entrance in Lat. 47° 45′ N. which, in 27 days' course, brought them to the vicinity of Hudson's Bay'.[53]

The task now facing Dalrymple was to persuade the East India and Hudson's Bay Companies, as well as the Government, of the advantages of his plan, and having so persuaded them, to see that the necessary surveys were carried out on the North-West Coast, in the interior, and in Hudson's Bay. The coastal surveys were required in order to demonstrate without ambiguity the truth or falsity of the de Fuca and de Fonte legends. The Arathapescow Lake would be the centre of attention for the survey of the interior of Canada. The de Fonte story could be interpreted to suggest a waterway from the lake to the Pacific coast, while it appeared, from the Indian maps,[54] 'that the Arathapescow Lake communicates with Hudson's Bay; it is therefore highly expedient', wrote Dalrymple, 'to examine what

52 Burney, op. cit., Vol. II, London, 1806, pp. 110–15. *N.B.* that Burney had served under both Captains Cook and Hugh Dalrymple, one of Alexander's elder brothers.

53 Dalrymple, *Plan for the Fur-Trade*, p. 22.

54 In the Hudson's Bay Company's Collection Dalrymple found 'a very curious map . . . made by two Indians, describing the parts to the North-westward and Westward of Churchill: It describes Rivers, or Inlets, still unknown to Europeans, and makes some of them communicate with the Arathapescow Lake, from whence the River Kiscachewan runs Westward into the Sea; which is comformable to the Map of the Canadian Traders. . . . There is also a sketch of those parts, drawn from the Reports of the Indians, by Moses Norton, and brought by him to England in 1760; in which the River called Kish-stoch-ewen disembogues from a great Lake; but this is too rude a Sketch to form any inference of positions or direction'. Both maps, he added, implied that Hudson's Bay communicated with the Hyperborean Sea.

SECTION OF DALRYMPLE'S MAP OF THE LANDS AROUND THE NORTH POLE

obstructions there are to navigate thither; for the lake is reported by Mr Hearne to be about 400 miles long; the most effectual manner of making the examination would be from the Arathapescow Lake, which, by the observation of the Longitude at Hudson's House, appears to be much nearer Hudson's Bay than Mr Hearne's Map represents'.[55] More knowledge was required of Hudson's Bay for two reasons. Dalrymple's primary interest, in this context, was to investigate the supposed water-communication between Bay and Lake. 'Mr Hearne mentions that the Esquimauds [sic] winter at a very great Lake, called Yathked, situated to the SW of the Chesterfield Inlet,' he wrote, 'and it is not improbable they may be induced under the English influence to accompany some of our People across those Lakes and by those Rivers which the Indian Maps represent as connecting Hudson's Bay and the Arathapescow Lake.'[56] Secondly, Dalrymple was anxious to discover whether Middleton had been correct in believing that the northern end of Repulse Bay was closed by a continuous coast, or whether a passage might be found through it to the 'Hyperborean Sea'.[57]

At the moment when his plan was published, a beginning had already been made in surveying the interior of Canada, for in May 1789 Philip Turnor departed from London, bound for the Athabaska country, where his main task, it seems clear, was to determine the exact position of 'Lake Arathapescow', and the best way of reaching it. After spending the winter of 1789 at Cumberland House, and that of 1790 at Ile à la Crosse, on 30 May 1791, exactly two years after he had sailed from London, he was again on the move, and two days later was camping on the shores of Buffalo Lake in the company of Alexander Mackenzie.

Mackenzie himself had spent the winter of 1787–8 with Peter Pond, and he had been much influenced by Pond's notions of the need to find a route to the Pacific in order to forestall the Russians and the Americans in the exploitation of

[55] Dalrymple, *Fur Trade Plan*, p. 32.

[56] P.R.O., *C.O. 42/72*, f. 249, 2 February 1790.

[57] Dalrymple, *Memoir of a Map of the Lands around the North Pole*, pp. 13–14.

the fur-trade. Pond had come to believe that a river flowed south-westwards from Great Slave Lake to the Pacific, perhaps to Cook's river. Three years later, Pond was to tell Isaak Ogden in Quebec how three Indians had arrived at Athabaska, in 1787, and had told him how they had come up a river from the north Pacific Ocean all the way to Slave Lake, carrying a blanket which they had received from ships which were at the mouth of the river.[58] It was in order to test Pond's new theory that Mackenzie had carried out his great exploration of the Mackenzie River in 1789, which had proved that it really flowed into the Arctic, and not into the Pacific as had been hoped. Turnor and Mackenzie had already met twice at Cumberland House in the summer of 1790, and the former had relayed to London an account of this exploration, so that by the end of the year the main details were known to Dalrymple. Thus Daines Barrington was soon telling Dr Douglas how Dalrymple had told him 'that Mackenzy found Cook's River to turn N: instead of the W: and that he hath proceeded to 70 degrees'.[59]

When Turnor and Mackenzie met beside the waters of Buffalo Lake, the latter was on his way to England to spend a winter's leave (1791–2) in London learning the arts of navigation. During this stay in London there does not appear to be any record of his meeting Alexander Dalrymple, though it is most unlikely that the latter would have missed such an opportunity. Whether they met or not, however, it is inconceivable that Mackenzie, after three meetings with Turnor, and his subsequent winter in London, should have been unaware of Dalrymple's fur-trade plan. It is highly probable, therefore, that his own scheme was inspired by that of his fellow-Scot. It was, indeed, soon after his return to Canada that the first suggestion of Mackenzie's plan was reaching London. Mackenzie had travelled up the Peace River in 1792, and the Lieutenant-Governor of Upper Canada was reporting that the explorer 'describes the communication between Upper Canada and this Pacific Ocean to be practicable . . . the height of the land between

58 P.R.O., *C.O. 42/72*, f. 245, David Ogden to Nepean, 23 January 1790.
59 Williams, op. cit., p. 235, quoting *Eg. Mss.* 2186, f. 18.

the Peace River which he ascended to its source and branches of the great River which he supposes to be the River of the West, not being more than 700 yards . . . it appears from the observations of Mr Mackenzie who seems to be as intelligent as he is adventurous, That to carry on this Commerce to National Advantages, the privileges and rivalship, the claims and monopoly of great Commercial Companies must be reconciled and blended in one common interest. His observations on this head which particularly attracted my attention were that the most practical Rout to the Northwest was through the territories of the Hudson's Bay Company. . .'.[60] This plan, in more developed form, was again brought to the notice of the Government when Mackenzie returned to London for the publication of his book in 1801, but was not pursued. In contrast to Dalrymple, Mackenzie was naturally sympathetic towards the Canadian traders. Dalrymple not only feared that if they reached the Pacific first they might join with the Americans and break with Britain, which employees of the Hudson's Bay Company would never do, but he also argued that their long and difficult routes made it impossible for them to carry British exports, so that weapons, ammunition and 'Proof Spirits to the destruction of the Indian' would be their only means of buying furs. To Mackenzie, their expert knowledge of living and travelling with the Indians was an essential element of his scheme, which envisaged 'a union, a pooling of interests, of the great commercial organisations operating under the British flag – the North-West and X.Y. Companies, the Hudson's Bay Company, the East India Company and the South Sea Company'.[61]

As a result of the discoveries on the North-West Coast and of Dalrymple's powerful advocacy, together with pressure from the pioneers of the Southern Whale Fishery, who were anxious

[60] A. S. Morton, *A History of the Canadian West to 1870–71*, London etc., 1939, pp. 419–20.

[61] Wade, op. cit., p. 264. For the Plan itself, see Ibid. Appendix II, pp. 314–17.

Dalrymple suggested that the Canadian Traders seemed 'scarcely less savage than the most savage of the Indians' (*Plan*, p. 31n); of Pond he remarked, 'He also pretends to the Sovereignty of the Lands adjacent to Arathapescow Lake, so that by encouraging him we may be fostering a Viper in our bosom'. (*C.O 42/72*, f. 249.)

for a permanent depot for their vessels in the South Pacific, the Government purchased a new ship in the autumn of 1789, which was named the *Discovery* in memory of Captain Cook, and of which Captain Henry Roberts was to have the command, with George Vancouver serving under him. The object of this new expedition was to find a suitable base for the whalers in the South Pacific, and then to survey the north-west coast of America.[62]

In the summer of 1789, before this action had been taken by the Government, George Dixon had been in conference with Dalrymple, and had afterwards written to Evan Nepean, the Under-Secretary for Foreign Affairs, to report that it was Dalrymple's opinion 'that a ship should be sent by Government as soon as possible round Cape Horn, and a Settlement made on the other side; and from thence the Journey should be taken. His Reasons for this are the Russians having got full possession of Cook's River, Prince William Sound; and he makes no Doubt but they will soon have Settlements to the Southward, as they are in possession of all the Information Mr Etches is enabled to give, who is at Petersburg on that Business at this present Time. The Americans last year had a ship on the Coast. . . . Two were under Portuguese colours, and I am told of one Swedish to say nothing of the Spaniards who we are sure are extending their Settlements Northwards. Upon the whole I am afraid if something is not done and that immediately this Valuable Branch of Commerce will be lost to this Country and in Consequence of that Loss the Traders from Hudson's Bay and Canada will find themselves in a bad Neighbourhood'.[63]

Now that preparations were going ahead, Dalrymple himself drew up a Memorial. After asserting that the present object of discovery was de Fuca's Strait in 48½° N., he went on to discuss the whole question of a North-West Passage of whose location 'The antient idea was by the Hyperborean Sea on the N° of America; altho' I am very far from meaning any

[62] Harlow, op. cit., Vol. II, pp. 438–9. For an account of the development of this whaling enterprise, see Ibid., pp. 293–328.

[63] P.R.O., *C.O. 42/72*, f. 243, Captain Dixon to Evan Nepean, 14 July 1789.

imputation on Captain Cook's memory or Abilities, I cannot admit of a Pope in Geography or Navigation'. He pointed out that the distribution of the eskimos was a significant pointer towards 'a Sea-Communication, navigable for their Boats, from Labrador and Greenland to the utmost extremity of America and Its Islands', since it was indisputable that they were confined to the sea-coasts and their immediate vicinity, and their presence had been alleged both on the west coasts and on the most remote northern coasts. 'Whether this Sea-Communication is navigable for more than Boats is a matter well worth examining.' He pointed out how the earliest maps, which had distinctly shown Hudson's Bay before its discovery by Hudson himself (though showing it much too small), had also shown a channel joining 'the NW part of that Sea, which corresponds to Repulse Bay, with the Hyperborean Ocean'. This agreed with all the Indian maps, that showed a sea-coast from Churchill, or Hudson's Bay, to the Copper River. It was not to be thought that the ice barrier which had stopped Captain Cook in Bering's Strait was an insuperable object to the existence of a navigable North-West Passage. Meares had suggested that a passage existed from Cross Sound to the 'Hyperborean Sea', an opinion founded on the fact that during his hard winter in Prince William's Sound he had found no 'High Islands of Ice' such as had been seen farther south in Cross Sound, and it seemed reasonable to assume that the latter had floated down from the north. Furthermore, Dalrymple argued that large formations of ice were most likely to appear where there were 'multitudes of drifts', which was the case off Northern Asia, where there were 'many great Rivers disemboguing into that Sea'. It was probable that the ice which had stopped Captain Cook had drifted from the coast of Northern Asia. But off North America, eastwards of the meridian of Cross Sound, Hearne's journey to the Coppermine River had revealed a land destitute of timber and lacking large rivers. Moreover, there was no reason to believe that this coast was anywhere farther north than 70° N., whereas the sea at Spitzbergen was known to be navigable as far as 80° N. And as he wrote, Dalrymple must have had at the back of his mind the reported opinion of Peter Pond that had Cook reached Bering's

Strait a month later, he would have found no barrier of ice. Isaak Ogden believed that by mid-September the seas from Bering's Strait around North America to the North Atlantic were free of ice.[64]

Dalrymple then turned to the land route which would need to be examined, in case the navigation westwards by the north of Hudson's Bay was impracticable. According to the Canadian traders, the distance from Quebec to the Great Slave Lake by way of Lake Superior was 5,250 miles, and however much this might be exaggerated the route by way of Hudson's Bay would be much shorter.

Finally, he suggested that 'the most eligible mode of promoting the Enterprise would be by sending one vessel round Cape Horn without delay and another to Hudson's Bay'.[65]

This was an imaginative plan for further discovery, made in accordance with the best knowledge of the time, which did not ignore, as has sometimes been suggested, the discoveries already made. But like all plans of action devised in time of urgency, it minimised the doubts and difficulties, and exaggerated the hopeful auguries; there would always be doubters at hand to voice objections.

It was during the preparations for this voyage that the Nootka Sound crisis broke. It had been intended that the *Discovery* should sail in March 1790, calling at Port Jackson, New South Wales, en route, where reinforcements would be picked up so that a settlement could be established on the North-West Coast.[66] In January, however, the first news of the arrest of a British ship at Nootka Sound by the Spaniards had been received, and when John Meares returned to England in April, with his own dramatic and partisan account of the affair, it was realised that the country was faced with a diplomatic crisis of major proportions, so the expedition was cancelled.

It appeared that in May 1789 the *Princessa*, a Spanish warship commanded by Don Estaban Martinez, had anchored in Nootka Sound, the first sign that the Spaniards intended to

64 P.R.O., *C.O. 42/72*, f. 245, D. Ogden to Nepean, 23 January 1790.
65 P.R.O., *C.O. 42/72*, f. 249, Dalrymple to Nepean, 2 February 1790.
66 Harlow, op. cit., Vol. II, pp. 439–40.

respond to Russian and British initiative on this coast by moving in to control what they considered to be Spanish waters. Two American ships, the *Columbia* and the *Washington*, which had wintered in the Sound, were left unmolested. Two British ships (one under Portuguese colours) were turned away, however, and when the *North-West American* appeared, also under Portuguese colours, she was seized and her crew were made prisoners. In July 1789 the *Argonaut* (Captain Colnett) arrived, as well as the *Princess Royal*, and Martinez took the rash decision of arresting Captain Colnett and his crew, and of sending the *Argonaut*, the *Princess Royal* and the *North-West American* to San Blas. Meanwhile, Martinez claimed the whole coastline as far as 60° N. as a Spanish possession.

A fierce diplomatic struggle now ensued, and a majority of the British Cabinet came to believe that war was inevitable. To Dalrymple the crisis must have been a cruel disappointment, threatening to undo all his efforts to initiate exploratory work in North America at the very moment of apparent success. Towards Meares, a central figure in the crisis, his feelings must have been mixed. He would have disliked Meares' opposition to the East India Company's monopoly, and Dixon had doubtless related many uncomplimentary things about this adventurer; on the other hand, Meares' warm support for his own ideas on a North-West Passage cannot have been unwelcome.[67] As the crisis developed, and anti-Spanish sentiment grew, Dalrymple published two pamphlets, wherein he sought to defend his own country's rights, while discouraging a resort to war; they were not the inflammatory writings that some have represented them to be.[68]

67 J. Meares, *Voyages . . .*, pp. xlv et seq. Dalrymple was kept well informed of Meares' statements on his return to England, for on the 12 March 1791 he wrote to Dundas as follows:

'Mr Dalrymple begs to caution Mr Dundas not to mention anything to indicate that Mr Dalrymple knew the particulars of the Examination of Lieut. Meares before the Privy Council; and in copying the Paper concerning the China Trade if there is any thing to that Effect Mr Dundas will be so good to omit that part if he means to communicate the Paper to any other Persons'. – Nat. Lbry. of Australia, Canberra, *MS. 43/7*.

68 His first pamphlet, 'The Spanish Pretensions Fairly Discussed' (11 May 1790), emphasized his devout desire for peace and his 'individual Experience

By 5 August 1790 it was clear that war had been averted, and on 28 October an Anglo-Spanish Convention was signed, which acknowledged that both British and Spanish subjects could trade and form establishments anywhere on the coast to the north of the Spanish settlements. The Spaniards also agreed to restore 'the buildings and tracts of land on the North-west coast of which British subjects had been dispossessed' in April 1789. It was therefore necessary to send a British representative to receive them in due form, and this allowed for the resumption of the plan to explore this coast. Thus, once more, the *Discovery* was prepared for her voyage, this time under the command of Captain Vancouver, who received his orders on 8 March 1791.

---

of the Liberality and Generosity of the Spaniards', which convinced him that the 'Good Faith and Honour of the Spanish Nation' would incline them, on conviction, to make full satisfaction for the indignities and losses suffered by the British. Then, after the Spanish Foreign Minister, Count Florida Blanca, had set out Spain's case in its most comprehensive form, claiming the west coast of America as far north as the Russian settlements, Dalrymple issued his second pamphlet, 'The Spanish Memorial of the 4 June Considered' (1 August 1790). He argued that the Spaniards were claiming more than they were entitled to for at a time when their own historian, Herrera, showed that they had not navigated farther than 44° N. on that coast, Drake had reached 48° N., and maps, from the Arcano del Mare and Le Clerc's map of 1602 down to those by De Lisle (1700) and Vaugondy (1750), had named this area 'New Albion'. Secret voyages could not be the basis for any claims, and the first authentic account of a Spanish voyage to the North-West Coast was that of 1775; but even then their explorations were concentrated on the coast between 55° N. and 58° N., and omitted the coast between 48° N. and 55° N. It was Captain Cook who had first described Nootka in 49½° N. War was wrong, for multitudes would be killed and 'calamities worse than death' would ensue. 'It would be extremely mortifying to suppose that the Ignorance, Arrogance or Insolence of Officers of either Government had involved the two Countries, frantickly into Hostilities, contrary to their mutual Interests and subversive to the Principles of Humanity.' The first British vessels had openly left England for the North-West Coast in 1785, and if Spain had then thought that she had a claim to the exclusive navigation of those seas she ought 'to have urged such claims amicably to the Court of Great Britain, and to have communicated Her intentions to enforce them, before Orders were sent to that Effect'. The extent of Spanish claims was vague; there could be no rightful dominion where there was no jurisdictive authority. To remind the Spaniards of their vulnerability in South America, he pointed out that their own intervention in the American War of Independence had established the doctrine 'that whenever Subjects have taken up arms, avow and are able to maintain their Independence, that then their actual Independence is to be acknowledged by all Nations!'

The coast between 30° N. and 60° N. was to be surveyed and a careful search made for any water-communication which would be of commercial value in opening a trade 'between the North-west Coast and the Countries upon the opposite side of that Continent' inhabited or occupied by the British.[69] It appears that Sir Joseph Banks was closely concerned in the planning of this expedition,[70] and it can be accepted as certain that in this he would have consulted Dalrymple.

Meanwhile, the Nootka Sound crisis had not delayed action in Hudson's Bay where, as a direct result of a request by Dalrymple, Charles Duncan was to be put in charge.[71] He was instructed, firstly, to seek for any possible water communication from Hudson's Bay to Yathked Lake, but if such could not be found he was then to proceed up the Chesterfield Inlet, find his way overland to the Yathked and Dobaunt Lakes, and then explore the land between these lakes and Hudson's Bay. With him was to go George Dixon,[72] and the plan was for Dixon to be landed, at Yathked Lake if possible, and to discover an overland passage from there to the Pacific, via Hearne's Arathapescow Lake (still believed to be Athabaska, instead of the Great Slave Lake)[73] and Pond's Slave Lake. Duncan left the Orkneys on this mission in May 1790, but when he arrived in the Bay, where the sloop which he was to command was already stationed, he found it unfit for the task and had to return to England in the autumn.

In 1791 he was fitted out from London in the Company's brig, the *Beaver*, and he was instructed 'to explore Corbet's Inlet, the only place to the southward of Marble Island which had not been explored; whence he was to proceed to the Chesterfield and, by means of his boats or by land, he was to survey the river which falls into the lake, at the head of it; which Norton had before examined, a few miles to the westward, in 1768, and found impassable'. When he arived at Corbet's Inlet, he soon found that it terminated in a bay, and that

69 Harlow, op. cit., II, pp. 419–81.

70 Ibid., p. 473n.

71 Williams, op. cit., II, p. 240.

72 Ibid., pp. 240, 242. This was a revival of Dixon's earlier suggestion to Banks for an overland crossing, though by a different route.

73 Williams, op. cit., II, p. 242.

the river flowing into it was navigable only for canoes. After wintering at Churchill, he proceeded to Chesterfield Inlet, where he left the brig in Lake's Harbour, and went on by boat to Norton's Falls. He then followed the river, on land, for some thirty miles, but finding that it came from the northward he was convinced that it could not be an outlet from the Dobaunt, and that to follow it farther could lead to no useful discovery.[74]

Duncan is said to have been so deeply disappointed and overwrought by his experiences that he tried to commit suicide on the return voyage.[75] Nevertheless, he still retained his faith in the essential authenticity of de Fonte's account, but suggested that the route had become impracticable at the present time because of the rising of the land in Hudson's Bay, where it was known that the sea, on the west coast, had retired considerably since settlements were first established there, the Indians declaring that at Churchill 'canoes have passed within their remembrance over rocks, where the highest tides do not flow at present by several feet'.[76]

Vancouver returned to England at the end of his voyage in the autumn of 1795. His arduous survey was an achievement of the highest order, but it had taken its toll of his health, and during the voyage his men had noticed an increasing tendency towards violent bursts of temper over apparently trivial incidents. He survived the voyage by only three years, and his biographer has suggested that he was suffering from a hyperthyroid condition known as Grave's disease, which would cause irritability and unexpected loss of temper.[77] Certain it is that a pronounced antipathy had developed between Sir Joseph Banks and Vancouver, and it seems probable that Dalrymple was caught up in this quarrel before ever the voyage started. This background may help to explain the animosity displayed in Vancouver's own account of the non-existence of a North-West Passage.

[74] W. Godson, *Observations on the Passage between the Atlantic and Pacific Oceans . . .*, Portsmouth, 1793, pp. 53–4. Godson claimed to have spoken personally with Duncan.

[75] Williams, op. cit., p. 248.

[76] Godson, op. cit., p. 248.

[77] B. Anderson, *Surveyor of the Sea. The life and voyages of Geo. Vancouver*, University of Washington Press, Seatle, 1960, pp. 66–7.

'These ideas,' he wrote, without any justification, '. . . have, it is much to be feared, been adopted for the sole purpose of giving unlimited credit to the traditionary exploits of ancient foreigners and to undervalue the laborious and enterprising exertions of our own countrymen in the noble science of discovery.' Treating the 'concurring opinions of modern traders' with withering contempt, he suggested that 'should any opening further to the Northward be discovered leading to a North-West Passage, the merit of such discovery will necessarily be ascribed to de Fuca, de Fonte, or some other favourite voyager of these closet philosophers'.[78]

Vancouver rightly concluded that his voyage had shown that a North West Passage could not exist within the limits of his survey, in just the same way that the 'indefatigable diligence of Captain Cook [had] completely subverted [the hypothesis] which gave as a counterpoise to the globe a southern continent'. Had not ill-health warped his judgement and drained his nature of magnanimity, he might have reflected that the voyages which brought undying fame to Cook and himself, and benefited their country, as well as the future dominions of Australia, New Zealand and Canada, beyond measure, would in all probability never have materialized but for the indefatigable and selfless labours of Alexander Dalrymple, the foremost of his so-called 'closet philosophers'.

[78] *Naval Chronicle,* Vol. 1, London, 1799, pp. 403 et seq.

CHAPTER IX

The Hydrographer

As a result of the five years which he had spent among the Eastern Islands, sometimes sailing in waters never before navigated by English vessels, and all the time in seas made dangerous by numerous but unknown reefs and currents, Alexander Dalrymple had been impressed by the urgent need for accurate charts.

In an earlier age the Dutch had done good work in this field, yet they had always been secretive lest competitors should benefit from their work, and in the eighteenth century their East India Company was in decline. Thus Captain Stavorinus, himself a Dutchman, when writing about a voyage to the East Indies in the 1770s, described his charts as being 'extremely defective'. With regard to the cartography of the seas to the eastwards of Batavia, he noted that 'none of the islands which I met with, except the group called the Hen and Chickens, are laid down in their true latitudes.... This inaccuracy not only renders these charts useless, but likewise extremely dangerous.... It is not impossible, but this may be purposely left so, and that it is an adopted opinion, that it is better to expose a few ships to the danger of shipwreck, than to correct errors which might operate to render the navigation towards the Spice Islands difficult and hazardous for other nations; for it cannot be pretended that this notorious faultiness is unknown to the Company...'.[1]

It was the French who gave a lead in providing more reliable charts. In 1720 the French Government had established the Depôt des Cartes et Plans de la Marine, and in 1745 D'Après de Mannevillette, himself an experienced sea-captain, published the first edition of his great *Neptune Oriental*. As a Swedish seaman,

[1] J. S. Stavorinus, trans. by S. H. Wilcocke, *A Voyage to the East Indies*, 3 Vols., London, 1798, Vol. II, p. 168.

Captain Carl G. Ekeburg, remarked, 'One would think, that the way to the East Indies, which most European nations so long have been [sic], ought to be well known; [yet] new discoveries are still frequently made.... Old imperfect Portuguese and Dutch manuscripts – (many of the old Dutch charts were drawn on parchment) – and sea charts, with English and Dutch pilot-books, were for a long time the guides of navigators. He who had once gone his way, or had a log-book, steered exactly the course therein prescribed, without troubling himself with new trials; until Captain D'Après de Mannevillette ... made this way better known by his ... Neptune Oriental'.[2] A warm friendship and sense of mutual esteem developed between D'Après and Dalrymple, and when the Frenchman died the latter expressed the opinion that 'In the enlightened Ages of Modern Times there has scarcely been one Hydrographer, deserving the appellation, but D'Après.'[3]

The English were backward in this field, and according to an early authority their main reliance for charts of the Eastern Seas, between *c.* 1675–1745, depended upon the *Old English Waggoner*, Seller's *English Pilot* and Captain Cornwall's *Collection*.[4] These Collections were wholly inadequate. The *Old Waggoner* got its name from the sea-atlases published by L. J. Waghenaer, the Dutch hydrographer, whose first edition of 1584 was followed by an English one, entitled *The Mariner's Mirrour*, in 1588. Seller's *English Pilot* had been taken over by John Thornton, the nearest approach to an official hydrographer that the East India Company possessed at the beginning of the eighteenth century, and from 1784 onwards it was being published by Messrs. Mount and Page. Its third book dealt with oriental navigation, and this was referred to in scurrilous fashion by a writer who stated that anyone comparing it with D'Après' *Neptune Oriental* would 'have a despicable opinion of our Indian Pilot, with which Messrs Mount and Page have long imposed on, and picked the pockets of, our Countrymen, and which are only fit for the Grocers and Chandlers Shops, or

[2] *United Service Journal*, Part 1, London, 1829, p. 346.

[3] A. Dalrymple, *General Collection of Nautical Publications*, London, 1783, p. 5.

[4] *United Service Journal*, ut supra.

posterior uses'.[5] Writing in 1772, Dalrymple mentioned that the only printed collections of East Indian charts with which he was familiar were 'the English Wagoner . . . Van Keulen . . . [and] the Neptune Oriental'.[6] Even the famous *Sailing Directions*, first issued by William Herbert in 1759, were originally in large part an English version of those issued by D'Après to go with his charts. Thus, during the first half of the eighteenth century the English contribution to the hydrography of eastern waters had been slight, and this was only to be rectified with the advent of Alexander Dalrymple.

During his youthful years in the Far East, the latter was already acquiring a reputation for being an eager collector of valuable navigational lore, and he received help not only from his own countrymen, but also from foreigners who were impressed by his zeal and ability. In this connection, he himself expressed gratitude for the generous help extended by Don Manuel Galves,[7] the Spanish Governor of Samboangan, and by the Swedish Captain Olbers.[8]

When Dalrymple reached England in July 1765, he found that the time was not favourable for pressing his Sulu enterprise. He was already hard at work on preparing his Collection of Voyages for publication, and was hoping that he might be employed on an expedition to the Pacific, but this did not bring his hydrographic labours to a standstill. On 31 March 1766 he informed the Directors of the East India Company that he hoped, in due course, to reduce to a general scale the 'large number of Charts of various parts of India' which he had collected. He therefore asked their permission to copy those

[5] C. F. Noble, *The French and English Marine Regulations Compared*, 1755, p. 3.

[6] A. Dalrymple, *Collection of Charts and Memoirs . . .*, London, 1772, p. xii. Jan Van Keulen published sea-atlases in Amsterdam in the last two decades of the seventeenth century, and the firm continued to operate throughout the eighteenth century.

[7] On his return to Madras, Dalrymple gave the copy of Correa's account of Luzon, which he had obtained from Galves, to his friend Sir Hyde Parker, then a captain in command of HMS *Grafton*. Before the latter left England in 1782, on his last fatal voyage in HMS *Cato*, he gave a translation of this document to Dalrymple, who published it in 1789, the year when Spain joined France against Britain in the American War.

[8] For details, see *United Service Journal*, Part 1, p. 348.

charts in their possession which could help in this undertaking.[9]

It was in the course of the year 1766 that Dalrymple went on board the *Nottingham* East-Indiaman to bid farewell to his friend Thomas Howe, who was off on another voyage to India. On the way down river they were joined, off Gravesend, by Thomas's brother, Lord Howe. 'It was observed, in conversation,' wrote Dalrymple, 'what a loss and shame it was, that there should be no Hydrographical Office established in this Country.' Thomas Howe asked his friend if such a post would appeal to him, and the latter replied that it would, if he did not return to India. Some time later, Lord Howe met Dalrymple and told him that as a result of this conversation he had urged Lord Egmont, the First Lord of the Admiralty, to establish such an office, mentioning that he had in mind a most suitable person whom he would name if the post were established. Lord Egmont backed the idea, and with the King's approval it was agreed to assign £500 p.a. for the purpose. Dalrymple mentioned this 'to a person in the Royal Navy, now dead, he immediately went to Lord Egmont, and got his Lordship's promise in his own behalf. However, the appointment did not then take place'.[10]

The first set of charts which Dalrymple published in 1772 included two of the China Sea, and four of the seas around Sulu and Balambangan. The latter waters, in particular, were almost unknown to European shipping. William Herbert's *Sailing Directions* contained no detail of them, nor were they included in the *Neptune Oriental*, and when Dalrymple sent a set of these charts to D'Après, complete with a dedication expressing his warm esteem, the Frenchman immediately incorporated the whole set in the new edition of his book, which was just about to be issued. Dalrymple also published a collection of memoirs to accompany these charts, as well as the first edition of his *Essay on Marine Surveying*, which was the pioneer work in English on this subject.

Another important publication of this year was his chart

[9] I.O. Lbry., *Miscellaneous Letters Received*, Vol. 48, f. 32. Dalrymple commonly included the whole of the East Indies in the term 'India', employing 'Hindostan' to describe the sub-continent itself.

[10] *European Magazine*, Vol. 42, London, 1802, pp. 324–5.

of the Bay of Bengal, and as he himself observed, it was an extraordinary circumstance, in view of the long period over which Europeans had traded with Bengal, that this was the first 'particular chart of the Bay . . . published in any language'. It was based on an original chart constructed in 1765 by Thomas Howe, who had asked Dalrymple to try to improve it by utilizing the materials which he had collected. Finding a discrepancy in the various latitudes given, Dalrymple had hesitated to have the chart engraved. However, after going over some Journals with a Captain William Smith, he laid down many soundings in the Bay, and gave copies of the chart to several persons, including two captains about to sail for India who, on their return to England in 1771, 'testified their highest appreciation' of its merits. During Thomas Howe's last illness, Dalrymple discussed the chart with him in the light of a new survey which Captain Richie had recently completed of the Bay, and Howe strongly recommended that it should be published, with a special note to give warning that the latitudes were uncertain. The Chairman of the East India Company supported Howe's pleas and promised that the Company would defray the cost. Dalrymple therefore revised and published his chart in the light of Richie's survey,[11] and he later had the satisfaction of knowing that it had been 'the occasion of saving the *Hawke* Indiaman from the French in the war'.[12] Dalrymple had also intended to accompany it 'with some Nautical Instructions and Observations, but', he had added, 'I am not yet master enough of the subject to attempt anything of this Nature . . . and although all plain matters of fact are useful, ill grounded deductions may be very prejudicial'.[13]

Encouraged by the response to this initial effort, he now began to work on a more ambitious scale, and in 1774 the list of subscribers for his forthcoming *Collection of Plans of Ports in the East Indies* included not only old personal friends like Robert Orme and Claud Russell, but senior naval officers, namely

[11] A. Dalrymple, *Memoir of a chart of the Bay of Bengal*, London, 1772.

[12] J. Nichols, *Literary Anecdotes of the Eighteenth Century*, Vol. VIII, London, 1814, p. 35.

[13] Dalrymple, *Memoir of a Chart of the Bay of Bengal*, ut supra.

Viscount Howe and Lord Mulgrave. It was natural that the East India Company should make a contribution, but it is more surprising to find the Earl of Bute on the list. With this backing, the first six numbers had appeared by the beginning of 1775, containing seventy-eight plans and many views from unpublished manuscripts.

This work was interrupted by Dalrymple's return to Madras as a Member of Council under Lord Pigot. He departed for India in April 1775,[14] in company with Lord Pigot and Claud Russell on board the *Grenville* East Indiaman, and since they began their nine-month voyage at almost the same time that Captain Cook arrived at Cape Town towards the close of his second circumnavigation, the track of the outward-bound India-man passed not far distant from that of the returning *Resolution.*

It was characteristic that Dalrymple made full use of this outward voyage to keep a detailed log of the *Grenville*'s progress, with separate columns to record the date, the thermometer and barometer readings, the weather and winds, the latitude and longitude, the 'Magnetic Variation and Remarks'.[15] In keeping a daily record of the thermometer readings, he may have had in mind the following passage in the account of Anson's circumnavigation: 'I cannot help wishing.' Walter had written, very possibly at Anson's behest, 'that all ships bound to the Warmer climates would furnish themselves with thermometers of a known fabric, and would observe them daily, and register their observations . . . it is incredible how very rarely anything of the kind hath been attended to . . . I do not recollect that I have ever seen any observations of the heat and cold, either in the East or West Indies, which were made by mariners . . . except those made by Mr Anson's order . . .'[16]

After the arrest of Lord Pigot by the dissident majority of his

[14] One of his last acts before leaving England was to send Franklin a letter of recommendation for an emigrant engraver, dated 17 April 1775.

[15] The log, which was sent back to the Hon. Henry Cavendish, who presented it to the Royal Society, is to be found in *Royal Society Letters and Papers*, Decade VII, Vol. 61, 8 January – 2 April 1778. For Dalrymple's 'Observations of the Dip of the Magnetic Needle made in a Voyage to Madras', see R.S. Lbry., *Miscellaneous Manuscripts*, Vol. 10, f. 9.

[16] R. Walter, *A Voyage Round the World in the Years 1740–44 by George Anson*, London, 1748, p. 184.

Council in the summer of 1776, it was Alexander Dalrymple who was chosen to return to England with Pigot's narrative of the course of events. The situation being critical, the utmost despatch was called for, and it was decided that the party should travel in the *Swallow* to the Red Sea, then overland to Alexandria and so back to England. This use of the Red Sea route was new, for Warren Hastings, as Governor-General, was the first to consider it as a means of rapid communication with Britain, in addition to being an important area for trade. In 1775 he had sent agents to Cairo to start the necessary negotiations.[17] Because of its novelty, Dalrymple realized the importance of discovering all that he could about this route, and the result was to be seen in his pamphlet 'Correspondence with India via Suez'.[18]

The repercussions of Pigot's imprisonment upon the personal career of Dalrymple were of great significance. Like other members of the minority in the Council who had supported the Governor, he was exonerated, while four members of the majority were recalled to England to stand trial, and were fined £1,000 each. The fact remained, however, that for the time being it would be impossible for him to return to Madras. He therefore decided to devote his whole time to hydrography. It

[17] H. L. Hoskins, *British Routes to India*, London, 1928, p. 7 et seq. See also his article 'The growth of British Interest in the Route to India' in *Journal of Indian History*, Vol. 2 (1922–3), pp. 165–77.

For a graphic contemporary account of this route, written by another supporter of Pigot, see Eyles Irwin, *A Series of Adventures in the Course of a Voyage up the Red Sea*, Dublin, 1780.

[18] I.O. Lbry., *Orme Mss.*, Vol. 88 : 11.

N.B. that George Baldwin, British agent in Cairo, had no chart of 'the Navigation of the Red Sea from Judda to Suez unfrequented by European navigators . . .' – B.M. *Add Mss.* 29,210, f. 422, 28 March 1776.

Dalrymple estimated that a message sent by ship and courier dispatch could reach Suez from Bengal in forty days, and continuing on its way via Alexandria and Trieste or Venice, would arrive in England within eighty-eight days, and might possibly take only seven weeks. Political difficulties, however, intervened, for the Porte was hostile to a scheme which promised to benefit only the local Beys. Certainly the East India Company was interested, and on 19 May 1786 the Chairman was informing the Court of Directors that it was the Government's intention 'to negotiate for opening the communication with India by way of Suez'. It was to take Napoleon's invasion of Egypt in 1798, however, to shock the British into taking decisive action to open this route.

was not his intention to forego all future claims to a post on the Madras establishment, for that would involve too great a financial sacrifice. Yet that is what did in fact happen, and he was never again to leave England for the East. It was entirely understandable that he should resent the lucrative promotions which were accorded to men who were his juniors. Even more did he resent the lavish rewards bestowed upon the heroes of the moment by a grateful Court of directors, while his own unremitting labours during the course of a long working life were taken for granted and given little recognition.[19] Yet it may well be that this enforced sacrifice and removal from the sphere of executive power enabled him to play a more significant part in the Company's affairs than would otherwise have been possible.

It was the news of the loss of the *Colebrooke* East-Indiaman on the Anvil Rock near the Cape of Good Hope which determined Dalrymple to renew his application to become Hydrographer to the Company. Therefore he submitted a Memorial on this subject on 28 January 1779, wherein he stressed that at present there was not 'in any language ... a tolerable set of charts for all parts of this very important Navigation (to India)', and that much needed to be done to complete the work so ably begun by D'Après. The Journals at the India House constituted 'a noble repository of nautical knowledge'; what was needed was an examination of 'all the Journals, from the earliest times to the present ... a work of infinite labour', which would enable good charts to be constructed. To underline the potential value of such work, he pointed out that the *Colebrooke* had been lost on the very rock on which the *Caesar* had struck on 25 February 1745, as well as the French ship *Mergé* at a later date, and that this misfortune would not have happened if information had been available to Captain Morris. This was a compelling argument for, as Sir George Wombwell, the Chairman, pointed out, 'the loss of the *Cole-*

[19] *European Magazine*, Vol. 42, p. *327, wherein he pointed out that his own pension of £500 p.a. was 'much less than what the Company have granted to military men, viz.

To General Sloper £1,500 per annum; Dalling £1,000; Lang £1,000; Nelson £1,000'.

brooke was more than the Expense of such an office to all Eternity'. The Committee of Correspondence considered this Memorial on 3 February 1779, and decided to employ Dalrymple in the position.[20]

When, at the year's end, Dalrymple applied to have the post put on a permanent basis, he submitted a report which shows the vast scope of the work he had undertaken. He stated that he had already examined 1,187 Journals, from which extracts had been made to show all the lands seen in the outward and homeward voyages, and all the dangers which had been recorded.[21]

That East India captains felt the need for this sort of work can be gauged from the remarks of Captain Thomas Forrest, who had more than a quarter of a century's experience to draw

[20] A. Dalrymple, *Collection of Plans, Ports . . . in the Indian Navigation*, London, 1783, Introduction and pp. 7 et seq.

See also *Memoranda of the Committee of Correspondence*, Vol. 27, entries for 3 February 25 February and 1 April 1779.

At first Dalrymple was to be employed on a probationary basis for one year, after which it was hoped that the evidence of what had already been accomplished would persuade the General Court of Proprietors to authorize his appointment on a 'much more liberal Establishment'. The scope of his work was defined as 'examining the Ships' Journals from the earliest times, that Notice may be given of every danger which has hitherto been discovered, and for publishing from time to time such Charts and Nautical Instructions as a Comparison of the various Journals and other Materials may enable him to do'. His salary was to be £500 p.a. and it was agreed that after the Company had received the first one hundred impressions of each plate, and the same number of all such printed instructions as he might prepare, the plates and publications would then become his personal property.

[21] See *Memoranda,* ut supra, entry for 7 June 1780, and *Miscellaneous Letters Received,* Vol. 66, f. 232, 20 May 1780. He had made a record of the times taken by ships to move from place to place at all seasons. He had also set down the winds reported for each day, showing not only their direction but also their velocity 'by means of the greatest and least distance run in an hour'. He had prepared twenty plans of ports and harbours in the East Indies, and '15 Plates of Views of Lands, which are intended as part of a complete series of all the Lands in the course of the Voyages of the Company's ships to and from India'. He had also collected the Journals of the various ships using the Mozambique Channel with the intention of making a chart of that passage. For this he would first have to draw up over one hundred plans, and from these he would then be able to draw one, comprehending the information of the whole. Later he meant to do the same for every other quarter 'by laying down the track of each ship, which has had soundings for any considerable extent'.

upon, including 'eighteen voyages from Indostan to the eastward', as well as four voyages from Europe to the sub-continent. In 'presuming' to give advice about the best track to pursue on a voyage to the East, Forrest affirmed his confidence that there were many more valuable hints than he could give 'locked up in journals of the skilful commanders in the East India Service, which not being collated together, not properly digested and published, the world is so far kept from much valuable knowledge on this subject.'[22]

On 24 December 1780 Kempenfelt thanked Dalrymple for the 'very valuable charts for particular parts of the East Indies'. The Admiral had known the Scot since 1762, when they had met at Madras at the conclusion of the latter's three-year voyage of reconnaissance among the Eastern Islands. Kempenfelt had been much impressed by the ability and strength of character which Dalrymple had displayed in that undertaking, and he now praised him for the 'infinite deal of pains' which lay behind this latest 'Herculean labour'. 'It is a proof,' he continued, 'what genius joined with industry is capable of . . . you have the pleasing reflection, that you have successfully laboured for the public good, the good of navigation, and that your memory will live for ever. Love of fame is a laudable ambition. Young calls it the universal passion; and yet how few pursue the true road to it.'[23]

Apart from these long-term tasks, the Company's hydrographer soon found himself occupied by duties more immediately concerned with the war-effort, for these were the dark days of the American War of Independence; not only were France and Spain already involved in the war on the side of the rebels, but on 20 November 1780 the British Government had felt compelled to declare war on the Dutch as well. In these circumstances, the routes normally followed by the East-Indiamen on their way to China were most vulnerable, and it was necessary to open up as many alternative routes as possible. One

[22] Thos. Forrest, *Treatise on the Monsoons*, London, 1783, Introduction. Forrest was in London on 1 February 1779, and was presumably the 'Mr Forrest' who dined at the Royal Society Club, as Dalrymple's guest, on 2 March 1780.

[23] *European Magazine*, Vol. 42, p. 421.

such track was the Pitt's Passage,[24] and on 20 February 1781 the Secretary of the Company was applying to Dalrymple for as many charts of that passage as he could spare.[25]

Dalrymple turned his attention to this problem, and in June 1782 produced his most informative *Memoir concerning the Passages to and from China*. Only a few copies were printed at the time, and these were issued by the Secret Committee of the East India Company to the Commanders of their China ships.[26] The purpose was to show what alternative routes were open to ships in place of the Straits of Malacca and Sunda, which they normally used but which were 'scarcely eligible' in a Dutch war. The Memoir described and assessed every possible route which could be negotiated by ships using the five main passages which he classified as the 'Direct Passage' to the westward of Halmahera; the Pitt's Passage, in which he included every route to the south of Halmahera and to the north of Australia; the New Zealand Passage, which included all the routes to the east of Australia; the passage to the south and east of New Zealand; and, finally, the passage round Cape Horn.

In writing about the China Sea, he stressed the need for chronometers, 'for the currents . . . are so strong and irregular that no Person can without the assistance of such Machines be sure of his position', and he urged that a survey should be made of its southern stretches. He noted that 'present ignorance' made a direct crossing from Poule Sapate[27] to Palawan out of the question. 'I do not believe,' he added, 'there is, on the face of the Globe, an equal number of dangerous shoals in the same space, as in the middle part between 8° and 12° N. called Karang-Bander.'

The large number of alternative passages which were avail-

[24] See Chapter II for an account of Captain Wilson's discovery of this route.

[25] *Miscellanies*, Vol. 25, f. 218, Mitchell to Dalrymple, 20 February 1781.

[26] He later added a supplement to this Memoir, 'Concerning the Passages at a late Season from India to China', and after the war both Memoirs were published, in 1785 and 1788 respectively. This was indicative of the Company's growing interest in the Eastern Archipelago – see Chapter VI.

[27] An island off South Vietnam ('Cochin China').

able through the chain of islands to the eastward of Bali gave the British a great advantage, since it would be impossible for enemy cruisers to patrol them all. To exploit this advantage, however, it was essential that the British should keep 'ringing the changes' in the choice of routes, a precaution which they had not adopted in the last war. 'Every different Passage', he concluded, 'should be different thro' the whole of it.'

Another wartime problem which engaged Dalrymple's attention was the need to find new places where ships could obtain water and provisions on the route to India. This became an urgent necessity after the failure of Commodore Johnstone's expedition to the Cape of Good Hope in 1781. That failure jeopardized the safety of St Helena, whose dependence upon the Cape was emphasized in a letter which the Chairman and his Deputy wrote to Lord Hillsborough in October 1781. There was a danger, they feared, that 'by leaving an enemy in possession of the Cape, we shall submit to lose the Island of St Helena . . . [and] be deprived of every place of refreshment and supply for the King's and Company's homeward-bound ships'. The Cape was the Gibraltar of India. 'No fleet can possibly sail to or return from India without touching at some proper place for refreshment . . . The places about midway are the Cape of Good Hope, Madagascar and St Helena'. Madagascar was dangerous and unhealthy, while 'The Island of St Helena, even in time of peace, has scarcely been able to accommodate the Company's ships. During times of war with France that island has been constantly assisted from the Cape. This resource being utterly cut off . . . not only the Company's possessions in India, but also the immense trade between Britain and that part of the world will be hazarded and in extreme danger'.[28]

In January 1782, shortly after the Ministry had rejected the proposal for a second attack upon the Cape, Dalrymple submitted a memorandum to the Chairman of the East India Company, in which he suggested an exploration of the South Atlantic in search for alternative sources of water and provisions on the route to India. In this memorandum he drew

[28] V. T. Harlow and F. Madden, *British Colonial Developments, 1774–1834*, Oxford, 1953, p. 6.

upon the knowledge he had acquired when he had been advocating a search for the supposed Southern Continent in this area. He suggested that Sierra Leone might prove a better choice for outward-bound ships than St Jago, in the Cape Verde Islands, which was a usual rendezvous for the French. Moreover, since a visit to Brazil added a month to the voyage, it would be worthwhile to make a careful examination of the island of Trinidada, where the first edition of the *India Pilot* (1675) stated that water could be found; in making this proposal he may not yet have learnt that Commodore Johnstone, on his return from the abortive attack on the Cape, had left a small settlement on this island in case Britain should wish to make it a permanent colony. Dalrymple also hoped that his proposed voyage of discovery would show whether the island of Ascencâo really existed, or was only the northern part of Trinidada. It was known that Tristan da Cunha provided water, and possessed a good roadstead where ships could anchor, but there were big discrepancies in the description of the island which needed to be cleared up. A thorough search should also be made for the very large island which was said to exist in 45° South and in about 30° or 40° West. This was thought to have a good harbour with plenty of wood and water, but the only description he had seen of it was in Seixas' account of La Roche's voyage in 1675. 'This island', added Dalrymple, 'is of the most essential Consequence as its difference of Latitude beyond the usual Track in a passage to India will not exceed ten days sail and is therefore much less out of the way than Brazil; besides being so much further advanced in the voyage, which is a very great advantage. Delisle's map makes it about the Meridan of Trinidada.' There was plenty of water at St. Helena's Bay in Patagonia. He did not know of anyone ever having examined Gough's Island. For the return voyage, he recommended that an examination should be made of 'the West Coast of Africa between the N° Extremity of the Dutch Districts and the South Extremity of the Portuguese Territory on the coast of Angola. They should confine their Observations to the Unfrequented Parts'.[29]

[29] P.R.O., C.O. 77/25, f. 16., January 1782.

The *Swallow* was instructed to carry out a voyage of discovery in September 1783, its orders being closely modelled on this Memorandum, but the Directors tied it down to so tight a schedule that the voyage was curtailed, and no useful discovery was made, and with the return of peace the immediate danger had passed.[30] The time had now arrived when the Company's hydrographer could devote all his energies to the production of his charts, and of their related memoirs.

Eighteenth century chart-makers were often subjected to fierce attacks from practising seamen, but they had a most difficult task to perform, for they were expected to produce accurate charts without being able to benefit from reliable surveys. Indeed, neither the East India Company nor the Royal Navy possessed a regular surveying service. In these circumstances, the information supplied by the seamen themselves was of the utmost importance, and Dalyrmple did his best to persuade them to carry out their own surveys. He also spent much time on the study of ships' journals, and on the patient correlation and correction of existing charts. This was exhausting, and sometimes heart-breaking, work. 'I have found in Poetry,' he wrote, 'the best relief to the Mind, in Researches so fatiguing as the investigation of Hydrographic Truth, amidst the variety of discordant authorities, all of them claiming implicit confidence.'[31]

To make the problem even more troublesome, there was the age-old difficulty over establishing longitude. Writing in 1783, Dalrymple asserted that there were only twelve places in the East, including the principal British, French, Dutch and Spanish bases as well as Peking and Canton, whose longitude had been positively ascertained by astronomical observations. Even reported latitudes could not be relied upon, since there were often contradictions, sometimes from different officers on the same ship.

[30] V. T. Harlow, *The Founding of the Second British Empire 1763–93*, Vol. 1, London, 1952, pp. 125–6, where it is stated that the Secretary of State addressed this memoir to the Chairman of the East India Company. There is no doubt, however, that the Memorandum was written by Dalrymple, and it seems more likely that it was referred to the Secretary of State by the Chairman.

[31] A. Dalrymple, *Collection of English Songs*, London, 1796, p. 6.

Dalrymple had taught himself to be an expert navigator and surveyor and was justified when he complained that 'not one navigator in a thousand ever attempts to make, or thinks it a part of his Professional Duty to make, a Chart: They are all ready', he continued, 'to exclaim against the badness of the charts made by others, indeed with sufficient reason, since those charts are constructed from the execrable materials afforded by their superficial Observations. Were the practice of Hydrography Universal amongst Navigators, the Improvement of Charts would rapidly approach to perfection; when the authority is produced for every line. Then the inconsistency and contradiction of Common Bearings, would stare a man in the face, and compell him to accurate precision.'[32]

Anxious to encourage seamen to send him all the material they could, he was always careful to acknowledge the help that he received, and would publish their observations when relevant. Sometimes men who were not in the Company's service responded, as in 1783 when he thanked Captain John S. Smith, R.N., for a chart of the Arabian coast 'with a most elegant set of views', and expressed his particular gratitude since he was 'an entire stranger to Captain Smith'. On another occasion, the captain of a country ship trading between Calcutta and Japan sent his Journal and a valuable chart 'to be delivered to Mr. Dalrymple or to Mr. Arrowsmith, that what they contained serviceable might be secured to Navigation'.[33] Other examples could be cited, but the response was erratic, and in 1783 he was complaining that the charts and remarks which he had previously been so pleased to get from Bombay had now ceased to arrive.[34] It was doubtless as a result of his pressure that the Directors gave strict orders to Bombay to send back 'copies of all Charts and Plans which you may be able to obtain likely to throw any additional lights on the Geography of India or

[32] A. Dalrymple, *General Collection of Nautical Publications*, London, 1783, p. 5.

[33] Jas. Burney, *A Chronological History of the Discoveries in the South Sea or Pacific Ocean*, Vol. III, London, 1813, p. 429.

[34] A. Dalrymple, *Collection of Ports . . . in the Indian Navigation*, London, 1783.

on the Indian Navigation'. Likewise, the commanders of the country ships were to be asked to co-operate.[35]

Dalrymple wished to impress upon people that the most unlikely materials could often be helpful. Old maps, 'however generally erroneous or imperfect', might contain something of value, 'were it only in shewing the application of names in Old Journals'. Similarly, even inaccurate plans could be of some use, for whereas 'General Charts' with hardly the least similiarity to the areas they covered were not uncommon, 'particular Plans are scarcely ever without some resemblance . . . but even the publication, in a General Collection, of a few plans without the smallest resemblance may be useful, because someone . . . may prevent the evil effects which might attend a confidence in an unknown plan, by declaring when they know on good authority such Plan is execrable'.[36] When he found discrepancies between charts, he would, on occasion, print alternative versions side-by-side, and when he found an old chart which contained data not to be found elsewhere, he would sometimes publish it separately.[37]

For these methods to be successful, it was essential that those who used the charts co-operated by sending back the necessary corrections, for, as he once wrote, 'I shall be much better pleased to learn from positive data that I am wrong, than remain in doubt, with however strong probabilities that I am right'.[38]

35 *Bombay Despatches*, Vol. 7 (1783–5), 8 January 1783, p. 89, paras. 37–9.

36 A. Dalrymple, *General Collection of Nautical Publications*, London, 1783, p. 31.

37 For an example of alternative versions printed side-by-side, see his chart of the shoals to the eastward of Billiton. An example of an old chart which he reproduced was 'The Chart of Banka and Billiton, found in the early editions of Van Keulen', which he reduced to the same scale as the rest of his set for ready comparison. The I.O. Lbry. has a large collection of his charts in bound volumes.

38 A. Dalrymple, *Memoir of a Chart from Cape Mons to Acheen*, London, 1785, pp. 10–11. Yet even when this co-operation was forthcoming, it was not always possible, he explained, to incorporate individual corrections, because 'in the Composition of a General Chart, the component parts must be taken from Authorities of various kinds, some deserving the utmost confidence; others, used for want of good materials, meriting no confidence:

Of the transient nature of much of his work he was only too well aware, and as he himself remarked, it was 'a misfortune, incident to the Science, that a Geographer must labour with doubtful, almost distracting materials, before he obtains certain data, when he finds almost all his Work to do over again... This obscurity will be no bar to our Successors, who, by the common use of Chronometers, will acquire, without labour, a precision to which all our Investigations cannot reach'.[39]

It was, indeed, the chronometer which was revolutionising this science. From the first, Dalrymple had been an enthusiastic champion of the instrument, and may well have been the first to give it its name.[40] He fully realized that its introduction marked a turning point in the history of navigation.[41]

---

and... even when Errors are pointed out, by actual and correct Observations: as there is a connexion between Place and Place, which would be totally destroyed by such alterations: therefore, that Plate must remain, at least, with many of its inaccuracies, 'till the accumulation of more precise Observations, warrants an entire new Construction of the Chart' – *Memoir of a Chart of the Indian Ocean*, London, 1787.

39 A. Dalrymple, *Memoir of a Chart from Cape Mons to Acheen*, ut supra.

40 According to the Oxford English Dictionary, the term chronometer was being applied to pendulum-type time-keepers as early as 1715 but the first use of the term for pocket time-keepers is credited to Arnold in 1780. Dalrymple was a great admirer and champion of Arnold, and at an early stage he wrote 'Some Notes useful to those who have Chronometers at Sea'; in a note on page 1 he wrote – 'The Machine used for measuring Time at Sea is here named Chronometer, my friend Mr Banks agreeing with me in thinking so valuable a Machine deserves to be known by a Name, instead of a Definition. The name Time-Keeper is only proper to a perfect Chronometer'. As Banks was made a baronet in 1781, this undated Memoir (B.M., ref. G.2198) was written before that year, and it seems highly probable that Arnold adopted the name from Dalrymple.

41 It was, he explained, the last of a series of advances which had been made in the methods of determining longitude. First, Halley had taken up the idea of using the variation of the compass to determine longitude, and had 'brought it into a practicable system [even though]... a perfect and comprehensive Theory of the Variation is still wanting'. This system had, in turn, been superseded by that of Lunar Observations. 'Dr Halley had the honour of being, I believe, the first who practically applied the Lunar Distances to determine the Longitude at Sea', though the idea had been thought of as early as the time of Magellan. The system had been perfected through the zealous efforts of Dr Maskelyne, the Astronomer Royal, and had 'been brought into common use in the India Navigation, and will in time doubtless become universal in the Royal Navy', an aside that serves to

Harrison had been the first to produce a successful marine chronometer, 'but the degree of precision to which they are now brought, by Arnold, would not, ten years ago, have been believed within the bounds of possibility'. As the price had been reduced from the original two hundred and forty guineas to twenty guineas, 'in a short time few officers in the Navy or India Service will be without them'. In this he was over-optimistic, so far as the Royal Navy was concerned, for in 1812, almost thirty years later, a naval captain was blaming the loss of 2,000 seamen in the North Sea to a want of good chronometers.[42]

Dalrymple was confident that within a few years navigation would gain 'a certainty and precision . . . which no inference could reach, however laborious the investigation'. He was therefore abandoning his original intention to postpone the publication of a set of charts until he had 'extracted all the journals'. He now meant to complete a set forthwith, and to publish it. Although these charts would be imperfect, they would be less defective than those which were currently in use, and would serve to show what observations were still needed 'to render them compleat'.

He suggested, too, that the return of peace offered a great opportunity to organize a voyage for the improvement of geographical knowledge by making full use of the chronometer, for 'more could be done in three years towards establishing the Longitudes of Places, than could otherwise be effected in thirty'. He would readily volunteer to lead such an expedition. The expense, though great, 'would be less than has been sometimes squandered by an Individual in one Parliamentary Election'. He proposed using one large and six small vessels 'for sounding, and for forming stations for the ready continuation of the Chain of Triangles by the Quincunx, which is the only certain mode

---

remind us that the East India Company was commonly ahead of the Royal Navy in its navigational techniques at this time. 'The more recent Improvement in Navigation', continued Dalrymple, 'which leaves the Lunar Observations as far behind, as they did the Variation, is by Chronometers'.

42 *The Naval Chronicle,* Vol. XXVII (1812), pp. 121–2. 'Every man,' wrote this correspondent, 'who has associated with naval officers for the last thirty years, must have heard their complaints of the want of good chronometers.'

of laying down Soundings, where the angles of objects on Shoar cannot be had'.[43]

Another problem which faced the cartographer was the nomenclature adopted by explorers for their discoveries. This was a subject on which Dalrymple had strong convictions, for he knew of the confusion which was caused by the use of different names for the same places, or of the same name for separate discoveries. His stand on this point had caused friction with the irascible Captain King, when they had both been engaged in preparing the maps for the official account of Captain Cook's third voyage, for Captain King did not have to struggle with this problem, day after day, as did a professional cartographer.[44] To demonstrate the confusion that was thus caused Dalrymple listed, in his *Memoir concerning the Passages to and from China,* which was first printed at this very time, a long series of different names which had been used for the same places, particularly when the Dutch and Portuguese charts were compared. He admitted that he himself was not blameless, for 'In the views . . . given to the Ships lately returned from China, I had named Gilybanta, by an unaccountable mistake, Gabylintan; This Error was corrected before their return. It has however propagated a false name'. Such confusion was all the harder to overcome because of the lack of international conferences, and on another occasion he expressed his regret that there was 'not a more ready communication amongst Geographers, in the various Countries of Europe; whereby none could be ignorant, for a considerable time after the Publication, of the Geo-

[43] A. Dalrymple, *General Collection of Nautical Publications,* London, 1783, pp. 6 et seq.

[44] This was why Dalrymple had entered on the map 'Kerguelen's Land called by Captain Cook the Island of Desolation', and 'Marions Isles called by Captain Cook Prince Edwards Islands'. In the case of Nootka Sound he refused to accede to King's request that he should again include Captain Cook's version, for in this case a native name was available which he always considered should have priority – *N.B.* his own use of Balambangan. – See B.M., Eg. MSS. 2180, f. 46, Captain King to Dr Douglas, 16 September 1782. Dalrymple's plea for more international co-operation amongst geographers was made at the end of his *Observations on M. Buache's Memoir* (1790).

graphical Publications of any Country . . .[45] He himself favoured the use of native names when these were available, and had been careful to do this in the case of Balambangan, though it was uninhabited and not shown on existing European maps, and so might easily have been given an anglicized name. 'Where Native names cannot be had,' he wrote, 'the Fittest Names are descriptive', for this minimized the risk of confusion. Captain Cook had adopted this principle when he had named the 'Bay of Inlets', the 'Bay of Isles', and 'Where the Endeavour Struck' on the eastern coast of Australia. As a result, when Dalrymple had discovered the ancient Dauphin map in Sir Joseph Banks's library, where the cartographer had used the same principle to name 'Baye Perdue', 'R. de beaucoup d'isles' and 'Coste dangereuse', he had been able to recognize these as referring to the same places, and to realize that this was an ancient map of Australia. It is ironic that modern writers, with preconceived views on Dalrymple's supposed life-long enmity towards Captain Cook, should have interpreted this passage as an attack on him, when it was surely the reverse.[46]

When considering these exhausting labours which Dalrymple so willingly undertook, and which resulted in Britain taking the lead in European hydrography, whereas previously she had lagged far behind, it is worth remembering that he was not in the best of health. Apart from the eye-strain through 'over-application' which occasionally forced him to rest, there were the erysipelas and 'bile' that were a result of his years in the East. 'I saw your brother two days ago,' wrote Lord Morton to Lord Hailes, 'at his old occupation of making charts and drinking tea. He had a little eruption on his skin, for which he is certainly the better, though he will not allow it.'[47] In his application to be considered for the vacant Governorship of Madras in 1792, Dalrymple referred to 'a return of that Erup-

[45] A. Dalrymple, *Observations on M. Buache's Memoir*, London, 1790, Conclusion.

[46] The passage in question is to be found in the footnote, starting on page 4, in Dalrymple's *Memoir concerning the Chagos Archipelago and the Adjacent Islands*, London, 1785.

[47] Nat. Lbry. of Scotland, *Newhailes Archives*, file 11-M, MS. 750, 18 January 1788.

tion, which confined him to the House for three months, and rendered him incapable of any business for some time'.[48] A naval surgeon of the time ascribed 'those fashionable Oriental diseases, the liver complaint [and] bilious fever' to 'beef-steaks in the morning, and sumptuous dinners at seven in the evening with a bottle of wine to crown the whole', an unwholesome diet in such a climate as that of Madras. His colourful description of the symptoms of 'bile', to which Dalrymple confessed he was 'very subject' on his return to England,[49] referred to 'an acrimony that seems absolutely to corrode the stomach . . . and when directed downwards, can be compared to nothing more appropriate than the sensation which one would expect from boiling lead flowing through the intestines'![50]

The original terms of Dalrymple's appointment as hydrographer to the East India Company made no reference to a power to initiate surveys. As a commercial undertaking, the Company could only be expected to sanction them in those cases where the repeated losses of ships threatened their profits. Once a safe route had been found, the tendency was for all ships thereafter to follow it. Captain Wilson's voyage in the *Pitt* and Dalrymple's reconnaissance in the *Cuddalore* were rare events indeed in the Company's maritime history.

Conditions, however, were now changing. The East India Company was becoming the sovereign power in India, and its need for maritime and land surveys was being increasingly felt. A particular reason for this was to be found in the great increase in the size of the East-Indiamen,[51] and the development of new

[48] Nat. Lbry. of Australia, Canberra, MS. 43/12, Dalrymple to H. Dundas, 2 November 1792.

[49] *Case of Alexander Dalrymple*, 31 May 1808.

[50] J. Johnson, *The Influence of Tropical Climates on European Constitutions*, (4th edition), London, 1827, pp. 11 et seq.

See also his *Oriental Voyager*, London, 1807. In February and September 1804 Dalrymple, in a letter to Earl St Vincent, was referring to frequent and severe attacks of erysipelas.

[51] See C. N. Parkinson, *Trade in the Eastern Sea, 1793–1813*, Cambridge, 1937, Chapter VI. He points out that it was customary for ships to be registered at 499 tons after 1750, but by 1773 ships of up to 800 tons had begun to multiply. By 1783 the normal tonnage was 758. But the Dutch and French ships were still larger, and for self-defence, as well as for the enormous increases in tea-imports after 1784, ships of over 1,000 tons were

routes like that of the Pitt's Passage, whose use had become more necessary and frequent during the American and French Revolutionary Wars. Furthermore, with the development of the Bombay Marine the Company was acquiring ships which could be used for this purpose.

The Bombay Marine had organized its first survey in 1772, when an examination was made of the coasts of Mekran, Scinde, Kattywar and parts of Persia and Arabia.[52] After his appointment as the Company's hydrographer, Dalrymple, with his office in India House, was in a position to have more influence when new surveys were being considered. One of the problems in which he was interested concerned the group of islands now known as the Chagos Archipelago. He had been in touch with D'Après de Mannevillette about this, and the journals of ships which had sighted the islands had been consulted, but great uncertainty remained. Most charts showed two islands and a shoal[53] some 4° to the eastward of this group, but Dalrymple was doubtful about them, and with justification, since they are now known not to exist. There were other problems, too, including the longitude of, and number of islands in, the Egmont Group, as well as the longitude of Chagos Island. Pending an elucidation of these mysteries, Dalrymple decided to publish D'Après' posthumous chart, even though he was convinced that a new one was needed. At the same time he published his *Memoir concerning the Chagos Archipelago and the Adjacent Islands*, in the hope, as he put it, that it would fall into the hands of 'Persons in India, who can add the necessary Elucidations . . . to enable me to publish a correct chart of the Islands'. Orders were also sent to Bombay to despatch vessels to ascertain 'the situation of the numerous Banks and Islands in the Southern

---

soon being constructed, with five vessels of 1,200 tons being launched in 1790. This became the standard size, and by 1810 there were thirty-four ships of this measurement.

[52] C. R. Low, *History of the Indian Navy (1613–1863)*, Vol. 1, London, 1877, pp. 185–6. Dalrymple was also consulted about a proposed survey between the Maldives and Madagascar – *Bombay Despatches*, Vol. 4, p. 217. 1 April 1772.

[53] The islands were named Ady and Candy, and the shoal was known as the London's Bank.

Passage from the Maldives to Madagascar as an accurate knowledge of those, hitherto much neglected, Seas is essential to the Security of the Navigation of the Company's Ships'.[54] These orders, of course, referred to the Chagos Archipelago, and it was a remarkable coincidence that twenty-seven days after the despatch of these orders, the ship *Atlas* was wrecked on this very group, with James Horsburgh on board. It was this experience which determined Horsburgh to devote himself to hydrography, and he was to be befriended by Dalrymple a few years later, and was eventually to succeed him as the Company's hydrographer.

Chagos Island itself, which the French knew as Diego Garcia, had been sighted by East-Indiamen from time to time, and in 1774 the *Drake* had been sent from Bombay to survey it and to put on shore some hogs, sheep and goats, for, as Dalrymple recalled in an historical memoir, the Company's ships 'going the outward Passage, had lost many men by the scurvy, for want of water and refreshments, [and the Company had therefore] determined to settle there that their ships might be enabled to get refreshments, after their long voyage from Europe, before they came into the low latitudes where the light winds, and tedious passages consequent to them, had so often proved fatal to the lives of the seamen before they could reach India'.[55] The orders to make this settlement had gone out from London on 8 July 1785, and on 18 March 1786 the ship *Admiral Hughes,* accompanied by a cruiser and 'advice boat', left Bombay to put these orders into effect. The island was a disappointment, however, since it was overrun by rats, and proved a difficult place in which to grow grain. The French had made a like attempt shortly before, with similar results.[56] In November 1786 the British therefore withdrew from the island. Nevertheless, Dalrymple had good reason to be satisfied that the attempt had been made, for it had resulted in the execution of an excel-

[54] *Bombay Despatches,* Vol. 8, 3 May 1786, pp. 145–55, para. 28. Particular attention was to be paid to the longitudes of the lines of equal variation.

[55] Nat. Lbry. of Australia, Canberra, MS. 43/6, Dalrymple to Lord Mulgrave, *Memoir relative to the Island of Diego Garcia,* 30 April 1787.

[56] I. O. Lbry., *Home Miscellaneous Series,* Vol. 606, pp. 5–15.

lent survey of the whole group by Archibald Blair, a lieutenant in the Bombay Marine.[57]

Another Scotsman in the service of the Bombay Marine who was soon attracting the attention of Alexander Dalrymple was John McCluer. In 1785 he had carried out a survey of the Persian Gulf, and had also written some Sailing Directions for that area, which were later to be used by Horsburgh in his East Indian Directory.[58] It was no surprise, therefore, when the Committee of Correspondence entrusted him with the command of a new survey which had been planned by Dalrymple.[59]

Its purpose was to gain 'a perfect Knowledge of the Soundings on the Bank to the Westward of Bombay' for the benefit of East-Indiamen approaching that port in thick weather. The latitudes and longitudes of coastal promontories between Bombay and Surat were to be carefully determined, and as a means of carrying out their full and detailed orders the Directors despatched from London one box and two pocket chronometers, an azimuth compass, a sextant and 'an artificial horizon for finding the Time by Altitudes of the Sun on Shoar'; and it was carefully laid down that while any necessary repairs to the pocket chronometers could be carried out in Calcutta, the box chronometer was not to be 'put into the hands of any artist in India', but must be returned to London! The hallmark of this survey was to be thoroughness: 'Let what is done', ran the orders, 'be done compleatly, and nothing left undetermined in this Space; if any doubt arises, let them repeat their Observations in such Part, that an Implicit Confidence may be safely placed in the work when finished.'

This was the first of a series of surveys of the west coast of India carried out by McCluer, covering the whole coast between the Gulf of Cambay in the north and Cape Comorin in the south. The results were incorporated in three charts drawn by Wedgborough, with smaller plans by McCluer, which, together with some views that had been obtained, were engraved

[57] *Remarks and Observations on a Survey of the Chagos Archipelago by Lieut. Archibald Blair in 1786 and 1787*, published by A. Dalrymple, London, 1788.

[58] Low, op. cit., Vol. 1, pp. 188–9.

[59] Dalrymple later published McCluer's account, and included the orders.

by Dalrymple. The latter expressed his appreciation of what McCluer had achieved by stating that his 'diligence has a just claim to our approbation . . .'[60]

With the completion of this examination of the west coast of India, Dalrymple now planned a new survey farther afield, for which the wreck of the *Antelope* in the Palau Islands in 1783 provided the pretext.[61] The instructions for this new voyage stated that because of 'the frequent occasion which our China ships lately have had to go by unfrequented Passages', and the probability that this state of affairs would continue, the most eligible passage was to be surveyed. Either Blair or McCluer was to be given the command, because of their proved hydrographic skill, and the expedition would consist of a Bombay vessel of not less than 150 tons, accompanied by a smaller one not exceeding 50 tons, the larger being fitted out with an extra supply of anchors, cables and chains.

'The accompanying Map', ran the instructions, 'published in the English translation of Leinschoten 1598, indicates that there is a Channel thro' Papua or New Guinea to the NEward of the Aroo Islands; which, if practicable for an Indiaman, would be the most eligible Passage for our Ships to China at a late Season', and the principal object of the present expedition would be to look for, and to explore, any such passage.

It was hoped that in the course of this survey the whole coast of New Guinea could be traced.[62] In practice, McCluer had to be content with a much more restricted performance, but the voyage accomplished the discovery of McCluer's Inlet, whose existence may have been the origin of Leinschoten's 'strait'. He was impressed with the possibilities of doing good trade in the Inlet, for 'canoes came from all quarters with Nutmegs

60 *Bombay Despatches*, Vol. 8, pp. 145–55, 3 March 1786. This survey was praised in a later despatch – Ibid., Vol. 11, p. 231, 21 April 1790, where Dalrymple's name is specifically entered by the copyist against this portion of the orders.

61 For details, see Chapter VI. These islands were then known as the Pellews.

62 *Bombay Despatches*, Vol. 11, pp. 129–58, 23 March 1790. It is possible that a search for Leinschoten's 'Strait' may have been a feature of the Instructions for the *Cuddalore's* voyage in 1759.

See Chapter VI for background to this survey.

and Massoy Bark', and so many nutmegs were brought that they could have loaded the vessel with them in a few days.[63]

This was the last of the surveys which Dalrymple was able to persuade the Company to undertake, for with the outbreak of the French Revolutionary Wars the Bombay Marine could no longer spare ships for such work. But Dalrymple could feel well pleased with what had been achieved in the few years of peace which had been available to him, and in 1793 the Company paid him a warm tribute when it testified that in consequence of his 'unremitting Attention, and voluminous Publications of Sea Charts, etc., the Navigation of the Indian and Chinese Seas are almost as well known to the Company's Officers as the British Channel'.[64]

In contrast to this growing activity by the servants of the East India Company, the record of the Royal Navy in this field had been uninspiring. Anson's chaplain had almost certainly been expressing his master's views when he had deplored the lack of skill displayed by most naval officers 'in drawing, and in the general principles of surveying'. This had resulted in an unnecessary ignorance about foreign countries, and in navigational hazards that could have been avoided, had these officers received the right sort of encouragement and guidance from the authorities.[65] James Cook had also referred to 'the few [seamen] I have known who are capable of drawing a chart or Sketch of a Sea coast'.[66] The fact was that the Royal Navy had no regular

63 Nat. Lbry. of Scotland, *Melville Papers,* MS. 1068, f. 40, McCluer to Dalrymple, Bencoolen, 25 May 1792.

In exploring this Inlet, McCluer observed that a 'huge chain of Mountains extended from N to SE'. He then entered a river at the head of the inlet, and, when it divided, took the most northerly branch, but was soon stopped by shoal water. At this stage he decided that he must lose no time in returning lest the health of his men suffer, for they were now 'almost surrounded with immense high Mountains, and in the mornings were almost suffocated with the fogs, which hung in clouds about the hills all day long'.

64 *The Third Report of the Select Committee of the East India Company,* London, 1793, p. 37.

65 R. Walter, *A Voyage Round the World . . .*, London, 1748, Introduction.

66 *Mariner's Mirror,* Vol. 40, London, 1954, p. 96, article by R. A. Skelton on 'James Cook as a Hydrographer'. The Navy was slow to mend its ways – see *The Naval Chronicle,* Vol. 34 (1815) for continuing criticisms on this score.

surveying service, and had failed to create a climate of opinion among its officers which would have made them wish to excel in this important task. Special arrangements were sometimes made for the survey of a specified area, like that carried out by Cook off Newfoundland, or those by Des Barres and others along the Atlantic seaboard of North America, which were later incorporated in the *Atlantic Neptune*. But no arrangements had been made for the systematic storage of hydrographic material, or for the compilation and issuing of Admiralty charts. The Navy had to rely on the services of the commercial chart-makers and chart-sellers, who were themselves restricted both by the lack of adequate surveys, and by those commercial considerations which often made it difficult or impossible for them to keep their charts up-to-date.[67]

During the Seven Years' War a directive went out from the Admiralty, of which Anson became the First Lord in March 1761, which noted how the King's Service had suffered greatly 'for want of due information and Knowledge of Harbours, Roads, and accesible Places on the Coast of France' and strictly required all officers, whether serving in foreign or home waters, to submit full information on all subjects that were likely to be of value to navigation or hydrography.[68] Such directives, however though they might help to alter the outlook of naval officers, could only be effective for a limited period of time, and were no substitute for a Hydrographic Office.

It is not clear why Lord Howe, who had suggested the establishment of such an Office in 1766, did not pursue the matter when he himself became the First Lord of the Admiralty in 1783. The need was as great as ever and Kempenfelt had given it expression. 'I wish,' he had told Dalrymple, 'you was placed in a situation that would afford you more means, and a greater latitude to pursue your favourite study. I mean at the Head of an Hydrographical Board, established by authority of Government, to which office encouragement should be given, to bring all surveys and discoveries of rocks, shoals, etc. and those found

67 *Mariner's Mirror*, Vol. 40, London, 1954, p. 100.

68 Vice-Admiral Sir A. Day, *Draft History of the Hydrographic Office*, Appendix B4.

good, printed at the public expence. It is no more than what the interest, as well as reputation, of the nation, as a great maritime state, requires should be done. By such an office, well conducted, what an increase of good surveys would the public be benefited with! And the good being stamped with the authority of the Board, would direct the purchaser to avoid those erroneous Charts, which, instead of serving to avoid dangers, too often fatally lead to them.'[69]

Another who stressed this need was J. H. Moore, 'teacher of navigation, hydrographer and chart-seller to H.R.H. the Duke of Clarence', and author of the best-selling *Practical Navigator*. 'When a voyage is finished,' he had written, 'the Journal of that voyage . . . is seldom regarded. Were the Lords of the Admiralty to establish a Repository for Observations, Drawings, Appearances of the Land, and other useful Articles, such Materials might be applied to the Improvement of Navigation. Proper Persons might be appointed to arrange and apply them in the constructing of useful Sea Charts; and such Charts, if not given to the Public, should be delivered to the Officers in the Royal Navy. . . .'[70]

It was on 12 August 1795 that an Admiralty Order in Council announced the decision to set up a Department of Hydrography in view of 'the great inconvenience which has constantly been felt by the officers of Your Majesty's Fleet, especially when ordered abroad, from the want of sufficient information respecting the navigation of those parts'. The scope of the office was, in the first place, to be limited to getting the plans and charts in the Admiralty's possession 'judiciously arranged and digested'. The hydrographer was to be paid a salary of £500 p.a., and from the materials now entrusted to his care he was to select and compile 'all such information as may appear to be requisite for the purposes of improving the navigation, and for the guidance and direction of the Commanders of Your Majesty's Ships'. Dalrymple was the natural choice for this post, and there is

69 *European Magazine*, Vol. 42, p. 421, Kempenfelt to Dalrymple, 24 December 1780.

70 J. H. Moore, *The Practical Navigator* (9th edition), London, 1791, pp. 250–1.

evidence that he was already working for the Admiralty before the official announcement was made.[71] When the offer came he immediately sought the East India Company's permission to accept it, pointing out that the new post would be 'rather an extension, than contradiction' to his post with them, since there were 'few parts of the world, in which the Navigation of your ships might not, at least eventually, be interested'.[72] The Company acquiesced in this arrangement.

The task of arranging the hydrographic material already in the Admiralty's possession must have been considerable, for the second half of the eighteenth century had seen the circumnavigations of Byron, Wallis, Carteret and Cook, the polar voyage of Phipps (later Lord Mulgrave), the discoveries of Flinders, Bass and others in Australian waters, and the survey of the north-west coast of America by George Vancouver, whose return to England almost coincided with Dalrymple's new appointment. Surveys in home waters had also been carried out in this period by the two Murdoch Mackenzies and Graeme Spence, and the work of Des Barres and others in North America has already been mentioned.[73]

After the materials in the office had been reduced to order, preparations were started for the Admiralty to issue its own charts, and on 22 March 1800 Dalrymple was informing

[71] P.R.O., Adm. 1/3522, 28 May 1795, where he was complaining that he had no money with which to pay an engraver's bill. 'I find you Admiralty folks are as tardy in payment as in other things,' he grumbled, observing that he found it 'very unusual and disagreeable that any workman I employ should ask twice for his money'.

[72] I.O. Lbry., *Miscellaneous Letters Received*, Vol. 92, f. 101, Dalrymple to Directors, 10 June 1795.

[73] There were various difficulties which Dalrymple had to face in his new post. It is probable that many serving officers resented having a civilian as their hydrographer, and there could be none of the team-work which he experienced when working in India House. There he was busily employed alongside men who had shared similar experiences to his own and who had a common outlook, and he had developed close friendships with a number of captains in the Company's service. This gave him the means of judging with accuracy the reliance to be placed on the materials he was using. But of American waters, or of the Mediterranean or Baltic, he had no personal experience, nor the help of friends on whose judgement he could depend. Another handicap was that he had no power to initiate or to control naval surveys in this new post.

Nepean[74] that, as soon as possible, he would draw up a list of the charts and plans in the Hydrographic Office which were, in his opinion, 'fit to be engraved'. At the same time he suggested that it 'would be very expedient to fit up a rolling press in the Admiralty both as least expensive and most convenient if a number of plates are intended to be printed'.[75] What plates were, in fact, engraved in this office at the time is not clear, but two years later he was proposing that impressions of plates engraved there should be issued to His Majesty's cruisers, which would provide an opportunity 'of verifying and correcting the Plates before they are printed off for general use'. To speed up the formation of a large collection, he pointed out that plates which were copied from foreign printed charts and plans could be 'executed out of the office' without any threat to security, which would allow his own engravers to 'employ their whole time in the Public Service'. This latter suggestion was not taken up, but orders were given for the plates to be sent to commanding officers for distribution 'among the most intelligent officers'.[76]

Dalrymple now began to concentrate his attention upon the waters he knew. It was natural that he should do so, since it was in supplying information about the eastern seas that he could make his own most significant contribution, and it is clear that this was an area in the world about which the Royal Navy was singularly ill-informed.[77] He found that the Admiralty's own materials on 'the East India Navigation' were 'too few in number to make anything like an Oriental Pilot'. He therefore sought permission to include them in the collection which he had made for the East India Company, and suggested that if the Admiralty should wish to supply His Majesty's ships with the plates in this collection, he would 'very

[74] Sir Evan Nepean (1751–1822) was Secretary of the Admiralty from 1795–1804.

[75] Adm. 1/3522. Dalrymple to Nepean, 22 March 1800.

[76] Ibid., 27 May 1803. In this letter, Dalrymple's signature is very shaky, instead of showing its usual neat form, suggesting one of his periodic illnesses.

[77] Vice-Admiral Sir A. Day, *The Admiralty Hydrographic Service, 1795–1919*, London, 1967, pp. 27–28, containing a report drawn up by Captain Hurd in 1814.

readily, on a reasonable Consideration for the use of the plates', permit as many to be printed for the Admiralty as their Lordships might desire, if they would meet the expense of the paper and printing.[78] This was a fair offer, for the Hydrographic Office in the Admiralty, working with such a small staff,[79] on a strictly controlled and minimal budget, and with the whole world to cover, could not hope to meet its own needs in this respect. The best professional advice would have been to purchase these same charts, which were generally acknowledged to be the best of that area. The listed price of his complete set of 52 charts, 57 views and 640 plans was £34 12s. 6d., one hundred sets costing £3,462. The Admiralty agreed to take one hundred sets, for which they would pay him one thousand guineas. This kept their copper-plate printer busy, and he was turning out about 140 impressions a day, finally completing the order on 31 October 1806.[80]

On one occasion Dalrymple used his knowledge of conditions in India to offer advice on a matter outside his own sphere of responsibility, for in 1801 he wrote to Earl St Vincent to suggest an alteration in the system of convoying the China ships of the East India Company. His proposal was that the convoy ship, on the return voyage from China, should proceed to India and there relieve one of the ships already on the India Station, for experience showed that 'when men have remained very long aboard without a prospect of returning home, they became enervated; and, in case of severe service, many die'. If the men on

[78] Adm. 1/3522. Dalrymple to Marsden, 13 June 1804. Marsden was the new Secretary to the Admiralty, and was a personal friend whom Dalrymple appointed as one of his executors, together with James Rennell.

[79] In 1797 it comprised one assistant, one draughtsman, two engravers and one printer.

[80] In September 1806 Dalrymple was also informing the East India Company that the Admiralty had directed that such of his Nautical Memoirs as he deemed proper for the use of His Majesty's Navy should immediately be reprinted. If the Company wished to profit by the occasion, he would agree to their printing whatever number they might desire, the expense of which would not be a quarter of the normal price. Any remuneration which the Company might decide upon would be entirely their affair. His only stipulation was that these copies should be only for their own use, and not for sale. – *Miscellaneous Letters Received*, Vol. 114, f. 67, Dalrymple to Directors, 10 September 1806.

the India station were allowed, annually, to draw lots to come home in the convoy ship, they would 'be relieved from Despondency without any loss to the Service or expense to the Publik'.[81]

That letter must have been written at about the time when he first heard ominous news which grieved him and the rest of the Dalrymple family. In October 1800 the *Earl Talbot,* an East-Indiaman of about 1,500 tons, had disappeared in the China Sea, and on board her, as a junior officer, was his nephew, Sir James Dalrymple. It was believed that the ship had been lost on the Paracels, a much feared group of islands and reefs, and the Bombay Marine decided to despatch two cruisers, the *Intrepid* and *Comet* to search this area, and to make a survey. On 19 January 1803, however, it was learnt in Canton that these two cruisers were also missing, and James Horsburgh, who was then in that port, was fairly certain that they had been wrecked on this same group, since he considered that they had chosen the wrong time of year to attempt a survey.

Horsburgh had become interested in hydrography after he had been wrecked in the Chagos Archipelago, on board the *Atlas,* in 1786. A Scotsman of humble birth, he had worked his way up from cook and cabin-boy to become the captain of an East-Indiaman, and he had devoted all his spare time, since that wreck, to studying navigation, astronomy, geometry and drawing.[82] Eventually he had constructed some charts which had won high praise from the captains of a number of East-Indiamen at Canton, and these had then been forwarded on to London for the attention of the hydrographer. Dalrymple had been much impressed and had published them, and it must have been on his advice that the Court of Directors, when forwarding a letter of thanks to Horsburgh, also sent him some money for the purchase of useful instruments with which to continue his hydrographic work. Then, when Horsburgh was in England in 1796, he met Dalrymple for the first time, and the latter introduced him to his friends, including Sir Joseph Banks, PRS, and Dr. Maskelyne, the Astronomer Royal.

[81] Adm. 1/3522. Dalrymple to Earl St Vincent, 29 April 1801.

[82] See the *Dictionary of National Biography,* and C. R. Markham, *A Memoir on the Indian Surveys,* London, 1871, pp. 279–80.

Horsburgh stressed the need to establish the boundaries and situation of the Paracel shoal, including all the shoals to the westward of the Macclesfield Bank. He judged their extent to be much more limited than was generally believed. He wanted the command of a small ship to trace the north-western and western limits of the Paracels, and he believed that if this was done all the returning ships from China, with their heavy cargoes, would prefer the inner passage where they could sail before wind and sea during the north-eastern monsoon.[83] The Superintendent of the Bombay Marine backed this plea for a careful survey of the China Seas, but stated that he was short of qualified men and ships for the job.

Reminding the Directors that he himself had recommended a survey of the China Seas in his *Memoir on the Passages to and from China* (1782), Dalrymple sent on these letters, together with an extract of one from Madras. This latter gave information about the Paracels which had been obtained from a former pirate, who declared that these islands, which Europeans so greatly feared, were 'perfectly free from danger'. The corsairs themselves lived among the northern-most islands, which had been fortified, and thither they took their prizes. The extract gave some details of this group, and of the considerable errors in the European charts which had sought to depict them.[84]

The authorities at Canton backed up these pleas by forwarding a letter which told how 'The China Sea, for the most part of the year, is subject to most violent and sudden Tempests which nothing can resist', so that 'scarcely a year passes without the losses of ships in some part of it: added to this Calamity it is encompassed with many dangerous and unknown Rocks and Shoals'. The supercargoes stated that it was a reproach that these seas should have remained 'in the same unexplored state as when we first navigated there', and suggested that the Directors should appoint Horsburgh to make this survey, and should approach 'Mr Dalrymple who is so eminently capable

[83] I. O. Lbry., *Boards Collections*, Vol. 181, paper 3380, Horsburgh to Dalrymple, Canton, 20 November 1802.

[84] Ibid. Dalrymple to Directors, 22 April 1803, pp. 1 et seq.

of giving them advices and information on the subject' for any further details they might require.[85]

Horsburgh delayed his return to England for many months in the hope of getting this appointment, but his hopes were disappointed and in December 1804 he left Canton for London. He had already sent on from Bombay some barometer readings, which formed the subject of a paper read at the Royal Society on 14 March 1805.[86] Now he received a letter from Dalrymple, thanking him for some charts. 'If it is agreeable to you,' wrote his friend, 'I will when the Society meets in November propose to Mr Cavendish, Mr Aubert and Dr Maskelyne to join me in a Certificate to propose you as a proper Person to be elected a Fellow of the Royal Society.'[87] Horsburgh, who had a most distinguished career before him, owed a great deal to this early encouragement and support from Dalrymple, and their combined contribution to the science of hydrography was truly immense. Nor was the survey of the Paracels forgotten, being undertaken by Captain Daniel Ross, from Bombay, in 1810.[88]

In his work for the East India Company, Dalrymple had always relied heavily on the information that had been sent back to him from serving officers in Indiamen and the Country ships, and from his friends in the various settlements in the East, and he wished to receive the same sort of help from the officers of the Royal Navy. It has already been noted that Anson had ordered information to be sent back during the Seven Years' War, and he had specified fortifications and watering-places as constituting the type of intelligence that was required. On 6 February 1804 this idea was revived, and a long memorandum was issued from the Admiralty Office, wherein it was considered 'highly important to the advancement of Nautical

85 I.O. Lbry., *Boards Collections*, Vol. 181, pp. 27–37.

86 See *Philosophical Transactions of the Royal Society of London for the year 1805*, Part 2, pp. 177–85. This paper was addressed to Henry Cavendish, to whom Horsburgh had been introduced by Dalrymple in 1801. The paper was entitled 'Abstract of Observations on a Diurnal Variation of the Barometer between the Tropics'.

87 University of Edinburgh Library, La II/589, Dalrymple to Horsburgh, 19 September 1805.

88 L. S. S. Dawson, *Memoirs of Hydrography*, Part 1, Eastbourne, 1885, p. 43.

Knowledge, and the safety of His Majesty's Ships, that the Reports on Coasts, Harbours, etc. which the Officers of His Majesty's Navy are directed to transmit to this Office, should be made with every possible degree of correctness', and for this purpose a most detailed form of Remark Book was devised, requiring full information under eight heads.[89] It was further stated that their Lordships had given directions to the hydrographer to examine such reports, and to state to them how far they appeared to him to have been made with a due attention to the objects of these instructions. The Journals, Nautical Descriptions, charts, etc., of any captured ships were likewise to be sent back for the use of the Hydrographical Office. The result, however, was derisory. Nearly three years later Dalrymple, recalling how 'their Lordships Orders, for every Man of War to give in a Report under established Heads, were revived during the time Earl St Vincent presided at the Admiralty', observed that 'only one Report has been sent to the Hydrographical Office, under the enjoined heads, and that one of a well known part of the Coast of England, in a very exceptionable stile'.[90] It seems strange that whereas many of the civilian officers of a commercial company went out of their way to co-operate, the serving officers of a disciplined navy entirely ignored these orders, especially when they had emanated from so redoubtable a source as Earl St Vincent!

The unsatisfactory materials which his office possessed even of Britain's own coastline were revealed, from time to time, in Dalrymple's official letters. On one occasion he was remarking that they had no 'Survey of any part of the S° coast of England between the S.Foreland and the Owers except Rye,

[89] These were:
1. Situation. Latitude, Longitude and Compass Variation.
2. Directions for sailing into, or out of Ports, and for avoiding dangers.
3. Marks for anchoring.
4. Wooding and Watering.
5. Provisions and refreshments.
6. Fortifications and Landing Places.
7. Trade and Shipping.
8. Inhabitants.

[90] Adm. 1/3522. Letters dated 6 February 1804 and 23 December 1806.

Pensey, Cockmere, New Haven, Shoreham and Arundel', and he drew attention to the inexpensive method which he and Rennell had proposed for carrying out such work on the Coromandel coast in 1785.[91]

He returned to the need for accurate surveys of home waters when he commented on Ainslie's map of Scotland,[92] which he found to be 'very circumstantial in detail', but with great defects in its construction. 'It is a great discredit to this Country,' he wrote, 'that so few places are determined in Latitude precisely, and still fewer in Longitude; notwithstanding the perfection to which Instruments and Chronometers are now brought: It is to be wished that the Commissioners would supply a Competent Person with a Hadley, Artificial Horizon and 2 Pocket Chronometers the expense of all of which would be under £200 and the necessary knowledge and practice for using them is easily attainable by any Person of common capacity.'[93] Similarly he found that the existing surveys of Falmouth and Dungeness conflicted in detail, and his suggestions that these could be verified at small expense, by Captains Hurd and Edmonds respectively, were agreed to.[94] He also emphasized the need for a survey of the Channel Islands, as parts of the existing charts were believed to be very defective, and the pilots untrustworthy; to ensure precision he urged that orders should be given to use a Hadley for taking angles. In the absence of a separate surveying service, the best he could do was to take every passing opportunity as it came. Where a need existed, and a ship with

91 Adm. 1/3522, Dalrymple to Nepean, 8 June 1801. At this time Graeme Spence, who had retired from active surveying, still had an office in the Admiralty and was engaged in altering Murdoch Mackenzie's Sailing Instructions for the north coast of Kent to suit present conditions, but here Dalrymple suggested that this would inevitably mean that the new Sailing Instructions would not match up with the charts, and that it would have been better to have reproduced them as written by Mackenzie, with the addition of a warning as to the alterations that had taken place since the survey was made, through the shifting of the sands and the changing of the channels. – Adm. 1/3522. Letter dated 17 January 1804. See also A. H. W. Robinson, *Marine Cartography in Britain*, Leicester, 1962, p. 102.

92 This was based on a survey made in 1784–5.

93 Adm. 1/3522. Letter dated 1 August 1805.

94 Ibid., letters of 15 June and 6 August 1805.

a well qualified man in command happened to be in that area, he would draw the Admiralty's attention to the case in point, and trust that action would be taken.

On 28 February 1807 he took the opportunity of the loss of HMS *Athenian* 'which mistook her landfall', not only to impress upon the authorities 'how expedient it is for Views to be taken of all Lands seen', but also to urge 'how necessary it is for HM ships to be supplied with Chronometers with which the whole Navy of England might be supplied at a less expense than the loss of this One Ship has occasioned not to mention the inestimable Lives lost to their Country by that event'.[95]

It was with the appointment of Lord Mulgrave[96] as First Lord of the Admiralty, in March 1807, that the personal tragedy which closed the great hydrographer's career began to take shape.

Two months after the new First Lord had taken office, Dalrymple received an order to purchase for the Hydrographic Office a complete set of all the charts published in England. Presumably the Royal Navy was experiencing a shortage of charts which it wanted to rectify. It is most unlikely that the Hydrographic Office, with its small staff, and starting from the very beginning, could have kept pace with the Service's requirements, and the emphasis had been on the routes to India and China, a task which had kept the copper-plate printer fully occupied until October 1806. The compilation of this new list was a big undertaking, as many plates had been destroyed, and sometimes the only available impressions from them were in private collections, but by 10 October 1807 Dalrymple was able to present a detailed list. He pointed out that he was unable to judge the merit of individual charts, but he suggested that ships could be issued with them provided they were accompanied with a caution. He also commended Kempenfelt's proposal of 1780, that where experience showed that these charts were

95 Adm. 1/3522. Dalrymple to Marsden 28 February 1807. As already noted, the Navy was slow to respond, and complaints about the lack of chronometers were being voiced in 1812 – see p. 239, n.(42).

96 He was the younger brother and heir of Alexander Dalrymple's deceased friend.

good, they could be distinguished by an Admiralty stamp of approval.[97]

It was at this stage that the crisis began to develop, for Dalrymple was being pressed to decide upon the suitability or otherwise of the charts to be issued, but, as he pointed out, he had no experience to guide him in European and American waters, and would incur 'odium and embarrassment' if he had to decide on the merits of charts 'without any data to guide or support' his judgement. This was an entirely reasonable and correct attitude, as was his proposal that a 'Committee of Officers who have the necessary experience' should be set up to select the charts to be used by the Royal Navy. As he explained, 'it was for enabling the officers of HM Navy to point out where they knew, by experience, charts to be good or bad, that I recommended printing the lists'. He also reverted to the eminently sensible suggestion which he had made four years earlier, that the engraving of foreign charts, where secrecy was not involved, should be entrusted to outside firms.[98]

The proposal to set up a chart committee was immediately taken up, its three members being Captains Sir Home Popham, Hurd and Columbine, with John Barrow as Secretary to the Committee.[99] There need have been no friction over this arrangement, had the Committee's terms of reference been carefully drafted to ensure that it did not encroach upon the hydrographer's wider duties. Unfortunately, the Committee made no attempt to concern itself only with the merits of individual charts. It operated in a tactless and even arrogant manner, and in view of Dalrymple's age, and his bad personal relationship with the First Lord, it is difficult to avoid the impression that an ambition to succeed the hydrographer was motivating one or more of its members. That suspicion is not lessened by the Com-

97 Adm. 1/3522. 10 October 1807. On 14 November 1807 he augmented this list with another recording all the plates engraved, and the charts and plans prepared for engraving, by the Hydrographic Office, but most unfortunately this list has disappeared.

98 Adm. 1/3522. 24 November 1807.

99 Hurd and Columbine had both made their names with surveys of the West Indies and America, which suggests that that was where the Royal Navy was most ill-equipped with charts.

mittee's Second Report, on 5 February 1808, which made a particular point of the fact that no charts of the American coast or the Bermudas, which were then required for a ship, were published by the Hydrographic Office; for had not Captain Hurd, who was to succeed Dalrymple, made his name with his survey of the Bermudas?

The three reports of the Chart Committee,[100] which so humiliated and angered Dalrymple, advanced from a discussion of the merits of individual charts to proposals for the future policy of the Hydrographic Office. Furthermore, Dalrymple was not asked to preside at these meetings, but was treated as a source of irritation and, where possible, ignored. He had always been hot-tempered and obstinate, and could be a difficult man to deal with, but in view of his age and his great record of achievement and selfless endeavour, this treatment was inexcusable and reflects no credit on its authors. The subsequent reports, in Parliament and elsewhere, about the chaos in his office and his own senility, should be treated with great reserve and scepticism. They were, at the very least, grossly exaggerated and came from those who were responsible for his downfall, and wished to defend themselves from the subsequent uproar.

It has usually been supposed that his dismissal was caused by the dispute over the charts of the d'Entrecasteaux expedition, which flared up in May 1808, and this was implied by the account given to Parliament which referred to his repeated refusal to respond to orders, a description which could only relate to that one case. But Dalrymple recorded how he had been called to the office of the Secretary, Mr Pole, on 26 April 1808, when the latter 'took great pains to assure me, that what he said did not come from himself'. He told Dalrymple that new arrangements were being planned for the Hydrographical Office, and that it was supposed that at his time of life it would not be agreeable to take charge of such work. He was therefore invited to retire. But Dalrymple was adamant. 'I would never agree,' he told the Secretary, 'to be superannuated, so long as I retained my faculties . . . if I was dismissed, I could

100 They were issued on 4 December 1807, 5 February and 10 March 1808, and are to be found in Adm. 1/3523.

not help it – but I would never resign. If I outlived my faculties, I must then submit to be taken care of.' He was officially informed of his dismissal one month later, and when he was told that he would be awarded a pension on half-pay, he promptly declined to accept it.[101]

The dispute over the French charts related to the expedition which had been sent out under the command of Joseph de Bruni d'Entrecasteaux to search for the lost ships of La Pérouse.[102] Sir Joseph Banks had been personally responsible for getting the Government to issue orders 'in favour of Le Pérouse, wheresoever our fleets should come in contact with that unfortunate navigator'. Safe conducts for scientific expeditions were customary at that time, as they were held to benefit all. La Pérouse's ships had been expected at Mauritius in 1788, and when they had failed to appear by mid-1789 anxiety began to grow. Early in 1791 the National Assembly had therefore authorized the despatch of this new search party, and Louis XVI had signed the necessary decrees. La Pérouse had vanished after leaving Botany Bay in February 1788, so d'Entrecasteaux had sailed out by way of Tasmania and in the course of his wanderings had circumnavigated Australia, had coasted along New Caledonia, and had sailed through both the St George's Channel between New Ireland and New Britain, and Dampier's Strait separating New Britain and New Guinea. The expedition had then sailed to Java, where the first news of the execution of Louis XVI had been received, an event that divided the crew into royalist and revolutionary factions and brought the enterprise to an end. D'Entrecasteaux had died and Rossel had taken over effective command. The ships had been retained by the Dutch as a security for French debts, and in 1795 Rossel had been on his way home in a Dutch ship, carrying with him the expedition's

[101] *The Case of Alexander Dalrymple*, London, 31 May 1808. There is a copy of this rare pamphlet in the Library of the Royal Geographic Society, London. Pole again showed his distress at the part he was called upon to play when the matter was raised in Parliament – on the first occasion he was conspicuous by his absence.

[102] For La Pérouse, see J. Dunmore, *French Explorers in the Pacific, Vol. I, The Eighteenth Century*, Oxford, 1965, pp. 250–82. For d'Entrecasteaux and the search for La Pérouse, Ibid., pp. 283–341.

papers and natural history specimens, when he had been captured by the British. Amongst the papers were the valuable charts made of these almost unknown waters by Beautemps-Beaupré.

Having been brought back to England, Rossel had been entertained to dinner at the Royal Society Club, as Dalrymple's guest, on 27 October 1796, and he was then employed as a temporary assistant at the Hydrographic Office. 'M. Roselle has been employed,' explained Dalrymple, 'in calculating the astronomical observations made in the late voyage of the French; certainly observations in seas so little frequented are useful to Navigation. . . .'[103] It is worth pondering whether Matthew Flinders, who left Spithead in July 1801 on the way to his great circumnavigation of Australia, was able to benefit from information supplied by Rossel; he was certainly armed with a memoir prepared by Dalrymple on the winds to be expected on the south coast of Australia, and would obviously have visited the Hydrographic Office when preparing for the voyage. Rossel had eventually returned to France during the Peace of Amiens, when émigrés were once more welcomed in their homeland.

When Captain Columbine of the Chart Committee realized that the charts were still in the safe keeping of the Hydrographic Office, he was taken aback. These 'valuable surveys of the coasts of New Guinea, New Britain, etc., etc.,' he wrote, were 'the principal authentic materials for these extensive but very little known coasts,' and he deplored the fact that they had been 'carefully concealed from the world in the Hydrographic Office', despite copies of them having been 'liberally communicated to the French Government'. To the mind of a serving officer engaged in a world war the issue was simple; the charts had been captured from the enemy and should be used.

To the scientist a matter of principle was involved which led to a different conclusion. It had been customary for eighteenth century voyages of exploration to be given protection, even by enemies in time of war. D'Entrecasteaux's expedition had been no exception. True, Sir Joseph Banks had originally intended to present the Natural History Collection to Queen Charlotte,

103 Adm. 1/3522. Dalrymple to Secretary, 25 August 1799.

since he had believed that the expedition had been a royalist enterprise, and that the scientists on board had forfeited their claim to these finds by joining the Revolutionary faction. But when he had learnt that the expedition had been under the direction of the Revolutionary Government throughout, he had changed his mind and had decided that the collection must be returned to France.[104] 'I confess I wished much to have from his [i.e. Labillardière's] specimens some of those discoveries in the Natural Order of plants which he must have made,' declared Banks, 'but it seemed to my feelings dishonourable to avail myself of the opportunity I had of examining them. I have not possessed myself of anything at all of his that fortune committed to my custody.'[105] It is also recorded that Sir Joseph 'sent to the Cape of Good Hope, to recover some charts belonging to Humboldt, which our cruizers had seized.'[106] The same strict code of honour dictated Dalrymple's course of action. "Entrecasteaux's charts etc.,' he wrote, 'are a secret[107] Deposit. The originals were sent to France, the copies were made to prevent accident in the passage to France and have never been communicated except some concerning Van Diemen's Land under strict injunctions of keeping them secret. I have always kept the key of the drawer where they are in my possession.'[108] On 13 May the Chart Committee got the Secretary to order the surrender of these charts, and when Dalrymple complied with this order on the following day, he took the occasion to submit a further letter explaining his views. 'In such Voyages of Discovery,' he wrote, 'the Public Faith has been mutual and even Bonaparte has given orders . . . for Capt. Flinders' Release.[109] The Charts of Entrecasteaux's

104 H. C. Cameron, *Sir Joseph Banks*, London, 1952, p. 212, and Lord Brougham, *Lives of Philosophers of the time of George III*, Glasgow and London, 1855, p. 369. According to Brougham, Banks restored them as if he feared that anyone should profit by any discoveries save their rightful owner, 'the author'.

105 Cameron, op. cit., p. 213.

106 Brougham ut supra.

107 or sacred? This word is difficult to decipher in the MS.

108 Adm. 1/3523. Dalrymple to Columbine, 11 May 1808.

109 Matthew Flinders, after his circumnavigation of Australia, was held as a prisoner-of-war on Mauritius from 1803 onwards. Dalrymple was one of the men whom he had asked his brother in England to approach for help on his behalf. Cultivating his acquaintance, he wrote, 'will do you

Voyage were on board a Dutch Indiaman.... This Indiaman was captured in the passage when no war was declared.... On no other pretence but Security against accident could copies have been honourably made, and on no account can they be published, till the French publish them, without a disgraceful and flagrant breach of Publick Faith.... Fully convinced of this Public Duty,' he concluded, 'I have abstained from making use of them myself altho' I have a chart partly engraved of those parts from Original Documents not published; but knowing M. Entrecasteaux's Discoveries exist I am prevented from publishing for the East India Company what I do know....'[110]

It should be borne in mind, when considering Dalrymple's attitude, that he knew that his old colleague Rossel was preparing an official account of the voyage, which was to be embellished by Beautemps-Beaupré's charts, and publication could be expected at any time; in fact, by a tragic irony this publication had already taken place (1807), though war-time conditions had prevented the news from reaching England. To a generation inured to world wars, and to governments which often paid little attention to public faith, his actions may seem to have been idealistic and impractical. Be that as it may, he had virtually won his fight on this matter of principle, for the Chart Committee now modified its attitude. It gave an assurance that the French charts would only be used for fixing the principal points on the coasts concerned, and only upon the general charts, without entering into detail or publishing a copy of the work. It rightly felt that there could be no impropriety in using the charts in this limited manner.[111] But Dalrymple's stand, though it did him great honour, probably hastened his dismissal, which occurred on 28 May 1808.

He himself foreshadowed the end. 'Nothing,' he wrote, 'is so apt to produce Bile as Chagrin! ... having through Life devoted myself to the Service of the Publick, and to gain fair Fame by

---

honour, and is only a tribute due to men who have so usefully distinguished themselves' – see S. J. Baker, *My Own Destroyer: biography of M. Flinders*, Sydney, 1963, p. 131, quoting letter of 6 December 1806.

[110] Adm. 1/3523. Dalrymple to Secretary, 14 May 1808.

[111] Adm. 1/3523. 21 May 1808.

my hydrographical Labours, in which I have been arduously employed these 49 years, having returned twice from India, poorer than I went thither, and having but a very limited income, Debarring my free exertions in the former, and diminishing the last, may produce Bile from Chagrin. . . .' He tried to comfort himself with lines from the poet Cotton—

> To be resigned if Ills betide,
> Patient if Favours are denied,
> And pleased with Bounties given;
> This is truely Wisdom's part,
> This is that Incense of the Heart,
> Whose fragrance mounts to Heaven.[112]

Patience and resignation, however, were foreign to his temperament, and his fears for his health proved only too well founded. He had lived for his work, and his dismissal was a sentence of death.

He had been dining weekly at the Royal Society Club during March and April, and Captain Beaufort[113] had been his guest. His last two dinners were on 2 and 9 June, at the former of which Sir Joseph Banks presided, and Henry Cavendish and

[112] *The Case of Alexander Dalrymple,* ut supra.

[113] Beaufort, like Horsburgh, owed much to Dalrymple's early encouragement. After recommending an immediate survey of the banks and shoals between England and the coasts of Holland and Denmark (4 April 1808), Dalrymple added: 'It is fortunate that a Vessel most admirably adapted for the Service proposed is at present unemployed, and her Commander unquestionably as fit as any Man living to be entrusted with the execution of the Service. I mean Captain Beaufort of His Majesty's Ship Woolwich. . . .' (9 April) – Adm. 1/3523.

According to the *Dictionary of National Biography,* Beaufort first conceived the notion of his Beaufort Scale when in command of this vessel. It is noteworthy that in 1807 Dalrymple was employing an engraver 'to make Drawings, from Pictures of Sea-Pieces, to show the progress of Wind from a Calm to a Storm'. In his Will (1798; codicil 1805) he had stated that 'it would be very useful to have a series of prints of Sea-pieces to explain the degrees and gradations of Wind from a Calm to a Storm which gradations are so well expressed in pictures in my Collection I bequeath those pictures . . . . to the . . . Admiralty for the Treatise of Navigation which I have printed wherein is the List for the said Gradations of Wind taken from the Sea Journals compared with Mr Smeaton's Scale from the Work on Windmills . . .' See my 'The Emergence of the Beaufort Scale', *Mariner's Mirror,* Vol. 53, No. 4, Nov. 1967, pp. 311–13, and Vol. 54, No. 4, Nov. 1968, p. 412.

Dr Maskelyne were present. These old friends were taking this first opportunity of demonstrating solidarity with their distressed colleague. At both these dinners 'Mr Barrow' was Dalrymple's guest, and one may assume that this was John Barrow, the Secretary of the Chart Committee. Forty years later, Barrow, who was never renowned for accuracy, wrote about Dalrymple's declining powers in his old age, and his unreasonable attitude towards retirement, but he himself had been closely involved in the Committee's disputes with the hydrographer, and probably felt remorse for the part which he had been called upon to play.[114]

A few years afterwards, William Marsden told Joseph Farington, the artist, that the real reason for Dalrymple's dismissal was his excessive rudeness to Lord Mulgrave, and that his obstinacy affected his own spirits and killed him.[115] Dalrymple died in his home in High Street, St Marylebone on 19 June 1808, just ten days after that last dinner at the Club. He was buried in the small cemetery alongside the Parish church, where no monument, or even gravestone, appears in his memory.

Kempenfelt had once told Dalrymple that British ministers had seldom been noted for encouraging men of genius. 'A genius in this country,' he had written, 'may remain unknown to our Ministers, though known and esteemed in every other State of Europe.'[116] These proved to be prophetic words, for on 8 March 1812, at the height of the Napoleonic Wars, M. Delambre wrote to Sir Joseph Banks, from Paris, to advise him that on 16 December 1811 Alexander Dalrymple, of whose death they had not heard, had been elected a corresponding member of the First Class of the Institut National[117] – a rare honour in the circumstances.

[114] John Barrow, *Sketches of the Royal Society and the Royal Society Club*, London, 1849, pp. 134–9. *The Farington Diary* (ed. Jas. Greig), Vol. V, London, 1925, p. 74, describes the Club's sympathy for Dalrymple at this last dinner.

[115] *Farington's Diary*, Vol. VII, London, 1927, p. 202.

[116] *European Magazine*, Vol. 42, p. 421, Kempenfelt to Dalrymple, 24 December 1780.

[117] Sir G. de Beer, *The Sciences were Never at War*, London, 1960, pp. 191–3.

CHAPTER X

Alexander Dalrymple and Captain Cook

THE historical significance of Alexander Dalrymple's career has been overlooked for two reasons, his exclusion from positions of executive power at an early stage of his career, and the ill-supported legend that he was the life-long enemy of Captain Cook.

His exclusion from an executive role began in 1768 when, through no fault of his own, he was deprived of the command of the *Endeavour*, and the great achievements of his successor so obscured his own vital contribution that even the memory of his name has been condemned to a shadowy oblivion. This setback was immediately followed by the East India Company's decision to entrust the management of the Balambangan settlement to other hands. Under a good leader Balambangan might have attained the fame of a Singapore. As it was, under Herbert's woeful leadership the settlement came to a disaster, which has diverted the attention of subsequent generations from the seminal importance of that experiment.

Whereas the overthrow of Balambangan has contributed to the neglect of Dalrymple's significance, however, the legend of his supposed enmity with Captain Cook has done his reputation positive harm. It has led to the belief that he was a small-minded, vindictive man, a misreading of his character that has resulted in a grave underestimate of the impact of his personality and influence upon the men of his time. It is therefore important to pay serious attention to the charge.

The evidence cited to support this view consists of Dalrymple's two letters to Dr Hawkesworth in 1773, a footnote in his *Memoir concerning the Chagos and Adjacent Islands* (1786) and a passage in his pamphlet entitled *A Serious Admonition to the Publick on the intended Thief Colony at Botany Bay* (1786). In weighing up this evidence it is most convenient to begin with the Memoir and the pamphlet, since in both cases the relevant passages refer to the so-called 'Dauphin' map which, in Dalrymple's view, provided evidence of the discovery of the east coast of Australia by unknown Europeans as early as the sixteenth century.[1]

As explained in Chapter V, Dalrymple saw the proposal to colonize Botany Bay as one of a series of steps aimed at undermining the monopoly of the East India Company. He was convinced that this monopoly was essential, especially for trade with the Eastern Islands, yet he was aware that the new administration of the Younger Pitt was much influenced by the free-trade doctrines of Adam Smith. He did not believe that Botany Bay would remain a mere convict settlement, for the fact that the project 'was at one time to have been protected by Imperial Colors as well as English . . . explains the true Prospects of the Undertakers; viz., to carry on an illicit Trade under pretext of a Colony'. This was what persuaded Dalrymple to muster every argument he could think of to put obstacles in the way of this experiment, including the suggestion (which he himself admitted to be far-fetched) that the prior discovery of this coast by unknown Europeans in the sixteenth century deprived the English of any legal claim to establish a settlement there. He introduced the Dauphin map as evidence of such prior discovery; his remarks had nothing to do with any supposed attack upon Captain Cook.

Dalrymple's other reference to the Dauphin map, in the footnote to the Memoir concerning the Chagos and Adjacent Islands, was written at this same time. In that memoir he was pointing out that though the Chagos archipelago and the Maldive Islands had been among the earliest Portuguese discoveries in the East, knowledge of them had been lost in subsequent years. He was stressing that knowledge was sometimes lost in this way through failure to observe clear principles when naming what were believed to be new discoveries. Dalrymple recommended that native names should always be used when they were available. When they were not known, or did not exist, he recommended the use

[1] For some comments on the sixteenth-century Dieppe maps, of which this was one, see *The Journals of Captain Cook* (ed. J. C. Beaglehole), Vol. 1, Cambridge, 1955, pp. xxx–xxxi.

of descriptive names. As evidence of the value of using descriptive names he cited, in this famous footnote, the examples of the sixteenth-century cartographer of the Dauphin map, and of Captain Cook. It was because they had both used this sensible procedure that he himself, when the Dauphin map came to light, had been able to recognize that they were both describing the same coastline. Thus Captain Cook's:

> Bay of Inlets is in the MS. called Baye Perdue
> Bay of Isles R. de beaucoup d'isles
> Where the Endeavour struck Coste dangereuse.

Strangely enough, it was R. H. Major, already quoted in the Preface as drawing attention to Dalrymple's significance in Britain's commercial history, who gave currency to the long-held view that this footnote constituted an attack upon Captain Cook, instead of recognizing it as the commendation that it really was. According to Major, Dalrymple had made 'an invidious insinuation . . . and his observation would seem to imply that Cook, who had been so successful in his discoveries on the coast of New Holland, might have been led thereto by an acquaintance with this pre-existent map'.[2] It never seems to have occurred to Major that Dalrymple would have been the last man to have resorted to insinuation. Nobody ever accused him of timidity. Not unjustifiably did he write in his last days that the crest of a rock and the motto 'Neminem Timeas' had been the 'Pole Star and Crozier of his course thro' life'. If he had wished to attack Cook, he would have done so in the most forthright terms. Not only would such insinuation have been wholly out of character, but it would have conflicted with Dalrymple's consistent practice, as a point of honour, never to attack the dead.

Major had adopted this view from an article written by a certain M. Frederic Metz and published in France in 1805. It is noteworthy that Metz, who entirely misunderstood Dalrymple's argument, failed either to quote Dalrymple's own words, or to name the Memoir in which they appeared. Furthermore, Metz implied that Dalrymple was suggesting that Cook could have

[2] R. H. Major (ed.), *Early Voyages to Terra Australis, now called Australia* (Hakluyt Society), London, 1859, p. xxxi.

studied the Dauphin map in the British Museum which was nonsensical, since Sir Joseph Banks only presented the map to the Museum in 1790. Major knew this, yet he adopted Metz's interpretation despite the fact that he included, in that same introduction, a categorical statement made by 'the celebrated geographer M. Barbié du Bocage' in 1807 that 'the English pretend that none of these charts [i.e., those of the Dieppe school of cartography, including the Dauphin map] were discovered till after the death of the celebrated Captain Cook and that they had no knowledge of them when this navigator set sail'.[3] This statement should have prevented Metz's interpretation, apparently based upon an imperfect grasp of the English tongue, from ever becoming established.

There is no question, of course, that Dalrymple was deeply disappointed at the turn of events in the spring of 1768; any man would have been. To appreciate his disappointment fully it is well to recall that there were good reasons why that particular expedition could have been under civilian command. As precedents Dalrymple himself cited Dampier and Halley who, as civilians, had led naval scientific expeditions at the turn of the century. Moreover, in the spring of 1768 a French naval expedition was actually exploring the South Pacific under the command of Bougainville, who was not even a scientist or a sailor, let alone a naval officer. Dalrymple himself could claim to be both scientist and sailor, and in his skill as a navigator, surveyor, cartographer and hydrographer he was second to none. Moreover, it is generally forgotten that the 1768 expedition of the *Endeavour* was only a naval undertaking by chance. This expedition was planned by and for the Royal Society, and Dalrymple had been nominated by that Society as its chosen commander. The *Endeavour* itself was originally a merchantman, and it was only the Royal Society's lack of funds that compelled it, through the

[3] Ibid., p. xxxv. The whole subject of this footnote is dealt with in greater detail in my article 'Early British interest in the Chagos Archipelago and the Maldive Islands', in *The Mariner's Mirror*, Vol. 53, 1967, no. 4, pp. 353–6. Contemporaries who shared Dalrymple's view that the Dieppe maps depicted the east coast of Australia included Rennell, Pinkerton, Jas. Burney, and the French geographer Buache.

king, to call for Admiralty assistance in purchasing and manning the ship.

Despite this great disappointment Dalrymple never criticized Cook personally in the months that intervened between the time of Cook's appointment and the sailing of the *Endeavour*, nor did he do so during the voyage or immediately after the vessel's return, though he was present when Cook delivered his journal and papers to the Royal Society, and presumably met him on various social occasions. It is inconceivable that a man of Dalrymple's warmth of temper would have waited for five years before giving expression to his bitterness had Captain Cook been the object of his wrath, yet the attack only came when the official account of the voyage was published in 1773.

Lord Sandwich, the First Lord of the Admiralty, had decided that the story of Britain's exploration of the South Pacific since 1764, including the voyages of Byron, Wallis, Carteret and of Cook in the *Endeavour*, should be told to the world. Yet he had felt that the original journals would make unattractive reading for the general public, for which reason he had appointed a successful writer of the day, Dr Hawkesworth, to edit them in more popular form. Under this arrangement, however, it had been agreed that Hawkesworth should be free to intersperse his own observations where he saw fit, and there was no way in which the reader could discover which portions were quoted from the journals, and which were Hawkesworth's interspersions.

The first of Hawkesworth's volumes to appear was the one dealing with Cook's voyage, and in view of its topical interest it was assured of a world-wide audience. When Dalrymple read it, however, he was justifiably upset. It will be remembered that in 1767, when the Royal Society had been considering whom they should appoint as commander of their expedition, Dalrymple had printed his *An Account of the Discoveries made in the South Pacific Ocean previous to 1764* to strengthen his own claim, and that when the *Endeavour* had sailed Dalrymple had given a copy of this work to Sir Joseph Banks, the Royal Society's representative on board the ship. This work had included Arias's account of Torres's voyage through Torres Strait. Then, while the voyage was under way, Dalrymple had published his *An Historical Account of the Several Voyages and Discoveries in the South Pacific Ocean,* the importance of which had been quickly appreciated by Benjamin Franklin and others, at whose instigation Dalrymple had thereupon been elected a Fellow of the Royal Society in recognition of his skill 'in Mathematical and Geographical Knowledge' and for this work of 'translation of Voyages to the South Seas and other Places from Spanish'.

These books had been written not merely as works of scholarship, but also with the specific intention of persuading his countrymen to persist in their search for the conjectural Great Southern Continent, lest their French rivals should get there first. Because of the urgency of this undertaking, where success might vitally affect the balance of sea-power in the years ahead, Dalrymple had depicted the potentialities of such a discovery in vivid terms. But in Hawkesworth's first volume Dalrymple now found that whereas his arguments in favour of a Southern Continent had been criticized with the wisdom of hindsight, his important contributions to the success of the expedition had been entirely ignored. Without his arguments in favour of a Southern Continent it is very possible, even probable, that Cook's instructions would not have stressed the importance of his searching for it, which was to lead to his circumnavigation of New Zealand to his exploration of the eastern coasts of Australia. Apart from that, Hawkesworth made no mention of his share in the choice of the *Endeavour,* or of his exceptionally important revelation of the existence of Torres Strait. This was both unjust and ungenerous, and Dalrymple's violent reaction was that of a man who found his highly-prized and hard-won reputation under sudden unprovoked attack, in a work that was bound to have a world-wide audience.

In his anger Dalrymple certainly went too far and, smarting under his own sense of injustice, was insensitive to the distress that he was bringing to others. 'The death of poor Dr Hawkesworth,' wrote Frances Burney, the sister of Dalrymple's later friend James Burney, 'is most sincerely lamented by us all, the more so as we do really attribute it to the abuse he has of late met with from the newspapers . . . Dr Hawkesworth said he had not yet made an answer to the torrent poured upon him, except to Dalrymple who had attacked him by name.' Both parties were to blame in this dispute, but Dalrymple has been censured for the wrong reasons. His two letters are good evidence of his recurring loss of self-control, but they are poor witnesses for a lasting enmity towards Captain Cook; there is a great difference between a passing and understandable storm of anger, and a life-long enmity dictating a man's attitude in after years.

The first letter was designed to set the record straight by showing that Hawkesworth had misrepresented Dalrymple's views and had made many careless errors. Knowing that he had been deprived of the command of the *Endeavour* by senior officers at the Admiralty, Dalrymple suspected that the unfair criticism to which he had been subjected had not been accidental, but deliberate. Hawkesworth's answer to the suggestion that he had allowed himself to be used as a tool by this 'influence' at the Admiralty was not calculated to mollify Dalrymple's resentment. 'I passed over Torres' track in silence,' he confessed, 'because I had never seen Mr Dalrymple's book in which it was laid down.'

In his first letter Dalrymple confined his attack on Cook to a criticism of his failure to search for the Southern Continent on the way to Tahiti. He had been irritated to read Cook's remark that 'It was a general opinion that there was Land to windward, but I did not think myself at liberty to search for what I was not sure to find'. To the impatient Dalrymple, who feared that foreign rivals might yet forestall the British, such lost opportunities were infuriating. 'Such a declaration, if not foisted in by you, would almost preclude me from taking any further notice of Captain Cook's conduct or opinions', he exclaimed in exasperation. He qualified his criticism in this way because he was not certain that Cook had written the offending words. They might represent one of Hawkesworth's own insertions which were admitted to be more frequent in the volume dealing with Cook's voyage than in the others of the series.

The real attack on Cook came after the appearance of the second edition, in which Hawkesworth assured Dalrymple that he had not advanced any sentiment or opinion of his own regarding the Southern Continent, and that it could be accepted that he had not misrepresented the views of the writers of the journals to whom his manuscript had been read and afterwards delivered. It was only after he had received this assurance that the unfair and inaccurate criticisms of his own views had originated with Captain Cook that Dalrymple decided to hit back hard in a second letter to Hawkesworth. He still suspected, however, that Hawkesworth might 'have suppressed what he found in the Journals to my credit; at least it was natural for me to have expected that if the Writers of those Journals had mentioned my name, they would have taken notice where they found me right, as well as when they thought me wrong'. With his usual candour, Dalrymple confessed that when he had shown his letter to Sir David, his eldest brother, the latter had warned him that it contained 'too much asperity'. Alexander had therefore held up its publication, and before he had had time to amend it Hawkesworth had died so that its publication was abandoned altogether and only the first printed copies remained.

Dalrymple was accustomed to write in the outspoken manner of eighteenth-century pamphleteers, and abhorred what he termed 'the flowery path of flattery and sycophancy', but had his original letter to Hawkesworth been couched in more tactful terms it is possible that the latter, in his second edition, would have made a more graceful acknowledgement of the just grounds for Dalrymple's resentment. As it was, however, Hawkesworth had responded to Dalrymple's tactlessness with a lofty and patronizing air and suggested that Cook should have been above criticism since he was 'universally allowed, except perhaps by Mr Dalrymple, to be as good an officer and as able a navigator as the world has ever seen'. It was this taunt, and the assurance that Cook's remarks had not been misrepresented, that goaded Dalrymple, who hated what he once termed 'the whistling of a name', into those criticisms of Cook, including his grounding of the *Endeavour*, that have led to the belief that he harboured a lasting feeling of enmity towards Captain Cook.

Even when launched into his attack upon Cook, however,

Dalrymple still qualified his remarks. He continued to feel that 'the jumble between Writer and Amanuensis may make it difficult to know . . . where we are to throw the blame; but I was unwilling to attack the absent[4] while I was not certain that the absent had attacked me'. This remark was significant. It implies that his argument with Cook only began with the appearance of Hawkesworth's volume, and the available evidence bears this out. It also appears that the dispute ended with Dalrymple's second letter to Hawkesworth. No earlier attacks by Dalrymple on Cook, written or verbal, have been recorded, nor were they repeated after 1773. His indignation in that year was primarily directed against Hawkesworth, and his irritation with Captain Cook was confined to two points; he was upset by the ungenerous treatment that he had been accorded in the present publication, and he was critical of the failure to make full use of the outward voyage to seek the Southern Continent. It is noteworthy that after the completion of the second circumnavigation he had no further grounds for complaint on either score, and he never again attacked Captain Cook in his writings.

The real cause of Dalrymple's resentment had been the unjustified harm that had been done to his reputation as historian and geographer, and it must be admitted that the manner in which writers down to the present day have derided his faith in a Southern Continent confirms that his fears were well grounded. He himself was an original thinker who believed that 'errors may lead to truth, but when all men's notions are ground in one mill, they serve no purpose of investigation or discovery'.[5] But he no doubt knew that this is not the common view, and that the world does not readily tolerate the man who has dared to be wrong.

Dalrymple himself confessed to a sense of grievance against the men who, at the very last moment, had wrested from his grasp the command of the *Endeavour* and thus denied him the greatest opportunity of his life. Contrary to general belief,

[4] Cook was then at sea on his second circumnavigation.

[5] A. Dalrymple, *An Historical Collection . . .*, Vol. 1, London, 1790, p. xvi.

however, Sir Edward Hawke who was First Lord of the Admiralty from December 1766 to January 1771, was not one of them. 'I am very far from intending the most distant insinuation or resentment to, or dissatisfaction with, the worthy and brave old officer who was at the head of the Admiralty when the *Endeavour* was purchased,' wrote Dalrymple in 1773, 'his ideas were clear and just in the only conference I ever had with him, and I have been told that afterwards "He lamented I did not go".' In his Memoirs (1802) he added that Hawke had been 'wrought upon by insinuation that he would be exposed to a parliamentary impeachment if he employed any but a Naval Officer'.

It was Kippis, the first biographer of Cook, who stated that Sir Edward Hawke had declared 'that he would suffer his right hand to be cut off before he would sign any [brevet] commission' for Dalrymple, but the truthfulness of this story is immediately made suspect when one notes that Palliser was one of Kippis's most important sources of information. Palliser was a controversial figure and an unreliable witness. It seems certain that he was one of the men whom Dalrymple held responsible for his own rejection. He was politically active, which would account for the reference to parliamentary impeachment. It was obviously Palliser who had prompted Philip Stephens[6] to suggest Cook as a likely commander for the *Endeavour* in 1768, and in his desire to help his protégé it is very possible that he had denigrated the merits of Alexander Dalrymple; it would not have been out of character.

Sir Charles Saunders was the other man most probably involved. He was the First Lord of the Admiralty in November 1766 when Dalrymple, in a letter to Lord Shelburne, mentioned naval opposition to the appointment of a civilian commander for the forthcoming expedition. Moreover, Hawke would have felt an especial obligation to respond to suggestions from Saunders, since the latter had warmly supported Hawke's appoint-

[6] In a private letter written during the famous dispute between Keppel and Palliser, Sir Joseph Banks summed up the latter's case as 'the iniquitous ambition of an iniquitous Admiralty Baronet'.

Philip Stephens was Secretary of the Admiralty in 1768, and remained a life-long friend of Dalrymple.

ment as First Lord in December 1766 despite bitter opposition from more senior admirals. Saunders would have wanted to see Cook in command of the *Endeavour*, since it was he who had chosen him, despite his 'very subordinate position in the fleet', to survey the Channel of the St Lawrence during the historic attack on Quebec.

In this context it is worth recalling an incident that Dalrymple mentioned in connection with the fitting out of the *Endeavour*. In his letter to Hawkesworth he wrote: 'When I gave as a reason for preferring the *Endeavour* to the other ship that was smaller that being able carry another anchor and cable might be of the utmost consequence, a navy Oracle told me I was much mistaken if I thought I should have just what stores I pleased, that there was an Establishment, although I might be allowed an anchor and cable extraordinary on such a voyage.' This sounds remarkably like Saunders' flat rejection of Captain Carteret's request for extra equipment when he was preparing for his circumnavigation with Wallis in 1766. Carteret rightly protested that the *Swallow* 'was neither a fit Vessell, or properly fitted out for such a Service', but he got no sympathy from Saunders, then First Lord of the Admiralty, whom he found both stubborn and hot-tempered. If Dalyrmple, who had a similar temperament, ever came up against Saunders, a clash would have been well nigh inevitable.

It is noteworthy that two early landfalls in New Zealand which Cook named after men other than members of his crew were Capes Palliser and Saunders. This reinforces the belief that it was they who were primarily responsible for insisting upon a naval appointment to the command of the *Endeavour*, and who represented the 'influence' at the Admiralty to which Dalrymple had referred in his letter to Hawkesworth. But Dalrymple was discriminating in his apportionment of blame, and while resenting the action of those who had forced his own rejection in 1768, and of the author who had gratuitously harmed his reputation, felt no sense of grievance against those who had merely been the tools of this policy – Philip Stephens, who remained a good friend for life, Admiral Sir Edward Hawke, or even Captain Cook, apart from the offending passages and omissions in his journal. Dalrymple's true attitude towards Cook is clear from scattered remarks in his various works; he respected his professional skill, but thought him no more infallible than other men. And had enmity really been known to exist between them, it is unlikely that Lord Sandwich would have invited Dalrymple to play an important part in preparing the official account of Cook's last voyage for publication.

Had there been any inclination towards a personal antipathy between the two men, of which there is no convincing evidence, there were personal links which would have had a moderating influence. In the first place, Dalrymple and Cook had a mutual friend in Commodore William Wilson, who responded to men of character. His fatherly treatment of the youthful Alexander has already been recounted, and the two men remained lifelong friends. On his retirement from the service of the East India Company, which he had served with such distinction, Wilson had settled in the village of Great Ayton in the North Riding of Yorkshire. This was conveniently situated for anyone travelling between London and Edinburgh, and in 1784, when he was arranging to send a letter of commendation on behalf of the commodore's son George, who was about to sail for India, Dalrymple assured Wilson: 'I shall never pass that way without paying my respects at Ayton'. The whole tone of his letter reflected the warmth of his attachment to the old man. By a curious chance Great Ayton had also been the boyhood home of Captain Cook, and when the latter was visiting the village to see his father after the return of the *Endeavour*, he is said to have stayed as the guest of the commodore. According to one of Cook's earlier biographers, Commodore William Wilson and Captain Cook 'felt powerfully attracted to each other, and formed a friendship which lasted during life'.[7]

[7] Rev. George Young, *The Life and Voyages of Captain James Cook*, London, 1836, p. 120.

There was another possible connection between Cook and Dalrymple in Great Ayton, where the lord of the manor, until his death in 1771, was Thomas Skottowe, the man who was the employer of Cook's father and who made himself responsible for James Cook's own boyhood schooling. Was Captain Nicholas Skottowe of the East India Company's maritime service and an old friend of Dalrymple, a relation, perhaps even a son, of Thomas?

A still more interesting personal link between Dalrymple and Cook is to be found in a friendly little letter that has hitherto escaped notice. When it is remembered that the Dalrymples were a particularly close-knit family, and that 'Sandy', as Alexander was known in the family circle, was rather a favourite, the significance of this letter becomes apparent. A friendly exchange of gifts and correspondence between Captain Cook and other members of the Dalrymple family would have been unlikely to have gone on at the same time as a feud with a favourite brother. The recipient of the letter was Captain Hugh Dalrymple, an elder brother of Alexander. Hugh, under whom James Burney had recently been serving, was then in command of HMS *Juno*, and while he was at Portsmouth he received a letter from Captain Cook, addressed from his home in Mile End and dated 22 January 1776. 'Yesterday,' wrote Cook, 'I received your sister's very curious and valuable present in which she has great merit. I should never have thought of applying Otaheito Cloth to such a purpose or that it would have looked half so well as this does. I beg you'll convey my thanks to her for this obliging favour which will remain myne when all my other Southern Curiosities are neglected. If I should make another trip and live to return home, it will give me great pleasure to add to your collection of curiosities. . . .'[8]

On this note of friendship between the Dalrymple family and Captain Cook on the eve of his final voyage, it is appropriate to end this book.

[8] National Library of Scotland, Edinburgh, *Newhailes Archives* (Microfilm). Otaheito was the original name of Tahiti.

Appendix: Genealogical Table

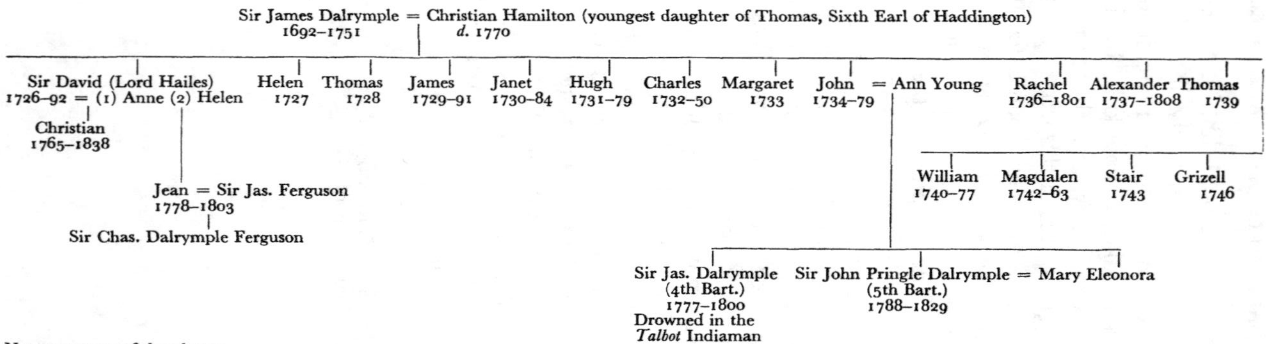

Notes on some of the above:

Sir David (3rd Bart.)
Admitted a member of the Faculty of Advocates, 24 February 1748. Elevated to the Bench, and took his seat as Lord Hailes on 6 March 1766. Appointed a Lord of Justiciary, 3 May 1766. Distinguished scholar and antiquary – wrote *Annals of Scotland*.

James
Lt.-Col. of 1st Bn. Royal Scots. 1773 married Elizabeth, d. of Chas. St Clair (friend of Lords Howe and St. Vincent).

Hugh
Captain of HMS *Canada*. Died at sea.

Charles
Died while a student of Medicine.

John
Merchant. Lord Provost of Edinburgh.

Bibliography

I. MANUSCRIPT SOURCES

ARCHIVES OF THE ADMIRALTY

HYDROGRAPHIC DEPARTMENT, CRICKLEWOOD

Historical Papers Miscellaneous 4, 6, 11, 23, 48.

BODLEIAN LIBRARY, OXFORD

5△ 203 List of Alexander Dalrymple's Nautical Memoirs (incomplete).

MS. Don. e. 55 Incognita, or Love and Duty reconciled. Drama by A. Dalrymple (1795).

MS. Don. f. 25 Dalrymple's annotated copy of *Extracts from Juvenilia.*

BOTANY LIBRARY, NATURAL HISTORY MUSEUM, LONDON

Sir Joseph Banks Correspondence, Vols. 3 and 14.

BRITISH MUSEUM, MANUSCRIPTS ROOM

Add. MSS. 19,295 Correa's account of the Philippine Islands (translated by Sir Hyde Parker).

19,298 Dalrymple's Plan for the Conquest of the Southern Philippines, 1762.

19,299 Rennell's *Journal of a Voyage to the Sooloo Islands and the North-West Coast of Borneo, 1762–3.*

19,300 Extracts from journal by Capt. John Sans of *A Voyage . . . 1610–12*, made by Alexander Dalrymple.

22,900 f. 255 Dalrymple to Geo. Chalmers re Lord Hailes, 16 August 1794.

22,901 f. 275 Dalrymple to Geo. Chalmers re James Dalrymple, 16 March, 1805.
29,210 Baldwin, from Cairo, re lack of charts of the Red Sea, 1776.
33,765 Dalrymple's Geographical Collection, Fort St George, 1758.
38,392 Liverpool Papers, Vol. CCIII (Minutes of the Committee of Trade, 1790 – Meares' evidence re Nootka Sound crisis).
Egerton MSS. 2,180 (preparations for publishing Cook's last voyage).
2,185
2,186

BRITISH MUSEUM, STATE PAPERS OFFICE

Admiralty Order in Council, 12 August 1795, establishing the Hydrographic Office.

INDIA OFFICE LIBRARY

Board's Collections

Vol. 181, Paper 3380. (Proposed survey of the China Seas).
Vol. 49, Paper 1109.
Vol. 74, Paper 1617.

China Miscellaneous

Vol. 7, Part 1, *Memoir on Intercourse with China, 1656–1818.*

China Records, Secret Consultations

Vol. 1, 1796–1800; Vol. 2, 1800–5.

Correspondence Reports

Vols. 5, 6, 8, 9, 12, 21–27.

Despatches to Bombay

Vols. 4, 7, 8, 9, 10, 11, 15.

Despatches to Madras

Vols. 1, 2, 16, 27.

Dutch Records

Vols. 1, 7, 8, 14, 15, 17, 21, 27.

Dutch Records – A

Vol. XVII.

Factory Records, Borneo (1648–1814)
Packet IX.

Factory Records, China and Japan
Vols. 18–20, 93, 195.

Fort St George Public Consultations
Range 240, Vols. 13–22 (1755–64).

Home Miscellaneous Series
Vols. 95, 97, 99, 100, 101, 102, 105, 107, 116, 118, 128, 134, 144, 146, 147, 174, 209, 210, 260, 494, 605, 606, 629, 714, 715, 771, 795, 800.

Letters from the Board of Control to the Company
Vols. 1 (1784–1801), 2 (1801–8).

Letters from the Company to the Board of Control
Vols. 1 (1784–8), 2 (1788–1805), 3 (1805–9).

Correspondence between the Company and the Board
Vol. 1 (1784–95).

Marine Miscellaneous
Vols. 1, 21–23, 26–7, 325, 379, 386, 492, 503–5, 530–4, 680–90, 901.

Marine Records
Ship Journals – the *Pitt* (1758–9), the *Griffin* and *Admiral Pocock* (1761).

Memoranda of the Committee of Correspondence
Vols. 17–18, 24, 25–34, 36, 38–41.

Minutes of the Board of Control
Vol. 1 (1784–93), 2 (1793–1804).

Minutes of the Secret Committee
Vol. 4 (1782–1806).

Miscellaneous Letters Received
Vols. 40–80 (1757–1808) inclusive.

Miscellanies (Home Letters Out)
Vols. 16–47.

Orme Collection
Vols. XV, XVII, XIX, 4, 6, 52, 65, 67, 71, 88, 171, 202, 222, 336.

Personal Records
Vols. XII, XIV.

Political and Secret Department Records (Minutes, etc., of Secret Committee)
Vols. 1 (1778–82), 4 (1782–1806).

References to the Committee of Correspondence
Vols. 1A (1783–1803), 2A (1803–15), 3A (1784–1817).

NATIONAL LIBRARY OF AUSTRALIA, CANBERRA
(Photostat copies in Cambridge University Library)

MSS. 43/1 to 43/21 Letters from Alexander Dalrymple to Henry Dundas, 1784–1802.

MSS. 43/22 Dalrymple to Chalmers; 43/23 Dalrymple to Lord Grenville;

MSS. 43/24 Royal Society Election Notice, 1800.

MSS. 9/55, 9/56, 9/57 Dalrymple to Banks 1783 (publication of Cook's last voyage).

MS. 72/12 Copy of the New Zealand Scheme of Dalrymple and Benjamin Franklin, 1771.

NATIONAL LIBRARY OF SCOTLAND, EDINBURGH

Melville Papers, MSS. 1067, 1068, 1069, 1071.
Newhailes Archives (Microfilm copy of correspondence of many correspondents with Lord Hailes.)

NATIONAL MARITIME MUSEUM, GREENWICH

San/T/7 Transcripts of Sandwich Papers.

Pocock Papers, General Correspondence. See Poc/1g and Poc/2c,

MS. 9956.

Original letters, collected by Wm. Upcott; Naval Characters, Vol. 4 (1803–26) W. Bligh to A. Dalrymple.

Board of Longitude Papers (microfilm copies).

ADM/B/180 (The *Endeavour*)

PUBLIC RECORD OFFICE

Adm. 1/3522, 1/3523. Hydrographer's correspondence with Admiralty, 1795–1808.

Adm. 2/540.

Adm. 51/379, Part. III, Captain Middleton's Log.

Adm. 55/146, Captain Colnett's Log.

Adm. 106/3315.

Chatham Papers 30/8 Vols. 31, and 128 (f.58).

C.O. 42/21, 42/47, 42/66, 42/72.

C.O. 77/19–21, 77/23, 77/25–27.

C.O. Maps 700/America/51. Dalrymple's Map of the Lands around the North-Pole, 1789.

C.O./700/America/49. Peter Pond's map of N.W. America, 1787.

Egremont Papers 30/47, Vol. 20/1 and Vol. 20/3 (Manila expedition, 1762–).

F.O. 41/1 and 41/2.

ROYAL SOCIETY LIBRARY, LONDON

Council Minutes, Vol. (1763–68), 6 (1769–81), 7 (1782–1810).

A. Dalrymple's Certificate of Election as F.R.S. (Elected 14 February 1771. Paid 31 guineas and admitted 14 March 1771).

Royal Society Dinner Club Registers.
Journal.

Letters and Papers, Decade VII, Vol. 61.

Miscellaneous MSS., Vols. 3 and 10.

JOHN RYLANDS LIBRARY, MANCHESTER

Melville Papers, Vols. 672, 673, 677, 692, 697, 927, 931.

Pitt Papers, Vols. 907, 931.

SOMERSET HOUSE

Dalrymple's Will, No. 555 (dated 24 December 1798; codicils and corrections 25 October 1805).

UNIVERSITY OF EDINBURGH LIBRARY

MS. La II 589, Dalrymple to Horsburgh, 1805.

II. PRIMARY PRINTED SOURCES

Dalrymple, Alexander. Printed Books and Tracts. (The place of publication is London unless stated otherwise).

'Memoirs of Alexander Dalrymple Esq.', *European Magazine*, Vol. 42, pp. 323–7* and 421–4, 1802).

A. DISCOVERIES

An Account of the Discoveries made in the South Pacifick Ocean previous to 1764 (Printed 1767; 1769).

An Historical Collection of the Several Voyages and Discoveries in the South Pacific Ocean, (2 Vols. (1770–1).

Proposition of a Benevolent Voyage to introduce Corn, etc. into New Zealand...(1771).

A Letter from Mr Dalrymple to Dr Hawkesworth occasioned by some groundless and Illiberal Imputations in his account of the late Voyages to the South (1773).

Observations on Dr Hawkesworth's Preface to the Second edition (1773).
(The opinion of Sir D. Dalrymple that there was too much asperity in this reply retarded, and the death of Dr Hawkesworth prevented, its publication).

Memorial of Dr Juan Luis Arias (in Spanish) (Edinburgh, 1773).

Proposition for printing, by subscription, the MS Voyages and Travels in the British Museum (1773).

Collection of Voyages, chiefly in the South Atlantick Ocean, from the original MSS by Dr Halley, M. Bouvet etc. with a Preface concerning a Voyage of Discovery, proposed to be undertaken by Alexander Dalrymple at his own expense; Letters to Lord North on the Subject, and Plan of a Republican Colony (1775).

A Collection of Reports in English and Dutch concerning Papua (post–1780).

Considerations on M. Buache's Memoir concerning New Britain and the North Coast of New-Guinea (1790).

'Relation of Luis Vaez de Torres, concerning the discoveries of Quiros . . . dated Manila, July 12, 1607.' A translation, nearly literal, by Alexander Dalrymple from a Spanish MS. copy in his possession. Burney, *Chronological History,* Vol. II (1806), pp. 467–78.

(For the Spanish Discoveries to the North of California, see G. Trade, *Fur-Trade Scheme,* below.)

B. EAST INDIA COMPANY AFFAIRS AND ORGANIZATION

A letter to the Court of Directors . . . concerning the proposed supervisorship (1769).

Second Letter – do. – 10 July 1769.

Vox Populi Vox Dei, Lord Weymouth's Appeal to the General Court of India Proprietors, considered (1769).

Considerations on a Pamphlet (by Governor Johnstone), entitled, *Thoughts on our Acquisitions in the East Indies, particularly respecting Bengal* (1772).

General View of the East India Company (written in January 1769), to which are added some Observations on the present State of the Company's Affairs (1772).

A Paper concerning the General Government for India.

Rights of the East India Company, N.B. This was printed at the Company's expense (1773).

An Historical Relation of the Several Expeditions, from Fort Marlbro' to the Islands off the West Coast of Sumatra (1775).

Copies of Papers relative to the Restoration of the King of Tanjour, the Imprisonment of Lord Pigot, etc. Printed by the East India Company, for the use of the Proprietors (4to, 1777). *N.B.* In this Collection are many Minutes of Council, and some Letters by Alexander Dalrymple.

Several other pieces on the same Subject, written by Alexander Dalrymple, were printed by Admiral Pigot and Alexander Dalrymple, but not sold (1777).

Notes on Lord Pigot's Narrative.

Letter to Proprietors of East India Stock (8 May 1777).

Account of the Transactions concerning the Revolt at Madras (30 April 1777). Appendix.

Letter to the Court of Directors (19 June 1777). *Memorial* (19 June 1777).

Account of the Subversion of the Legal Government of Fort St George, in Answer to Mr. Andrew Stuart's Letter to the Court of Directors (1778).

Considerations on the East India Bill, 1769 (1778).

State of the East India Company... and Sketch of an equitable Agreement (1780).

Reflections on the present State of the East India Company (1783).

A Short Account of the Gentoo Mode of collecting the Revenues on the Coast of Coromandel (1783).

A Restrospective View of the Antient System of the East India Company, with a Plan of Regulation (1784).

Postscript to Mr. Dalrymple's Account of the Gentoo mode of collecting the Revenues on the Coast of Coromandel; being,–Observations made on a Perusal of it by Moodoo Kistna (1785).

Fair State of the Case, between the East India Company and the Owners of Ships now in their Service, to which are added–Considerations on Mr Brough's Pamphlet, concerning East India Shipping (1786).

Review of the Contest concerning Four New Regiments, graciously offered by his Majesty to be sent to India, etc. (1788).

Observations on the Copper Coinage wanted for the Circars (Printed for the use of the East India Company, 1794).

C. LITERARY AND HISTORICAL

Extracts from Juvenilia, or Poems by George Wither (1785).

Plan for the Publication of a Repertory of Oriental Information (1790).

Oriental Repertory, Vol. 1st. April 1791 to January 1793. (This work was re-issued in 1808.)

Oriental Repertory. Vol. 2d. 1794– (This work was re-issued in 1808.)

A Collection of English Songs, with an Appendix of Original Pieces (1796).

D. PERSONAL MEMORIALS

Memorial to the Proprietors of East India Stock (1768).

Case of Alexander Dalrymple [A claim to be exempted from the operation of a Bill relating to the East India Company] (1784).

Memorial of Alexander Dalrymple (1791).

Case of Alexander Dalrymple Esq. (1808).

E. POLITICAL TRACTS

Considerations on the present State of Affairs between England and America (1778).

Parliamentary Reform, as it is called, improper, in the present State of this Country (1793).

Mr Fox's Letter to his Worthy and Independent Electors of Westminster, fully considered (1793).

The Poor Man's Friend (1795).

Thoughts of an old Man of independent Mind, though dependent Fortune (1800).

F. RELIGION

A Letter to a Friend on the Test Act (1790).

G. TRADE

(*i*) *The Sulu Enterprise*

Account of what has passed between the East India Directors and Alexander Dalrymple (1768).

Plan for extending the Commerce of this Kingdom, and of the East India Company, by an Establishment at Balambangan. *N.B.* Although printed in 1769, it was not published till 1771.

A full and clear Proof that the Spaniards can have no claim to Balambangan (1774).

To the Proprietors [a proposal to undertake the management of the Settlement at Balambangan] (1775).

(*ii*) *General*

A serious Admonition to the Public, on the intended Thief Colony at Botany Bay (1786).

A Fragment on the India Trade, written in 1791 (1797).

(*iii*) *Fur-Trade Scheme*

Plan for promoting the Fur Trade, and securing it to this Country, by uniting the Operations of the East India and Hudson's Bay Companys (1789).

Memoir of a Map of the Lands around the North Pole (1789).

An Historical Journal of the Expeditions by Sea and Land, to the North of California, in 1768, 1769, and 1770, when Spanish Establishments were first made at San Diego and Monterey, translated from the Spanish MS. by William Revely, Esq. to which is added – Translation of Cabrera Bueno's Description of the Coast of California, and an Extract from the MS. Journal of M. Sauvague le Muet, 1714 (1790).

The Spanish Pretensions fairly discussed (1790).

The Spanish Memorial of 4 June considered ((1790).

H. NAUTICAL MEMOIRS AND PAPERS, WRITTEN, OR EDITED AND PUBLISHED, BY ALEXANDER DALRYMPLE

[C. F. Noble] *The French and English Marine Regulations compared* (No date).

Memoir of a Chart of the Southern Ocean (1769).

Essay on the most commodious methods of Marine Surveying (1771). This was the first work on this subject, and was re-issued in 1786. A revised and enlarged edition appeared in 1806.

A Collection of Charts and Memoirs (1771–72), including:

Memoir of a chart of the China Sea.

Memoir of the chart of part of the coast of China, and the adjacent islands, near the mouth of Canton River.

Journal of the Schooner Cuddalore, *on the coast of China, near Honghai* (in 1759).

Journal of the Schooner Cuddalore *on the coast of Hainan* (1760).

Memoir of a chart of the west coast of Palawan (the *Cuddalore,* 1761). (Re-issued 1786.)

(Later editions in 1786 and 1806, with Larkins's observations on a passage from St. John's to Macao.)

General Introduction to Charts and Memoirs (1772).

Memoir of a Chart of the Bay of Bengal. (Appendix pub. 1787) (1772) (3rd. ed. 1807).

Collection of 40 coastal views of Africa, Arabia, Persia, India and China, and of various islands in the Atlantic, Indian and Pacific Oceans (1771–89).

Collection of 475 charts of Africa, Arabia, Persia, India and China including various plans of Islands and Harbours in the Atlantic, Indian and Pacific Oceans (1772–89).

A Collection of Plans of Ports in the East Indies, with introductory Explanation. (1775). Later enlarged editions in 1782 and 1787.

The Journal of the Grenville, *on a voyage from London to Madras in 1775.* Published in the Philosophical Transactions (1778).

Explanation of the Map of the East India Company's Lands on the Coast of Choromandel (1778).

[Robertson's description of] *The Strait of Allass, during a passage in the* Vansittart (1780).

[Payne's] *A Voyage in the* Flying Eagle *from Bantam to Baber, and other islands...eastward of Timor, in 1672* (1781).

The Journal of Captain Richard Pinnell, commander of the Jane *Frigate, bound through the Straits of Baly and so to Timor, in 1706* (1781).

[Porter's]*Remarks on the Bloachee, Brodia and Arabian coasts* (1781) (2nd ed. 1787).

Collection of Views of Land and of Plans of Ports in the East Indies (1781).

Journal of the ship London, *Captain Walter Alves, along the north coast of Magindanao, in October 1764* (1781).

A brief statement of the Prevailing Winds; from M. D'Après de Mannevillette (1782).

[Capt. Taylor's] *Remarks in Ship* Ceres *on the Navigation of the Indian Ocean* (1782).

Introduction to a General Collection of Nautical Publications (1783).

An Account of the loss of the Grosvenor *Indiaman, commanded by Capt. J. Coxon on the 4 August 1782* (1783).

General Introduction to a Collection of Plans of Ports...in the Indian Navigation (1783).

A Collection of Views of Land in the Indian Navigation (1783).

Memoir of a Chart of the East Coast of Arabia, from Dofar to the Island Maziera. From an eye-draught taken by Capt. J. S. Smith (1783).

[Capt. Ritchie's] *Hydrographical Survey of the Bay of Bengal* completed in 1770–1, with Appendix (1784–5).

Explanations to Plans of Ports, etc. (1781–2) (1784) (2nd ed. 1787).

Memoir of a Chart from St John's, on the coast of India, to Cape Arubah, on the coast of Persia, containing the Gulphs of Cambay and Cutch, with the coasts of Guzerat and Scindy, from the latitude of 19° 40′ N to 25° 40′ N (1784).

Proposition for a survey of the Coast of Choromandel (1784).

Collection of Nautical Papers concerning the Bay of Bengal (1784–5).

Memoir concerning the Passages to and from China, written in 1782, and then issued to selected ships by the Secret Committee (1785).

Memoir of a chart from Cape Mons to Acheen...(1785).

Memoir of a chart of the Straits of Sunda and Banka... (1786).

Memoir of a Chart of the Natunas, Anambas, and Adjacent Islands (1786).

General Introduction to the Charts and Memoirs published by Alexander Dalrymple (1786).

Memoir concerning the Chagos and Adjacent Islands (including a Memoir of a chart of the islands and dangers to the North-East of Madagascar..., by M. D'Après. Translated from the French by A. Dalrymple) (1786).

Mr Larkins's Observations concerning the Chart and Passage from St John's to the Ladrones (1786).

List of classes into which are distributed the Plans of Ports, etc.: published on or before April 1786 by Alexander Dalrymple (1786).

[Petrie's] *An Account of the Shoal to the Eastward of the Cape of Good Hope,* edited, with notes by A. Dalrymple (1787).

[McCluer's] *An*...*Account of the Navigation between India and the Gulph of Persia.* (1786).

[McCluer's] *Description of the coast of India (Malabar)*... (1789).

[McCluer's] *Continuation of the description of the coast of Malabar* (1791).

Memoir of a Chart of the Indian Ocean, exhibiting the coasts, islands, rocks and shoals from Madagascar, to India, Sumatra and Java, composed from various materials and published by A. Dalrymple (1787).

[Thos. Howe's] *Description of Madeira (c. 1762)* (1787).

Memoir of a Chart of the South-East coast of Arabia (1784–7).

Appendix to Capt. Ritchie's survey of the Bay of Bengal, containing Capt. Hayter's instructions for the west coast of Ava, with notes by Capt. Walter Alves. Capt. Alves' Journal in the Snow Victoria, *1759 . . . Mr Plaisted's instructions for the coast of Chittagong,* 2nd ed. (1787).

Memoir of a chart of the south coast of Pegu (1787).

Memoir concerning the Passages, at a late season, from India to China, supplement to *Passages to and from China* (1788).

[Thos. Forrest's] *A Journal of the* Esther *Brig in a Voyage from Bengal to Quedah, 1783* (1788).

Remarks and Observations on a Survey of the Chagos Archipelago [by Archibald Blair] (1788).

Strait of Sinkapore; An account of a voyage through the Strait in 1712 (1788)

[Larkins'] *Account of the Passage of the Ship* Warren Hastings *by the Macklesfield Strait, on the east of Banka* (1789).

[Cooper's] *Account of the Passage of Ship* Atlas *to the Eastward of Banka* (1789).

[Lestock Wilson's] *Remarks on a Passage from P° Wawoor to the Strait of Sunda, by the Macklesfield Strait on the East of Banka, with the Journal of the* Carnatic (1789).

An exact and True description of the Coasts, Ports, Islands and shoals . . . on the coast of Luzon . . . with a description of the Babuyanes Islands by Don Manuel Correa. Translated from the Spanish MS. by the late Sir Hyde Parker. (Revised and published by A. Dalrymple) (1789).

[J. H. Cox's] *A Description of the Island called St Paul's by the Dutch, and by the English Amsterdam . . .* (1790).

Journal of the Schooner Cuddalore *through the Strait of Sapy, and on the south coast of Mang-e-rye* [i.e. Flores] *in February, March and April 1761* (1793).

Some remarks made [by C. F. Noble] *in Mauritius and Bourbon, 1755* (1794).

Collection of Papers concerning the Navigation, Winds and Weather at the French islands, Mauritius and Bourbon (1794).

[Goldingham's] *A Survey of the Pulicat Shoals*...(1794).

[Horsburgh's] *Observations on the Navigation of the Eastern Seas* (1797).

[Palmer's] *Memoir of a chart from the Strait of Allass to the Island Bouro* (1799).

General Remarks for the use of those who have not been accustomed to navigate unfrequented seas (1806).

Longitude. A Full Answer to the advertising concerning Mr Earnshaw's timekeeper...(1806).

Memoir concerning the Pirates on the coast of China, with supplement [Drawn up at the desire of the Chairman of the East India Company] (1806).

Collection of Nautical Papers concerning the Bay of Bengal (1807).

Catalogue of authors who have written on Rio de la Plata, Paraguay & Chaco (1807).

Memoir concerning the Geography of the countries situated in the Rio de la Plata (1807).

[Bonverie's] *Directions for the Mouth of the Rio de la Plata* (1808).

Charts and Plans. In addition to the above, Dalrymple published 58 charts, 740 plans and 57 views of land, and had many unfinished at the time of his death. From 1800 there was a sharp decline in his publications, as he had ordered that none were to be issued after 31 January 1799 on his own account because of Income Tax. In 1805 he suggested a new scheme for tax which would be better for publishers, and mentioned that he had renewed publication to meet the needs of the East India Company and of the Navy. (P.R.O. 20/8, Vol. 128, f. 58.)

JOURNALS OF VOYAGES

A. CONTEMPORARY EDITIONS

BOUGAINVILLE, L. DE (trans. by J. R. Forster). *A Voyage Round the World performed in the Years 1766, 1767, 1768 and 1769* (London, 1772).

BERESFORD, W. (Introduction by Capt. G. Dixon). *A Voyage Round the World, but more particularly to the North-West Coast of America performed in 1785, 1786, 1787 and 1788 in the* King George *and* Queen Charlotte, *Captains Portlock and Dixon* (London, 1789).

CARVER, J. *Travels through the Interior Parts of North America, in the Years 1766, 1767 and 1768* (London, 1778).

COOK, CAPT. J. (ed. J. Douglas). *A Voyage to the Pacific Ocean undertaken by command of His Majesty for Making Discoveries in the Northern Hemisphere. To determine the position and extent of a northern passage to Europe. Performed...in the Years 1776, 1777, 1778, 1779 and 1780.* Volumes 1 and 2 written by Captain Cook, Vol. 3 by Captain James King. Illustrated with Maps and Charts from the original drawings made by Lieut. H. Roberts. 3 Vols. (London, 1784).

DODWELL, G. A. *Narrative of the principal Transactions betwixt the Agents and Officers of the East India Company and George Dodwell...respecting a voyage to Sooloo in 1765 and 1766* (London, 1770).

FORREST, CAPT. THOMAS. *A Voyage to New Guinea and the Moluccas, from Balambangan: including an account of Magindano, Sooloo and other islands ... performed in the* Tartar *galley...during the years 1774, 1775 and 1776* (London, 1779).

FORREST, CAPT. THOMAS. *A Voyage to ... the Mergui Archipelago* (London, 1792).

HEARNE, SAMUEL. *A Journey from Prince of Wales's Fort in Hudson's Bay to the Northern Ocean, Undertaken by order of the Hudson's Bay Company, for the Discovery of Copper Mines, a North West Passage, etc. In the Years 1769, 1770, 1771 and 1772* (London, 1795).

MACKENZIE, SIR A. *Voyages from Montreal, on the River St Laurence, through the Continent of North America, to the Frozen and Pacific Oceans, in the Years 1789 and 1793. With a preliminary account of the rise, progress and present state of the fur trade of that country* (London, 1801).

MEARES, J. *Voyages made in the years 1788 and 1789 from China to the North West Coast of America* (London, 1790).

MORTIMER, G. *Observations and Remarks made during a voyage to the North-West Coast of America... and from thence to Canton in the Brig* Mercury *commanded by John Henry Cox* (London, 1791).

VANCOUVER, G. *A Voyage of Discovery to the North Pacific Ocean and Round the World. Principally with a View to ascertain the existence of any navigable communication between the North Pacific and North Atlantic Oceans,* 3 Vols. (London, 1798).

B. MODERN EDITIONS (Hakluyt Society. All volumes in this series are provided with a long scholarly Introduction in addition to the text.)

Commodore Byron's Journal of his Circumnavigation, 1764–6 edited by R. E. Gallagher (Cambridge, 1964).

Captain Philip Carteret's Voyage round the World, 1766–9, edited by H. Wallis, 2 Vols. (Cambridge, 1965).

The Journals of Captain Cook, edited by J. C. Beaglehole, 4 Vols. (Cambridge, 1955–67).

MORGA, A. DE (translated and edited by the Hon. E. J. Stanley.) *The Philippine Islands, Moluccas, Siam, Cambodia, Japan and China, at the end of the sixteenth century,* including a letter from Luis Vaez de Torres describing his voyage through the Torres Straits (London, 1868).

QUIROS, P. F. DE (translated and edited by Sir C. Markham.) *The Voyages of ... 1595–1606,* 2 Vols. (London, 1904).

[WALLIS] *The Discovery of Tahiti,* a Journal of the second voyage of HMS *Dolphin,* written by her master, George Robertson, edited by Hugh Carrington (London, 1948).

III. SECONDARY WORKS

AIKEN, J. *Annals of the Reign of King George III 1760–1815*, 2 Vols. (London, 1816).

ALI, A. YUSUF. *The Making of British India* (London, 1925).

AMERICAN HISTORICAL ASSOCIATION REPORT FOR 1904, Part XVI, pp. 279–478. Manning, W. R. 'The Nootka Sound Controversy'.

AMHERST, LORD AND BASIL, T. (eds.). *The Discovery of the Solomon Islands by Alvaro de Mendana*, 2 Vols. (Hakluyt Society, London, 1901).

ANDERSON, A. *An Historical and Chronological Deduction of the Origin of Commerce*... (a later edition), 4 Vols. (London, 1787–9).

ANDERSON, B. *Surveyor of the Sea: the life and voyages of George Vancouver* (University of Washington, Seattle, 1960).

THE ANNUAL REGISTER (from 1758 onwards).

ANSTEY, V. *The Economic Development of India* (London, 1929). (Good for geographical background.)

D'ARBLAY, MADAME (i.e. Frances, or Fanny, Burney). *Diary and Letters of Madame D'Arblay* (ed. C. Barrett) (London, 1891). (See also under Burney, F.)

ASHTON, T. S. *An Economic History of England: the eighteenth century* (London, 1955).

ASSEY, C. *On the Trade to China and the Indian Archipelago, with observations on the insecurity of British interests in that quarter* (London, 1819).

AUBER, P. *China: an outline of its Government, Laws and Policy, and of the British and Foreign Embassies to, and Intercourse with, that Empire* (London, 1834).

Australian Encyclopaedia, 10 Volumes (Sydney, 1958).

Australian Quarterly
Tregonning, K., 'Alexander Dalrymple – the man whom Cook replaced', Vol. 23, no. 3, pp. 54–63 (1951).

BAGROW, L. (ed. R. A. Skelton). *History of Cartography* (London, 1964).

BAKER, J. N. L. *History of Geographical Exploration and Discovery* (London, 1931).
History of Geography: collected papers (Oxford, 1963).

BAKER, S. J. *My Own Destroyer: A biography of M. Flinders* (Sydney, 1963).

BARLOW, G. *The Story of Madras* (London and Madras, 1921).

BARRETT, C. L. (ed.). *The Pacific: Ocean of Islands* (Melbourne, 1950).

BARRINGTON, DAINES. *Miscellanies* (London, 1781).
The Probability of Reaching the North Pole Discussed (London, 1775).

BARROW, J. *A Voyage to Cochin China in the Years 1792 and 1793* (London, 1806).
Travels in China, 2nd ed. (London, 1806).

BARROWS, D. P. *A History of the Philippines* (New York, 1905).

BASTIN, J. AND ROOLVINK, R. (eds.). *Malayan and Indonesian Studies: Essays presented to Sir Richard Winstedt* (Oxford, 1964).

BAYLDON, F. J. 'Alexander Dalrymple'. Royal Australian Historical Society, 1927, Vol. 13, pp. 41–59.

BEAGLEHOLE, J. C. *The Exploration of the Pacific*, 3rd ed. (London 1966). (See also under Cook, J.)

G. DE BEER. *The Sciences were Never at War* (London, 1960).
'The Relations between Fellows of the Royal Society and French men of science when France and Britain were at war' – Notes & Records of the Royal Society of London, Vol. 9, no. 2 (1952), pp. 244–99.

BEATSON, R. *Naval & Military Memoirs of Great Britain from 1727–1783*, 6 Vols. (London, 1804).

The Beaver Outfit (published by Hudson's Bay Company, Winnipeg). Wilson, J. T. 'New Light on Hearne' (No. 280, June 1949). Glover, R. 'Hudson Bay to the Orient' (No. 281, Dec. 1950, pp. 47–51).

BESANT, W. *London in the Eighteenth Century* (London, 1902).

BIDDULPH, J. *The Pirates of the Malabar Coast* (London, 1907).

BLAIR, E. H. AND ROBERTSON, J. A. (eds.). *The Philippine Islands, 1493–1898,* 55 Vols. (Cleveland, Ohio, 1903–9).

BLEWITT, M. *Surveys of the Seas* (London, 1957).

BLOK, P. J. (trans. by O. A. Bierstadt). *A History of the People of the Netherlands,* 5 Vols. (New York and London, 1912).

BONNER, W. H. *Capt. William Dampier* (London, 1934).

BOWDEN, K. M. *George Bass, 1771–1803* (Melbourne, 1952).

BOXER, C. R. *The Dutch Seaborne Empire, 1600–1800* (London, 1965).

BREBNER, J. B. *The Explorers of North America, 1492–1806,* 2nd ed. (London, 1964).

C. DE BROSSES. *Histoire des Navigations aux Terres Australes,* 2 Vols. (Paris, 1756).

BRYCE, G. *The Remarkable History of the Hudson's Bay Company* (London, 1900).

BUACHE, P. *Éclaircissemens géographiques sur la nouvelle Bretagne et sur les côtes septentrionales de la nouvelle Guinée* (Paris, 1789).

BURNEY, FRANCES (see also D'Arblay). *The early diary of* (ed. Ellis, A. R.) (London, 1907).

BURNEY, J. *A Chronological History of the Discoveries in the South Sea or Pacific Ocean,* 5 Vols. (London, 1803–17).

BURROWS, M. *The Life of Edward Lord Hawke,* 3rd ed. (London, 1904).

BUTTINGER, J. *The Smaller Dragon: a political history of Vietnam* (New York, 1958).

CADY, J. F. *The Roots of French Imperialism in Eastern Asia* (New York, 1954).

CALLANDER, J. *Terra Australis Cognita* (London and Edinburgh, 1766).

Cambridge History of the British Empire, Vols. 1, 2, 4, and 7 Cambridge, 1929–40).

Cambridge History of India, Vol. V (ed. H. H. Dodwell), British India 1497–1858 (Cambridge, 1922).

CAMERON, H. C. *Sir Joseph Banks* (London, 1952).

CAMPBELL, J. *A Political Survey of Britain* . . ., 2nd ed., 4 Vols. (London, 1775).

CAMPBELL, J. (ed., with large additions). *J. Harris's Navigantium atque Itinerantium Bibliotheca; or, A complete collection of voyages and travels,* 2 Vols. (London, 1744–8).

CAMPBELL, M. W. *The North West Company* (Toronto, 1957).

Canadian Historical Review. Mills, L., 'The Real significance of the Nootka Sound Controversy', Vol. 6, no. 1, pp. 110–22.

CARRUTHERS, J. *Captain James Cook, 150 Years After* (London, 1930).

CHATTERTON, E. KEBLE. *The Old East Indiamen,* 2nd ed. (London, 1933).

THE CHINESE REPOSITORY. Canton, etc., 1832–51.

CLAPHAM, J. H. *An Economic History of Modern Britain,* 3 Vols. (Cambridge, 1926–38).

CLARKE, J. S. *The Progress of Maritime Discovery* (London, 1803). (Useful summary on early collections of voyages.)

CLODD, H. P. *Malaya's First British Pioneer* (London, 1948).

CLOWES, W. LAIRD. *The Royal Navy: A history,* Vol. VI (London, 1901).

COATS, W. (ed. Sir J. Barrow). *The Geography of Hudson's Bay* (Hakluyt Society, London, 1852).

COATES, W. H. *The old 'Country Trade' of the East Indies* (London, 1911).

COLLINGRIDGE, G. *The Discovery of Australia* (Sydney, 1895).

CORBETT, SIR J. *England in the Seven Years' War,* 2 Vols. (London, 1907).

CORNEY, B. G. (ed.). *The Quest and Occupation of Tahiti by the Emissaries of Spain, 1772–76,* 3 Vols. (London, 1913–18).

The Voyage of Don Felipe Gonzalez to Easter Island in 1770–71 (London, 1908).

COTTON, SIR H. E. A. (ed. Sir C. Fawcett). *East Indiamen: the East India Company's Maritime Service* (London, 1949).

COUPLAND, R. *The American Revolution and the British Empire* (London, 1930).
Raffles, 1781–1826 (Oxford, 1926).

COWAN, C. D. *Early Penang and the Rise of Singapore, 1805–32*, JMBRAS, Vol. 23 (March 1950), pp. 1–205.
Nineteenth Century Malaya: the origins of British Political Control (London, 1961). ('Prelude', pp. 1–27, gives useful introduction to 1785 period.)

COXE, W. *Account of the Russian Discoveries between Asia and America* ... (London, 1780).

CRAWFORD, J. *A Descriptive Dictionary of the Indian Islands and adjacent countries* (London, 1856).
A History of the Indian Archipelago, 2 Vols. (Edinburgh, 1820).

CRONE, G. R. *Maps and their Makers*, 3rd edition, Paperback (London, 1966).
'Early books and charts in the Royal Geographic Society's Collection', *Institute of Navigation Journal*, Vol. VI, 1953.

CRONE, G. R. AND SKELTON, R. A. 'English Collections of Voyages and Travels, 1625–1846', in *Richard Hakluyt and his Successors* (ed. E. Lynam), Hakluyt Society, London, 1946).

CUNNINGHAM, W. *The Growth of English Industry and Commerce*, 5th ed. (Cambridge, 1917).

MISS DALRYMPLE of Hailes. *Private Annals of My Own Time (1765–1812)*. Privately printed 1914 (copy in the Edinburgh Central Library).

DANVERS, F. C. *Report to the Secretary of State for India in Council on the Records of the India Office*, Vol. 1, Part 1, (London, 1887).

DAVIES, C. C. *Historical Atlas of the Indian Peninsula* (Oxford, 1949).

DAVIES, R. English Foreign Trade 1700–1774, *Economic History Review*, 2nd Series, Vol. XV (1962).

DAWSON, L. S. *Memoirs of Hydrography*, 2 Vols. (Eastbourne, 1885).

DAY, VICE-ADMIRAL SIR A., *The Admiralty Hydrographic Service, 1795–1919* (London, 1967).

DAWSON, W. R. (ed.). *The Banks Letters: a calendar of manuscript correspondence* (British Museum, London, 1958).

DÉ, BARUN. *Henry Dundas and the Government of India*, unpublished D. Phil. thesis (Oxon) (1961).

DEANE, P. AND COLE, W. A. *British Economic Growth, 1688–1959* (Cambridge, 1962).

DEWAR, D. *Bygone days in India* (London, 1922).

DICKINSON, R. E. AND HOWARD, O. J. R. *The Making of Geography* (Oxford, 1933).

DIXON, G. *Remarks on the Voyages of John Meares, Esq., in a letter to that Gentleman* (London, 1790). *Further Remarks* ...

DOUGLAS, SIR R. K. *Europe and the Far East* (Cambridge, 1913).

DOWDELL, H. *The Nabobs of Madras* (London, 1926).

DRAGE, T. SWAINE. *The Great Probability of a North-West Passage* (London, 1768).

DUNMORE, J. *French Explorers in the Pacific*, Vol. 1, The eighteenth century (Oxford, 1965).

EAMES, J. B. *The English in China 1600–1843* (London, 1909).

EAST INDIA COMPANY, The First, Second and Third Reports of the Select Committee, printed 1793.

EAST INDIA EXAMINER (London, 1766).

EAST INDIA OBSERVER (London, 1766).

EDGELL, VICE-ADMIRAL SIR J. A. *Sea Surveys: Britain's contribution to Hydrography* (HMSO, London, 1965).

EDGELL, T. C. P. *English Trade and Policy in Borneo, 1667–1786*, unpublished London MA thesis, 1935.

ELLIS, H. *A Voyage to Hudson's Bay by the* Dobbs *Galley and* California. *In the Years 1746 and 1747, For Discovering a North West Passage* (London, 1748).

ELMORE, H. M. *The British Mariner's Directory and Guide to the Navigation of the Indian and China Seas* (London, 1802).

English Historical Review
Morse, H. B., 'The Supercargo in the China Trade', Vol. 36 (1921), pp. 199–209.
Sutherland, L. S., 'Lord Shelburne and East India Company Politics', Vol. 49 (1934), pp. 450–86.
Philips, C. H., 'The New East India Board of Directors, 1784', Vol. 55 (1940), pp. 438–46.
Norris, J. M., 'The Policy of the British Cabinet in the Nootka Crisis', Vol. 70 (1950), pp. 562–80.

ENNIS, T. E. *French Policy and Developments in Indochina* (Chicago, 1936).
Eastern Asia (Chicago, 1948).

ETCHES, C. *An Authentic Statement of the Facts relative to Nootka Sound* (London, 1790).

European Magazine, Vol. 42, Memoirs of Alexander Dalrymple, Esq. (London, 1802).

FARINGTON, J. *The Farington Diary,* 8 Vols. (London, 1922–28) (ed. P. J. Greig).

FAVENC, E. *History of Australian Exploration* (Sydney, 1888).

FIDLER, W. *The East India Company... leading events 1599–1858* (London, 1875).

FLEURIEU, C. DE. *Discoveries of the French in 1768 and 1769, to the South-East of New Guinea,* trans. from the French (London,1791).

FLINDERS, M. *A Voyage to Terra Australis,* 2 Vols. (London, 1814).

FORREST, T. *Treatise on the Monsoons in the East Indies* (Calcutta, 1782).

FORSTER, J. R. *History of the Voyages and Discoveries made in the North* (London, 1786).

FOSTER, SIR W. *England's Quest of Eastern Trade* (London, 1933).
The Founding of Fort St George (London, 1902).

A Guide to the India Office Records, 1600–1858 (London, 1919).
John Company (London, 1926).
The East India House, its history and associations (London, 1924).

FRANKLIN, B. *Works of . . . Benjamin Franklin: consisting of his life, written by himself* (Dublin, 1793).

FURBER, H. *Henry Dundas, First Viscount Melville, 1742–1811* (London, 1911).
John Company at Work (Cambridge, Mass. and London, 1948).
'Abortive Attempt at Anglo-Spanish commercial co-operation in the Far East in 1793', *Hisp. Amer. Hist. Rev.*, XV (1935), pp. 448–63.

GEIKIE, SIR A. *Annals of the Royal Society Club* (London, 1917).

Gentleman's Magazine. Old Series, 77 Vols. (London, 1735–1807). New Series, Vol. 78, Part 1, p. 556. Dalrymple's Obituary (London, 1808).

Geographical Journal (Journal of the Royal Geographical Society) (London, 1832).
Horsburgh, J., 'Some remarks relative to the Geography of the Maldive Islands', Vol. II (London, 1832), pp. 72–80).
Jervis, Capt. T. B. 'Origin, Progress and Present State of the Surveys of India', Vol. II (1837), pp. 127–43.

Geographical Magazine (ed. C. R. Markham). 'Indian Marine Surveys of India' Vol. VII (1837), pp. 127–43.

GILL, C. *Merchants and Mariners of the eighteenth century* (London, 1961).

GODWIN, G. *Vancouver, a life: 1757–1798* (London, 1930).

GOLDSON, W. *Observations on the Passage between the Atlantic and Pacific Oceans*. . . (London, 1793).

GRAHAM, G. S. *The Politics of Naval Supremacy* (Cambridge, 1965).

GREENBERG, M. *British Trade and the Opening of China, 1800–42* (Cambridge, 1951).

HALL, D. G. E. *Early English Intercourse with Burma 1587–1743* (London, 1928).

Europe and Burma (London, 1945).

History of South-East Asia (London, 1958).

HAMILTON, CAPT. A. *A New Account of the East Indies* (ed. Sir W. Foster), 2 Vols., originally published Edinburgh, 1727, London, 1744 (London, 1930).

HAMILTON, C. J. *The Trade Relations between England and India* (Calcutta, 1919).

HARDY, C. *A Register of Ships Employed in the Service of the Honourable the United East India Company, from the union of the two Companies, in 1707, to the year 1760 ... to which is added from the latter period to the present time* (London, 1799).

HARLOW, V. T. *The Founding of the Second British Empire*, 2 Vols. (London, etc., 1952–64).

HARLOW, V. AND MADDEN, F. *British Colonial Developments (Select Documents) 1774–1834* (Oxford, 1953).

HAWKESWORTH, J. *An Account of the voyages undertaken ... for making discoveries in the Southern Hemisphere, and successively performed by Commodore Byron, Capt. Wallis, Capt. Carteret, and Capt. Cook*, 3 Vols. (London, 1773).

HEAWOOD, E. *A History of Geographical Discovery in the Seventeenth and Eighteenth Centuries*, new edition (New York, 1965).

HEWSON, J. B. *A History of the Practice of Navigation* (Glasgow, 1951).

HILL, S. C. *Episodes of Piracy in the Eastern Seas, 1519–1851*, supplements to the *Indian Antiquary*, Vols. 52–7 (Bombay, 1923–8).

JACK-HINTON, C. 'Alexander Dalrymple and the Rediscovery of the Solomon Islands', *Mariner's Mirror*, Vol. 50, no. 2, May 1964.

Hispanic American Historica Review. Furber, H., 'Attempt at Anglo-Spanish Commercial Cooperation in 1793', Vol. 15 (1935), pp. 448–63.

HISTORICAL MANUSCRIPTS COMMISSION. Fourth Report, London,

1874, pp. 529–33, 'The manuscripts of the late Sir David Dalrymple, Lord Hailes, in the Library at New Hailes'.
Report on the Palk MSS. (London, 1922).

Historical Studies, Australia and New Zealand.
Tregonning, K. G. P., 'Steps in the acquisition of North Borneo', Vol. 5, pp. 234 et seq.
Atkins, B., 'Australia's place in the swing to the east 1788–1810', Vol. 8, p. 315.
Roe, M., 'Australia's place in the swing to the east 1788–1810', Vol. 8, p. 202.
Spate, O. H. K., 'Terra Australis-Cognita?', Vol. 8, p. 1.
Kelly, Celsus, 'Geographical Knowledge and Speculation in regard to Spanish Pacific Voyages', Vol. 9, p. 12.

History. Marshall, P., 'The First and Second British Empires: A Question of Demarcation', Vol. VLIX (1964), pp. 13–23.

History Today
Woodcock, G., 'Fur Empires of the North', Vol. 4 (1954) pp. 251–9.
Harcourt-Smith, S., 'The Emperor Ch'ien Lung, 1735–99', Vol. 5 (1955), pp. 164–73.
Harris, R., 'Indo-China and the French', Vol. 5 (1955), pp. 84–94.
Boxer, C. R., 'The closing of Japan 1636–9', Vol. 6 (1956), pp. 830–9.
Thornton, A. P., 'The British in Manila, 1762', Vol. 7 (1957), pp. 44–53.
Boxer, C. R., 'Jesuits at the Court of Peking, 1601–1775', Vol. 7, pp. 580–9.
Godwin, G., 'Captain George Vancouver, 1757–98', Vol. 7, pp. 605–9.
Wright, E., 'Henry Dundas', Vol. 8, pp. 155–63.
Boxer, C. R., 'The Manila Galleon, 1565–1815', pp. 538–47.
McAleavy, H., 'The Manchus', Vol. 10, pp. 32–43.
Charnley, W., 'The Founding of Sydney', Vol. 12 (1962), pp. 105–15.
Woodcock, G., 'Alexander Mackenzie and the River of Disappointment', Vol. 14 (1964), pp. 334–43.

PINGTI-HO. *Studies in the Population of China, 1368–1953* (Cambridge, 1959).

HOLZMAN, J. M. *The Nabobs in England* (New York, 1925).

HONOR, H. *Chinoiserie, the Vision of Cathay* (London, 1961).

HOSKINS, H. L. *British Routes to India* (New York, 1928).
'The Growth of British Interest in the Route to India', *Journal of Indian History*, Vol. 2 (1922–3), pp. 165–77).

HOWAY, F. W. (ed.). *The Dixon-Meares Controversy* (Toronto, 1929).
'Early Days of the Maritime Fur-Trade on the North-West Coast', *Canadian Historical Review*, Vol. IV, no. 1 (1923), pp. 26–44.
The Journal of Captain James Colnett aboard the Argonaut *from April 26 1789 to November 3, 1791* (Champlain Society, Toronto, 1940).

'A List of Trading Vessels in the Maritime Fur-Trade, 1785–1794', *Transactions of the Royal Society of Canada*, 3rd series, Vol. XXIV (1930), pp. 111–34.

HUDSON, G. F. *Europe and China: a survey of their relations from the earliest times to 1800* (London, 1931).

HULOT, BARON. *D'Entrecasteaux 1737–93* (Paris, 1894).

HUNT, J. Sketch of Borneo . . . 1812 [*Malayan Miscellanies*, Vol. 1, no. 8, Bencoolen, 1820].
Some Particulars relating to Sulu, in the Archipelago of Felicia, collected partly from a parcel of shattered and torn memoranda, and recited partly from memory . . . 1815 [*Malayan Miscellanies*, Vol. 1, no. 10, Bencoolen, 1820].

ILBERT, SIR C. *The Government of India: a brief survey of Parliamentary legislation relating to India* (Oxford, 1922).

IMAGO MUNDI. *Yearbook of old cartography* (London, etc., 1935).

INNIS, H. A. *Peter Pond, Fur Trader and adventurer* (Toronto, 1930).
The Fur Trade in Canada (Toronto, 1956).

Institute of Navigation Journal.

Crone, C. R., 'Early Books and Charts in the Royal Geographical Society's Collection', Vol. 6, pp. 38–43.

May, W. C., 'Navigational Accuracy in the Eighteenth Century', Vol. 6, pp. 71–3.

Schüller, J. A., 'A History of the Dutch Nautical Chart', Vol. 6, pp. 194–9.

Skelton, R. A., 'The Hydrographic Collections of the British Museum', Vol. 9, pp. 323–34.

IRVING, B. A. *The Commerce of India, being a view of the routes successively taken by the commerce between Europe and the East* (London, 1858).

Journal of Economic History

Deane, P., 'The Output of the British Woollen Industry in the Eighteenth Century', Vol. VII, no. 2 (New York, 1957).

Journal of the Indian Archipelago (ed. Logan, J. R.), 9 Vols., (Singapore, 1847–55). Some of the important articles included in these volumes are:

Vol. I, Detail respecting Cochin China.

Vol. II, Notices of Malacca. History and Present State of Malacca.

The geographical group of Borneo.

European intercourse with Borneo Proper prior to the establishment of Singapore in 1819.

Vol. III, Piracy in the Indian Archipelago.

Sulu (including reprint of Dalrymple's 'Essay towards an account of Sooloo').

Can a Christian merchant engage in the opium trade?

Vol. IV, Origin and Progress of the British Colonies in the Straits of Malacca.

Notices of Penang.

Vol. V, Geographical group of Celebes.

Vol. VI, Palawan. Cambodia.

Vol. IX, Life and service of Sir Stamford Raffles.

Journal of the Malay Branch of the Royal Asiatic Society (Kuala Lumpur).

Tarling, N., 'British Policy in the Malay Peninsula and Archipelago, 1824–71', Vol. 30, Part 3.
'Historical Sketch of Penang', Vol. 32, Part 1.
Lamb, A., 'British Missions to Cochin China, 1778–1822', Vol. 34, Parts 3 and 4.

JULIAN, E. A. *British Projects and Activities in the Philippines, 1759–1805,* unpublished Ph.D. (London) thesis, 1963.

KEATE, G., *Account of the Pelew Islands . . . composed from the journals and communications of Captain Henry Wilson . . . who in August 1783 were there shipwrecked in the* Antelope (London, 1788).

KIPPIS, A. *Life of Captain Cook* (London, 1788).

KIRWAN, L. P. *A History of Polar Exploration* (Penguin Books, Harmondsworth, 1962).

LEE, IDA. *Commodore Sir John Hayes* (London, 1912).

LIPSON, E. *The Economic History of England,* Vol. II, 5th ed. (London, 1948).

LOVE, H. D. *Vestiges of Old Madras* (*Indian Records Series*) (London, 1913).

LOW, C. R. *History of the Indian Navy,* 2 Vols. (London, 1877).

LYONS, SIR H. *The Royal Society 1660–1940: a history of its administration under its charters* (Cambridge, 1944).

LYNAM, E. (ed.). *Richard Hakluyt and His Successors* (Hakluyt Society, London, 1946).

MACALISTER, CAPTAIN N. *Historical Memoir relative to Prince of Wales Island in the Straits of Malacca, and its Importance, Political and Commercial* (London, 1803).

MCCULLOCH, J. R. *Dictionary . . . of Commerce and Commercial Navigation* (London, 1832).

MACGREGOR, J. *Commercial Statistics,* Vol. IV, Section XX: Oriental Commerce (London, 1848).

MACKANESS, G. *Sir Joseph Banks: His relations with Australia* (Sydney, 1936).

The Life of Vice-Admiral William Bligh, F.R.S., 2 Vols. (Sydney, etc., 1931).

MACPHERSON, D. *Annals of Commerce* (London, 1805).
The History of the European Commerce with India (London, 1812).

MAIDEN, J. H. *Sir Joseph Banks, the Father of Australia* (Sydney, 1909).

MAJOR, R. H. (ed.). *Early Voyages to Terra Australis, now called Australia* (Hakluyt Society, London, 1859).

MANNING, R. W. 'The Nootka Sound Controversy', *American Historical Association Annual Report*, 1924, pp. 279–478.

MANWARING, G. E. *My Friend the Admiral ...* (London, 1931). (Biography of James Burney.)

MARCUS, G. J. *A Naval History of England*, Vol. 1 : *The Formative Centuries* (London, 1961).

Mariner's Mirror.
Knight, C., 'H.M. Bark *Endeavour*', Vol. 19, pp. 292–302.
Skelton, R. A., 'Captain James Cook as Hydrographer', Vol. 40, pp. 91–119.
Skelton, R. A., 'Copyright and Piracy in Eighteenth Century Chart Publication', Vol. 46, pp. 207–12.
Jack-Hinton, C., 'Alexander Dalrymple and the Rediscovery of the Solomon Islands', Vol. 50, no. 2 (May 1964), pp. 93–114.

MARKHAM, SIR C. R. *A Memoir of the Indian Surveys*, 2nd ed. (London, 1878).
Life of James Rennell (London, 1895).

MARSDEN, W. *Memoir of the Life of William Marsden*, privately printed (London, 1838).

MENDOZA, J. G. DE (trans., with Introduction, by R. Parke). *The Historie of the Great and Mightie Kingdome of China and the situation thereof: together with the great riches, huge citties, politike governement and rare inventions in the same*, originally published 1588 (Hakluyt Society, London, 1853). (*N.B.* that Dalrymple drew particular attention to Parke's Introduction in his letter to Pitt, 1761.)

MILBURN, W. *Oriental Commerce*, 2 Vols. (London, 1813).

The Monthly Review, 81 Vols. (London, 1749–89).

MORRELL, W. P. *Britain in the Pacific Islands* (Oxford, 1960).

MORSE, H. B. *The Chronicles of the East India Company trading to China, 1635–1834*, 5 Vols. (Oxford, 1926–9).
The Gilds of China (London, 1909, pp. 65 et seq.).
International Relations of the Chinese Empire, Vol. I (London, 1910).

MORTON, A. S. *A History of the Canadian West to 1870–1* (London, 1939).

Naval Chronicle, 40 Vols. (London, 1799–1818).
D'Entrecasteaux's Circumnavigation, Vol. 6, pp. 41–2.
Fur Trade, advantages offered by the N.W. coast of America to Great Britain, Vol. 11, pp. 108–13.
Alexander Dalrymple, account of, Vol. 20, pp. 210–5.
Sir Hyde Parker snr., biographical memoir, Vol. 20, pp. 337 ff.
James Horsburgh, biographical memoir, Vol. 28, pp. 441–51.
James Horsburgh, letter, Vol. 31, pp. 398–9.
Alexander Dalrymple, biographical memoir, Vol. 35, pp. 177–204.

NICHOLS, J. *Literary Anecdotes of the Eighteenth Century,* 9 Vols. (London, 1812–5).

NOBLE, C. F. (ed. A. Dalrymple). *The French and English Marine Regulations Compared* (1755).

O'BRIEN, E. *The Foundation of Australia,* 2nd Edition (Sydney, 1950).

ORME, R. *Historical Fragments of the Mogul Empire . . . and the Morattoes, and of the English Concerns in Indostan, from the Year 1659,* reprinted Calcutta, 1905 (London, 1782).
History of the Military Transactions of the British Nation in Indostan, 2 Vols. (London, 1763, 1778).

OROSA, S. Y. *The Sulu Archipelago and Its People* (Yonkers-on-Hudson, 1923).

OSBECK, P. *A Voyage to China and the East Indies by Capt. C. G. Eckeberg* (London, 1771).

Oxford History of India, by V. Smith, revised by P. Spear (Oxford, 1958).

Pacific Historical Review
Pritchard, E. H., 'The Struggle for Control of the China Trade during the eighteenth century', Vol. III (1934), pp. 280–91.
Williams, G., 'An eighteenth century investigation into the apocryphal voyage of Admiral Fonte', Vol. 30, pp. 319–28.

PACK, S. W. C. (ed.). *Anson's Voyage Round the World, 1740–44,* by R. Walter (Penguin Books, England, 1947).

PANIKKAR, K. M. *India and the Indian Ocean* (London, 1945).

PARKINSON, C. N. (ed.). *The Trade Winds* (London, 1948).
Trade in Eastern Seas, 1793–1815 (London, 1937).
War in the Eastern Seas, 1793–1815 (London, 1954).

PARRY, CAPT. J. F. 'Historical Sketch of the Exploration and Survey of the Waters of British Columbia', *Hydrographic Annual for 1913,* no. 2 (Hydrographic Dept., Admiralty, London, 1914).

PAUL, J. D. S. *The East India Company: a study of its early trading organization and commerce* (London and Madras, 1933).

PHILIPS, C. H. *The Correspondence of David Scott, Director and Chairman of the East India Company... 1787–1805,* Camden Third Series, Vols. 75, 76, R. Hist. Soc. (London, 1951).
The East India Company 1784–1834 Manchester, 1940).

PORTLOCK, N. *A Voyage Round the World, but more particularly to the North-West Coast of America...* (London, 1789).

PRIESTLEY, H. I. *France Overseas through the Old Regime,* Vol. I (New York and London, 1939).

PRITCHARD, E. H. *Anglo-Chinese Relations during the seventeenth and eighteenth centuries* (Urbana, Illinois, 1929).
The Crucial Years of early Anglo-Chinese Relations, 1750–1800, Research Studies, the State College of Washington, Vol. 4, nos. 3 and 4 (Pullman, 1936).

QUIASON, S. D. *English 'country trade' with the Philippines, 1644–1765* (Quezon City, University of Philippines Press, 1966).

RAINAUD, A. *Le Continent Austral* (Paris, 1893).

RAINBOW, S. G. *English Expeditions to the Dutch East Indies during the Revolutionary and Napoleonic Wars,* unpublished London M.A. thesis (1933).

RAMSAY, G. D. *English Overseas Trade during the centuries of emergence* (London, 1957).

RENER, C. F. *The Foreign Trade of China* (Shanghai, 1926).

RICH, E. E. *History of the Hudson's Bay Company, 1670–1870* (London, The Hudson's Bay Record Society, 2 Vols. 1958–9).

RICHMOND, SIR H. W. *The Navy in India, 1763–83* (London, 1931).

ROBERTS, P. E. *History of British India under the Company and Crown,* 3rd ed. completed by P. Spear (London, 1952).

ROBINSON, A. H. W. *Marine Cartography in Britain. A History of the Sea Chart to 1855* (Leicester, 1962).

ROBINSON, F. P. *The Trade of the East India Company, 1709–1813* (Cambridge, 1911).

ROGERS, J. D. (revised Kershaw, R. N.). *Historical Geography of Australasia* (Oxford, 1925).

ROSSEL, E. P. E. DE *Voyage de D'Entrecasteaux*... (Paris, 1808).

ROYAL AUSTRALIAN HISTORY SOCIETY: *Journal and Proceedings.* Bayldon, F. J., 'Alexander Dalrymple', (Sydney, 1927), Vol. XIII, pp. 41–59.

Royal Society of London, the Record of (London, 1940).

ST JOHN, H. R. *The Indian Archipelago: its history and present state*, 2 Vols. (London, 1853).

SALEEBY, N. M. *The History of Sulu* (Manila, 1908).

SARGENT, A. J. *Anglo-Chinese Commerce and Diplomacy* (Oxford, 1907).

SARIS. *The Voyage of John Saris to Japan, 1613* (ed. Sir E. M. Satow) (Hakluyt Society, London, 1900).

SCHLOTE, W. *British Overseas Trade from 1700 to the 1930's* (Oxford, 1952). (Trans. by Henderson, W. O. and Chaloner, W. H.)

SCHUMPETER, E. B. *English Overseas Trade Statistics, 1697–1808* (Oxford, 1960).

SCHUYLER, R. L. *The Fall of the Old Colonial System: a study in British Free Trade, 1770–1870* (London, 1945).

SCOTT, E. *Life of Matthew Flinders* (Sydney, 1914). *Terre Napoléon* (London, 1910).

CHONG-SU SEE. *The Foreign Trade of China* (New York, 1919).

SHARP, A. *The Discovery of Australia* (Oxford, 1963).
The Discovery of the Pacific Islands (Oxford, 1960).

SKELTON, R. A. *Explorers' Maps* (London, 1960).

SMITH, E. *The Life of Sir Joseph Banks* (London, 1911).

SMITH, V. A. See *Oxford History of India.*

SOOTHILL, W. E. *China and England* (London, 1928).
China and the West (Oxford, 1925).

SPARKS, JARED. *Life and Travels of John Ledyard, 1751–88* (London, 1828).

SPEAR, P. *A History of India*, Vol. 2 (Penguin Books, Harmondsworth, 1965).

STAVORINUS, J. S. (trans. S. H. Wilcocke). *Voyages to the East Indies*, 3 Vols. (London, 1798).

STEUART, A. E. *The Founders of Penang and Adelaide* (London, 1901).

STEVENS, H. N. *New Light on the Discovery of Australia* (Hakluyt Society, London, 1930).

STEVENSON, W. *Historical Sketches of the Progress of Discovery, Navigation and Commerce from the earliest times to the beginning of the nineteenth century* (Edinburgh, 1824).

SUTHERLAND, L. S. *The East India Company in Eighteenth Century Politics* (Oxford, 1952).

TARLING, N. *Anglo-Dutch Rivalry in the Malay World, 1780–1824* (Cambridge and Sydney, 1962).
Piracy and Politics in the Malay World . . . (Melbourne, 1963).

TAYLOR, A. C. *Le Président de Brosses et l'Australie* (Paris, 1938).

TAYLOR, E. G. R. *The Haven Finding Art* (London, 1956).

THIERY, M. *Bougainville, Soldier and Sailor* (London, 1932).

THOMPSON, DAVID. *Thompson's Narrative* (ed. R. Glover) (Champlain Society, Toronto, 1962).

THORNTON, E. *The History of the British Empire in India*, 6 Vols. (London, 1841).

TOUSSAINT, A. (trans. J. Guicharnaud). *History of the Indian Ocean* (London, 1966).

TREGONNING, K. G. *North Borneo* (London, 1960).

TURBEVILLE, A. S. *English Men and Manners in the eighteenth century* (Oxford, 1926).

TYRRELL, J. B. (ed.). *Samuel Hearne: A Journey from Prince of Wales's Fort in Hudson's Bay to the Northern Ocean in the Years 1769, 1770, 1771 & 1772* (Champlain Society, Toronto, 1911).
The Journals of Samuel Hearne and Philip Turnor . . . (Toronto, 1834).
David Thompson's Narrative of his Explorations in West America 1784–1812 (Toronto, 1916).
New edition, with Introduction by R. Glover (Toronto, 1962).

The United Service Journal, Part 1, (London, 1929), pp. 345–8, 469–73. 'The works of the late Alexander Dalrymple Esq.'

Universal Modern History, Vol. 9 (London, 1759).

VERELST, H. *A View of the Rise, Progress and Present State of the English Government in Bengal* (London, 1772).

VLEKKE, B. H. M. *Nusantara: A History of Indonesia* (revised edition) (The Hague and Bandung, 1959).
The Story of the Dutch East Indies (Cambridge, Mass., 1946).

WADE, M. S. *Mackenzie of Canada* (Edinburgh and London, 1927).

WAGNER, H. R. 'Apocryphal Voyages to the North-West Coast of America', *Proceedings of the American Antiquarian Society*, Vol. XLI (April 1931), pp. 179–234.
The Cartography of the North-West Coast of America to the Year 1800, 2 Vols. (Berkeley, Calif., 1937).

Spanish Explorations in the Strait of Juan de Fuca (Santa Ana, Calif., 1933).

WALTER, R. *A Voyage Round the World in the Years 1740–44 by George Anson Esq.* (London, 1748).

WELD, C. R. *History of the Royal Society* (London, 1848).

WILBUR, M. E. *The East India Company and the Britsh Empire in the Far East* (Stanford, Calif., 1945).

WILLI, J. OF GAIS. *The Early Relations of England with Borneo to 1805* (Langensalza, 1922).

WILLIAMS, G. *The British Search by Sea for the North-West Passage, 1719–94* (London, 1962).

WILLIAMSON, J. A. *Cook and the Opening of the Pacific* (London, 1946).

The Observations of Sir Richard Hawkins (with Introduction dealing with the Dieppe Maps) (London, 1933).

A Voyage to New Holland by William Dampier (London, 1939).

WILLIAMSON, CAPT. THOS. *East India Vade-Mecum* (London, 1810).

WISSET, R. *A Compendium of East Indian Affairs*, 2 Vols. (London, 1802).

A View of the Rise, Progress and Present State of the Tea Trade in Europe (London, 1801).

WOOD, G. A. *The Discovery of Australia* (London, 1922).

WOOLF, H. *The Transits of Venus: a study of eighteenth century science* (Princeton, 1959).

WRIGHT, H. R. C. *Indian Economic Problems of the Age of Cornwallis and Raffles* (London, 1961).

WROTH, L. C. 'The Early Cartography of the Pacific', *Papers of the Bibliographical Society of America*, Vol. 38 (New York, 1944).

YORK, H. AND BURNELL, A. C. (eds., new edition by Crooke, W.). *Hobson-Jobson: A Glossary of colloquial Anglo-Indian words and phrases* (London, 1903).

IV. GEOGRAPHIES, MAPS AND SAILING DIRECTIONS OF THE PERIOD

D'APRÈS DE MANNEVILLETTE. *Le Neptune Oriental* (Paris, 1745) (2nd ed. 1775).

BEAUTEMPS-BEAUPRÉ. *Atlas du Voyage de Bruny-Dentrecasteaux* (Paris, 1807).

BELLIN, J. N. *Carte Reduite des Mers comprises entre L'Asie et L'Amerique ... 1742 ... corrigée en 1756*, L'Hydrographie Francoise (Paris, 1756).

BOWEN, E. *A Complete System of Geography*, 2 Vols. (London, 1747).

The Maps and Charts of the Modern Part of the Universal History (London, 1766).

DUNN, S. *A New Directory for the East Indies* (London, 1780). (In effect this was the 5th edition of Herbert's Directory, revised and enlarged.)

HERBERT, W. *A New Directory for the East Indies* (London, 1759).

HORSBURGH, J. *Directions for Sailing to and from the East Indies, China, etc.*, 2 Vols. (London, 1809–11).

Memoirs comprising the Navigation to and from China (London, 1805).

Observations on the Navigation of the Eastern Seas (London, 1797).

MOLL, H. *Atlas Geographus; a Complete System of Geography, Ancient and Modern*, Vol. V (Chapter One 'Terra Australis') (London, 1717).

NORDENSKIOLD, A. E. *Facsimile Atlas (of the Early History of Cartography)* (Stockholm 1889).

PINKERTON, J. *Modern Geography* (London, 1802).

ROBERTS, J. *The Elements of Navigation* (London, 1754).

VARENIUS. *A Complete System of Geography*, 3rd ed. (London, 1736).

INDEX

For Product Safety Concerns and Information please contact our EU representative GPSR@taylorandfrancis.com
Taylor & Francis Verlag GmbH, Kaufingerstraße 24, 80331 München, Germany

www.ingramcontent.com/pod-product-compliance
Lightning Source LLC
LaVergne TN
LVHW010551300926
849162LV00002B/306
9780415381659